AUTHORITARIANISM AND THE INDIVIDUAL

THE BROOKINGS INSTITUTION

The Brookings Institutions—Devoted to Public Service through Research and Training in the Social Sciences—was incorporated on December 8, 1927. Broadly stated, the Institution has two primary purposes: the first is to aid constructively in the development of sound national policies; and the second is to offer training of a supergraduate character to students of the social sciences.

The responsibility for the final determination of the Institution's policies and its program of work for the administration of its endowment is vested in a self-perpetuating board of trustees. It is the function of the trustees to make possible the conduct of scientific research under the most favorable conditions, and to safeguard the independence of the research staff in the pursuit of their studies and in the publication of the results of such studies. It is not a part of their function to determine, control, or influence the conduct of particular investigations or the conclusions reached, but only to approve the principal fields of investigation to which the available funds are to be allocated, and to satisfy themselves with reference to the intellectual competence and scientific integrity of the staff. Major responsibility for "formulating general policies and co-ordinating the activities of the Institution" is vested in the president. The by-laws provide also that "there shall be an advisory council selected by the president from among the scientific staff of the Instiution."

Authors of studies published by the Institution have had the advice, criticism, and assistance both of an administrative officer and of a co-operating committee selected from the staff. In manuscript accepted for publication, the author has freedom to present his final interpretations and conclusions, although they may not necessarily be concurred in by some or all of those who co-operate with him or by other members of the staff. The Institution in publishing the work assumes the responsibility that it meets reasonable tests of scholarship and presents data and conclusions worthy of public consideration.

Authoritarianism
and the
Individual

By

HAROLD W. METZ

and

CHARLES A. H. THOMSON

Washington, D.C.
THE BROOKINGS INSTITUTION
1950

Set up and printed
Published January 1950

Printed in the United States of America
George Banta Publishing Company
Menasha, Wisconsin

PREFACE

Since the dawn of political society, the issue of human freedom has turned for the most part on man's relation to political authority. Man's potential and actual freedom in all fields of life—social, economic, or political—has been set by his relation to the city-state, world empire, feudal authority, or the national sovereign state. Within these limits the issues of church and state, voluntary groups and the state, and business organization and economic activity and the state, have been adjusted in varying ways to meet varying demands and conditions.

The current century is marked by the rise of totalitarianism and the mass state. So strong has been the tradition of democracy, social justice, and human freedoms that even the totalitarians (with the exception of Fascist Italy) have had to couch their platforms and appeals in terms of democracy and human welfare. The totalitarians have emphasized in their propganda the economic, not the political forms of democracy; they have tried to capture for themselves the role of chief champion of democracy on the grounds that they distribute economic products more equitably than do their capitalist contemporaries. At the same time they have glossed over the cost in political freedom, or have explained it away by saying that there is no value in any formal freedom which does not guarantee work and income. Clarification obviously is needed.

The object of this book is to state the price of totalitarianism in terms of human liberty. A vast expansion of the power and functions of government is tolerable only when political authority is genuinely responsible to the demands of the people. There are areas which the state must not enter at all, if the individual is to retain real freedom, and there must be constitutional or traditional limitations on the sphere of state action to ensure this. There must, moreover, be courts or other instrumentalities which can keep government servants within the limits of subject and procedure authorized by law.

The bulk of this book is devoted to demonstrating the ways in which authoritarian societies, medieval and modern, voluntary and involuntary, have dealt with these critical areas of political and human freedom. We are not concerned here with the relative capacity of the various forms of organization to produce and distribute economic goods.

The authors of the book are Harold W. Metz and Charles A. H. Thomson of the staff of the Institution. Mr. Metz is chiefly responsible for the chapters on feudalism, the absolute monarchies, and voluntary societies in America. Mr. Thomson is chiefly responsible for the chapters on communism, fascism, and naziism. The preliminary drafts of the introductory and concluding chapters were prepared by Mr. Metz, but in their final form these sections represent the joint work of the authors. In the nature of the case, the authors have had to rely largely on the work of authorities in these fields. Mr. Thomson in particular wishes to acknowledge his debt to those scholars who have made fundamental materials available in English, without which it would not have been possible to make a serious appraisal of the nazi and communist systems. The works of Franz Neumann and Vladimir Gsovski are especially noteworthy from this standpoint.

The study was suggested by and made possible through a grant from the Alfred P. Sloan Foundation.

HAROLD G. MOULTON
President

December 1949

CONTENTS

CHAPTER I

INTRODUCTION

The whole world is now torn by the struggle between nations and groups of nations, and between individuals and groups within nations, over the basic principles underlying free societies and controlled societies. This conflict is illustrated every day by the ever-recurring, never-ending disputes between the United States and Soviet Russia; it was dramatized earlier by the challenge of Fascist Italy and Nazi Germany not only to international peace, but to free institutions everywhere. It is further emphasized, perhaps in more critical fashion, by the arguments within customarily free societies between those who would give aid and comfort to the philosophies and systems of the dictators, and those who hold to the values and principles of freedom for all individuals. The conflict is involved and often too little dramatized in the proposals for extension of societal control, which in themselves represent no great derogation to the dignity or scope of the individual, but collectively mark the road to total domination.

The main ways in which these controlled societies differ from their free counterparts is in the value, position, and role of the individual in his relation to society. A free society rests on the basic premise that it is organized solely to facilitate the efforts of each individual to conceive and to achieve his ends. In it society as such has no life, values, or ends apart from those of the individuals which compose it. The controlled society, on the other hand, rests on the premise that the social organization has reality, ends, and values of its own, and that individuals are valuable only as a means to achieve society's purposes. In other words, the individual is a tool or a means, not an end in himself. These two opposing views of the position of the individual in society have long made conflicting claims on the allegiance of thinking men.

The main objective of this study is to reveal how systems

founded on the supremacy of society have controlled the life of the individual. To do this the treatment of the individual by a number of controlled societies will be examined. In this inquiry we are concerned chiefly with practice, but also with theory: with practice, to show how the rulers of controlled societies have actually trammeled and trampled the individuals within their power; to show how far those leaders would have gone (or, in Russia's case, want to go) had they been able to push their systems to logical conclusions.

The fortunate inhabitants of free societies are prone to underestimate the rigor and completeness of control within totalitarian ones. They often assume the universality of their own liberties, and lack first hand knowledge of totalitarian regimentation. They often discount the reports of those who do have firsthand knowledge, and disbelieve the frank statements of totalitarian leaders about the measures they apply to the regimes they dominate. They fail to understand the integral nature of totalitarian society, and consider it possible to incorporate certain desirable features of such systems without concomitant personal regimentation or increased temptation to shore them up by further features of less honorable character. Or others among them may admit extension of control, but justify it by arguing that such losses of liberty are transitory, and more than offset by achieving a higher and more meaningful freedom.

The evidence shows that the governments of controlled societies characteristically establish far-reaching regulations—many of them arbitrary and capricious—that touch upon every aspect of the life of the individual.

In this introduction four problems will be considered. First, the basic elements embodied in the attitude of the free society toward the individual are summarized with major stress being placed upon the underlying assumptions. Second, there is developed a list of questions concerning the various activities and rights of individuals that might be subjected to government interference in a controlled society. In considering each of the experiments at regimentation that are included in the subsequent chapters of this study the discussion will be designed to present the answers to these queries. Third, there is presented an explanation of why the controlled societies included were selected. Fourth, an effort is made to set specific bounds for this study by indicating some of the problems that will not be considered in it.

A word of explanation is required to make clear why at the very outset the basic elements of a free society are described. First, such a description might serve throughout the study to indicate the completely different philosophies of the controlled and free groups. Second, and more immediately, it is needed as background for the second part of this introduction. In describing how totalitarian regimes regulate the individual, it will be necessary to concentrate the presentation on certain specific activities of the citizen that are subjected to public control; and to ensure that the analysis will be meaningful, attention will be focused on the restraints imposed by controlled groups on those rights that are considered to be fundamental in a free state. This discussion of the major assumptions of a free society will be of assistance in determining which of the multitude of rights that we enjoy are actually fundamental to our way of life. Then in considering totalitarian regimes we shall direct our attention to those controls which limit the more significant activities of the individual.

I. THE NATURE OF THE FREE SOCIETY

In our view, there are a number of assumptions basic to the idea of the freedom of man in society.

One of these is that the sole legitimate role of the state is to make possible the maximum self-realization of each individual by creating an environment in which he can develop in his own way, primarily by applying his own efforts and resources. This basic goal and its necessary conception of method rests on the belief that each man is a rational thinking person who knows better than anyone else what things contribute to his enjoyment and to his highest welfare. The free society does not assume equality of tastes, talents, or capacities, but recognizes that men differ on these points. Taken together, these propositions form the basis of equality of rights and of procedures in making group decisions. So far as possible, all persons must have equal opportunity to develop their own facilities in their own way.

Diversity of individual capacities leads to a desirable diversity of interests. Since individual interests are varied, dissimilar things give satisfaction to different people. Individuals pursuing various interests make new developments, new scientific and technological discoveries, and new products. Ideas germinate, and a variety of economic, social, and cultural institutions and practices flower. Where there is success, others will seek to match or improve; the failures warn intelligent people not to make the same mistakes again. Obviously, a diversity of tastes cannot fit into the uniformity and rigidity that are generally found in programs of government control over the individual.

Genuine individual improvement can come only through the efforts of the individual himself, working alone or in groups of his choosing. Insofar as government tries to do for the individual what he should do for himself, it diminishes his scope to improve himself by his own efforts. This may not be so important in the material realm as in the realm of mind and spirit. Only as government by its provision of services and its administration of social discipline makes it possible for the individual to better his position, can it be said that government contributes to progress. The individual cannot be forced to be wise, to be good, or to be free.[1]

The freedom of individuals is not unlimited. No individual should exercise his legitimate freedom in such a way as to diminish the freedom of others. Every individual, in his own interest, needs regular, just, and efficient means for controlling and resolving the conflicts inevitable in human association. Unlimited freedom for each and every person would result in complete anarchy, involving the utter destruction of the freedom of all

[1] The classic exposition of this argument is in T. H. Green, *Lectures on the Principles of Political Obligation* (1880).

men. In a society without public authority adequate for keeping the peace, each individual would have to devote most of his efforts and time to protecting himself from the encroachments of others. Where peace and order are wanting, physical might and intelligent cunning become the prime requisites for survival. Civil society provides an environment wherein the individual is in a position to develop and exercise more varied and valuable talents.

The scope and functioning of the state must be limited. The most important limitation is stated in our first and fundamental assumption. Other limitations of nearly equal importance are the requirements that the state must act only as authorized by law, and solely as an agent of the sovereign people. The citizen is always the master, the government the servant. Hence freedom requires that government act in accordance with clear legal authority. Public officials are responsible not alone for broad results, but also for the legality of all their public acts.

The existence of personal rights against the government is a necessary part of the idea that government is only an agent. Such rights are not inherent in democracy as such. It is conceivable that a democracy might provide by democratic procedures that the state is supreme within certain areas, and the individual has no right which he can urge against it. But personal rights against the government, procedural or concrete, are an inescapable element of the free society which insists that political freedom rests on limitation of government and rejects the totalitarian assertion that no individual interest is ever more important than the interest of the state.

For such personal rights to have substance, the state must provide to the citizen machinery adequate for testing the legality of the acts of government servants. Courts must be in operation where the individual can test the propriety of any act of government against the established law of the land. The state may arrest, imprison, search the domicile, or seize property, but it may not do so arbitrarily or without regard to the objects and procedures established by law. To have it otherwise is incompatible with free society.

The form of government of a nation does not of itself guarantee freedom. The quality of political freedom depends on the position of the individual with respect to his government. Democracies are commonly supposed automatically to guarantee freedom, since they are assumed to operate according to the will of the people. Actually, democracies unfettered by constitutional restraints may indulge in some of the worst forms of domination and exploitation of individuals. Democracies frequently operate on the assumption that each and every individual or minority group can be rightfully subjected to any decision of the state because its determinations represent the will of the majority of society, and the majority knows what is best for the group as a whole. Thus an unlimited majoritarian democracy could suppress freedom of speech on the ground that no individual should be permitted to question or criticize the will of the majority. It might arbitrarily arrest and imprison as a means of imposing on the intransigent individual the will of the then preponderant group.

In a free society the state is only one of many forms of social organization. The claims of the state on the individual are not necessarily prior to those of any of the other organizations which make up society. This results both from the nature of the individual personality, from the view of the primacy of the individual, and from the very form and methods of operation inherent in the state. The individual cannot attain his maximum self-realization without participation in groups. Many of the interests of men can best be attained through voluntary associations composed of like-minded people. Only in such groups can most people satisfy their craving for fellowship, pursuit of common interests, and spiritual solace. By organizing groups with a common purpose, members of society can increase their resources and power and can attain objectives impossible to individuals acting independently. Labor unions, business corporations, agricultural co-operatives, and universities exemplify this role of groups for the individual.

The purposes of group life, so conceived, cannot be achieved by the state alone. No single pattern of association will fit the diversity of human nature and the variety of interests of men. Membership in several organizations enables the citizen to give expression to the many facets of his personality and to the changing significance of his various interests under rapidly shifting conditions. It enables the citizen to choose whichever of his interests is dominant as against any other, and to support the group that furthers the one he favors. Being a member of a labor union and a consumers' co-operative, he might support the latter against the former. Being a member of a church and a fraternal organization, he might support the former, in any temporary conflict of interest, or withdraw from one or the other, if his interest and conscience so moved him because of an enduring rift.

Two inherent aspects of the state make desirable a multiplicity of voluntary associations. The first of these is its nonvoluntary universality. The state embraces every person within its boundaries, whether he wills it or not. If the state treats all citizens equally, as it must to be just, it cannot give appropriate emphasis to the differing wants of diverse individuals. Second, the state is the only organization which by right can utilize physical force as a sanction to enforce its decisions. The potentiality of physical compulsion reduces the usefulness of the state as a social device in some fields. This is especially true in those fields where faith, belief, and reason are involved. The state, by force, should not and cannot impart real religious conviction or intellectual agreement. To use force for such purposes creates more antagonism than good. Outward conformity may be purchased at the price of inner disrespect, resentment, and disaffection.

Finally, the claims of the state on the individual cannot be presumed to be prior to those of any voluntary organization, or of the conscience of the individual. The state, as guarantor of the conditions of a good life, makes claims which are entitled to high consideration, but these claims must be judged by individuals and groups according to their merits. Furthermore, the state is not a mystical body, acting infallibly through human agencies. The state in effect is government, and is no better or wiser than the servants acting for government, or the people participating as legislators, executives, judges, or citizens in forming the decisions or carrying out the processes of government.

Authority and power must be diffused among groups and individuals. No one group or section of the community—corporation, labor union, religious group, or the state itself—can enjoy so much power that it can dominate individuals or other groups to the point where their formal freedoms become a mere sham. Such power need not be public or political in the ordinary sense of the term; it can be economic, social, or religious. If it is over-concentrated, it spells the death of freedom. A free society will remain free only so long as the control of the means of production is divided among numerous people acting with a large degree of genuine autonomy. If the direction of all means of production, or all of a key sector of production, is in a single hand, be it government or be it trust, that authority has complete power over all the people.

In a free state, as we have seen, the individual and his own satisfaction or pleasure is the supreme objective of the social structure. This goal is to be attained primarily through the application of the individual's own efforts and capacities. This does not mean that in a society thus constituted government has only an insignificant role. It has a most important role—the provision of an environment wherein maximum individual development and satisfaction can be attained by those persons who desire them. But it must be clear that these fundamental preconceptions of a free society influence not only the form of government that it must have, but also the functions that the state ought or ought not to perform as well as the very spirit and attitude underlying its every act. They also clearly indicate the types of rights or liberties that must be secured for every one of its members if the free society is to be a reality with substance and not merely an empty form.

II. RIGHTS TO BE CONSIDERED

The problem of the impact of a controlled society on the individual will be approached primarily from the standpoint of the restraints imposed by such a group upon those rights of the individual that we consider to be fundamental to a free state. This method will bring out most fully the contrasting positions of the individual in the two opposing forms of social organization. Here we will only enumerate the questions concerning individual rights that we will attempt to answer in connection with each of the controlled societies to be studied. Solely for purposes of exposition, the rights will be divided into three groups: political, personal, and economic. Without doubt such classifications are arbitrary because it is impossible to define hard and fast lines of demarcation between these different classes of rights.

Many of our accepted political rights arise from the basic premise that the government is an instrumentality of the people. The government is merely their agent for accomplishing certain objectives that individuals acting separately cannot attain. As a result we normally assume that every citizen who has reached the age of discretion should have a right to participate in the choice of public officers. Therefore we shall inquire:

Do controlled societies permit all mature individuals owing them allegiance to participate in government?

Do all individual citizens take part in the selection of the government?

Does the citizen have a vote?

What limitations are imposed on the individual's right to hold elective and appointive offices?

Since we consider that government responsibility is fundamental we ask:

Is each person in a position to criticize the government and take effective measures to hold it responsible for its activities so far as they affect his rights?

Many relatively personal rights are fundamental to freedom because their existence is a prime requisite of the development of the personality of the individual. Among such rights freedom of speech and expression are basic. With freedom of speech goes the right to study, to investigate, and to publish opinions on such problems as the student might wish.

Does the totalitarian state ensure that the individual has freedom of speech and the right to assemble and to exchange views.

Can any person express his opinion of the government?

Can like-minded citizens gather to discuss problems of common concern?

Does the totalitarian state prohibit its subjects from engaging in any scientific or scholarly studies that might question the fundamental philosophy underlying its concept of society?

Does the all-embracing state maintain that it has a duty to ensure that individuals engage only in such studies as will produce the higher good as the state sees it?

As a part of freedom of speech goes freedom of belief especially in the religious sphere.

Does every individual have the right to follow such religious beliefs as he might wish and to attempt to win converts to his faith?

Does the political society consider that it is imperative that individuals should be restricted from giving expression to their religious convictions where the government believes that such beliefs might conflict with the goals of the state?

Is the individual permitted to proclaim actively that there are no basic religious ideas and principles?

Are special privileges given to adherents of certain religious groups while burdensome discriminations are visited upon those who profess other faiths?

Also of a personal nature are those rights that exist primarily for the purpose of protecting other liberties—that is the so-called procedural rights.

Are individuals protected from arbitrary government action not authorized by law?

Can public officers arrest the individual at will, search his property, and imprison him without a trial by a duly constituted court?

Is machinery available for the judicial review of every activity of the government that might injure the rights of individuals?

Are all persons equal before the law?

Are some men placed in special legal categories because of their race, religion, birth, or economic status?

Limitations imposed on the economic liberty of the individual are of basic importance both to him and the community as a whole. How an individual earns his living and invests his money not only affects his own personal satisfaction and advancement but it has repercussions on the economic organization of society. Limitations imposed on such rights will affect the very organization and operation of the economic system. They can influence what is produced, how it is made and at what cost, how efficiently the economy operates, and how the products of the economy are distributed to the various groups in the community.

In a controlled society is the individual generally free to follow such economic pursuits as he sees fit and at such places as he may wish?

Can he work at any trade, calling, or profession that he desires, or is the prior approval of some public body required?

Can he move about within the country and even depart from it at will?

Is industrial production guided and directed by the state or does public authority itself monopolize the major forms of productive enterprise?

Are the types of goods to be produced and the methods of production prescribed by public authority?

Is the utilization of new mechanical devices restricted?

Can new products be developed and marketed without prior government approval?

Are the prices of commodities determined by the government?

Can the farmer plant the crops that he wishes, cultivate his land as he desires, and market his crops when and where he pleases?

The worker as well as the producer in a free society is vested with basic economic rights, and how a totalitarian state treats them is of great interest to us.

Do such regimes permit workers to organize associations designed to improve their economic position?

Can individuals engage in concerted activities designed to strengthen their bargaining position?

Can the worker choose his own trade and select his own employer?

Does the state prescribe the wages that laborers are to be paid and decree the hours that they must work?

There is no need to decide which of these rights are the most significant. Some will assert that the economic rights are the most important; others will contend that certain political or personal rights are most important; still others will take the position that the only basic rights are those concerned with freedom of religion. A diversity of interests, and hence of values, is taken for granted. It is important to point out, however, the integral nature of rights and freedoms in the modern state. This means that political rights are in jeopardy if economic rights fail; religious freedom, positive or negative, is challenged if the state imposes rigorous controls over freedoms of speech, publication, or association. Control of the freedom to utter threatens the freedom to think and to believe. Control of the manner of working and the distribution of livelihood shapes the political choices and paths of the citizen.

There might be a tendency to regard as unimportant those rights that are of a procedural nature: equality before the law, freedom from arbitrary arrest, imprisonment, and search. A right is no less significant merely because it is procedural in the sense that its objective is to preserve or protect other rights. It does not become subordinate merely because it is used to make other rights a reality. What is the use of freedom of speech, freedom of religion, and freedom of inquiry if the state fails to provide machinery for their enforcement, and if public authorities are able to imprison at will any person who dares to exercise them? The substantive rights are but a hollow shell and a mockery without machinery adequate for their enforcement.

III. SOCIETIES TO BE STUDIED

Six controlled societies will be examined to determine the extent to which they regulate individual rights. We believe the comparative approach yields more comprehensive evidence as to the ways in which controlled societies deal with the individual than would a minutely detailed study of only one or two of such experiments. In each of the examples included only so much of the institutional and philosophical background of the program of regulation will be presented as is necessary to understand the objectives of the program and methods of operation.

1. *Feudalism.* We have paid special attention to a survey of the rights and privileges enjoyed by the individual in feudal society as it existed primarily in England in the thirteenth century. The desire for protection from physical violence was the basis for many of the controls imposed. Other restraints were imposed for religious reasons—to ensure salvation for the individual. Public rights and private rights were thoroughly intermixed. Partly as a consequence public power was widely diffused; numerous government functions were performed by private individuals or groups. Many of the limitations on personal liberty were imposed by custom rather than by a conscious program of legislation. This customary form of society, where public and private rights were merged and control decentralized, offers an interesting contrast to some of the more centralized modern experiments at regimentation.

2. *European absolute monarchies.* The absolute monarchies of the sixteenth and seventeenth centuries constituted examples of totalitarian states that differed from feudalism.[2] The bare, naked, political power of the then newly developed national state was considered of itself to be sufficient justification for imposing detailed regulations for the control of the individual. Only in the economic sphere was a rationalization for such state power developed; this was known as the merchantile system. Despite their lack of any systematic political, economic, or social justification those absolutistic states sought to impose a more far-reaching program of control over the individual than did some of the more recent experiments that equipped themselves with a fully rationalized program.

For the modern examples, we have chosen Soviet Russia, Fascist Italy, and Nazi Germany. We have not analyzed here the lesser examples of Spain or of Argentina. Spain might

[2] A. D. Lindsay, *The Modern Democratic State* (1943), p. 73, calls this form the first attempt at totalitarianism.

teach us something of the accommodation of an authoritarian political regime with a hierarchical religious authority. Argentina might teach us something of the possible conditions under which a fascist dictatorship might emerge in a major Western Hemisphere country. Otherwise these regimes do not exhibit special characteristics. We have not dealt with China, where totalitarian phenomena are still too recent and too obscure to warrant the effort to draw lessons for our own society—lessons which in any case would be vitiated by the vast differences in social conditions and technological level between them and ourselves. Nor have we dealt with the imposition of control by the postwar communist regimes in Eastern Europe. These have much more to teach us of the methods of communist imperialism of Moscow than they have to add to our knowledge of how a totalitarian government controls its supporting society.

3. *Russia.* Russia is our chief modern example, because it remains as a system in being, in course of development, and finally as the greatest remaining threat to freedom elsewhere in the world. Paradoxically, Russian communism inverted the objectives and emphases of Marxist and Leninist theory. Marxism aimed to establish human freedom by destroying violently the tyranny of the capitalist class, and its instrument, the bourgeois state. Marx promised a short transitional period of the "dictatorship of the proletariat," which, according to Lenin, would use violence to smash the bourgeois apparatus, and erect afterwards a spontaneous and voluntary administrative authority which would run economic and social affairs without more than sporadic discipline of occasionally aberrant elements in society. But Lenin soon discovered that he could not run a modern state in that way, and after his death, Stalin demonstrated that the dictatorship of the proletariat would not be a passing phase, but would exist so long as the country of the revolution was threatened by "capitalist encirclement." Today and for the future, Russia as the dictatorship of the Communist party, has emerged as a full-fledged, thoroughgoing totalitarian system in which nothing is left outside the ambit of state management or control. Yet the communist system retains the attractiveness for

many well-meaning people of its elements of idealism, and its completely rationalized philosophy. Our analysis asks how the rights of individuals have been shaped by the application of these theoretical principles, whether they have resulted in a consistent program of controls advantageous to the individual, and whether the rationalization has become a mere justification for naked state authority.

4. *Nazi Germany.* We have analyzed Hitler's Germany to show how the individual fares in a regime founded on unadorned, brute force, exercised in the name of a tribe, a leader, and a movement, resulting in an unlimited program of regimentation. The basic philosophical justification was the claim of race superiority. The basic emotional underpinning was the opportunity for supporters of the regime to indulge in sadism, blackmail, and violence to a degree unparalleled in modern history. Opportunities for violence and looting at home were more than matched by chances for violence and looting among the nations. The principle guiding all decisions within Nazi regimentation of the state and spoliation of its internal and external victims, was maximum improvement of fighting effectiveness. The Nazi system was geared for war. Finally, the Nazi system surpassed its two compeers in the efficiency of the administrative machine—party or government—used to enforce the restraints it engendered upon the individual.

5. *Fascist Italy.* We have dealt with Fascist Italy as the most forthright theoretical attack on the principles and practice of individual freedom, even though Italian practice was less rigorous than German or Russian. Fascist Italy proclaimed unequivocally the subordination of the individual to the state, although it did not set up either the class or racial distinctions on which German and Russian inhumanity was founded.

6. *Voluntary groups.* A study of the voluntary attempts to create small controlled communities within a nation yields interesting contrasts. In the United States during the past century and a half, a number of people of their own free will have attempted to set up planned communities designed to attain religious, social, or economic objectives. For the purpose of

reaching these goals many phases of the lives of the members were subjected to detailed regulations. These idealistic groups constituted islands of control in what we like to think of as the vast sea of freedom existing in this country. Why were people willing to give up the freedom they normally enjoyed and to accept in its stead the restraints imposed by these special groups? Did these associations succeed in attracting adherents over any period of time? In what ways did the communities restrict their members?

In some of these totalitarian regimes (for instance, Communist Russia) a well-organized systematic philosophy was developed to justify the subordination of the individual to the state while in others such a rationalization was absent. The whole program of control in a few of the experiments flowed almost logically from certain philosophical assumptions. Russia has developed a rationally consistent system that is supported by detailed intellectual explanations. These justifications are presented in the official literature and in the speeches of communist politicians. In other experiments attempts at rationalization are almost completely lacking. In feudalism the customary nature of the controls exercised largely explains this absence. The mass of regulations was developed over a long period of time and never embodied into formal laws.[3] Another reason is that in part feudal thinkers were largely preoccupied with other questions, primarily religious, that were considered to be more fundamental. The philosophical study of political institutions was subordinated to the consideration of problems of theology. Consequently, our discussion of feudalism cannot be as well-rounded and as systematic as our analysis of Communist Russia. Likewise the consideration of the absolute monarchies and mercantilism will have systematic shortcomings.[4]

[3] "We do not hear of a feudal system until long after feudalism has ceased to exist." F. W. Maitland, *Constitutional History of England* (1920), p. 142.

[4] One writer on mercantilism cautioned, ". . . We must be careful to assume that what we see in perspective was seen by the actors in the drama, not that they were conscious of any guiding principle more profound than what they would themselves have called practical common sense." Conyers Reid, "Mercantilism; The Old English Pattern of a Controlled Economy," *The Constitution Reconsidered* (1938), pp. 63, 65.

IV. PROBLEMS NOT CONSIDERED

Of necessity many questions will be unanswered by this study. Some of these are excluded because they are not germane to the major objective; others are not considered because of a want of creditable evidence on which to base conclusions. Still others involve such imponderables that to consider them would call for mere philosophizing.

Beyond our purview are controls imposed by groups other than the major source of political authority. Obviously numerous groups, associations, and institutions in the community restrict the rights of individuals in many ways. Only when these sources of power operate implicitly or explicitly as agents of the state shall we consider the restrictions exercised by them. Such limitations on personal liberty are not included because in practically all instances the groups imposing them lack the right to utilize physical authority to enforce them. Not infrequently religious organizations establish far-reaching restraints upon their adherents, but generally such regulations are not enforced by physical sanctions. In most instances any person can escape from them simply by withdrawing his affiliation from the organization concerned if he can endure the resulting crisis of conscience. But such a right of disassociation did not effectively exist for adherents of the Catholic Church in the Middle Ages. Through its control over the temporal state, that Church in effect exercised physical sanctions over individuals, for it was then impossible to distinguish clearly between what we now call the state on the one hand and the church on the other.

Some private groups do control certain activities of individuals who do not belong to them and who desire not to become so affiliated. A present-day example might be a labor organization that has closed-shop agreements with employers. In such a situation a person who does not belong to the union and who does not wish to become a member cannot be employed in occupations covered by such agreements even though employers might wish to hire him. During the Middle Ages and in the mercantilist period, guilds frequently exercised a comparable control over employment. But then guilds were acting tacitly or explicitly as agents of the government, and consequently their activities restricting individuals are considered to be within our purview.

The political dynamics of control will not be included because requirements of time and space do not permit. In any society where there is a large number of well-organized and politically articulate groups struggling for power, the individual is less likely to be subjected to unrestrained exploitation by one of them operating through the state than where one particularly powerful organization monopolizes the control of public authority.[5] Thus, if a church is the only group able to make its influence felt politically, the policies of the state will be more readily shaped to meet its demands than if other articulate groups are able to make effective demands on government. Again, if agricultural interests have a pre-eminent voice in the formulation of policy, all individuals might be subjected to extensive state controls designed to further the demands of rural residents. The enactment of the Statute of Apprentices by sixteenth-century England is an example of the results of such influence. These problems of the balance of interests within the state and of policy motivation are alluring; but their consideration would not help to determine what controls the state exercises over the individual; it would merely explain how the system of restraints took the form that it did.

No attempt will be made to consider whether a higher standard of living was developed in controlled societies than in free societies. The prevailing standard of living affects the physical well-being of the individual but it does not necessarily affect his liberty or his personal satisfaction; since it is possible for individuals to have a great deal of freedom and a low standard of living or a high standard of living and no liberty. Our major objective is to study the effect of a controlled society on the rights of the individual, and as a consequence an inquiry into the prevalent plane of living is extraneous to the primary goal.

[5] John N. Figgis, *Studies in Political Theory from Gerson to Grotius, 1414-1625* (1923), p. 126.

In any case, the relative standard of living in different countries at different times is not a result of the form of government. It is determined by the resources of the nation, its form of economic organization, and by the state of its technological development.

We have not concerned ourselves with the question of the degree of satisfaction and contentment experienced by individuals within controlled societies. This test of the value of a society is not germane to our major problem of describing the rights the individual is permitted to exercise. Individual gratification or sense of well-being is to a large extent relative. A man may well be contented in a society if he is not made aware by the knowledge of conditions elsewhere that his own lot could be vastly improved; totalitarian censorship is in part founded on this way of increasing the stability of the state. Furthermore, many men are so accustomed to what another place or age would call tyranny, that they are unaware of domination or exploitation, and inclined by inertia to accept it in any case. However far-reaching the restraints imposed on the individual by the absolute monarchies of the seventeenth century, royal institutions were venerated by the great mass of people. The crown often protected the little man against the inroads or encroachments of local landowners or the local guild.[6] State propaganda as well as censorship contribute to this satisfaction—propaganda which often could celebrate genuine accomplishments of the regime as seen in the eyes of the common man. Hitler expanded the Third Reich, and conquered unemployment, in the view of most Germans; thus he revindicated national honor and gave fresh cause for an upsurge of national pride, while re-establishing a feeling of economic security.

Whether controlled societies are more warlike than free societies is another query that must go unanswered.[7] This problem cannot be brushed off as being irrelevant to a consideration of the problem of personal liberty. The far-reaching wartime controls imposed by western countries twice within the last half century will not soon be forgotten by most people; but it

[6] Walter L. Dorn, *Competition for Empire* (1940), p. 11.
[7] Walter Lippmann, *The Good Society* (1937), Chap. 8.

would take us far afield into the philosophy of history to speculate concerning either the forms of government that are most conducive to war or the effects of war on individual rights. Our attention must be confined to the simpler problem of the consideration of the specific rights themselves rather than directed toward the conditions that affect those rights. In short, this book is designed to meet the relatively simple objective of describing the restraints actually imposed on individuals by controlled societies. In what ways do totalitarian states limit the rights of the individual?

CHAPTER II

FEUDALISM

Western European feudalism in the late Middle Ages is an excellent example of a controlled society that greatly affected the fundamental rights of practically all individuals. Protection both from external attack and from internal disorder was probably the major objective of feudal society, while the attainment of spiritual salvation in the next world was a second objective. Generally, the task of protection was performed through decentralized government agencies rather than by a unified public authority. Since central government was almost uniformly weak, authority to control the individual was divided among the manors, guilds, towns, and the Church, as well as the central government.

One of the major reasons for the decentralization of authority was the absence of adequate means of transportation and communication. Poor roads were the rule, and where adequate physical means of transportation existed, tolls all too frequently constituted a tremendous barrier to travel. These were heavy and they were applied in a capricious manner. Another basic cause of political decentralization was the prevailing system of natural economy. The difficulties of transportation and the prevalence of civil disorders compelled most communities to become relatively self-sufficient, and this in turn impeded the development of a strong central government. It was too costly to transport the food and other supplies necessary to maintain a government that was largely concentrated at a single point. The royal court traveled around the country because it was easier to bring the courtiers to the food than the food to them. Also the relative scarcity of money encouraged decentralization. Because of the monetary dearth, it was not unusual for taxes to be paid in kind.

Probably the most significant force in this period that tended to reduce the authority of the central government was the Roman Catholic Church. Almost everywhere its power rivaled that of the state. It was practically the only religious organization that operated in western Europe. Throughout this area it propagated many of the basic social, economic, and political ideals that were prevalent. It was not, according to present day ideas, purely a religious body, but was able to direct and guide government action. As a result, it had the capacity to get its philosophy embodied in public policy.

Since western Europe consisted of many countries and independent cities, there existed no uniform system of controls. Both the objectives and the means of control varied from place to place. For reasons of simplicity and brevity, attention will be directed primarily, but not exclusively, to how England controlled the individual in the period from the twelfth through the fourteenth century.

First, an attempt will be made to show the nature of feudalism and its significance to the individual. Then some of the major prevailing devices for exercising control will be considered. Most attention will be devoted to the manors and the guilds both because of their importance and because of our lack of current experience with them. Since the Church occupied a significant position in the system of government control, an effort will be made to explain its role. On the basis of this background the specific political, personal, and intellectual controls imposed in the feudal period will be discussed, and then the limitations on economic liberty will be examined.

I. THE NATURE OF FEUDALISM

What was feudalism? Maitland described it as:

> . . . A state of society in which the main social bond is the relation between lord and man, a relation implying on the lord's part protection and defence; on the man's part protection, service and reverence, the service including service in arms. This personal relation is inseparably involved in a proprietary relation, the tenure of land—the man holds land of the lord, the man's service is a burden on the land, the lord has important rights in the land, and (we may say) the full ownership of the land is split up between man

and lord. The lord has jurisdiction over his men, holds courts for them, to which they owe suit. Jurisdiction is regarded as property, as a private right which the lord has over his land. . . .[1]

In return for protection individuals placed themselves under the personal authority of a lord. The individuals promised to obey, to protect, and to work for him; in return they received certain rights to some of his land. The need for mutual protection was the major motivating force of both lord and vassal.

War was the cause of feudalism. The central government was too weak to keep the peace. Nobles, especially in France and Germany, fought among themselves since the royal government was not strong enough to control them. "War was the function, the profession of the noble; he was above all else a soldier."[2] As a consequence, brutality and insecurity permeated the society. Rights were generally insecure; adequate machinery for their enforcement did not exist.[3]

Feudalism developed and persisted because of the weakness of the central government. For various reasons the king sometimes granted limited authority over an area to a lord, who by various means extended the authority into a title of possession. Such an encroachment upon the authority of the central government was possible only because that government was weak. And because of its weakness individuals were willing to place themselves under the authority of a great lord so that he might protect them against barbarians or the attacks of other lords. "The protection of the central authority in the State was, even at its best, not sufficient to provide for the needs of individuals."[4] The lord was anxious to have individuals place themselves under his jurisdiction both because he desired to increase his own strength in fighting his fellow lords or to stave off an invasion and because he needed a ready supply of labor.

Government authority often arose out of private landholding,

[1] F. W. Maitland, *The Constitutional History of England* (1920), p. 143.

[2] Achille Luchaire, *Social France at the Time of Philip Augustus* (1912), p. 261.

[3] Charles Howard McIlwain, *The Growth of Political Thought in the West, from the Greeks to the Middle Ages* (1932), pp. 198-200.

[4] *Cambridge Medieval History*, Vol. 3 (1922), p. 460.

and as a result, feudalism involved a wide dispersal of public authority. As a part of his property rights the lord of the manor had the authority to hold court for his vassals.[5] The manorial court handled relations between the lord and his vassals that were not subject to the king's law. In England the authority of the king's justices was much broader than elsewhere; but even there it was relatively narrow. In addition, the lord of the manor might even be vested with the authority to execute the king's justice. Where such a grant of jurisdiction extended to all persons on the manor, irrespective of whether or not they held land under the lord or whether they were freemen or villeins, it was easy for royal and private jurisdiction to become confused in the lord's mind, for the right to hold court was a valuable possession. It yielded revenue, and it was a means of control.

Contract and status were confused in the feudal system. Some individuals had certain rights and duties because of the tenure by which they held land, but other individuals had the same or comparable duties because of their status. For example, a freeman might have to perform labor services because he was holding his land by villein tenure. Others persons were born villeins and had to perform the same tasks because of their birth.

Economically feudalism was pre-eminently a self-contained agrarian society. Over 90 per cent of the population of western Europe lived in rural areas.[6] The lack of means of transportation and the absence of any central authority adequate to keep the peace meant that local agricultural units had to be self-sufficing. The landholders were anxious for their land to be cultivated; consequently, they were interested in securing dependents attached to the soil to perform this work; in return such dependents were protected by their lord.[7] The nature of the landholdings and the organization of the agricultural economy were the major factors influencing the type of controls exercised over the individual in rural areas.

[5] Maitland, *The Constitutional History of England,* p. 151.
[6] P. Boissonnade, *Life and Work in Medieval Europe* (1927), p. 203.
[7] Maitland, *The Constitutional History of England,* p. 145.

II. MANOR, GUILD, AND CHURCH

Control over the individual was decentralized; it was not exercised by a single central government. In most countries in western Europe there was no single government that had sufficient authority to enforce its decisions effectively throughout its territory. England had a more unified and centralized government than any other country; but even here authority was divided among a large number of public and semipublic bodies, each of which imposed far-reaching restraints over the individuals within its particular sphere of action. In the rural areas the manorial system was a primary instrument of control. Within the towns frequently guilds exercised far-reaching economic authority.

In addition, the Church exercised significant temporal powers. In theory the earthly jurisdiction of the Church was only incidental to its spiritual role. Nevertheless, for several reasons its authority had significant repercussions upon individuals of all ranks. First, almost everyone was a communicant of the Church. Second, the state was not necessarily considered to be superior to the Church in the temporal sphere. Third, the Church itself was permitted to exercise significant temporal powers. Before attempting to present in a systematic manner the types of controls that were exercised over the individual, the significance of the manor, the guild, and the Church as instruments of control will be examined.

THE MANOR

The major form of economic and social organization in feudal society was the manor; and in rural areas this formed the pre-eminent instrument of public control. Essentially, it was an agricultural unit organized on a feudal basis. A village and the agricultural lands cultivated by its inhabitants were usually embraced in it. Over the manor a lord presided, and the greater part of its residents were his personal dependents. Normally, most of them, freemen as well as villeins, held land from the lord and were subject to his jurisdiction. Part of the land was directly occupied by the lord as demesne land, and was cultivated for him by villeins or freemen. Most of the remaining land was cultivated by villeins (and a few freemen) for their own benefit. The tilling of the soil either for themselves or for the lord was the principal work of the inhabitants.

The villeins who constituted the major portion of the manorial residents were under the personal control of the lord. In England at the time of the Domesday survey (1086), approximately 70 per cent of the rural population were villeins, and throughout western Europe they probably constituted more than 50 per cent of the population.[8] The villeins were personally dependent upon the lord of their manor, for legally the essence of villenage was personal dependence on a lord and the obligation to furnish him labor services. "The value of a manorial estate depended in fact upon the number of tenants which it contained, and the extent of their services and contributions, rather than upon the fertility of the soil." The work done by the villein on the lord's property might consist of a fixed number of days plowing and harvesting each year. If additional work was performed, as a rule food and drink were provided by the lord.[9]

The cultivation of the land on the so-called open field system facilitated the development of manorial control over the individual. All of the arable land in the manor was divided into three open fields, and in these fields the land was divided into strips allocated among the lord, his dependent villeins, and freemen. The strips were of approximately uniform size; the number of strips held by any individual depended upon the extent of his total holdings. In some places the location of these strips was not fixed. They were not necessarily assigned permanently; for apparently there were some efforts at rotation so as to provide for a more equitable distribution of the fertile land.[10]

On all the land in each of these three fields a uniform system

[8] E. Lipson, *An Introduction to the Economic History of England,* Vol. 1 (1923), pp. 32, 43; Boissonnade, *Life and Work in Medieval Europe,* p. 132.

[9] Paul Vinogradoff, *Villainage in England* (1892), pp. 44, 281; Lipson, *An Introduction to the Economic History of England,* Vol. 1, p. 37.

[10] The same, p. 66.

of cultivation was imposed. Each year one field was allowed to lie fallow: in one of the fields grain was planted and in the other root crops. The types of crops to be planted and the times of planting and harvesting were largely communal decisions made by the manor. Since all the land in each field was divided into small strips the ownership of which was intermingled, "no one was free to manage his own land in his own ways."[11] As a result of both the uncertain possession of land and of central control over the management of agriculture, no individual could afford to take any interest in the development of the soil of the strips of land cultivated by him or in the improvement of his own crops.

A significant portion of the manor was cultivated for the interest of the lord. From the lord's standpoint villenage existed to provide him with an adequate labor supply. His land was of little value if he did not have sufficient workers to cultivate it. In a system of natural economy such labor could most easily be secured by exchanging the use of some land for services to be performed in cultivating the remainder. The lord's "home farm" or demesne land was not separated from the remainder of the manor. It was in the form of strips interspersed with those of the villeins and freemen. Like theirs it was distributed among the three fields.[12]

The greater part of the decisions concerning the conduct of the manor were made by the community as a whole and not by the individual cultivators. They were arrived at in the manorial court which was really a meeting of the village community presided over by the lord or his steward. These communal decisions included: "The rotation of crops, and regulation of the ploughing, sowing and reaping, the allotment of meadows and treatment of the common waste, the rules for fencing and removal of hedges, the decisions as to rights of way over the 'communal fields' and the maintenance of roads and paths."[13]

[11] The same, pp. 56-57; Vinogradoff, *Villainage in England,* p. 230.
[12] Frederic Pollock and F. W. Maitland, *History of English Law before the Time of Edward I* (1920), Vol. 1, p. 364.
[13] Lipson, *An Introduction to the Economic History of England,* Vol. 1, pp. 67-68.

"Not only the free, but also the servile tenantry are ruled in accordance with the views and customs of a congregation of the tenants in their divers classes."[14]

The lord controlled the economic life of the manor. No one could operate a mill, an oven, or a wine press without his approval, but he generally sold the right to engage in these activities. All of the dependent residents of the manor had to patronize the enterprises thus established. A person could not carry on such activities even for his personal use,[15] for that would reduce the value of the monopoly to be disposed of by the lord.

The lord's jurisdiction over the manor frequently extended to all persons residing on it. Over the villeins his authority was close to being absolute. Over the freemen, legally the lord's competence was much more limited. Actually, his power over freemen was generally very extensive both because of the type of agriculture pursued and because the central government was not able to protect them from the lord's arbitrary acts.

THE GUILDS

In many towns the major device for economic control was the guilds. These were quasi-public bodies charged with the task of protecting the trade monopoly of the town. In this respect urban communities resembled the manor, for internally it too sought to monopolize trade for its own benefit. In Germany in particular the cities developed for themselves a monopoly over the subordinate trading areas that surrounded them. In this area no handicrafts were allowed to exist, and all goods had to be bought and sold in the town.[16] A guild was a public or quasi-public association of the producers of or the traders in a given commodity or a group of commodities. Generally, each guild was a monopoly, for it was "an institution that blindly

[14] Vinogradoff, *Villainage in England,* p. 361.
[15] C. G. Coulton, *The Medieval Village* (1925), pp. 55-56.
[16] Boissonnade, *Life and Work in Medieval Europe,* pp. 196, 203; Eli F. Heckscher, *Mercantilism,* Vol. 2 (1934), p. 86; and Charles Gross, *The Gild Merchant* (1890), Vol. 1, pp. 43-47.

aimed to reduce competition to a minimum."[17] All persons in a given town who desired to engage in a specific activity had to belong to the appropriate guild if one existed.[18]

The guild merchant was the form taken by such organizations as they first developed in the English towns late in the eleventh century. This was an association of all traders and producers in the community. Probably over one third of the cities of England had guild merchants, but the institution was not nearly as prevalent on the Continent. It operated under a municipal or a royal charter, and the grant of such a privilege was a source of royal revenue. In many municipal charters one of the major liberties given by the king was the right to establish guilds. Individual craft guilds began to develop shortly after the guild merchant made its appearance. In many places where the guild merchant already had been established, the new craft guilds slowly broke off from it as specific crafts increased in importance.[19]

The guild merchant was not only a product of municipal authority but in many instances it constituted the basic element in the government of the city. In some towns in England the guild merchant ultimately became the municipal government; in others the governing body of the city was composed of representatives of the craft guilds. Not infrequently the only way to become a citizen of a town was to become a member of a guild.[20]

The guilds were monopolies established among the producers of or traders in given commodities. They were organized to control production and distribution primarily for the benefit of their members and only secondarily in the consumers' interest. "The Gild was the department of town administration whose

[17] The same, Vol. 1, pp. 37, 50.

[18] Sir William Ashley, *An Introduction to English Economic History and Theory,* Vol. 1, Pt. 2 (1920), pp. 13, 15, 29.

[19] Gross, *The Gild Merchant,* Vol. 1, pp. 22, 114-17, 284; Lipson, *An Introduction to the Economic History of England,* Vol. 1, p. 194.

[20] Gross, *The Gild Merchant,* Vol. 1, p. 161; Sidney and Beatrice Webb, *English Local Government from the Revolution to the Municipal Corporations Act: Manor and Borough* (1924), Vol. 1, pp. 74, 187, 188, 297, 302; Vol. 2, pp. 449, 495, 512, 579.

duty was to maintain and regulate the trade monopoly." As proof that the guilds were under municipal control, it should be recalled that Parliament in 1437 required that their charters, bylaws, and regulations be registered with the town government before they became binding.[21] To implement its monopoly, each guild generally enjoyed the authority to exercise far-reaching controls on all who sought to carry on activities within its field. As institutions "that blindly aimed to reduce competition to a minimum,"[22] the guilds regulated the conditions of production, the quality of goods, the time when shops could be opened, and the conditions of apprenticeship.

The types of restraint created by guilds will only be summarized here, for at this point the purpose is merely to make clear that the guilds were basic instruments of control. The specific limitations imposed by them will be discussed more fully later.

The authority of the guilds often extended to the activities of persons who attempted to ply the craft without having been admitted to the group; and to ensure compliance, the guilds frequently enjoyed a general authority to search and to destroy all goods not produced under their rules. Severe limitations were imposed on the admission of new members, an obvious requirement for preserving their monopoly position. The duration of apprenticeship was controlled, and the qualifications, fees, and wages of apprentices were regulated. The relations of guildsmen with nonmembers were restricted. "The primary purpose of the craft was to establish a complete system of industrial control over all who associated together in the pursuit of a common calling."[23] Consequently, all conditions of production were within the purview of the guilds. Goods had to be produced in the open, night work was forbidden, quality was controlled. The objective of the regulations concerning the

[21] Gross, *The Gild Merchant,* Vol. 1, p. 43; Stella Kramer, *English Craft Gilds and the Government* (1905), p. 45.

[22] Gross, *The Gild Merchant,* Vol. 1, p. 50.

[23] Lipson, *An Introduction to the Economic History of England,* Vol. 1, p. 295.

quality of the goods was to ensure that the craft should not be damaged by poor workmanship and to protect the consuming public from goods of poor quality.[24]

Throughout the thirteenth and fourteenth centuries the guilds acting as semipublic bodies were the prime instrument of the municipalities for exercising economic control over the individual. They affected the entire range of economic and social relationships in the centers of trade. The primary objective of regulations was to increase the income of the guild members by regulating production, and to promote the trade monopoly of the town wherein they operated. "The underlying principle of the gild system was order rather than progress, stability rather than expansion."[25]

THE CHURCH

The Roman Catholic Church was one of the most important instruments of control over the individual in feudal society. The only centralizing force extending over western Europe was the Church, for it alone transcended national boundaries. One cannot consider the Church as something entirely separate from the state; for it too was in effect an instrument of government.

The Church considered itself superior to the state. In the thinking of the Church fathers, it was more important than the civil government, since salvation was its exclusive concern and the supreme objective of life.[26] In the Middle Ages "the relations between the Church and the State are those of two independent though closely related powers. . . ."[27] The most far-reaching claim of the Church to domination of all persons is contained in the Bull *Unam sanctam* of 1302; "Moreover we

[24] The same, p. 298; William Cunningham, *The Growth of English Industry and Commerce*, Vol. 1 (1890), p. 342.

[25] Lipson, *An Introduction to the Economic History of England*, Vol. 1, pp. 276, 287; Georges Francois Renard, *Guilds in the Middle Ages* (1919), p. 69.

[26] R. W. Carlyle and A. J. Carlyle, *A History of Mediaeval Political Theory in the West*, Vol. 1 (1903), pp. 190-91.

[27] The same, pp. 175-76.

declare, we affirm, we define, and pronounce that for every human creature it is absolutely necessary for salvation to be subject to the Roman Pontiff."[28] The Church viewed the state as only a secondary instrument for civil control in the temporal sphere. Civil rulers largely admitted the superior claim of the Church to authority.

Only with difficulty can one actually draw a clear line of distinction between the Church and the state in this period. Each was only a different aspect of society. Complete separation was not a part of the thinking of either the Church or the state "for neither of them could conceive of a society that was not at the same time both Church and State."[29]

The Church was in a position to exercise significant control over the rulers of the state. In the last resort its authority was enforced through its power of excommunication. Since all holders of political power were professed Catholics, excommunication to them had tremendous spiritual and temporal effects. The subjects of an excommunicated monarch were not spiritually obligated to obey him, and they suffered no spiritual consequences for such disobedience. The tremendous feudal landholdings of the Church were a further source of temporal power. In Germany probably half of all land was in its hands.[30] Hence its economic and military strength enabled it to exercise great power over the civil government.

Many functions now considered to be within the purview of the state, in the Middle Ages were carried on by the Church. Education was almost entirely its monopoly. Very little teaching was done outside of the Church, and in the rare cases where this happened, educational activities were subject to the jurisdiction of the Church courts.[31] All forms of poor relief and

[28] Quoted in McIlwain, *The Growth of Political Thought in the West,* p. 245.

[29] The same, p. 205.

[30] Boissonnade, *Life and Work in Medieval Europe,* p. 124.

[31] Sir William Holdsworth, *A History of English Law* (1924), Vol. 1, p. 165; "Education in the Fourteenth and Fifteenth Centuries," *Cambridge Medieval History,* Vol. 8, p. 688.

medical services were in ecclesiastical hands. Marriage and divorce were subject to Church control exclusively.

The control of the Church over education was one of its principal sources of power. It was practically the sole center of intellectual activities throughout the Middle Ages. Although learning was nurtured only as an adjunct to the spiritual role of the Church, its intellectual activities had significant temporal results. Obviously, the Church was in a position to use teaching for its own ends. All educated persons were indoctrinated with the idea of the superiority of the Church. With a monopoly of learning in the hands of the Church, the state frequently had to turn to clerics when it required trained public servants.

The Church claimed and was able to enforce exclusive temporal jurisdiction over persons in ecclesiastical orders. Its courts alone had jurisdiction over the criminal acts of persons in holy orders. This claim of criminal authority over clerics gave rise to what was known in England as "benefit of clergy." Persons in holy orders charged with felonies were actually tried in Church courts, and there the trial was a mere formality. Only if the Church failed to acquit the accused, was he turned over to civil authorities for punishment. Ultimately, benefit of clergy was extended to anyone able to read and write.[32]

No divergence or dissension from the teachings of the Church was tolerated. Throughout western Europe there was no such thing as religious freedom. Apostasy and heresy were hunted out, generally with the assistance of the state, for the Church considered that it was a duty of the government to hunt down and destroy heretics. The policy of the Church toward heretics was the cause of the almost universal persecution of Jews. Members of this race were considered to be apart from the social and political fabric of western Europe. For example, since they could not take an oath, they were excluded from the system

[32] Holdsworth, *A History of English Law,* Vol. 2, pp. 294-300; Pollock and Maitland, *The History of English Law Before the Time of Edward I,* Vol. 1, p. 445.

of feudal landholding, and as a rule they could not be admitted to the guilds.[33] The special position of the Jews will be considered in more detail later.

In shaping many of the economic controls imposed by the state on the individual, the teachings of the Roman Catholic Church constituted a most significant force. The first principle underlying the economic ideas of the Church was that money making was a means not an end in itself, and that limits were imposed upon it as a result of the basic purposes for which the money was being earned. Its second basic precept was that trade and commerce must be carried on honestly and well. This probably was one of the major causes for the insistence of the guilds that a relatively high degree of craftsmanship must be maintained. Third, there should be a just price at which articles should be sold, and that this price should be determined by law. This was also a logical derivation from the first principle that money making was not an end in itself. To the medieval theologian "trade was sinful if conducted for sake of gain or greed."[34] And in the fourth place, the Church definitely disapproved of usury.

III. POLITICAL RIGHTS

Modern ideas of political rights of individuals are inapplicable to the Middle Ages, for the relationship of the government to the individual was entirely different than that we are now familiar with. No one thought of the government as being responsible to the great mass of individuals. True, the idea of "limited" government was prevalent, but there was an absence of effective means of controlling it to ensure that it was limited and responsible. Broad popular responsibility for government could hardly exist in most medieval states. The development of rapid means for communicating ideas was still far in the future, and without articulate organs of public opinion, responsi-

[33] W. E. H. Lecky, *History of the Rise and Influence of the Spirit of Rationalism in Europe,* Vol. 2 (1914), p. 38; Pollock and Maitland, *The History of English Law Before the Time of Edward I,* Vol. 1, p. 473; Renard, *Guilds in the Middle Ages,* p. 43.

[34] Bede Jarrett, *Social Theories of the Middle Ages* (1942), p. 164.

ble popular government cannot exist in a country with a large area.[35]

The prevalent attitude toward law was, however, a much more significant element conditioning medieval ideas of popular participation in government. "In its strictly 'feudal' connotation, 'law,' in the highest sense of that term, was nothing but the immemorial custom of a community defined territorially."[36] Since law was custom, it was found and not made.[37] Hence the idea of making new law or legislation was not a part of the climate of opinion of the Middle Ages.

> The idea of "making" law is alien to then existing modes of thought, and when changes occur, as they must, if consciously made, they are usually only the correction of defects in the machinery for administering the ancient customs, or they purport to be the restoration of these customs after a period of wrongful desuetude, or the abolishing of abuses that have contravened the ancient rules; or finally, if the changes cannot be brought conveniently under any of these, they are concealed under a fiction. Changes must inevitably occur in any system, and in a system of law and government which is developing as rapidly as was the case in mediaeval England, such changes must be great and fundamental. But the fact that these developments, great as they were, were so carefully covered up shows the attitude of men's minds towards "legislation." . . .[38]

Not even the king could make law—he could approve it, find it, and preserve it, but not make it.[39] When people did not think of new laws as coming from the government (even though some were actually enacted), ideas of popular participation in government or of government responsibility were not relevant.

This attitude toward law affected the medieval idea of kingship. All of the great feudal states of western Europe were monarchies. "Their kings were actually both irresponsible and absolute, and absolute because irresponsible." "In the middle

[35] McIlwain, *The Growth of Political Thought in the West,* p. 363; A. F. Pollard, *The Evolution of Parliament* (1920), pp. 337-39.

[36] McIlwain, *The Growth of Political Thought in the West,* p. 186.

[37] Charles Howard McIlwain, *The High Court of Parliament and its Supremacy* (1910), pp. 42-43.

[38] The same, pp. 46-47.

[39] McIlwain, *The Growth of Political Thought in the West,* p. 188.

ages a king must be 'absolute' in administration if he is to fulfil his obligation to preserve the law and ensure peace and justice." And by the term absolute is meant that he is "without a superior, associate, or companion, to whom he is in any manner responsible."[40]

The medieval king was also a feudal lord, and out of the duties and obligations resulting from his feudal role developed the idea that limits could be imposed on him. "In the mass of changing reciprocal rights and obligations existing between a medieval king and his people it is not always easy to distinguish clearly between the ones arising solely out of feudal custom and those based upon the relation of king and subject."[41] As feudal lord some things were beyond his competence, even though adequate machinery for enforcing such limitations did not exist.

In his role as chief feudal lord some checks did develop on the king's royal power. He was generally aided and assisted by a council composed of his chief feudal vassals or tenants. This council performed administrative and legal work for the king. Out of the feudal rights of these tenants and advisers came the first checks on the king, but these restraints had to develop outside the system of law for "against him the law had no coercive process; there was no legal procedure whereby the king could either be punished or compelled to make redress. . . . If the king breaks the law then the only remedy is a petition addressed to him praying him that he will give redress. . . ."[42] On occasion when the king transgressed upon the feudal rights of his principal tenants, they took steps outside of the law to enforce their rights.

> . . . It was, then, the legal fact that the king's rights as overlord did not make him sole proprietor of his subjects' lands and goods, that they were beyond his legitimate authority to take, to destroy, or disturb, and the further fact that his vassals were within their lawful rights in renouncing his authority and openly defying him if he did so; it was this which explains the nature of medieval king-

[40] The same, pp. 364-65, 372-73.
[41] The same, p. 388.
[42] Maitland, *The Constitutional History of England,* p. 100.

ship and the way in which it was in course of time made subject to the control of the people. . . .[43]

Magna Carta granted by King John in England in 1215 is an illustration of feudal limitations imposed upon the king. This granted a number of basic rights to the major feudal lords; but it was not a grant of rights to the great mass of subjects.[44]

As a means of enforcing such limitations rebellion by the principal tenants was on occasion legalized. For example, Article 61 of Magna Carta authorized it, and a half century later the Provisions of Oxford reaffirmed it.[45] In the fourteenth century several English kings were deposed by the major feudal tenants for transgressing their rights. The barons were merely enforcing their rights against their feudal lord—the king.

National grievances, especially in England, began to be redressed through the High Court of Parliament, which was an outgrowth of the king's council. This body consisted of the lords, the clergy, and representatives of certain other groups of the population. As a court of law its function was to find the law, not to legislate. The representatives in Parliament presented to the king petitions of grievances that they sought to have redressed. Representation was not a means of protecting individual rights or forwarding individual interests.[46] Members of the House of Commons were chosen to bind the constituency. They performed a duty to the king, and the major reason the king desired that any popular interests should be represented was to enable him to secure their financial support for new taxes. And since one of the major tasks of Parliament was to levy taxes, and it engaged in but little law making, hardly anything was to be gained by being a member. In addition, traveling to the seat of government was burdensome and time consuming. As a result in the late Middle Ages many persons refused to stand for election, and some were even compelled to

[43] McIlwain, *The Growth of Political Thought in the West,* p. 368.

[44] Holdsworth, *A History of English Law,* Vol. 2, p. 211.

[45] McIlwain, *The Growth of Political Thought in the West,* pp. 374-76.

[46] C. H. McIlwain, "Medieval Estates," *Cambridge Medieval History,* Vol. 8 (1932), Chap. 23, p. 668; Pollard, *The Evolution of Parliament,* p. 328.

serve against their wishes.[47] Taxes voted by Parliament in England in the late Middle Ages generally consisted of one fifteenth of the value of real property in rural areas and one tenth in cities which had special representation. Because of the increased taxes resulting from borough representation, the cities were not anxious to select representatives as separate constituencies. Hence borough representation actually declined in the Middle Ages. Since the king needed revenue in addition to his feudal income, frequently he was forced to grant the petitions of Parliament in return for its grant of taxes.[48] Not until the end of the fifteenth century was the participation of all of Parliament—the commons as well as the lords and clergy—required in the process of making laws designed to redress grievances.[49]

Even in England the parliamentary franchise was highly restricted. "The idea that anyone had a right to vote would have been unintelligible in the fourteenth century."[50] By the fifteenth century the commoners representing the various shires were chosen by electors who held real property of a value of not less than 40 shillings a year. The 40 shillings requirement, established in 1430, was first used in 1294 as the basis for determining who was obligated to serve on juries. Then its purpose was to free the poor from this burdensome obligation. Where boroughs were independently represented in Parliament, their members were chosen by a restricted franchise. They were selected by whatever means the borough might determine, and in many a town this meant that they were selected by the borough council, and in a number of towns this consisted of the guild leaders.

The task of serving as a member of Parliament was regarded as a duty not a privilege. Thus during the Middle Ages the individual was highly restricted in his right to hold office and to select representatives. Often the only office regularly open to the villeins was that of reeve. Women were generally re-

[47] McIlwain in *Cambridge Medieval History*, Vol. 8, pp. 687-88; Pollard, *The Evolution of Parliament*, pp. 154-55.

[48] The same, p. 373.

[49] Pollard, *The Evolution of Parliament*, p. 328.

[50] The same, p. 154.

stricted from holding office and so were the Jews and all other disbelievers. Not infrequently, in the English towns the franchise was limited to guild members.

There was no popular right to criticize the government. Obviously, in a manor the villeins were not in a position to criticize their lord, for he could punish them as he wished, provided he did not maim or kill them. As one writer put it, between the serf and the seignior "there was no other judge but God."[51] Hence the lord was able to run the manor in his own way. Under such conditions no right of assembly existed. Effective criticism of the king was not feasible for the great mass of the population. He was in a position to imprison at will since there was no means of questioning his authority to do so. The idea of any form of a responsible government was foreign to the medieval mind. The reins of authority were in the hands of a very small clique of persons who acquired their positions largely by birth.

IV. PERSONAL RIGHTS

Only a few problems of personal rights will be considered—freedom from arbitrary arrest and imprisonment, equality before the law, sumptuary legislation, and religious and intellectual freedom. The discussion will be illustrative rather than definitive.

FREEDOM FROM ARBITRARY IMPRISONMENT

As a rule, there was no protection of the individual from arbitrary arrest. The large mass of villeins could be thrown into jail at any time by their own lord. If the lord did not kill or maim his villeins, there was little that he could not do to them, for they were not protected by the common law.[52] The existence of the status of villenage was a valuable weapon in the hands of the overmighty subject. "Under such a claim [of villenage] a powerful lord could be guilty of false imprisonment and of all kinds of extortion."[53]

[51] Jean Bressaud, *A History of French Public Law* (1915), p. 319.
[52] See above, p. 26.
[53] Holdsworth, *A History of English Law,* Vol. 3, pp. 500-01.

Someone may say, "Yes, this is true of villeins—but were not free men better off?" Even the feudal nobility was fined and imprisoned arbitrarily without trial. That is one of the major reasons they demanded and secured Magna Carta in 1215. Did not Magna Carta protect all freemen when it provided in Section 39 that no man should be deprived of liberty or property except in accord with the judgment of his peers and the law of the land? Of course this only benefited the principal feudal tenants and not even all freemen. Nevertheless, if the king arbitrarily arrested a person covered by this clause, there were available to him almost no legal remedies to meet the situation. Not until late in the seventeenth century was the writ of *habeas corpus* developed to secure judicial review of such cases.[54] Concerning the availability of remedies for arbitrary imprisonment in England, Pollock and Maitland asserted,

> We may also beleve that if a man who thought himself unlawfully imprisoned by the sheriff or by some lord of a franchise made his voice heard in the king's court, the justices had power to order that his body should be brought before them and to liberate him if they were persuaded that his detention was unlawful. But we have seen no definite machinery provided for this purpose.[55]

Not until the end of the fifteenth century was it believed that a member of Parliament should be free from arrest during the session, but even then no effective means existed to protect him from such action.[56] There was no method for protecting a person from illegal searches by the crown or by his immediate feudal superior. Although now we consider freedom from illegal arrest and freedom from illegal searches fundamental, such civil rights were unknown in the Middle Ages.

EQUALITY BEFORE THE LAW

Equal treatment under the law for all persons was nonexistent in the Middle Ages. Special privileges, unusual rights,

[54] Holdsworth, *A History of English Law,* Vol. 2, p. 211; and Maitland, *The Constitutional History of England,* pp. 271-75.

[55] Pollock and Maitland, *The History of English Law Before the Time of Edward I,* Vol. 2, p. 586.

[56] Maitland, *The Constitutional History of England,* p. 241; S. B. Chrimes, *English Constitutional Ideas in the Fifteenth Century* (1936), pp. 71-141.

and burdensome limitations on various groups were the rule rather than the exception. "That there were different classes of society that should be governed by different laws would have appeared a truism to the medieval legislature."[57] Special privileges were given to the French nobility. The highest ranks in the army were reserved to them; they were exempt from the major tax—the taille. Trial in special courts and less burdensome criminal penalties were provided for them. They had certain honorary privileges—precedence and the exclusive right to wear a white plume and they alone could wear armor. Generally, a special pew was reserved for them in church. But a few limitations were imposed on the nobility. If the French nobility engaged in agriculture, handicrafts, trade, or commerce, their noble rights were temporarily suspended.[58]

There were probably fewer distinctions between the different classes of persons in England than in the continental countries, but even there significant distinctions existed. Society was divided into different groups—the king, peers, knights, yeomen, villeins, merchants, laborers, artisans, all had definite places. Nevertheless, "It might be possible—and in fact it was more possible in England than in any other country in Europe—to step from one class to another."[59]

For various classes of English freemen different rights existed. Pollock and Maitland observed, "Our law hardly knows anything of a noble or a gentle class; all freemen are in the main equal before the law."[60] "But there were many rules of law peculiar to each class."[61] The nobles did have some special rights. They had a right of judgment by their peers—that is, they could not be judged by men of lower rank. But this applied only to felony and treason. They had some freedom from civil arrest, and various delays were open to them in answering summonses.

[57] Holdsworth, *A History of English Law,* Vol. 2, p. 464.

[58] Bressaud, *A History of French Public Law,* pp. 300 and 303; Sydney Herbert, *The Fall of Feudalism in France* (1920), p. 33; and J. W. Thompson, *Feudal Germany* (1928), p. 312.

[59] Holdsworth, *A History of English Law,* Vol. 2, p. 464.

[60] Pollock and Maitland, *The History of English Law Before the Time of Edward I,* Vol. 1, p. 408.

[61] Holdsworth, *A History of English Law,* Vol. 2, p. 464.

Although "all freemen are in the main equal before the law," many and possibly most men were not free. Probably over half of the population of western Europe were villeins of one type or another. Other groups such as the Jews had only limited rights. Here only the special position of villeins and Jews will be considered.

The essence of villenage was the personal dependence of the villein on a lord to whom he was attached.[62] This personal dependence characterized and permeated all phases of the status. The villein "was merely the chattel of his lord to give and sell at his pleasure." "The lord may beat or imprison his serf, though of such things we do not hear much." As against his lord the villein had no rights—he could not sue him, nor could he have property rights against him. In England the villein could not bring a criminal appeal against his lord.[63] One French historian said that, "The only judge there was between the villein and his lord was God."[64]

Villeins acquired their status in three ways: (1) by birth, (2) by prescription, and (3) by acknowledgment of the status in a court of law. But in the period under consideration few freemen in England became villeins.[65] In the period before recorded history persons became villeins either by commending themselves to a lord to receive his protection or by the illegal extension of the lord's authority over freemen.

The economic essence of villenage was the obligation of the villein to render labor service to his lord. Generally, this was of an indeterminate character. The lord could determine what work was to be done and when it was due. Supposedly the labor service of villeins was determined by the custom of the manor, but it is problematic whether the custom of the manor ever effectively bound the lord. The personal dependence of the vil-

[62] Vinogradoff, *Villainage in England*, p. 44.

[63] Pollock and Maitland, *The History of English Law Before the Time of Edward I*, Vol. 1, pp. 414-16.

[64] Bressaud, *A History of French Public Law*, p. 319.

[65] Vinogradoff, *Villainage in England*, pp. 59 and 63; Pollock and Maitland, *The History of English Law Before the Time of Edward I*, Vol. 2, p. 425.

lein on his lord precluded him from objecting too strenuously if the lord demanded additional services. Besides, the king's justices offered no protection to the villein who charged that the manorial custom was violated. Villenage was almost exclusively confined to agricultural work.

A man who was of villein status could not leave the manor without the approval of its head. During a short period after his departure the lord could seize him any time without resorting to legal processes. But should the villein return to the manor even after the expiration of that period, he still could be impressed. If a villein remained in a town for a year and a day he became a freeman; consequently the lord generally required that a villein must secure his permission before leaving the manor. On occasion this permission was granted only on the condition that the villein's father would continue on the manor.[66] Thus, in effect the parent became a hostage to guarantee the return of his son.

A villein had no property or goods that the lord could not acquire through possession. But against all persons other than his lord the villein could defend his property as a freeman. The head of the manor did not of himself have full possession of all goods of the vassal; but he could take possession of them if he so desired. Under such circumstances it is not surprising that a villein could not sell cattle or other produce without the lord's consent. Whatever the villein bought he bought with the lord's money.[67] The villein could not transfer property to his heirs without permission from the lord. The right to inherit property from a villein was a privilege granted by the lord for a fee. To inherit real property from a villein, one normally had to pay a fee equal to one year's income from it. High fees were also required for permission to inherit personal property.[68]

The villein "was merely the chattel of the lord to give and

[66] The same, pp. 417-18; Vinogradoff, *Villainage in England,* pp. 157-58.
[67] Herbert, *The Fall of Feudalism in France,* pp. 4-5; Vinogradoff, *Villainage in England,* p. 67; Pollock and Maitland, *The History of English Law Before the Time of Edward I,* Vol. 1, p. 419.
[68] Vinogradoff, *Villainage in England,* pp. 161-62.

sell at his pleasure." But he was rarely sold apart from his land.[69] Villeins or their children could not become apprentices or follow any trade or craft without previous approval of the lord, and both civil and canon law forbade him to take holy orders.[70] Should a villein want to educate his children, he had to secure the approval of the head of the manor. Thus in 1372 a villein was fined heavily by his lord—a bishop—for sending his son to school without permission.

Probably the most degrading element in the status of villenage was the requirement that before the villein's daughter could marry the lord must give his permission. A regular fee known as merchet had to be paid to the lord to secure his permission. The reason for this was that if the daughter married outside of the manor the lord would lose her services. Her services constituted a valuable property right.[71]

Villeins were not slaves. Unlike slaves the lord was not responsible for feeding and clothing them. Although they could be bought and sold by their masters, there was no general market for their sale. But in their relations with all persons other than their lord they were freeman, and they had the normal rights of freeman.[72]

Although villenage may resemble slavery in some respects, actual slavery was not common in western Europe. At the time of Domesday book less than 10 per cent of England's population were slaves. In the ensuing centuries slavery declined still further. One reason the institution was not common in medieval Europe was because there was no central government with authority to prevent slaves from escaping. Since it was so easy for slaves to escape, this form of property was not profitable.[73]

[69] Pollock and Maitland, *The History of English Law Before the Time of Edward I*, Vol. 1, pp. 414-19.

[70] Vinogradoff, *Villainage in England*, pp. 153-54, 157; F. W. Maitland, *Collected Papers*, Vol. 2 (1911), p. 399; and Pollock and Maitland, *The History of English Law Before the Time of Edward I*, Vol. 2, p. 429.

[71] Vinogradoff, *Villainage in England*, p. 153.

[72] The same, pp. 151-52; Holdsworth, *A History of English Law*, Vol. 3, p. 495; Pollock and Maitland, *The History of English Law Before the Time of Edward I*, Vol. 1, p. 414.

[73] Lipson, *An Introduction to the Economic History of England*, Vol. 1, p. 45; Vinogradoff, *Villainage in England*, p. 152.

The Jews constituted another group that had strictly inferior rights and that suffered from onerous limitations. Their religion was the cause for discrimination. From the standpoint of theology the Jews were in a peculiar position. Obviously, they were not Christians, but they were not regarded as infidels. They were permitted to hold their own religious services; but they could not attempt to win converts.[74] Since they could hold no position involving control over Christians, they could not keep Christian servants. Their inability to take a Christian oath and their lack of authority to control Christians excluded them from owning land under the feudal structure, and as a result they were able to engage only in such pursuits in the towns as were not organized into guilds.[75] However, one line of activity was open to them that was closed to Christians. That was the lending of money at interest. This remained open to them because originally the only penalties attached to this pursuit were ecclesiastical, and being non-Christians they were not subject to the Church courts. Ultimately, usury was forbidden by civil law. For example, in 1275 England forbade Jews to engage in usury.[76]

Many other vexatious discriminations were applied to the Jews. They were not permitted to marry with Christians. Their place of residence was carefully delimited in many countries. Some English cities forbade Jews to dwell within their limits. In Germany they were required to live in a specified section of the cities so that they could be controlled more effectively and so that Christians would not be contaminated by them.[77] In many countries they had to wear a specific symbol—a yellow stripe or patch on their gowns.[78] In some places they were not permitted to enter Christian churches.

[74] "The Jews in the Middle Ages," *Cambridge Medieval History,* Vol. 7 (1932), Chap. 22, p. 646; Marvin Lowenthal, *The Jews of Germany* (1936), pp. 92-93; and Pollock and Maitland, *The History of English Law Before the Time of Edward I,* Vol. 1, p. 474.

[75] Lowenthal, *The Jews of Germany,* p. 15; *Cambridge Medieval History,* Vol. 7, p. 642.

[76] Pollock and Maitland, *The History of English Law Before the Time of Edward I,* Vol. 1, p. 471.

[77] The same, p. 473; Lowenthal, *The Jews of Germany,* p. 94.

[78] *Cambridge Medieval History,* Vol. 7, Chap. 22, p. 643.

In most countries Jews were considered to be villeins of the king or servants of the Treasury. As such they received the king's special protection insofar as he desired to extend it to them. Since they were completely subject to his power, he could tax them as he saw fit and confiscate their property whenever he desired. The king took all from them that a far-sighted self-interest would permit him. In order to make it possible for the English crown more effectively to seize their property, evidences of indebtedness that were held by them had to be reduced to writing and deposited at central recording offices. Thus when the king seized the Jews' property, he was able to appropriate the outstanding credits due to them, and these then would be payable to the king. Thus the borrowers were not able to escape their obligations when the king seized the property of the Jews.[79]

In dealing with all persons other than the king, Jews frequently had most of the civil rights of freemen. In England "when the interests of neither the king nor any other Christian are involved, the Jews may arrange their own affairs and settle their own disputes in their own way and by their own Hebrew law."[80] Since the Jews were completely under the control of the king, they could be expelled from a country at his will, as happened in England in 1290, in France in 1394, and in Spain in 1492.[81] This proved to be advantageous to the monarchs when they found themselves greatly in debt to the Jews. Thus throughout most of medieval Europe the Jews were set apart from the rest of the community by burdensome discriminatory regulations. Their lives and property were always at the mercy of the king. In general, their position was almost as disadvantageous as that of the villeins.

Aliens constituted another group with limited civil rights. There was a tendency to regard all aliens as enemies. In England they could not own land nor could they inherit property; but

[79] Lowenthal, *The Jews of Germany*, p. 72; Bressaud, *A History of French Public Law*, p. 198; and Pollock and Maitland, *The History of English Law Before the Time of Edward I*, Vol. 1, pp. 469-72.

[80] The same, p. 469.

[81] Lowenthal, *The Jews of Germany*, p. 82.

by the later Middle Ages alien merchants could own chattels and could lease houses for trade purposes. An English statute forbade them to engage in retail trade, and foreign traders had to reside with designated hosts. Probably they could not bring either personal or real actions.[82] The discrimination against foreigners may have been a result of a desire to preserve trade in the hands of the natives.

Burdensome limitations were placed on other groups of individuals. A person who had been excommunicated by the Church was an ecclesiastical outlaw, and apparently was very close to being legally dead. He could perform no valid legal act. He could not sue but he could be sued. Other persons could not talk, eat, or pray with him.[83] The rights of women at public law were highly circumscribed, although their rights under private law were extensive. Concerning the legal position of women in medieval England, Pollock and Maitland observed, "Private law with few exceptions puts women on a par with men; public law gives a woman no rights and exacts from her no duties, save that of paying taxes."[84] They could sue and be sued, but they could not serve on juries nor could they give evidence. Unmarried women could hold land even by military tenure. But the property rights of a married woman were an entirely different matter; they were exercised by her husband.

Equality before the law was unknown in medieval Europe. The population was divided into many distinct groups, and different rights were granted to these several segments of the community. Nobles, villeins, the clergy, aliens, Jews, and women constituted classes that were treated differently. Invidious distinctions under the law were the rule rather than the exception.

SUMPTUARY LEGISLATION

The dress and personal conduct of the individual were generally subjected to state regulations during the feudal period. Al-

[82] Holdsworth, *A History of English Law,* Vol. 2, p. 471; Pollock and Maitland, *The History of English Law Before the Time of Edward I,* Vol. 1, pp. 459-61.

[83] The same, p. 478.

[84] The same, p. 482.

though the full flowering of sumptuary legislation did not come until the sixteenth and seventeenth centuries, many controls of this type had been imposed by a number of countries before the end of the thirteenth century. For example, in 1294 Philip the Fair of France prescribed in detail the clothing to be worn by all classes. No common citizen was to wear precious stones, gold, or fur. Dukes and counts who had an income of less than 6,000 lire a year could have only four robes annually, and a lady of this class might have but a single gown a year. It was also provided that at dinner only two courses could be served in addition to the soup. In the next century the King of France attempted to restrict luxury by limiting the prices of clothing.[85]

Many cities adopted such legislation. Florence in the fourteenth century forbade women to wear excessive dress and established a special officer "to repress the luxury of women." To illustrate the minuteness of the regulations, the women were prohibited from wearing more than two finger rings at the same time. In 1375 Zurich made illegal the use of embroidery on women's dresses. In the same century Nürnberg regulated in detail many forms of wearing apparel. Women were not allowed to wear garments of silk, or gold, or silver. They were not permitted to have more than two garments made of fur, nor were they to wear ornaments of gold or silver. Men were not overlooked. They were forbidden to wear red buckram, nor could they wear their hair parted.[86]

England in the middle of the fourteenth century (1363) adopted legislation regulating clothing in detail. The law was designed primarily to check extravagance and to demarcate clearly the several classes of society. It contained specific regulations applicable to the clothing of servants and artificers. The cloth for the clothing of all persons in these categories was not to cost more than two marks. Yeomen and handicraftsmen could

[85] James M. Vincent, "European Blue Laws," *Annual Report of the American Historical Society* (1897), pp. 355, 358.

[86] Lecky, *History of the Rise and Influence of the Spirit of Rationalism in Europe,* Vol. 2, p. 275; James M. Vincent, *Custom and Conduct in the Laws of Basel, Bern, and Zurich, 1370-1800* (1935), p. 44; and Kent R. Greenfield, *Sumptuary Legislation in Nürnberg* (1918), pp. 108-09.

not wear cloth that cost more than 12 shillings. Such persons were also forbidden to wear gold, silver, stones, buttons, or chains.

Squires below the rank of knight and whose income was no more than 100 pounds a year were not supposed to wear cloth costing more than 4.5 marks. Cloth of gold or silver, silk, furs, and gems were forbidden to them. Different requirements were applicable to squires with incomes of more than 200 pounds a year. Knights worth from 400 to 1,000 pounds a year could wear anything they wanted with the exception of ermine. Carters, oxherds, shepherds, and swineherds were permitted to wear only blanket cloth that cost not more than 12 pence a yard. "Every custom was to some extent a uniform revealing the rank and condition of its wearer."[87] There is no evidence of the actual enforcement of this statute. Although it was repealed the following year, significant portions of it were embodied in legislation enacted during the ensuing years.

The sports of various classes of people were also regulated. In 1363 a royal ordinance was issued in England forbidding the playing of quoits, handball, and football under pain of imprisonment. Cock fighting and tennis were prohibited. In 1388 Parliament directed that servants in husbandry and laborers should practice with bows and arrows on Sundays and holidays, and they were directed not to play tennis, football, dice, or quoits. Hunting was also regulated by custom in many countries. The lord of a manor usually had the exclusive right to hunt on it.[88] By law England declared that only persons with specified incomes could hunt. The English Parliament provided that only those persons could have hawks who were "of an estate to have the hawk."[89]

There were probably three motives behind this sumptuary legislation. First, the regulation of clothing was impelled by a general desire to preserve class distinction so that any stranger

[87] Frances Elizabeth Baldwin, *Sumptuary Legislation and Personal Regulation in England* (1926), p. 53.

[88] The same, pp. 70, 71, 83, and 94; Herbert, *The Fall of Feudalism in France*, p. 28.

[89] Holdsworth, *A History of English Law*, Vol. 2, pp. 465-66.

merely by a glance at a man's clothing could determine his rank in society. A second objective was to check what were considered to be the deleterious consequences of certain individual actions. Luxury and extravagance were considered to be wicked in themselves and generally harmful to the morals of the people. Third, economic objectives were present in some cases. There was a wish to encourage home industry and to discourage the buying of foreign goods. This probably was the reason for English legislation against wearing foreign cloth.[90] Another economic objective was to encourage the people to save their money so that they could help the king in time of need. The sumptuary ordinances of the continental cities were aimed at eliminating the superfluous, suppressing vanity, and discouraging activities harmful to good character.[91]

FREEDOM OF THOUGHT AND EXPRESSION

There was no general right of freedom of speech, of assembly, or of religion. No one, whether he was a noble or a villein, was in any position to exercise freedom of speech and thereby to criticize the government or his feudal superiors, since there was an absence of legal means for preventing arbitrary arrests and imprisonment. A great mass of the people were villeins who had no rights against their lord, and as a consequence they could be put in jail or fined at the lord's pleasure if they so much as criticized him. Even the nobility was in no position to criticize their superiors. In the Italian cities anyone who dared to criticize the government would shortly find himself in jail or in exile.[92]

Religious freedom was unknown. No deviation from the dogmas of the Roman Church was permitted to Christians. The Church insisted that the civil government must assist it in suppressing all attempts to deviate from the theology that it

[90] Baldwin, *Sumptuary Legislation and Personal Regulation in England,* p. 30.

[91] The same, p. 10; Greenfield, *Sumptuary Legislation in Nürnberg,* pp. 132-33.

[92] Bressaud, *A History of French Public Law,* p. 319; Walter B. Scaife, *Florentine Life During the Renaissance* (1893), p. 224.

decreed. The Roman Catholic Church was pre-eminent both spiritually and temporally, and any form of heresy or apostasy could be punished by the Church courts. "The supremacy of God made heresy the supreme sin."[93] Fines, imprisonment, penance, and excommunication were all punishments that the Church had available, and in cases where the death penalty was considered to be desirable, the culprits were turned over to the civil authorities since the Church was squeamish about imposing that penalty.[94] This severe punishment was provided in Spain, France, Italy and the Holy Roman Empire.[95]

Those who did not adhere to the Church had only very limited rights. In France pagans could not engage in public worship nor could they attempt to win converts. Neither could they own property or engage in trade. Since they could not take an oath, infidels did not fit into the feudal structure. Jews and the members of other nonbelieving groups could not hold office nor could they be admitted to the guilds. Heathens were not subject to punishment by the Church courts for heresy or apostasy unless they had at some time been converted to Christianity.[96]

All educational activities were either directly carried on by the Church itself or under its control. The content of all teaching was directed toward the major objective of the Church—salvation. The main aim of education was the preparation of the clergy, and consequently the curriculum was shaped to meet this objective. Even where educational activities were conducted outside of the Church, they were subject to the control of the ecclesiastical courts.[97] Large segments of the population had no right to be educated even though they wanted it and were in a position to pay for it.

[93] M. Serle Bates, *Religious Liberty: An Inquiry* (1945), p. 143.
[94] Lecky, *History of the Rise and Influence of the Spirit of Rationalism in Europe,* Vol. 2, p. 38; "Heresies and the Inquisition." *Cambridge Medieval History,* Vol. 6, Chap. 20, p. 715.
[95] Bates, *Religious Liberty,* p. 144.
[96] Lowenthal, *The Jews of Germany,* p. 180; Bressaud, *A History of French Public Law,* pp. 192, 197.
[97] *Cambridge Medieval History,* Vol. 8, p. 688.

Freedom of investigation and publication had little significance both because printing was yet to be developed and because this was an era when intellectual curiosity was at a low ebb. All manuscripts were executed in handwriting. An individual could develop his own manuscript, but its wide distribution was almost an impossibility. The Church, and the civil state following its lead, took steps limiting scientific research and teaching.

The persecution of magic by the Church was detrimental to experimental science. Magicians were greatly feared; popes ordered the inquisition to be applied to them, and probably 100,000 people were killed for practicing magic.[98] As a result, both physics and chemistry were regarded as devilish arts, and their study was forbidden to ecclesiasts. In the latter part of the thirteenth century Roger Bacon was imprisoned for his work in experimental science. Many countries (France, England, Spain, and Venice) made illegal the possession of furnaces and other apparatus used in chemical research.[99]

Doctrines of the Church also were barriers to surgery and medicine. The belief that the body must remain unmutilated for the resurrection and the idea that the Church abhorred the letting of blood were the chief causes for opposition to such work. Anatomy was not studied, and surgery was a despised profession. Early in the thirteenth century the Church required that medical treatment could be given only with its advice, and this was still being enforced two and one half centuries later.[100]

The restrictions on learning and investigation that were implicit in the domination of the intellectual scene by the Church could not have been a great burden to most of the people in the Middle Ages. The intellectual outlook of the Middle Ages was thoroughly shaped by the Church. Religious institutions completely pre-empted all intellectual activities. There was practically no spirit of dissent or criticism because almost any

[98] A. D. White, *The History of the Warfare of Science with Theology* (1910), Vol. 1, p. 385.
[99] The same, p. 391.
[100] The same, Vol. 2, pp. 31-55.

person who was educated had been indoctrinated thoroughly in the tenets of the Church, and after many generations had been inculcated with only one viewpoint, there could be no real desire for innovation, dissent, or criticism.[101]

V. ECONOMIC CONTROLS

Far-reaching economic controls were the rule in the Middle Ages. Many of these were established by local institutions such as manors and guilds rather than by the national government. Although they were exercised by many jurisdictions, they were nonetheless significant. Controls imposed upon agriculture, business enterprises, trade, industry, cloth making, and labor will be considered in this section. The sole objective of this inquiry into the regulation of economic activities is to show how they affected the individual's freedom. Their implications for the economic system are beyond the scope of this study.

AGRICULTURE

Farming was probably the most important single economic activity in feudal Europe, but in its pursuit little room was left for individual freedom and initiative.

> A most important feature of the mediaeval system of tillage was its compulsory character. The several tenants, even when freeholders, could not manage their plots at their own choice. The entire soil of the township formed one whole in this respect, and was subjected to the management of the entire village. The superior right of the community found expression in the fact that the fields were open to common use as pasture after the harvest, as well as in the regulation of the modes of farming and order of tillage by the township. . . .[102]

The prevalent methods of owning and tilling the soil limited the freedom of the cultivator. Most of the arable land in a manor was divided into small strips, and the number of strips held by each owner was determined by the total size of his hold-

[101] Lecky, *History of the Rise and Influence of the Spirit of Rationalism in Europe,* Vol. 2, p. 37.
[102] Vinogradoff, *Villainage in England,* p. 230.

ings. In some cases these strips were redistributed annually so that the good land would be rotated and so that all persons would have strips close to as well as far from the village. This meant that no one would have sufficient interest in any one strip of land to encourage him to improve its fertility. Even where strips were not rotated, it was difficult to cultivate, plant, and harvest widely scattered strips.

The land was cultivated on the basis of the so-called open field system. This generally involved the use of three fields. Obviously (as explained on page 27), under this system of tillage the owner of any piece of land could not himself determine the use to which he would put it in any year. What was to be done in each of the fields was determined by custom or by the manor as a whole. The times of plowing, of planting, and of harvesting were all determined by central action. The lord, freemen, and villeins on a manor were all subjected to this form of centralized control.[103] All of the major decisions in the process of cultivation were made by the manor. Little room was left for individual judgment and choice. Since the land was split up into a large number of small strips that were intermingled, it was difficult for individuals to carry on cultivation in complete independence of the activities of their fellow owners and cultivators.

Communal action in cultivating land was required partly because most of the small owners (freemen as well as villeins) did not individually have all of the instruments of production needed for their own land. Frequently, a villein did not have enough oxen to plow his land; co-operation with his neighbors was imperative. Under these circumstances it was practically impossible for anyone to engage in experimentation in agriculture. It was most difficult for an individual to plant new crops or to modify the system of cultivation in any significant way. The breaking up of the field into a large number of small tracts precluded the development of new methods of cultivation.[104]

[103] The same, p. 230.
[104] Lipson, *An Introduction to the Economic History of England,* Vol. 1, p. 67.

The raising of livestock was also subject to significant controls imposed by the manor.

> . . . In the vast majority of cases the pasture is used in common, and none of the tenants has a right to fence it in or to appropriate it for his own exclusive benefit. It ought to be noted, that the right to send one's cattle to the pasture on the waste, the moors, or in the woods of a manor appears regularly and intimately connected with the right to depasture one's cattle on the open fields of the village. . . .[105]

The meadows were owned in common, and the number of cattle that could be pastured was determined by the size of each individual's agricultural holdings. This precluded the practice of animal husbandry exclusively or on an extensive scale.[106] Comparable rules governed the pasturing of cattle in open fields after the harvesting of crops. This intermingling of cattle in pastures of course made it impossible for any individual to improve the breed of his domestic animals.

FREEDOM TO ENGAGE IN BUSINESS ENTERPRISES

Before an individual could engage in various forms of enterprise, he generally had to secure permission from some governmental authority. Most production and distribution activities in the towns were subject to the control of the guilds, and the right to form guilds was granted by the towns, kings, and lords. The organization of guilds was closely regulated, and admission to a guild in one city did not mean that a person could engage in the activity involved in any other city.[107] Individuals, not members of the guild, could not carry on these business activities. For instance, the guild of bird fanciers of Paris sought to prevent private citizens from raising birds for their own pleasure, even though they were never to be offered for sale.

In most towns strangers were prohibited from carrying on business or were permitted to do so only within most clearly demarcated limits. They were not permitted to trade with other strangers unless a local burgess acted as an intermediary, and

[105] Vinogradoff, *Villainage in England,* p. 261.
[106] The same, p. 261.
[107] Bressaud, *A History of French Public Law,* p. 310; Renard, *Guilds in the Middle Ages,* pp. 36-37.

strangers were not allowed to keep open shop and sell at retail.[108] In the rural areas the right to engage in the various forms of handicrafts was strictly controlled by the lord of the manor. It was customary for him to sell monopolies of various kinds. He often sold the exclusive right to run a grist mill, bake oven, wine press, or brew house. Where such franchises had been sold, individuals had to patronize these establishments—they could not bake their own bread or press their own grapes.

The methods of organizing business enterprises were not as varied as they are today. Most business was carried on by a single individual. Normally partnerships could not be formed between a member of a guild and a nonmember. The limited liability corporation was not generally known in private law in the feudal period, for it was not until the late Middle Ages that it began to emerge in banking enterprises in Italy.[109] The limitations on the form in which business activities could be conducted was not highly significant in the Middle Ages because of the limited market available and because little capital was required for handicraft trades. Businesses were small and involved but limited investments.

FREEDOM OF TRADE

The freedom of the individual to carry on commerce was regulated minutely. Much of the trade was carried on in markets, and these were thoroughly controlled to protect both the monopoly of the market and the interest of consumers of the goods sold. Medieval markets first developed in the ninth century when the Frankish kings concentrated all trading in commodities between buyers and sellers in weekly markets to encourage the exchange of local products. As a rule the right to establish a market was bestowed by the king, or it was conferred by a lord exercising local jurisdiction. The right to hold a market was usually given to a church, a borough, or an individual, either as a favor or for a consideration.[110] These franchises were

[108] Gross, *The Gild Merchant,* Vol. 1, p. 45.

[109] J. W. Thompson, *Economic and Social History of the Middle Ages* (1928), p. 449; and Gross, *The Gild Merchant,* Vol. 1, p. 46.

[110] Vernon A. Mund, *Open Markets, An Essential of Free Enterprise* (1948), pp. 14, 32.

regarded as valuable rights because tolls could be charged for the privilege of doing business at the market. Consequently, the holder of the franchise guarded it from enroachment. Individuals were not allowed to set up a new market at will. The creation of a market close to an existing one would tend to destroy the monopoly conferred upon the person holding the market. Thus in England it was an unwarranted disturbance of an existing market for a person to set up a new market within approximately six and two-thirds miles of an existing one.[111]

On market day many towns required that individuals must carry on all trade in the market place. Frequently, merchants were forbidden to sell in their shops on those days. Thus an ordinance of the City of Worms provided that "all shoemakers in buying and selling of their shoes must go to the public market or where they are being ordered and no one is allowed to sell shoes on market days anywhere else, not in his house or under his house gates in any way."[112] The purpose was to ensure full publicity for all transactions. It was generally considered undesirable to have more than one market in a community because this would result in the scattering of buyers and sellers.

Efforts were made to ensure that the markets were free and open to all persons. The English courts held that "every person has of common right a liberty of coming into any public market for the purpose of buying and selling" and "every person has of common right a liberty of bringing his goods to a fair or market for a sale."[113]

Persons engaged in trade and commerce were subject to many far-reaching limitations and regulations. They had to pay many

[111] The same, p. 36.

[112] Quoted in the same, p. 20.

[113] Quoted in the same, p. 39. To ensure that no impediments were placed on the movement of goods to the market and on their sale there, the law declared a number of practices illegal. One of these was the offense of forestalling. This generally consisted of the private purchase of goods before they had a chance to reach the market, as well as any activity tending to mislead a seller or tending to dissuade him from bringing his goods to market. Engrossing constituted another offense. This involved buying up the whole or a large part of a commodity by a person or group of persons for the purpose of increasing its price by controlling and limiting its supply. Regrating was the purchasing of foodstuffs in a market for the purpose of reselling them in the same market. The same, pp. 44-45.

heavy tolls. Each city and each local lord had the right to impose a duty or charge on persons or goods entering his jurisdiction. Such charges were very prevalent in France, Germany, Italy, and central Europe. Late in the Middle Ages there were no less than 62 tolls levied on traffic on the Rhine River alone.[114] These tolls were not levied primarily for the purpose of improving the highways or waterways, they were charged merely for the permission to enter the jurisdiction of the city or the territory of the lord. In some cases the tolls were so heavy that it was advantageous to move goods by overland routes. As a result of such efforts to avoid tolls, individuals were forbidden to transport goods on specific designated trade routes because they thereby were by-passing the points where the tolls were levied. In England, the existence of a strong central government made such burdensome charges almost nonexistent.

Persons desiring to export or import goods were limited in many ways. They encountered more often general prohibitions of or tariffs upon exports than duties levied on imports. For example, early in the thirteenth century France forbade all exports; but this prohibition was largely a pretext to justify licensing the right to export; obviously, the sale of such licenses could be lucrative to the crown and its officers. In the same period no one was permitted to export wool and grains.[115] The export of unfulled cloth was forbidden, and on several occasions the import of foreign cloth was also prohibited. Frequently, England decreed that no one could export gold or silver coins. Late in the fifteenth century England forbade the importation of most foreign manufactured goods.[116]

The institution of the staple also limited the right of the individual to engage in trade. Where a staple existed, all trade in a given area or in a given direction must pass through a

[114] Heckscher, *Mercantilism,* Vol. 1, pp. 45-110.

[115] The same, pp. 89-91; and Lipson, *An Introduction to the Economic History of England,* Vol. 1, p. 396. The regulations were not uniform; they were subect to constant revision.

[116] Lipson, *An Introduction to the Economic History of England,* Vol. 1, pp. 400-02 and 461-62; and Holdsworth, *A History of English Law,* Vol. 2, p. 472.

specified city. The purpose of this of course was to give a monopoly to the inhabitants of that city. For example, Genoa, at the beginning of the twelfth century, set out to become the sole center for all trade directed to the south of France.[117] It also sought to exclude all of the Italian cities in that area from maritime trade with the Levant. Any ship from the other cities on the west coast of Italy bound for the Levant had to set sail from Genoa and on its return to unload its cargo at that city.

Strangers were limited in their right to trade, and the term stranger included not only aliens but also persons who resided in other towns in the country. Most cities and countries attempted to restrict the right to trade to their own subjects. Limitations on nonresident traders were possibly first prescribed by the charter of the City of Cologne in 1103. From there such limitations spread rapidly through Germany and Italy in the next century. Frequently, merchant strangers were required to live with specific local residents known as hosts, who were charged with the task of controlling them. For example, Venice even kept them locked in their hostel at night. In England retail trade was closed to them.[118] Often they could make a deal only through an intermediate local trader, and they generally were forbidden from dealing with each other directly. The English law tended to regard all aliens as enemies, and it was a significant concession when they were permitted to rent houses for trade purposes.[119] These limitations on the activities of strangers were largely designed to establish a trade monopoly for the local residents.

CONTROL OF INDUSTRY

Detailed regulation of what was produced and how it was produced was the rule rather than the exception. "The old law was founded on the view that it was for the state to regulate the conditions of trade." "The burden of proof in medieval times

[117] Heckscher, *Mercantilism,* Vol. 2, p. 63.

[118] The same, p. 74; and Holdsworth, *A History of English Law,* Vol. 2, p. 471.

[119] Pollock and Maitland, *The History of English Law Before the Time of Edward I,* Vol. 2, pp. 459-65.

was on those who denied the right of the state to intervene in such matters."[120] Much of the regulating was actually done by the guild acting as the agent of the state or the municipality. The minute systems of control were to protect both the guild members and the consumer. But where the interests of these two groups conflicted, the producers usually were protected at the expense of the consumers.

The prices at which individuals could buy and sell goods, especially foodstuffs were frequently fixed. Control over the quality and price of food was common, and it was exercised directly by public authorities. In 1202 an assize of bread was proclaimed in England providing for public control of the price of breadstuffs throughout the land. The price that a baker might charge for it was tied to the price of wheat; thus as the price of the basic raw material rose or fell the price of bread was changed. The enforcement of the assize was the task of municipal authorities. The price of ale was also fixed; here the legal price of ale was tied to the market price of barley.[121] Maximum prices for wine were set by the central government of England after 1199. Many towns fixed the price of and controlled both the quality and the sanitary condition of all varieties of meat, poultry, and fish.[122] Late in the fourteenth century Parliament passed a general law regulating the price of all food products. Sellers were to sell all foods at a "reasonable price," and a "reasonable price" was to be determined by the prices prevailing in the "places adjoining." The purpose was to ensure that "sellers have moderate gains and not excessive."[123]

The extent of the control exercised over industry can be illustrated by a description of the regulations covering the production and sale of cloth (primarily wool) since it was the major article of medieval commerce. By all means available to the government those who made and sold cloth were regulated. The major objectives of these regulations were the protection of the consuming

[120] Holdsworth, *A History of English Law,* Vol. 2, pp. 468-69.
[121] Ashley, *An Introduction to English Economic History and Theory,* Vol. 1, Pt. 1, pp. 188-91.
[122] The same, pp. 191-93.
[123] Holdsworth, *A History of English Law,* Vol. 2, p. 469.

public and the promotion of domestic manufacture. From the close of the twelfth century various attempts were made in England to regulate the size of the pieces of cloth that a producer could weave; the purpose was to protect the public from misrepresentation. Article 35 of Magna Carta (1215) specified the dimensions of cloth. Not infrequently such minute regulations merely constituted a source of revenue for the government and its agents because licenses were sold to the makers of cloth permitting them to produce and sell cloth not made in conformity with the regulations.

To enforce the assize of cloth and to ensure that all cloth was of the prescribed minimum quality, the office of the alnager was established probably by the time of Edward I (1272). The function of this official was to test both the quality and measurements of pieces of cloth and to fix his seal only on such pieces as were of satisfactory quality and of the legal size. When the cloth did not conform with the requirements, he was authorized to destroy it. His work was financed by fees that he collected from the makers of each of the pieces of cloth that were inspected. For short periods in the fourteenth century cloth could be made of any size, and the alnager merely determined and stated its accurate measurements, but foreign cloth always had to conform to specific limitations as to size.[124]

The freedom of individuals to carry on foreign trade in both raw wool and cloth was regulated to protect the native manufacturers. Parliament in 1258 and 1271 prohibited anyone from exporting raw wool to ensure a relatively large supply of domestic wool for the local manufacturers. In the middle of the fifteenth century no one was allowed to export unfulled cloth. This was to encourage the local cloth finishing industry. As another form of protection the use of foreign cloth was limited. In 1332 the king forbade anyone to wear foreign cloth unless he had 100 marks of land or rent; and five years later the import of all wool cloth was forbidden.[125]

The buying and selling of wool cloth in the various towns

[124] The same, pp. 406-07, and 431-32.
[125] The same, pp. 396, 400, 402.

was extensively regulated by local authority. Strangers were specifically forbidden to sell their cloth except at a designated market which was maintained only on specific days of the week. The establishment of a central sales place operating at fixed times was a means of enforcing the prohibition against strangers selling cloth either at retail or to nonburgesses. Such ordinances also served to "prevent disorderly and deceitful bargains against the franchise and liberties of the city."[126]

FREEDOM OF LABOR

In general freedom to work was nonexistent under feudalism. The emphasis was largely on the individual's duty or obligation to work. The villeins, who constituted the great mass of workers in most countries, were obligated to give such services to their lord as he demanded. Apprentices also were legally bound to serve their masters. The English king had the right to impress labor for his own personal use. For example, Windsor Castle was constructed largely by impressed artisans.[127]

In medieval times it could hardly be said that there was any freedom of the individual to choose his own line of work and to engage in it free from the approval of some public or quasi-public authority. One student of French public law summed up the situation in that country:

> The State . . . did not recognize freedom of labor; it sold the right of engaging in the crafts and granted them as fiefs. The corporations came to constitute no longer a protection for the individual (whom the state protected sufficiently) but establishments of public utility, labor organizations by the State, a form of state socialism.[128]

As was stated earlier (p. 28), in the rural manors the right of individuals to engage in the various crafts and occupations was definitely under the control of the lord. The villein in performing agricultural and other labor was completely under his con-

[126] The same, p. 408.

[127] J. E. T. Rogers, *Six Centuries of Work and Wages* (1884), p. 329; and D. Knoop and Y. P. Jones, "The Impressment of Masons for Windsor Castle, 1360-1363," *Economic History,* Vol. 3 (1937), p. 350.

[128] Bressaud, *A History of French Public Law,* p. 310.

trol. The right of free individuals to engage in the pursuits customary to a manor also depended upon the lord. The privilege to operate bake ovens, wine presses, mills, and the like was granted by the lord, and generally a person who had no franchise was unable to operate such facilities even for his personal use.[129]

In the towns permission to carry on various skilled pursuits—as master, journeyman, or apprentice—was granted by the guilds (see p. 30), and the right of the guild, acting in a governmental capacity, to control the entrance into a craft was generally accepted. In France it was not unusual for the king or for the lord who had jurisdiction over the town to sell memberships in the crafts to individuals. Once a person had received the right to work at a specific craft he could not readily change to another one. He would have had to serve another apprenticeship, and in all probability he would have had to renounce membership in the guild to which he belonged. The city of London was most peculiar in this regard. If an apprenticeship was served in one of the major crafts in the city the individual could follow any other major craft in the city. An English statute of 1363 provided that an individual could follow only one craft at a time.[130]

The freedom of the individual to sell his labor where desired and at whatever wage he wished was generally limited. Villeins as stated earlier (p. 43) were not free to leave the manor to which they were attached, for the right of pursuit existed, and many punishments could be inflicted by the lord. Freemen could be restricted by the lord from following such pursuits on the manor as he considered undesirable. Urban dwellers also suffered significant limitations upon their freedom to move about. Generally the right to engage in a significant trade in any town was restricted to citizens of that town. The limitations imposed

[129] Coulton, *The Medieval Village,* p. 55; Herbert, *The Fall of Feudalism in France,* pp. 25-28.

[130] Boissonnade, *Life and Work in Medieval Europe,* pp. 192-94; Bressaud, *A History of French Public Law,* pp. 311-12; and Lipson, *An Introduction to the Economic History of England,* Vol. 1, p. 317.

on strangers (see p. 55) constituted important barriers to the right of workers to move about.[131] The mere fact that an individual had received permission to follow a certain trade or craft in one town did not mean that he was in a position to follow it in another town without special license or without serving another apprenticeship.

After the Black Death in the middle of the fourteenth century additional restrictions on the freedom of rural laborers became general. Restrictive legislation was adopted in England, France, Prussia, and Italy. The English Statute of Laborers (1351) illustrates the type of controls imposed by such laws. All able-bodied persons, whether free or bond, who had no definite means of support were compelled to accept employment if offered to them at wages prevailing in the period before enactment of this law. No one was to give or to receive higher wages than were customary. Workers covered by it were forbidden to leave their employer during their contract of employment unless they had adequate cause.[132] All agricultural wage workers as well as craftsmen, such as shoemakers, tilers, masons, and curriers were forbidden to move from place to place without permission of their employers. An English statute of 1388 provided that artificers whose crafts did not need to be pursued during the time of harvest could be compelled to work in the fields. It also required all who followed agriculture at the age of twelve to continue at it.[133]

Under feudalism workers had no right to organize and to strike. Apprentices and journeymen belonged to the same guilds as the masters, and these were dominated by the masters. Journeymen's guilds were frowned upon, although it was not easy to suppress them. Whenever workers attempted to organize or to strike, government agencies took steps to put down the

[131] Kramer, *English Craft Gilds and the Government,* p. 134; and Lipson, *An Introduction to the Economic History of England,* Vol. 1, pp. 239-41.

[132] "Peasant Life and Rural Conditions," *Cambridge Medieval History,* Vol. 7, p. 734; and Bertha M. Putnam, *The Enforcement of the Statute of Laborers* (1908), p. 71.

[133] Holdsworth, *A History of English Law,* Vol. 2, p. 461; and Lipson, *An Introduction to the Economic History of England,* Vol. 1, p. 163.

activities. In 1377 the English Parliament forbade associations of villeins that were organized to attempt to win their freedom.[134] The English Statute of Laborers forbade workers from leaving their employment before their contract ended and required them to work if offered the legal wage; these provisions precluded all forms of work stoppages.

Wages were not fixed by anything resembling either individual bargaining or collective bargaining. Many of the agricultural workers were not paid regular wages, since most of them were villeins. Instead of wages, they enjoyed the use of land; in return for certain labor services they received specific privileges relative to land. On such land as they held they produced the products necessary for their subsistence, and in return for the use of the land they gave certain labor services to their lord. Only after the Black Death did free agricultural labor begin to be an important factor, and with its appearance came wage-fixing legislation. By the Statute of Laborers of 1351 the wages of British workers were fixed in relationship to the wages customarily paid in the period before its enactment, but with some variations as a result of changes in the cost of living. Comparable legislation was enacted in other countries. Obviously, such laws did not apply to agricultural tenants and villeins because they received no wages; the legislation applied only to hired servants.[135] Wages in most of the trades and crafts were fixed by the guilds. Remuneration of apprentices and of journeymen was determined by the guilds; the masters of course worked for their own account and received a profit not a wage. From the time of Henry II on, some municipalities in England fixed wages, and municipal action in this field was very prevalent by the fifteenth century.[136]

[134] L. F. Salzman, *English Industries of the Middle Ages* (1923), p. 345; Cunningham, *The Growth of English Industry and Commerce,* Vol. 1, p. 443; Boissonnade, *Life and Work in Medieval Europe,* pp. 305-07; Luchaire, *Social France at the Time of Philip Augustus,* p. 311; and Holdsworth, *A History of English Law,* Vol. 3, p. 500.

[135] Putnam, *The Enforcement of the Statute of Laborers,* p. 73; and *Cambridge Medieval History,* Vol. 7, p. 738.

[136] Kramer, *The English Craft Gilds and the Government,* pp. 91-95.

Thus to the medieval period our current ideas concerning freedom to labor were inapplicable. Workers had no right to follow whatever calling they might desire. Frequently, many of the conditions of employment were fixed by persons exercising public power, and employees had no right to organize or to engage in concerted action to modify the terms under which they served.[137]

VI. CONCLUSIONS

The general personal insecurity that prevailed in the Middle Ages largely conditioned the controls imposed upon the individual by feudal society. In the temporal sphere this was the main force that caused people to view the right to govern as a form of property. In the spiritual realm this caused people to be pre-eminently interested in salvation in the hereafter. Since life on earth was brutish and insecure, people were very anxious to make certain that life in the next world would be pleasant. The absolutist, irresponsible feudal government had its roots in property. In English law the very kingdom itself was the property of the king,[138] and from the king on down to the feudal tenants-in-chief, lords of manors, and to the borough corporations the right to govern resulted from ownership of property. Since the right to govern was considered to be property, few limitations were imposed on its exercise. The right to govern went with the title to land, and the holder of the land could do anything he wished to that land or the people attached to it unless he interfered with the right of other landholders. Few, if any, responsibilities went with the possession of public authority since the power to govern was not derived from the people subjected to its authority. As a result, government was absolute as well as irresponsible, for the owner of the property was responsible only to himself for what he did with his property.

Since public law hardly existed, efforts were made to bring all phases of government within the concepts of the private law of property. Even taxation was regarded as a form of private in-

[137] Boissonnade, *Life and Work in Medieval Europe*, p. 209.
[138] Chrimes, *English Constitutional Ideas in the Fifteenth Century*, p. 344.

come. The taxes voted to the king by Parliament were considered to be a part of the profits of the crown derived from the income of its court—the High Court of Parliament. Taxes voted to the king by Parliament were considered in the same way as the revenues that the lord of a manor secured from his manorial court.[139] That court was the great instrument of control on the manor, and the right to hold it was a property right. A similar confusion of property and government is evident relative to the control of serfs. When it comes to the bases for the lord's authority over his villeins "we find it difficult to decide where ownership leaves off and jurisdiction begins."[140]

The very idea that the right to govern was a form of property affected the significance and content of some of our basic political terms. A good example is to be found in the term liberty. To the medievalist, liberties essentially were property rights granted by a superior authority (be it the king or the lord of the manor) that exempted some persons or places from the jurisdiction of some other authority. Thus, "liberties were always attached to particular persons or places; there was nothing general or national about them. They were definite concrete priviliges, which some people enjoyed, but most did not." They were immunities or franchises conferred upon the holders of the liberty, and as a part of the privilege the possessor could do certain things to his subordinates. "The liberty of a town consisted largely in its right to rate its inhabitants and to levy tolls on all who frequented its markets. The liberty of a baron consisted in his authority over others, in the court he owned, and in the perquisites of his jurisdiction."[141] It was quite logical that the Commons in 1348 petitioned the king to grant no more liberties, for they limited the area of the common law.

The practice of viewing government as a property right was largely a product of an environment in which personal security was at a premium. The cruel brutishness of a society torn by

[139] The same, p. 13.

[140] Pollock and Maitland, *History of English Law Before the Time of Edward I,* Vol. 1, p. 527.

[141] Pollard, *The Evolution of Parliament,* pp. 169-70.

war made people willing to subordinate themselves to the authority of a superior in return for a modicum of physical security from attack by other overmighty lords or from invaders. The hard facts of physical insecurity led to a complete subjugation of the individual to the authority of certain property holders. No highly rationalized philosophy was required to explain why absolutistic, irresponsible power was exercised by government over individuals.

The other major force influencing the controls imposed upon the individual was the Church. Its primary objective was the salvation of human souls in the next world. Life in this world was merely a prelude to eternity, and it was the objective of the Church to promote salvation by ensuring that life in this world would be so lived as to ensure salvation. Whatever temporal action that was necessary for this purpose ought to be undertaken by the government. Since salvation was the primary objective, what did it matter if the individual was harassed or regimented in this world by government action designed to promote salvation? Any limitations imposed upon the individual were of course secondary and necessary for a higher objective. Obviously, the Church alone knew what was required for salvation. Finally, one must always remember that it was impossible in the Middle Ages to distinguish in modern terms between Church and state, and that as a matter of practice the Church was in a position to ensure that the state would follow its wishes.

Many limitations on human liberty were imposed largely as a consequence of the teachings of the Church. The persecution of heretics was a product of its doctrine. Limitations on intellectual activities were an outgrowth of its theology. Discriminatory treatment of Jews, although probably not imposed by the Church, was a logical result of its philosophy. The just price, the opposition to usury, the requirement that goods be of a high quality were all largely outgrowths of the theology of the Church.

The significance of the individual was minimized both by the idea that government was a form of property and by the dogmas of the Church devised to promote salvation. The need for personal protection caused the individual to subordinate himself to the holders of certain property rights. The widespread existence of war, civil disorder, and violence tended to make individual life and happiness something that was cheap and insignificant. It also encouraged the individual to look to the hereafter as the time when he would attain personal satisfaction. The emphasis of the Church on the importance of salvation and on the promotion of an earthly life solely designed to attain it tended to limit the individual's inclination to do as he pleased. The basic idea of the Church that salvation was solely and exclusively in its hands subordinated the individual to the Church and its hierarchy, for salvation was not something that could be obtained through the believer's own efforts; it could only be won through the intervention of the priesthood.

CHAPTER III

THE ABSOLUTE MONARCHIES

Extensive controls over the individual were exercised by the absolute monarchies of western Europe in the sixteenth and seventeenth centuries. Authority was highly concentrated in the central government, thus contrasting with feudalism where public power was exercised by a legion of public and private bodies. Generally, the mere existence of the might and power of the new nation state of itself constituted a sufficient justification for the exercise of power by government in any area that fancy might dictate. "Was anything wrong, the king should, and could, remedy it. Did an abuse exist, the king could annihilate it by an edict. Was an undertaking desirable, the king could initiate it and make it a success."[1] The vast mass of controls imposed on the individual by these new unified states was justified only partially through a resort to any form of a systematic theory; mercantilism was the pre-eminent example of a philosophical rationalization of state action.

This chapter will first consider how the development of the sovereign state contributed to this all-prevailing system of controls. Then the essence of mercantilism will be summarized, and its relation to the problem of control will be indicated. Against this background will be presented some illustrations of the limitations that were imposed on the political, personal, and economic freedom of individuals. England and France will serve as the sources of examples considered. This analysis will involve a consideration of some of the instruments of control that were encountered in the discussion of the feudal system (for example, the guilds). If one is to get a fair picture of the restraints imposed on the individual under both feudalism and the absolute monarchies some repetition is inevitable; but every effort has been made to keep it at a minimum.

[1] Charles Woolsey Cole, *Colbert and A Century of French Mercantilism* (1939), Vol. 1, p. 25.

I. THE SOVEREIGN STATE

The unified sovereign state had just emerged from the chaos of feudalism at the beginning of the sixteenth century. The great centralized monarchies were successfully suppressing the feuding factions that had disrupted their lands. The central governments were supreme in the sense that no higher source of authority existed within their bounds. From this evolved the idea that the competence of the state was unlimited and its authority sovereign.[2] Such a central supreme power was necessary to overcome the particularism of feudalism. Peace and order were devoutly desired. Since the state was the sole compulsory organization embracing the whole nation, it was assumed that it alone could bring internal order. Under such conditions power must therefore be the first interest of the state.[3]

The sixteenth century was an era of great social, economic, and political change that affected the power of the state. The commercial revolution required a strong state. Trade and commerce began to revive in the fifteenth century, facilitated by the use of money as the primary medium of exchange. The end of self-sufficiency that followed the decline of the feudal economy made imperative the maintenance of peace and stability. With the rise of commerce, not only was the state more necessary to maintain peace but commerce itself offered a new instrument of rivalry and warfare between states. The commercial class became more significant in government. These groups were increasingly able to influence the government. Thus in seventeenth century England when the king failed to govern in conformity with their wishes, they were able to spearhead a successful revolution.

The use of regular armies in place of the feudal levies contributed to the power of the state, while at the same time their support imposed unprecedented burdens on its treasury. The new armies meant greater physical power of the state as against the individual, and it made war more deadly and costly. While

[2] C. H. McIlwain, *The Growth of Political Thought in the West from the Greeks to the End of the Middle Ages* (1932), p. 387.

[3] Eli F. Heckscher, *Mercantilism,* Vol. 2 (1934), p. 15.

they made the state stronger, they also required more revenue from the government to keep them going. The maintenance of commercial prosperity was imperative for the state to ensure the revenues to pay for the armies.

The development of printing in the middle of the fifteenth century constituted both a threat to state supremacy and an added cause for state action. The spread of printing opened up new possibilities of individual intellectual action. As books became cheaper and more plentiful, ideas could be disseminated more widely, even views contrary to the wishes of the government. The ease of questioning authority made more necessary state action for controlling the spread of ideas.

The Reformation reduced and enfeebled the major rival of the state, increased the importance of the individual, and as a consequence paved the way for additional state action. In the Middle Ages the Catholic Church and the state were as inseparable as the two sides of a coin. The claims and power of the Church were a restraint on the state. The Reformation, where it was successful, swept away this rival source of authority. "By the destruction of the independence of the Church and its hold on an extra-territorial public opinion, the last obstacle to unity within the State was removed. . . ."[4]

The Reformation did not mean religious toleration. In a world of rival sovereign states the multiplicity of churches attached to various states called for state action to maintain religious orthodoxy. The state could not permit its subjects to adhere to a religion that was embraced or propagated by the head of a rival state. To differ from the king's religion was to question his authority. Loyalty required religious conformity in each state. Consequently, tolerance of diverse religious beliefs was the exception rather than the rule.

The individual became more significant as a result of the religious upheaval. The teaching of the new Protestant sects placed great emphasis on the individual's own faith. His salvation was in his own hands; he needed no church or clergy to

[4] John Neville Figgis, *Studies of Political Thought from Gerson to Grotius, 1414-1625* (1923), pp. 55-56.

intercede for him. A great impetus to education resulted, for people themselves had to be able to read and understand the sacred literature.

These economic, social, cultural, and religious changes of the sixteenth century had a great importance for the state as well as the individual. They both became more significant. More and more attention was focused on these two opposite poles. The power and prestige of intermediate groups such as the manors, the guilds, the towns, and the Church declined relatively. The manor as a means of personal control disappeared in England because royal officers, the justices of the peace, took over the functions of its court, the prime instrument by which the lord exercised personal jurisdiction.[5] In both France and England the guilds became more and more devices through which the central government controlled trade and industry. The church in many places, as in England and the German states, became in effect a state church and organ of government. All intermediate groups were subordinate to the state—they could not be independent for then they would be rivals—"lesser commonwealths." All other groups were "like worms in the entrails of a natural man."[6]

The justification of individual obedience to the state was the central problem of sixteenth century politics. The significant questions of political thought were not what tasks should the state perform and what were the appropriate rights of the individual. Its major interest was to justify the individual subject's complete obedience to the will of the state.[7]

Pragmatically the major justification for obedience was that without the centralized authority of the state anarchy would reign. Thus nothing could be worse than disobedience. As Hobbes said, man if left to himself only sought after individual personal power, "a restless desire after power, that ceaseth only

[5] Kenneth W. M. Pickthorn, *Early Tudor Government: Henry VII* (1934), pp. 136-68.

[6] Thomas Hobbes, *De Cive,* Chaps. 5, 6 quoted in George H. Sabine, A History of Political Theory (1937), p. 469.

[7] J. W. Allen, *A History of Political Thought in the Sixteenth Century* (1928), p. 512.

in death,"[8] and without civil power there would be a "war of every man against every man." Consequently, to Hobbes any government that governs is better than anarchy. The authority of the king is limited only by his power. The need for suppressing war and local disorders, for eliminating tolls and barriers to trade, for controlling coinage and weights, and for protecting the country against foreign aggressors all made state power imperative. Government power was a good in itself, because where it was absent things were always more disturbed irrespective of what the state did.

The divine right of kings was the official theory advanced in many countries to justify complete obedience on the part of the subject. In 1681 Charles II of England well summarized the idea: "We will still believe and maintain that our Kings derive not their title from the people but from God; that to him only they are accountable; that it belongs not to subjects, either to create or censure, but to honour and obey their sovereign, who comes to be so by a fundamental hereditary right of succession, which no religion, no law, no fault or forfeiture can alter or diminish."[9]

This theory, designed to justify complete obedience to unlimited state action, consisted of four elements. First, the monarchy was a divinely ordained institution. Second, the office was hereditary. The right acquired by birth could not be forfeited by usurpation, incapacity, or disposition. Third, the king was accountable to God alone; and as a result he could not divide or alienate his sovereignty. Fourth, "non-resistance and passive obedience are enjoined by God. Under any circumstances resistance to a king is a sin, and ensures damnation."[10] Thus with all royal authority derived from God, and with the king accountable to God alone, there was no limitation on royal power. The obligation of the subject to obey was absolute. It was the prevailing idea of sovereignty re-enforced by religious sanctions.

[8] *Leviathan,* Chap. 11.

[9] Quoted in J. N. Figgis, *The Theory of the Divine Right of Kings* (1896), p. 6.

[10] The same, pp. 6-7.

The newly found power of the state became an end in itself—since power of itself was good. The results of power no matter how it was used, were much more beneficial than the anarchy that resulted where it was absent; consequently, its repercussions on the individual were given hardly any consideration. A well-developed rationalization of the need for state action was almost unnecessary when those who controlled government accepted power as an independent good. Only in the economic and social sphere was a justification of state authority developed. This was the mercantile system. But here again the power of the state was rationalized as a good in itself. Since mercantilism was the only significant prevailing explanation of state control over the individual, the content of this idea will be considered before attention is directed to the specific controls imposed by government.

II. MERCANTILISM

"Mercantilism would . . . have had all economic activity subservient to the state's interest in power." It was "primarily a system for forcing economic policy into the service of power as an end in itself."[11] The state's "regard for its power must preclude all other considerations." Individuals were significant only insofar as they contributed to this end. "The well-being of the subject had the function of furnishing the necessary support for the power of the state." "Power was an end in itself" and "economic life was mobilized for political purposes." Thus Colbert explained to Louis XIV:

> It was essential to the lofty ambitions which the king set himself "to limit all the industrial activity of Your subjects, as far as possible, to such professions as may be of use in furthering these great aims, that is to agriculture, trade, . . . war at sea and on land." Everything else ought to disappear.[12]

Wealth was of pre-eminent importance because the power of the state depended upon it. This emphasis on wealth coupled with a static view of society produced international rivalry and war which resulted in greater demands for state revenue. The

[11] Heckscher, *Mercantilism,* Vol. 2, pp. 15-17.
[12] Quoted in the same pp. 17 and 20-21.

mercantilist believed that the sum total of wealth in the world was limited. Thus only at the expense of its rivals could any state have a large mass of wealth. To build up the power of the state involved increasing its strength externally as against all others. The net result of this quest for power was international rivalries and war. The state must be strong so as to carry on such wars. Colbert epitomized the whole idea in a few words, "trade is the source of [public] finance and [public] finance is the vital nerve of war."[13] This use of economics for political objectives came to be known as the mercantile system. The following paragraphs summarize its major elements as they related to the problem of control.

In pursuing this broad policy of power embodied in mercantilism, two basic methods were utilized by governments. The first involved direct state action designed specifically to build up political and military power. The second consisted of "creating a kind of reservoir of economic resources generally from which the policy of power could draw when it required."[14] This involved building up a strong and efficient domestic economy on which the state could draw when war demanded it. In mercantilist thought a healthy domestic economy was one that would yield the revenue necessary to support the armed forces required for war.

Many illustrations are available of the policy of state intervention in economic affairs specifically undertaken for the purpose of directly building up military potential. For many years England required that anyone who imported goods from Venice must bring into the kingdom at least four bow staves.[15] In the sixteenth century the export of copper alloys was forbidden because of their utility in making cannon, and likewise the export of cannon was specifically forbidden.[16] Royal action was taken to develop mines that would yield useful metals for

[13] The same.
[14] Heckscher, *Mercantilism,* Vol. 2, p. 31.
[15] The same, p. 32.
[16] E. Lipson, *An Introduction to the Economic History of England,* Vol. 2 (1931), p. 124.

war. Persons could be impressed to work in the royal mines. The production of saltpetre, required in the manufacture of gunpowder, was encouraged by creating a monopoly for its production, and the monopolists were even given the right to search private property to discover the so-called saltpetre mines.[17] Here again exportation was forbidden.

Many controls were instituted to build up the navy. Since there was then little difference between merchant ships and war ships, anything that encouraged the former was useful for war. By many laws the trade of England and France was restricted to ships of native registry. Similar restrictions were imposed on the trade of the colonies. Ultimately the ships carrying on both colonial and foreign trade had to be of domestic construction. Since the fisheries were a great source of potential seamen, they were encouraged by law. With the Reformation in England the consumption of fish declined. In order to keep up the demand for fish Parliament in 1549 required all to eat fish on specified days of the week.[18]

Colonial dependencies were utilized to promote military power. The newly discovered lands had to be appropriated and settled to prevent other countries from acquiring them and thus growing richer relatively. The quest for self-sufficiency made colonies attractive. It was considered to be advantageous to have all raw materials produced in one's own territory. The colonial trade had to be monopolized to make self-sufficiency a reality and to prevent rival states from making a profit from it. Manufacturing in the colonies was forbidden to ensure dependence upon the home land, for self-sufficiency might ultimately encourage independence. As a small concession the colonies were frequently given a monopoly of the production of specific products. Both England and France gave their American colonies a monopoly of growing tobacco for the home market. Each went so far as to forbid actually the growing of tobacco

[17] J. V. Nef, *Industry and Government in France and England 1540-1640* (1940), pp. 59, 88.
[18] William Holdsworth, *A History of English Law* (1921), Vol. 4, p. 328.

at home. In France many persons were killed for growing tobacco contrary to law, and in England tobacco fields were destroyed by military action.[19]

The prevalent monetary policies were in part shaped by the potential requirements of war. One tract writer declared that "Money is the sinews of war," because the troops must be paid in it.[20] Another writer explained that treasure was of great need for war because the state could not buy foreign supplies without it. England imposed restrictions on the export of coins. Both France and England prohibited the export of bullion. Foreign exchange was strictly regulated and licensed.[21]

Second, as said on page 76, many forms of regulation were adopted to build up a generally strong economy to constitute a vast reservoir of potential national power for trade rivalry and war. This was one of the major reasons for the detailed regulation of industrial production. Obviously, a thriving national economy would yield increased tax revenues, thus making possible a greater war potential. But the entire system of regulation cannot be justified exclusively on the basis of such a general philosophy. Not all of the controls were designed solely to increase the power of the state for the sake of war. Special interests clamored for attention. In an era that believed that state power was an end in itself and that had not developed any philosophy of limitations on government action, it was relatively simple for the state to take action when some significant interest in the body politic clamored for a privilege or for regulation to correct a situation that it considered undesirable.

To promote and encourage this general state of economic

[19] Cole, *Colbert and A Century of French Mercantilism,* Vol. 2, pp. 22, 525; George Louis Beer, *The Origins of the British Colonial System 1578-1660* (1922), pp. 126, 136, 403.

[20] Heckscher, *Mercantilism,* Vol. 2, p. 47.

[21] The early historians did realize the significance of mercantilism as a system designed to build up the power of states—especially their military power, but recent students generally give support to this interpretation. See Lawrence Stone, "State Control in Sixteenth Century England" *Economic History Review,* Vol. 17 (1947) pp. 103, 110; Heckscher, *Mercantilism,* Vol. 2, pp. 13-49; Philip W. Buck, *The Politics of Mercantilism* (1942), Chap. 5; and Lipson, *An Introduction to the Economic History of England,* Vol. 3, pp. 1 and 67.

well-being, the mercantilists imposed rights and duties upon the major groups in the population. The laborers, the rich, the land-owners, and the merchants were all expected to fulfill certain obligations to the body politic. "A beneficent harmony of interests assured them all of rewards suited to their station in the community."[22]

Labor was given a very important but strictly subordinate role. The key to understanding the mercantilists' ideas concerning labor is found in their idea of national wealth. Wealth consisted of "a stock of goods useful to the nation in the achievement of its aims and purposes." Any inflow of precious metal to a country appeared to increase in its national wealth. Consequently, maximum production within the country was desired to lessen the need for imports and to make possible exports. One of the basic objectives of the system was to stimulate the manufacture of goods domestically for export. This would permit a net inflow of bullion. In their thought "the entire value of the exported product was gain to the nation." To attain this objective it was necessary to ensure a large and cheap supply of labor. It was usually assumed "that the majority must be kept in poverty that the whole might be rich." An increase in the number of laborers meant an increase in national prosperity.[23] Hence it was imperative to keep a large number of workers very busy. The workers had a duty to labor, but with it there went a general right to employment. "It was the fate of the workers to be poor that the nation might be rich, and to be ceaselessly diligent that the nation might be powerful."[24]

On the upper classes more pleasant duties were imposed. "They were to spend while the poor labored. They were not, however, to spend wantonly, carelessly, or prodigally."[25] The wealthy were encouraged to spend on goods produced domestically, thereby assisting in promoting a favorable balance of trade. They must also spend for the purpose of providing employment

[22] Buck, *The Politics of Mercantilism,* p. 87.
[23] E. S. Furniss, *The Position of the Laborer in a System of Nationalism* (1920), pp. 7, 8, 14, and 30.
[24] Buck, *The Politics of Mercantilism,* p. 88.
[25] The same, p. 96.

for the poor workers. Those with money were counseled to put laborers to work upon houses and gardens. By making employment for the poor, the rich contributed to the strength of the realm. But expenditures should only be made for desirable objectives. Thus there was general unanimity that sumptuary legislation was desirable.

The merchants and manufacturers were to direct and manage the industry and trade of the nation. The employment of the people and the promotion of the treasure of the kingdom depended upon their energy and ingenuity. The activities of the merchants were very significant in promoting a favorable balance of trade.

The owners of agricultural land had the specific function of producing food for the workers and raw materials for industry. The mercantilist regarded them as being highly significant to the community. "The welfare and strength of the state required an active class of husbandmen and proprietors, who would supply a sufficient quantity of raw materials and foodstuffs, and still not demand too high a price nor exact exorbitant rents."[26] It was not easy to attain both a cheap food supply for the workers and a high return to the agricultural landowner.

A well-organized national community was one of the mercantilist's goals. Statesmen supporting this theory believed that if the prosperity and strength of the realm as a whole was assured, "the participation of its subjects in those benefits could be taken for granted, whatever their station in the community."[27] The mercantilists envisaged an ordered national community with every group and individual performing his appointed function and receiving his due reward in a share of the general welfare. Each would be rewarded in a manner suitable to his station. Although the wages of the laborer were small, employment was certain for the spending of the wealthy provided employment for the worker. The landlord's income was allowed to reach a level which would stimulate the production of subsistence for the working classes. The intellect of the

[26] The same, p. 106.
[27] The same, p. 107.

merchant and the manufacturer supplied the directing force for the activities of the nation, subjected of course to public supervision and control.[28] All classes performed their specific roles for the purpose of increasing the power of the state. Industry, labor, and agriculture were all regulated by the government to attain the major objective of greater state power. The detailed controls imposed by the state to ensure that the tasks of these groups were performed will be considered in the remainder of this chapter.

III. POLITICAL RIGHTS

There was little popular participation in government in most countries in western Europe. Generally, governmental power in the last analysis was exercised by the king. As the institutions and vitality of feudalism declined, the restraints and limitations that it had imposed on the monarch as chief feudal lord disappeared.[29] Absolute monarchies were the rule, and there was a general trend toward absolutism in most countries. "In the greater states men felt perfectly helpless without a king to rule the anarchical chaos into which society would have dissolved with him."[30] The estates or parliaments, which in many countries had constituted some limitation on the absolute power of the crown, declined in the sixteenth century, and in many states they disappeared completely.[31] The main role of these bodies was to vote special taxes and to protest to the king to secure the redress of grievances. But in these bodies "the majority of the population, the poor were unrepresented."[32] Thus all restraints on the monarch tended to disappear, and he was in a position to rule in an irresponsible and absolute manner.

The trend in France was toward complete absolutism. The subject was devoid of political rights, according to one of the leading students of the history of French public law.[33] The king

[28] The same, p. 112.
[29] McIlwain, *The Growth of Political Thought in the West,* Chap. 7.
[30] Preserved Smith, *The Age of the Reformation* (1930), p. 477.
[31] G. N. Clark, *The Seventeenth Century* (1931), pp. 86-88.
[32] Smith, *The Age of the Reformation,* p. 478.
[33] Jean Bressaud, *The History of French Public Law* (1915), p. 337.

could legislate on any matter subject to registration of his edicts by the *parlements* (law courts).[34] He ruled without the Estates General during most of the sixteenth century. Since he could levy taxes without it, he found it unnecessary.[35] It met last in 1614. There was little popular representation in it. Even in the Third Estate the guilds had the dominant voice in the selection of delegates from the towns.[36] The *parlements* became increasingly subservient, until by the mid-seventeenth century they had lost all significance as a check on the royal power.[37] "The king was, through devious means, becoming master of both the customary law and the property rights of his subjects."[38] Most of the important administrative positions in the government were reserved for the nobility. Many were sold and some were occupied on a hereditary basis.[39]

The government of England was also absolutistic. Although there was a movement for broader public participation in the government, the absolute monarchy was still pre-eminent. Not until the end of the seventeenth century did England become a constitutional limited monarchy. Throughout this period "the lower classes had small means of asserting what little political will they possessed."[40]

The government was essentially the king's affair to the extent that he wanted to make it so. He could name his own advisers and his administrative staff,[41] and at least up to the seventeenth century they were solely responsible to him. The king could issue royal ordinances that could be enforced in the prerogative courts although not in the common law courts. Through his dispensing power he could set the common law and statutes

[34] W. F. Church, *Constitutional Thought in Sixteenth Century France* (1941), pp. 136-50.
[35] The same, pp. 174-75.
[36] Bressaud, *The History of French Public Law*, p. 364.
[37] Clark, *The Seventeenth Century*, p. 86.
[38] Church, *Constitutional Thought in Sixteenth Century France*, p. 177.
[39] H. Hauser, "The Characteristic Features of French Economic History from the Middle of the Sixteenth to the Middle of Eighteenth Century," *Economic History Review*, Vol. 4 (1933), pp. 257, 262.
[40] A. F. Pollard, *The Evolution of Parliament* (1920), p. 164.
[41] Kenneth Pickthorn, *Early Tudor Government: Henry VII* (1934), Vol. 1, pp. 28-30.

aside. Although he was not able directly to levy domestic taxes, he could increase customs duties, demand forced loans, and impose additional taxes on shipping. Under the Petition of Right of 1628 he was forbidden to imprison his subjects at will; nevertheless he still did it because there was no way of enforcing the prohibition until the Habeas Corpus Act of 1679.[42] The law courts were under his control. Until 1689 he could and did remove the judges who displeased him. Before the Civil War he had the authority to establish prerogative courts that were able to enforce his personal will.[43]

Although Parliament rose in stature, not until the end of the seventeenth century did it become the only source of law. Not until then was it able to control the king, although a century before it managed to impeach the royal ministers who did not have its confidence.[44] As an indication of its increased stature it should be remembered that it managed to conduct a revolution in 1643-48,[45] and as a result of the Glorious Revolution of 1689 it became the only source of law and the king became responsible to it.

Parliament was far from being a body that actually represented the people. Even the domination of Parliament over the king in 1689 did not mean responsible government in the modern sense of the term. That term implies responsibility of the executive to the legislature and of the legislature to the people. Parliament was not responsible to the people. Obviously, the House of Lords was not responsible, but the Commons was as irresponsible as the lords. "Its criterion was its own privilege and it had little respect for anyone else's liberty. Each election was a local and personal contest, and not a political contest of principles." "The Revolution had transferred power from the crown to parliament, but not from parliament to the people."[46] Responsibility could not exist, of course, while the printing

[42] F. W. Maitland, *The Constitutional History of England* (1920), pp. 314-15.

[43] The same, p. 311.

[44] The same, p. 317.

[45] Pollard, *The Evolution of Parliament,* p. 335.

[46] The same, pp. 338-39.

of parliamentary debates and the votes of members was forbidden as was the case until well into the eighteenth century.[47]

The franchise for electing the Commons was still limited. The requirement of a forty-shilling freehold in the counties was not highly restrictive because of the increase in prices in the sixteenth century. But in the boroughs a very limited franchise for parliamentary elections was still the rule. In many places members of Parliament were elected by the governing body of the city, and frequently that body was elected by the guilds.

The individual was not free to express an unfavorable opinion concerning the government or even to receive information about it. Parliament as well as the king punished those who criticized governmental action.[48] Criticism of the public officials was regarded as seditious libel. This crime consisted of "the intentional publication of a writing which reflects on the government";[49] a slander of the queen was considered to be of such a nature. As late as 1704 any criticism of the government was seditious. During much of this period all printing was licensed. Even after the restoration of Charles II, the publication of news about the government required a license, and in 1675 the king closed the coffee houses to restrict the dissemination of news concerning the government. Although the laws for licensing the press expired in 1695, the law of seditious libel still continued to limit publications.[50]

IV. PERSONAL FREEDOMS

With the development of printing the control over individual thought and expression became more important than when communication was difficult. With the rise of many religious sects the maintenance of religious conformity became both more necessary and more difficult for the state. The problems involved in freedom of speech and expression were more significant than they were under feudalism.

[47] Lucy M. Salmon, *The Newspaper and Authority* (1923), p. 107.
[48] J. R. Tanner, *English Constitutional Conflicts of the Seventeenth Century* (1937), p. 48.
[49] Holdsworth, *A History of English Law,* Vol. 6, pp. 260, 368; and Vol. 8, p. 340.
[50] The same, pp. 312, 376-77.

FREEDOM OF SPEECH

Freedom of speech in our present sense of the term did not exist. The individual had little right of self-expression in these centuries. Only a few years after the introduction of printing the control over publishing began to develop. The Archbishop of Mainz first instituted a system for licensing printing in Gutenberg, and shortly thereafter Pope Alexander VI extended it to all Christendom. In 1557 the Inquisition at Rome issued the first list of books to be burned, and a few years later excommunication was decreed for those who read forbidden books. Many countries enacted laws to enforce these ecclesiastical prohibitions.

In France a most rigid form of censorship was set up under royal control. "Previous authorization was required for publishing every writing."[51] Even private letters were inspected and censored by the government authorities. In 1557 the death penalty was imposed on those who imported forbidden books. A decree of 1630 regulating the book trade in Paris declared that "experience has shown the kings of France how prejudicial to the state is the liberty of the press." The Parisian press was made subject to license in 1649, and from 1660 to 1665 practically all newspapers excepting official ones were suppressed.[52]

Freedom of speech and of the press was regulated in England in at least three different ways. First, the publication of any treasonable, seditious, heretical, or blasphemous statement was a criminal offense. All utterances critical of the government were regarded as criminal. Second, great powers over printing and publishing were conferred upon the Stationer's Company, and third, publications were regulated under comprehensive ordinances issued by the government from time to time.

To the Stationer's Company the crown in 1556 gave a monopoly of all printing.[53] Any book to be printed had to be registered with the company. This extensive control was given to the company so that it would be able to prevent the publication

[51] Bressaud, *The History of French Public Law,* p. 340.
[52] Preserved Smith, *A History of Modern Culture,* Vol. 1, pp. 512-17.
[53] Holdsworth, *A History of English Law,* Vol. 6, p. 362.

of undesirable books. By royal ordinances issued in the late sixteenth and early seventeenth centuries, printing could only be done in London, Cambridge, and Oxford. The Archbishop of Canterbury and the Bishop of London were to determine the number of printing presses that were necessary. All books to be published had to be licensed by these ecclesiasts, except law books which had to be approved by the justices. The powers of the Stationer's Company to regulate printing were ultimately embodied in a statute in 1643, and in 1662 Parliament passed a comprehensive law for licensing all books. This program for the control of printing continued with several renewals until 1695. Only then was anyone free to publish what he wished, except for the limitations imposed by the law of criminal and seditious libel, which has been previously mentioned.[54]

FREEDOM OF RELIGION

Religious freedom became more significant to the individual with the Reformation, for only then within the Christian faith were real choices of belief available to him. But actually rulers of the states alone enjoyed freedom of religion. Church and state were so closely connected in the minds of the ruling authorities that any deviation from the established church amounted to treason to the state. At the very time that religious freedom became of real importance to the individual, the maintenance of religious conformity became more significant to the jealous state. It has been well said that from 1500 to 1700, "Unity of faith secured by compulsion where necessary was the accepted tradition and principle."[55]

In Germany, where the Reformation began, the only religious freedom allowed was to the heads of the various principalities. In selecting their respective state religions they could choose only between the Catholic and Lutheran dogmas, but no tolerance was permitted to the subject once the ruler expressed his choice. Dissenting Catholics or Lutherans were subject only to banishment if the ruler elected the other religion, but the

[54] The same, pp. 368-77.
[55] M. Serle Bates, *Religious Liberty: An Inquiry* (1945), p. 148.

adherents of all other sects were subject to severe penalties. After the Peace of Westphalia in 1648, wider tolerance was permitted to followers of the two recognized religions but not to other groups. Full religious freedom first came to a country in Europe after Frederick the Great became King of Prussia in 1742.[56]

The Netherlands, once the Spaniards were expelled, enjoyed much wider religious freedom than was the case elsewhere in Europe. And there for a time Catholic worship in public was forbidden after 1573. But even here non-Christian beliefs were subject to severe penalties. For example, a deist was sentenced to ten years imprisonment in 1668.[57]

In France persecution was widely practiced. Here catholicism was the state religion, and with few exceptions dissenters were persecuted. On St. Bartholomew's Eve, 1572, no less than 10,000 Huguenots were slaughtered by secret orders of the King.[58] In 1598 by the Edict of Nantes limited toleration was allowed for some Protestants; but only the Huguenots benefited from it. They were permitted to establish places of worship in designated areas, and they were not discriminated against politically. This edict was revoked in 1685 by a most severe decree putting an end to even limited tolerance. Under this new decree all Protestant Churches were to be destroyed, heretical church services were forbidden, non-Catholic clergymen were expelled, all other Protestants were forbidden to leave the country. Subsequently, they were deprived of civil rights; only Catholic marriages were legal; and Huguenot children were to be taken from their parents at the age of five to be raised by Catholic families.[59] As a result, the number of Protestants declined from 2,000,000 in 1685 to 400,000 in 1756.[60] This spirit of intolerance continued until 1787, when a limited religious freedom was again granted to Protestants.[61]

[56] J. B. Bury, *A History of Freedom of Thought* (1913), p. 120.
[57] Smith, *A History of Modern Culture,* Vol. 1, pp. 472-73.
[58] Smith, *Age of the Reformation,* pp. 217-18.
[59] Smith, *A History of Modern Culture,* Vol. 1, pp. 465-67.
[60] Bates, *Religious Liberty,* p. 164.
[61] Bury, *A History of Freedom of Thought,* p. 118.

In England dissenters from the established church were generally discriminated against or punished. Sometimes they were punished as heretics, at other times as traitors. After 1560 the laws against Catholics were more severe than those against dissident Protestants. It was made a crime in 1580 to celebrate or to hear mass. Five years later all Jesuits were expelled. By a law enacted in 1593 those who frequented irregular churches were imprisoned until they conformed. The Puritans, when in control during the Commonwealth were as intolerant as the Anglican and Catholics before them. After the Restoration the King was tolerant of Catholics while Parliament imposed severe penalties on them. All holders of municipal office had to be Anglicans, and ultimately this requirement applied to the holders of any public office including members of the House of Commons.

After the Glorious Revolution most of the laws against Protestant dissenters were repealed. Nevertheless until 1778 the law called for the perpetual imprisonment of Catholic priests and full political equality did not come for Catholics until 1829. It was only in 1871 that Parliament opened Oxford and Cambridge to all dissenters.[62] When the Jews were permitted to return to England under the Commonwealth, they were allowed to conduct religious services. No laws were applied to them that were not imposed on other dissenters, but the Jews won absolute political equality only in 1846.[63]

As was natural, the Reformation inspired the Catholic Church to fight back against heresy. The Church imposed severe penalties on its adherents who deviated from its promulgated dogma. The Inquisition was established at Rome in 1542. Heresy, witchcraft, and "the least idle word against the Pope, the Church, or religion" resulted in severe punishments. In Spain Ferdinand and Isabella set up an inquisition that was

[62] E. S. P. Haynes, *Religious Persecution* (1904), p. 122; A. V. Dicey, *Law and Public Opinion in England* (1920), p. 351; Maitland, *The Constitutional History of England*, pp. 518-20.

[63] W. E. H. Lecky, *A History of the Rise and Influence of the Spirit of Rationalism in Europe* (1914), Vol. 2, p. 79; Holdsworth, *A History of English Law*, Vol. 7, p. 413.

renowned for its cruelty.[64] Since there were few Protestants there, the preservation of Catholic purity was its main task. In 1525 the Pope relieved Charles V from his oath to the Cortes not to convert by force the Spanish Jews, and almost a century later all Moors were expelled from Spain under penalty of death.[65]

FREEDOM OF INVESTIGATION

In many areas of intellectual activity scientific investigation and publication were forbidden. Religious considerations were the governing factor. Investigations that might tend to disprove or question religious teaching were absolutely forbidden, and those who indulged in such studies were persecuted by the church or the state.

Those who studied and taught astronomy were restricted and hampered in many ways. Copernicus only escaped the consequences of persecution for his ideas on the solar system because he stated them as a mere hypothesis.[66] The Inquisition at Rome murdered Bruno for supporting the nebular hypothesis.[67] Galileo was persecuted for his astronomical work. He was regarded as impious for saying that Jupiter had moons. He called attention to mountains on the moon, and he pointed out the existence of sun spots. In 1615 he was summoned before the Inquisition at Rome; after imprisonment he renounced these irreligious views. His books were placed on the Index. As a result of such persecution, throughout the seventeenth century no one dared to teach the Copernican theory in France. Comets were another cause of difficulty. In a large part of Europe, in Protestant as well as Catholic states, professors of astronomy had to take an oath that comets were not heavenly bodies subject to natural law.[68]

Individual inquiry in many other scientific fields was practi-

[64] Smith, *A History of Modern Culture,* Vol. 1, pp. 461-63.
[65] Bates, *Religious Liberty,* p. 161.
[66] A. R. White, *History of the Warfare of Science with Theology,* Vol. 1, p. 121.
[67] The same, Vol. 1, p. 15.
[68] The same, pp. 142, 154, and 183.

cally forbidden. The Church regarded many forms of science as magic, and the state helped the Church to prohibit such activities. Thus from the mid-fifteenth to the mid-sixteenth century, in Germany alone more than 100,000 persons were killed for indulging in magic. This policy was highly injurious to work in the entire field of the physical sciences. Thus in some places individuals were forbidden to engage in work in chemistry and physics. For example, in 1624 the *Parlement* of Paris forbade all chemical experimentations, and in Italy several cities did likewise. The attitude of the Church toward the dissection of the human body hampered the study of anatomy and medicine well into the sixteenth century.[69] Mutilation of corpses was considered to be improper, because the Church believed that they should be left intact for the resurrection.

Arbitrary searches, arrests, and imprisonments were not illegal in either France or Germany. Before the Petition of Right of 1628 arrest and imprisonment on the mere order of the English king were sanctioned by the law. Although the Petition of Right made such restraints illegal, there was no adequate machinery to protect the subjects' rights until the Habeas Corpus Act of 1679.[70] Protection of the French subject against arbitrary seizure by the government under so-called letters of cache never was developed.

SUMPTUARY LEGISLATION

Laws regulating dress and personal conduct were the rule throughout western Europe. No form of personal conduct was too insignificant for the state to regulate. Although the Reformation was not the original cause of this legislation, it did much to encourage the development of tendencies that already existed.

In numerous German and Swiss cities many forms of social celebrations were regulated. Municipal ordinances specifically controlled the festivities that could be indulged in to celebrate

[69] The same, Vol. 1, pp. 385, 390-93; and Vol. 2, pp. 31-44.

[70] J. R. Tanner, *English Constitutional Conflicts of the Seventeenth Century* (1937), pp. 62-64.

engagements, weddings, christenings, and funerals. Nürnberg, in 1485, issued a complete wedding manual. "From the celebration at the time of the engagement to the tips and doles of wine lawful to give to the servants in attendance, nothing, it would seem, was exempted from supervision."[71] Stag parties before weddings were forbidden; the gifts to the bride were carefully specified; the number of guests who could be present at the wedding was also prescribed.

Clothing in all forms was regulated. The use of cloth of gold and silver was frequently forbidden in both France and England to prevent the wasteful use of precious metals.[72] By repeated laws and edicts both countries forbade the wearing of foreign cloth. This was to protect domestic industry and to prevent money from being spent abroad.[73] The use of printed calico was forbidden in order to promote the domestic cloth trade and to protect the existing inefficient methods of dyeing cloth.[74] An English law in 1581 provided that every person above the age of six living in a town or village must on Sunday wear a hat made of English wool. From its application a number of groups of people were exempt—ladies, gentlemen, and noble persons, together with every lord and knight with an income from land of twenty pounds per year or more.[75] To encourage the domestic cloth trade all corpses in England had to be buried in woolen cloth.[76] The protection of the button industry was also not overlooked, for the wearing of any woven or cloth buttons was forbidden in England.[77] In some cities the use of finger rings was outlawed; the use of fringes was forbidden; and the wearing of pearls was frowned upon.[78]

[71] Kent R. Greenfield, *Sumptuary Law in Nürnberg* (1918), p. 46.
[72] Cole, *Colbert and a Century of French Mercantilism,* Vol. 1, pp. 6-8.
[73] The same, pp. 6, 260; and Frances Elizabeth Baldwin, *Sumptuary Legislation and Personal Regulation in England* (1926), p. 115.
[74] Heckscher, *Mercantilism,* Vol. 1, pp. 172-73.
[75] Baldwin, *Sumptuary Legislation and Personal Regulation in England,* pp. 211-12.
[76] Heckscher, *Mercantilism,* Vol. 1, pp. 265, 297.
[77] The same, pp. 265, 298.
[78] John Martin Vincent, *Costume and Conduct in the Laws of Basel, Bern, and Zurich, 1370-1800* (1935), pp. 53-60.

Even food and refreshments were subject to sumptuary legislation. A British proclamation of 1517 regulated the number of courses that were permissible at a meal. If a cardinal was a guest, nine courses could be served; if a member of Parliament, six courses; but if a person with an income of 500 pounds a year was present, only three courses could be served.[79] As was said earlier, England established a political lent by requiring the eating of fish on specific days of the week.[80]

The use of profanity was forbidden and the observance of Sunday was also specifically regulated. In Spain in 1566, persons convicted of the use of profanity were to be sent to the galleys for ten years. French legislation prohibited swearing, cursing, blasphemy, imprecations, and other villainous oaths "against the honor of God." In 1647 the use of such profanity was punished by cutting off the lips or piercing the tongue, and by death for repeated offenses. In many places Sunday amusements and work were prohibited. A Scottish statute of 1551 forbade gaming, playing, passing to taverns and alehouses, selling of meat and drink, as well as the "willful remaining away from kirk in time of sermon."[81]

Various reasons existed for this assortment of sumptuary legislation. In some instances the only justification or explanation was pure conservatism—a prejudice against novelty and change. In other cases the objective was to preserve class distinctions. "To make the vulgar know their places, it was deemed necessary to define the dress and diet of every rank." Economic objectives were prevalent. The protection of certain local industries was frequently a reason. Another motive was the general desire to encourage saving. In some cities the governmental authorities took sumptuary legislation so seriously that they actually prohibited individuals from visiting places where such laws did not exist. The town fathers of Zurich specifically for-

[79] Baldwin, *Sumptuary Legislation and Personal Regulation in England,* pp. 167-68.
[80] Holdsworth, *A History of English Law,* Vol. 6, p. 328.
[81] Smith, *The History of Modern Culture,* Vol. 1, pp. 501-02, 504.

bade its residents to make trips to Baden because thereby they escaped the sumptuary controls applied in Zurich.[82]

EQUALITY BEFORE THE LAW

With the increased power of the state, differences between classes tended to diminish somewhat but not to disappear. This was especially true in England. The discriminations against such classes as villeins and Jews declined. When Jews were readmitted to England in the mid-seventeenth century, they suffered no disability that did not apply to other religious nonconformists.[83]

Some elements of English villenage still continued into the sixteenth century—many of its attributes had disappeared. The labor services of villeins were being converted into money rents because with the growth of enclosures, labor was not so vital and because of the increased availability of currency. But the decline of the manorial court was possibly the major factor leading to change, for this was the main instrument of the lord in controlling his villeins. The new justices of the peace took over most of their jurisdiction, and thereby the lord lost his primary instrument for controlling his villeins. But this did not mean the complete extinction of the lord's power. Even late in the sixteenth century villeins were paying for the privilege of living away from the manor and of marrying off their daughters.[84]

Not infrequently English statutes classified individuals on the basis of their income. Only a few illustrations can be cited. The Statute of Apprentices of 1563[85] provided that persons with specified trades but who did not have £10 of property or an

[82] Vincent, *Costume and Conduct in the Laws of Basel, Bern, and Zurich 1370-1800*, pp. 96-97.

[83] Holdsworth, *A History of English Law*, Vol. 9, p. 3.

[84] I. W. Page, *The End of Villainage in England* (1900), p. 93; Pickthorn, *Early Tudor Government, Henry VII*, pp. 169-72; N. S. B. Gras, *The Economy and Social History of an English Village* (1930), p. 94.

[85] Text is in R. H. Tawney and Eileen Power (eds.), *Tudor Economic Documents* (1924), Vol. 1, pp. 338-50.

income of 40s. annually could be made to work if unemployed. Only a person with income of at least 40s. annually could apprentice his children, and in some areas even a higher income was required. The Statute of 1571 making it obligatory to wear wool caps on Sunday exempted ladies, gentlemen, noble persons, and every lord, knight, and gentlemen with land of the value of £20. An act of 1554 forbidding certain uses of silk did not apply to peers, knights, or persons worth at least £200.[86]

In France class distinctions continued right up to the Revolution. Four major classes existed: villeins, bourgeois, clergy, and nobility. The number of villeins declined rapidly from the sixteenth to the eighteenth centuries so that there were probably not over 150,000 at the time of the Revolution.[87] Late in the sixteenth century the amount of labor service that could be demanded of a villein was limited to twelve days a year. The right of pursuit did not end until 1779, but after the seventeenth century it was more nominal than real. The last incidents of serfdom were not eradicated until August 4, 1789.

The French nobility mainly acquired their specially privileged position by birth. At the time of the Revolution they numbered not more than 400,000.[88] As was explained earlier, they alone could own manors and exercise justice over others. Many public offices and most of the commissioned posts in the armed forces were reserved for them. Generally, commerce or handicrafts were closed to them. They were exempt from direct taxation, the lot for military service, the obligation to quarter troops, and compulsory road work. On the manors they often owned monopolies like the oven, the wine press, and the mill.

The clergy, although small, constituted another class. They had their own courts and also were exempt from direct taxation.[89]

The great mass of the population, between the nobles and

[86] Baldwin, *Sumptuary Legislation and Personal Regulation in England,* pp. 188, 211.

[87] Bressaud, *The History of French Public Law,* p. 296.

[88] Georges Lefebvre, *The Coming of the French Revolution* (1948), p. 7.

[89] H. See, *Economic and Social Conditions in France in the Eighteenth Century* (1927), pp. 58-75.

the villeins, made up the bourgeois or third estate. This class constituted at least 96 per cent of the population.[90] They were subjected to the manorial jurisdiction where it existed. The taille, the main form of direct taxation, applied to them. They had to billet troops and perform road work, and they could be conscripted into the army by lot.

Discrimination against Jews continued on the continent. With the Reformation their persecution declined somewhat from the extremes prevalent in the Middle Ages. Both the craft guilds and landholding in the feudal structure were closed to them. Many German cities did not even permit them to dwell within their limits. Even when admitted into the urban precincts, they frequently were required to live in segregated areas. In some cities only one son and one daughter in a family could marry—a regulation designed to restrict the Jewish population. It was well into the nineteenth century before many of the limitations on Jews were relaxed.[91]

Favoritism and special privilege permeated the actual administration of the minute system of social and economic controls. Monopolies, subsidies, and tax exemptions were given at the will of the French king. Masterships in guilds were sold by the government. Exceptions from export and import prohibitions could be bought. Dispensations were granted to violators of the law by the English king before the Revolution of 1689. All of such practices indicated that equality before the law was not prevalent.

V. ECONOMIC RIGHTS

Control was exercised over all phases of economic activity that the state or any influential interest in it believed to be in need of regulation. Any apparent difficulty could effectively be corrected by state action. Hardly more than a sample of the regulations can be given here. The discussion will include examples in the fields of agriculture, business enterprise, trade, industrial production, and labor.

[90] Lefebvre, *The Coming of the French Revolution*, p. 41.
[91] In general see Marvin Lowenthal, *The Jews of Germany* (1936).

AGRICULTURE

Agriculture was still the primary form of economic activity in western Europe. The types of controls involved were changed because production for use was waning. As a device for consciously controlling agriculture the manor was losing its significance. In France it persisted as a form of social organization practically up to the Revolution. The requirements for payments in kind continued in many places and were a significant hindrance to the abandonment of crops no longer desirable.[92]

But the end of the manor and the abandonment of compulsory labor service as a part of villenage did not mean that the average agriculturalist became a truly independent farmer. In the first place he did not necessarily become a landowner. The preponderant part of the land in England was still in large holdings and cultivated by agricultural workers on the basis of long-term leases.[93] But in France, at least by the seventeenth and eighteenth centuries, the greater part of the land cultivated by the peasants "must be looked on in the light of hereditary property, burdened only by the dues and rights of the seigneur."[94] But the power of each farmer to till his land in his own way was limited by its division into small strips grouped in open fields, and by the existence of common pasture.

The right of individuals to use agricultural lands for various purposes was regulated. The persistence of strip holdings made it difficult for an individual to cultivate land in large fields or to use it for raising sheep. The enclosure of land for cultivation was not frowned upon in England. It was permitted if sanctioned by agreement among the users or by private acts of Parliament. But the English government tried repeatedly throughout the sixteenth century to restrict land owners from converting arable land to pasture. A long series of acts from 1499 to 1597 sought to discourage enclosure for pasture. Several laws required the reconversion to tillage of recently enclosed

[92] G. Renard and G. Weulersse, *Life and Work in Modern Europe* (1926), p. 224.

[93] Lipson, *An Introduction to the Economic History of England,* Vol. 1, p. 371.

[94] Henri Gee, "The Economic and Social Origins of the French Revolution," *Economic History Review,* Vol. 3 (1931), pp. 1, 5.

pasture and the re-establishment of decayed houses of husbandry. Late in the century no house in agricultural areas could be let unless at least four acres of land were attached to it, and Parliament provided that all land that had been in tillage for twelve consecutive years had to continue to be cultivated.[95]

Many of these restrictive laws were repealed in 1624 because they were used only for the purpose of extortion; nevertheless the Star Chamber still continued to take steps designed to prevent depopulation.[96] Other laws prescribed how agricultural land could be used. By an act of 1533 no one could have more than 2,000 sheep. Another statute in force from 1533 to 1593 required that all who cultivated more than sixty acres must grow flax and hemp. During the first half of the seventeenth century forcible steps were taken to prevent the cultivation of tobacco in both France and England.[97]

Complete freedom of labor did not exist for agricultural workers. A major objective of the labor policy of the English government was to secure an adequate supply of farm labor. Steps were taken to prevent workers from drifting away from the farms. The Statute of Apprentices of 1563 required that all persons between the ages of 12 and 60 not employed in certain occupations and without visible means of support could be compelled to work by the year in agriculture. When needed for the harvest, certain classes of workers could be required to do such work. In some cases persons who were under 21 could be compelled to become apprentices in agriculture.

In France the regulation of agriculture sought to preserve the existing practices and to promote certain special interests. Here conversion of pasture and waste to arable land was frowned on. In most of the country, to preserve the market for the colonies, the right to grow tobacco was denied. The planting of buckwheat was also forbidden, and to prevent the con-

[95] These were not repealed until 1863. R. H. Tawney, *The Agrarian Problem of the Sixteenth Century* (1912), pp. 355, 363.

[96] Lipson, *An Introduction to the Economic History of England,* Vol. 2, p. 405; Tawney, *The Agrarian Problem of the Sixteenth Century,* p. 406.

[97] Holdsworth, *A History of English Law,* Vol. 6, p. 365; Lipson, *An Introduction to the Economic History of England,* Vol. 2, p. 109; G. L. Beer, *The Origins of the British Colonial System 1578-1660* (1922), pp. 404-08.

version of wheat land to grapes the planting of new vines was barred in 1731.[98]

THE RIGHT TO ENGAGE IN BUSINESS

Many laws and regulations severely restricted the right of the individual to enter into or to carry on a business. In England a would-be merchant frequently had to be both a freeman of the town and a local guildsman, and generally the municipalities forbade strangers from following any business. For example, in Grimsby no one could set up a shop without the permission of the mayor and his brethren. It was not until the Municipal Corporation Act of 1835 that any person could follow any calling within any city in England.[99]

In many lines of activity only guildsmen could engage in business, as was shown in the discussion of feudalism. This was largely a product of municipal action in England; in only a few fields, like textiles and leather, was guild membership required by national law.[100] In France it was made compulsory by a number of national laws passed between 1581 and 1663. These laws required that in towns where no guilds existed the workers had to form guilds and only persons who were members of the guilds could follow the major callings. The extent to which the royal authority was willing to go in creating guilds may be seen in the case of the lemonade makers of Paris. The dispensers of this refreshment had never formed a guild. In fact they did not want one, but the central government actually made them form a guild and buy a charter from the Crown. Usually the members of French guilds could practice their callings in only limited areas. Those who were admitted to guilds in Paris could practice their calling any place in France. Those who were admitted in other major cities could follow their trades in an intermediate area around those places, and those in lesser cities only in a much smaller area. It was not unusual for the law

[98] Cole, *Colbert and a Century of French Mercantilism,* Vol. 2, p. 524, Renard and Weulersse, *Life and Work in Modern Europe,* p. 224.

[99] Lipson, *An Introduction to the Economic History of England,* Vol. 3, pp. 344, 346, 351.

[100] The same, pp. 337-43.

to fix a definite limit on the number of persons who could follow a given line of business. At one time in France, the number of goldsmiths was limited by law to 300.[101]

The extent of public control over the right to carry on a business is seen in the printing trades in England. The central government specifically limited the number of printing presses, and no new ones could be set up until some went out of operation. Presses could be operated only in London, Oxford, and Cambridge. Later a few other cities were added. The presses had to be owned and operated by members of the Stationer's Company, and this guild was given the authority to destroy unauthorized presses. One of the objectives of these regulations was to facilitate censorship. The number of enterprises engaged in brewing, iron making, smelting, and sugar refining was also limited in England.[102]

In some cases the limitation on the right to set up a business was designed to protect the fuel supply, while in others the objective was to protect a limited monopoly. Thus the construction of new iron furnaces was restricted in specific areas in France and England with the object of preventing the destruction of the forests which were used for fuel.[103] In 1668 France forbade the resumption of the operation of once abandoned soap works. Here the objective was to protect the rights of a limited monopoly that had been established by the king.[104]

The English government in its efforts to prevent the movement of the textile trade from the cities to the rural areas restricted the individual in his freedom to carry on business where he wished. Statutes prohibited people from establishing new manufactures of woolen goods in certain counties outside the towns where such enterprises already existed. New enterprises were forbidden, and both the number of looms and of apprentices in old establishments were also prescribed. An act of

[101] Cole, *Colbert and a Century of French Mercantilism,* Vol. 2, p. 443.

[102] Holdsworth, *A History of English Law,* Vol. 1, pp. 367-72; Nef, *Industry and Government in France and England, 1540-1640,* pp. 28-30.

[103] The same, pp. 28-30, 76.

[104] Cole, *Colbert and a Century of French Mercantilism,* Vol. 2, p. 353.

1523 (repealed in 1623) required that in specified counties cloth woven in the country had to be finished in the market town of the county.[105]

A most significant limitation upon the right of individuals to carry on various forms of business was the practice of granting monopolies to an individual or to a specific group of individuals. The use of monopolies was most prevalent in England from the mid-sixteenth century to the Restoration. In France they were widely used in the sixteenth, seventeenth, and eighteenth centuries. The practice of granting such restrictive privileges was an extension of the feudal practice of conferring an exclusive right to operate specific enterprises on the manor. The utilization of monopolies for activities necessitating large enterprises seems to have been commenced by the popes who granted such privileges to specific persons to develop the alum workings of the Papal States.[106]

The monopolies were of four major types. First, a monopoly might be granted as a reward for a new discovery or as a means of encouraging the introduction of a new product from abroad. France used monopolies of this kind to secure the introduction from abroad of the production of new types of cloth. Second, a monopoly might consist of the grant of an exemption from the operation of existing laws. In England, despite a general statutory prohibition, an exclusive grant was made of the right to export unfinished cloth. Third, the government on occasion conferred upon an individual the privilege of supervising and licensing a whole industry. Thus Sir Walter Raleigh was given the authority to supervise taverns. Under the fourth and most objectionable type, an individual or a group of individuals was given the exclusive authority to engage in a settled trade or industry. This form sometimes developed out of monopolies that were originally established to encourage either new inventions or the introduction of new processes from abroad. At

[105] George Unwin, *Industrial Organization in the Sixteenth and Seventeenth Centuries* (1904), p. 91; Heckscher, *Mercantilism*, Vol. 1, p. 239.
[106] V. A. Mund, *Open Markets* (1948), p. 29; Lipson, *An Introduction to the Economic History of England*, Vol. 3, p. 352.

times they were designed to correct abuses in manufacturing as in the production of vinegar and starch in England.[107] One of the major reasons for the use of monopolies was the king's need for revenues, especially when he found it expedient to attempt to rule without Parliament. Although at one time James I canceled all monopolies, he soon found it advantageous for the royal purse to issue an entirely new set of them.

Many articles of common use were supposedly made only by such monopolies in England during this period. Among these products were salt, starch, steel, vinegar, glass, tin, playing cards, alum, soap, cloth finishing, and the production of saltpeter. The saltpeter monopoly was for the purpose of assisting in the production of gunpowder in which saltpeter was a significant ingredient. The monopolists had an exclusive right to make saltpeter. They alone could develop the "saltpeter mines." To discover the raw material, the right to search private property was conferred upon them. Individuals were forbidden to conceal deposits on their property, and the monopoly even had the right to impress workers.

In France practically no monopolies were granted except for a limited period of time. The only exceptions were a few theatrical enterprises.[108] Frequently, they were only applicable to a limited part of the country. Monopolies were granted at various times for lace making, gunpowder, saltpeter, glass, iron, beer,[109] tin plate, cloth finishing and bleaching, silk ribbons, soap, mirrors, and stockings. In only a few cases was a monopoly made applicable to all of France; in such cases it was for a specified number of years. Thus in 1665 the exclusive right to make tin plate was granted for a period of thirty years, and in the same year a twenty-year monopoly was established for the production of Venetian mirrors, window glass, and beads.[110]

[107] The same, pp. 352-55.

[108] Cole, *Colbert and a Century of French Mercantilism,* Vol. 2, p. 135.

[109] Nef, *Industry and Government in France and England, 1540-1640,* pp. 20, 59, 61, and 86.

[110] Cole, *Colbert and a Century of French Mercantilism,* Vol. 2, pp. 142, 192, 193, 214, 239, 309, 321, and 349.

The monopoly granted for the making of Venetian and Genoa lace illustrates the far-reaching extent of control over individuals that at times was involved in such a privilege. In 1665 a company received a grant of the exclusive right to make such lace for a period of nine years. Only those connected with the company could make this lace. Two years later the sale and even the use of lace not made by this company was forbidden. Even the wearing of such lace not made by this group was prohibited. Persons not registered by the company were restricted from making such lace in their own homes for their own use.[111]

REGULATION OF TRADE AND COMMERCE

Many hindrances were imposed on persons carrying on trade and commerce. As under feudalism tolls, tariffs, and embargoes, prohibitions against merchant strangers, monopolies, foreign exchange controls, and detailed regulations of the grain trades were prevalent. Tolls continued to burden freedom of movement on the continent until the end of the eighteenth century.[112] The restraints on strangers and foreign merchants also remained prevalent. It was customary for British towns to punish severely any guild that had admitted nonfreemen to its ranks.[113]

Persons desiring to move goods between nations were burdened by heavy tariffs as well as by detailed export and import prohibitions. Tariffs on exports were more prevalent than on imports. In some instances the exportation of all goods was illegal, especially raw materials (France 1572). England forbade the export of most minerals, especially copper.[114] Very stringent regulations forbade the exportation of leather. In order to stimulate the export of finished and dyed cloth England on occasion prohibited unfinished or gray cloth to leave the country. It was not unusual to make illegal the exportation

[111] The same, pp. 239-77.

[112] Thus on the Elbe River 54 out of every 60 planks transported over its navigable reaches were taken by tolls. Heckscher, *Mercantilism,* Vol. 1, pp. 68-80.

[113] Lipson, *An Introduction to the Economic History of England,* Vol. 3, p. 346.

[114] Holdsworth, *A History of English Law,* Vol. 4, p. 334.

of material useful in war. This included such things as cannon, saltpeter, gunpowder, and horses. It should not be forgotten that governments frequently sought to augment their treasury by selling licenses to export goods in violation of law.

The exportation of raw wool was strictly forbidden in England for over 150 years in this period. The government was anxious to preserve a large supply of relatively cheap wool for the domestic industry. No steps were regarded as too severe to enforce this prohibition.

> In order to prevent exportation, the whole inland commerce of wool is laid under very burdensome and oppressive restrictions. It cannot be packed in any box, barrel, cask, case, chest, or any other package, but only in packs of leather or pack-cloth, on which must be marked on the outside the words *wool,* or *yarn,* in large letters not less than three inches long, on pain of forfeiting the same and the package, and three shillings for every pound weight, to be paid by the owner or packer. It cannot be loaden on any horse or cart, or carried by land within five miles of the coast, but between sun-rising and sun-setting, on pain of forfeiting the same, the horses and carriages.[115]

Since fuller's earth was used in finishing cloth, England subjected its exportation to heavy penalties. In order to enforce this, the law even forbade the export of pipe clay solely because it resembled fuller's earth.[116]

Importation of many kinds of manufactured goods was often entirely forbidden. The objective was to protect local industries and to prevent money from being spent outside the country. France forbade in 1516 the importation of satin, velvet, taffeta, damask, as well as cloth of gold and silver. This prohibition was repealed in 1572.[117] An English statute of 1563 barred the importation of girdles, rapiers, daggers, knives, blades, pommels, scabbards, and gloves.[118] Such goods were relatively more important than now.

Persons engaged in foreign exchange transactions were con-

[115] Adam Smith, *The Wealth of Nations,* Edwin Cannan, ed. (1922), p. 614.
[116] The same, p. 619.
[117] Cole, *Colbert and a Century of French Mercantilism,* Vol. 2, p. 15.
[118] Reprinted in Tawney and Power, *Tudor Economic Documents* (1924), Vol. 1, p. 126.

trolled by many regulations. Numerous attempts were made to prohibit the movement of money out of the country. Even as late as 1600 England was still enforcing the medieval Statute of Employment which required foreign merchants to spend in England money realized from the sale of foreign goods imported into the realm. The export of bullion and local currencies was often punished—even by death. In England under the Tudors the rates of foreign exchange were determined by the government, and the state monopolized all activities relative to foreign exchange.[119]

It was not unusual to require that goods could be imported only in ships of the importing country or in the ships flying the flag of the country of origin. Not infrequently trade with the colonies was restricted to natives of the mother country. England required that such trade should be solely in vessels that were of British registry, British built, and manned by British men.[120] Goods from the English colonies could be shipped only to the mother country. France enacted not dissimilar regulations.[121]

In the field of foreign trade state established monopolies were common. These special privileges obviously restricted other individuals from carrying on such activities. In some countries foreign trade was regarded as the exclusive preserve of the state and could not be carried on by anyone but the government—that is the king. This was true in Portugal and Spain. France created a number of trading companies on which it conferred monopolies; in some of these the crown held the predominant financial interest, and on occasion the government used various forms of coercion to persuade private individuals to subscribe to the securities of such ventures.[122]

[119] Lipson, *An Introduction to the Economic History of England,* Vol. 3, p. 469; Holdsworth, *A History of English Law,* Vol. 4, p. 332; Cole, *Colbert and a Century of French Mercantilism,* Vol. 1, p. 77; Thomas Wilson, *A Discourse Upon Usury* (Tawney, ed. 1925), p. 137.

[120] Lipson, *An Introduction to the Economic History of England,* Vol. 3, pp. 116 ff.

[121] Cole, *Colbert and a Century of French Mercantilism,* Vol. 2, pp. 6-114.

[122] Heckscher, *Mercantilism,* Vol. 1, pp. 341-45; Cole, *Colbert and a Century of Mercantilism,* Vol. 2, pp. 1-32.

England granted a large number of foreign trade monopolies. The Merchant Adventurers from early in the sixteenth century enjoyed such an exclusive right to trade with the Low Countries, primarily handling cloth. The Russian Company, established in the mid-sixteenth century, enjoyed a monopoly of the trade with Russia. A monopoly was given to the Eastland Company for trade in the Baltic area. The Levant Company was permitted to monopolize trade with the Eastern Mediterranean. Trade monopolies were conferred upon the African Company, with the Hudson Bay Company, the French Company, the Spanish Company, and the South Sea Company, covering the geographical regions evident in their names. Thus in England much of the area of foreign trade was exploited by monopolies. Where such grants were held by regulated companies, apprenticeship or the payment of a high fee was required as a prerequisite to admission to the rights of the monopoly.[123]

Persons who engaged in the retail and wholesale trade in specific commodities were subject to minute regulation in order to further a particular government objective. In the late seventeenth century the French government found that its revenue from taxes on the sale of alcoholic beverages was being cut down through the use of new refreshments such as coffee, tea, chocolate, and sherbet. Consequently, in 1692 the king issued a decree conferring a monopoly of the retail and wholesale trade in these commodities.

The edict provided that henceforth coffee ground or in beans, tea, sherbet, and chocolate, together with "cocoa and vanilla which enter into the composition of chocolate," were not to be sold at wholesale or retail in France save by the monopolist or his agents. Moreover, drinks made from the above articles were to be sold only by persons having from the monopolist written permission, for which he might charge 30 livres a year in Paris and 10 livres a year in the provinces. All persons were forbidden to engage in the wholesale or retail trade in the enumerated articles under the penalty of the fine of 1,000 livres, and for a second offense twice that amount. The monopolist

[123] Lipson, *An Introduction to the Economic History of England,* Vol. 2, p. 184.

could enforce his rights by making searches. All merchants possessing the monopolized goods were to declare the quantity and quality of their stocks. They were then to be inventoried, weighed, sealed, and deposited in the warehouses of the monopolist, who would pay for them at prices to be agreed on. Supplies at seaports might be sold to the monopolist by agreement or exported.[124]

PRODUCTION AND PRICES

The major phases of industrial production were minutely regulated to promote the main mercantile goals. The types of goods to be produced, their size and quality, the industrial processes employed, the machinery used, and the prices at which the product was sold were all regulated. Control was much more thorough and far-reaching in France than in England. "Little room was left in French industry for private initiative except within the framework of the royal enactments and under the supervision of the royal officials."[125] One of the major reasons for such a thorough system of regulation was a belief that the production of high quality products was required to promote exports, and a large volume of exports was desired to ensure a favorable balance of trade.[126] It was also believed that industry properly organized and functioning would yield greater tax returns for the state.[127] The establishment of a system of public regulation could best ensure a high level of production. One consequence of this program of regulation was to protect existing products and methods. It placed a premium on conformity and made difficult any innovation.

The regulation of manufacturing in France was both thorough and extensive, although not well enforced. "No measure of control was considered too severe." The regulations governing the operation of industry during the period from 1660 to 1730 covered four large volumes containing 2,200

[124] Charles Woolsey Cole, *French Mercantilism 1683-1700* (1943), p. 184.
[125] Nef, *Industry and Government in France and England, 1540-1640,* p. 88.
[126] Lipson, *An Introduction to the Economic History of England,* Vol. 3, pp. 319-21.
[127] Heckscher, *Mercantilism,* Vol. 1, p. 178.

pages; in addition three volumes of supplementary orders were issued.[128] Although major attention was directed to regulating the production of woolen cloth, most of the other forms of production were also regulated in detail; these included linen, silk, iron, paper, leather, shipbuilding, and beer.[129]

The body of regulations covering the production of woolen cloth will serve to illustrate the extent and minuteness of the system of government direction. This industry was singled out for most thorough control because it produced what was probably the most significant single item of domestic and foreign commerce. The detailed code prescribed the methods to be followed in handling the raw material and in weaving, fulling, and dyeing the cloth. No phase of production was too insignificant for this minute system of regulation. The exact size and weave of each type of cloth was laid down, and only the kinds prescribed in the regulations could be made. The limitations on production applied even to household fabrication for personal use. Changes in the design of cloth were frowned on. A regulation of 1666 provided that before a cloth of a new design could be produced the permission of the judges of the town must be secured, and these judges could grant such permission only after consultation with four of the oldest weavers and four of the oldest merchants.[130] The regulations of 1669 (apparently based upon those of 1571) contained 53 articles. The first 29 fixed the length and breadth of all types of cloth. Even the length of the selvages was fixed. The cloth could not be stretched. All looms had to be adjusted to the determined sizes; looms of other sizes were not permitted. The maker's name had to be woven into each piece. All cloth had to be inspected by the guilds and government agents, and its size had to be specifically stated. To approved pieces of cloth the inspectors attached rosettes of lead bearing their seal. In the period before the Revolution, ordinary cloth had

[128] The same, p. 162.

[129] Cole, *Colbert and a Century of French Mercantilism*, Vol. 2, pp. 197, 328, 356, 397; Nef, *Industry and Government in France and England, 1540-1640*, p. 21.

[130] Heckscher, *Mercantilism*, Vol. 1, pp. 159, 171.

to have six seals on it, and no merchant could accept it for sale until it had been passed by the appropriate inspection bureaus.[131] The petty thoroughness of the controls imposed by the central government can be seen in regulations governing the bleaching of cloth in the Lyons area. The bleachers were

> . . . bound to spread linen on the fields moist, to carry it on their shoulders, to put it through the water troughs piece by piece, and to carry it in book form and not in bundles (? *angeller*). It proceeds, It is particularly forbidden to leave cattle in the meadows while linen is spread there, and (we order) the soaking to be carried out in the old style, without a covering of chalk. Moreover the said bleachers must hold the wash-cloths for the soaking ready on the tub, instead of using for that purpose the linen which they are given to bleach. All this under threat of a 100 *livres* fine.[132]

The dyeing of cloth was regulated by a code of 317 articles. Dyers were divided into two groups according to the colors that they used; those in each group were forbidden to handle the colors used by the other group. The ingredients used by each group of dyers were specified. The employment of some coloring substances was forbidden. Indigo was barred, for it was the policy to encourage the domestic production of woad. The use of alum in setting the colors was controlled. Any single dyer could handle only one kind of fabric—linen, wool, or silk; if he chose one he could not handle the others.[133]

The production of other fabrics was covered by regional regulations promulgated by the national government. Linen, cloth of silver and gold, and silk were thus controlled. The silk regulations were even more technical than those for wool, and they became ever more detailed as the eighteenth century progressed.[134]

England did not organize the control of industrial production with the same thoroughness as did France. The laws were simpler and more often were uniform throughout the country.

[131] Cole, *Colbert and a Century of French Mercantilism,* Vol. 2, pp. 382-94; Heckscher, *Mercantilism,* Vol. 1, p. 163.
[132] The same, pp. 161-62.
[133] Cole, *Colbert and a Century of French Mercantilism,* Vol. 2, pp. 405-07.
[134] The same, pp. 397-401.

Although many products were regulated, major attention was directed to the production of wool cloth. This concern for the cloth industry is not surprising, for it was by all odds the most significant single item of export, and most of the cloth produced was exported. The use of different kinds of fibers in the same piece of cloth was forbidden. The stretching of cloth was illegal as was the use of gig mills in its finishing. The size of cloth was regulated, but this was hard to enforce, since frequently the country of destination imposed its own conflicting regulations. Obviously, conformity to the regulations decreed by the country of destination was imperative.

Many other lines of production were subject to state control in England. The regulation of leather manufacturing was probably even more thorough than that decreed for the production of cloth. Here general enforcement powers were vested in the guilds by the national government; these producers' associations enjoyed the power of search by virtue of acts of Parliament. Among other lines of business regulated in detail by the government were beeswax, honey, gold and silver thread, and even feather beds. Again, the government did not fail to overlook the production of bricks; their size was specifically decreed.[135]

The right of the individual producer to utilize new processes and to develop new products was thwarted by the vast mass of regulations and by the guilds. As a result the consumers were not free to secure such new products as they might desire. The general objective was to maintain the existing situation and to protect vested interests. When fashion and demand changed, it was difficult to get the regulations modified so as to permit the production of different goods. New products were frowned upon. As was shown earlier, the French regulations concerning the cloth industry restricted the development of new patterns and made impossible the use of new techniques in finishing and dyeing cloth.

[135] Lipson, *An Introduction to the Economic History of England,* Vol. 3, pp. 321, 331; Heckscher, *Mercantilism,* Vol. 1, p. 264; Nef, *Industry and Government in France and England, 1540-1640,* p. 28.

The barriers imposed on the production and use of printed calicoes constitute a startling but not an atypical illustration of the efforts that were made to control a new product for the purpose of protecting an existing industry, in this case the weaving and dyeing of wool cloth (as well as silk and linen). The weaving of cotton fabrics was slow to develop in Europe, and neither France nor England managed to discover good methods of printing instead of dyeing cloth. Consequently, when printed cotton cloth began to be imported from India late in the seventeenth century, consternation resulted in the textile industry. In France the importation, printing, and use of calicoes was forbidden from 1686 to 1759. For a time the printing of any kind of cloth was illegal. These regulations were ruthlessly enforced; it is estimated that about 16,000 persons met their death as a result of the attempts to execute these laws. England followed a slightly different course. The importation but not the production of calico was forbidden in 1700. Even the use of such cloth was forbidden twenty-one years later, but its production was never forbidden. Manufacturing for the export trade was permitted to go on, and thus the industry was in a position to improve its technology. As a result, the British producers were able to take the export market away from the French who were not permitted to fabricate it even for export. Not until 1774 did England permit the use of calico.[136]

There are other illustrations of the attempt to prohibit individuals from making innovations. For a time France forbade the production of half beaver hats, for their manufacture both reduced the consumption of beaver, a product of the Canadian colony, and required the employment of some materials that were disapproved of on principle. The use of cloth or woven buttons was prohibited in both France and England since their production interfered with the existing button industry.[137] Producers had to secure permission from the government to modify their product to meet changes in fashion. It took the

[136] The same, Vol. 1, pp. 172-74.
[137] The same, pp. 171, 265.

weavers in one French town four years to get permission to weave cloth with black warp.[138]

Producers were forbidden to utilize various new machines and processes largely because their employment would interfere with existing production methods. Gig mills for finishing cloth and machines for stretching it were forbidden in England in the sixteenth century. The wearing of brass buckles was made illegal because their use interfered with the production of iron ones. Brass buckles were made in molds, a simpler process than was involved in the fabrication of iron ones which were wrought. The English government at first disapproved of the use of frames for knitting stockings, although it subsequently reversed its attitude. In the seventeenth century the Council in England ordered the destruction both of machines for making needles and of needles that had been produced by them. A similar fate awaited machines for making pins. Machines for weaving ribbons were forbidden in many countries because they reduced the amount of labor required.[139]

Government price fixing was not unusual. In England the assize of bread was enforced generally. Prices of beer, wine, and coal were also regulated by national authority. An act of 1489 fixing the retail price of cloth was not repealed until 1624.[140] Considering the great change in prices that took place during this century and a third, one may wonder whether it was well enforced. After the great fire of London of 1666, Parliament provided machinery for fixing the price of building materials in the vicinity of the metropolis.[141] Many other prices were fixed by municipal action. In France prices were regulated whenever the national government found it expedient. The price of cloth was fixed by the general code of regulations

[138] Heckscher, *Mercantilism,* Vol. 1, p. 170.

[139] Lipson, *An Introduction to the Economic History of England,* Vol. 3, pp. 51-52; Heckscher, *Mercantilism,* Vol. 1, p. 264; Clark, *The Seventeenth Century* (1931), p. 64.

[140] F. J. Nicholas, "The Assize of Bread in London During the Seventeenth Century," *Economic History,* Vol. 2, p. 323 (1932); E. Lipson, *The History of the English Woolen and Worsted Industries* (1921), p. 113; Holdsworth, *A History of English Law,* Vol. 6, p. 346.

[141] The same, p. 348.

imposed on the industry in 1571. When it suited the fancy of the king, he fixed any price, even that of flowers used merely for decorations.[142]

As devices for implementing and executing this extensive and intensive program for controlling industry, the central governments increasingly turned to the guilds thereby transforming them from municipal agencies to arms of national administration. Often in France it was illegal to sell goods unless they had been marked by the guilds as being of proper standard; in performing such inspection activities, these associations were subject to the supervision of the government commissioners of manufacture. To make government control more effective, their wardens became state officials in 1681.[143] Ultimately as was said before, membership became compulsory, and the royal government decreed that it alone could charter them. Not only did this increase the royal control, but it meant increased money for the king through the sale of charters and masterships. The same thing was going on to a lesser degree in England. After 1503 all of the bylaws of the guilds had to be approved by the king's justices, and a little later Parliament forbade them from charging excessive admission fees.[144] In a number of cases the right to search was conferred on them, thus enabling them to ensure that all goods met government specifications and were produced under guild auspices.

LABOR

A general obligation to work underlay the mercantilist's attitude toward labor. This was clearly revealed in the English Statute of Apprentices of 1563. One of its main objectives was to eradicate the sturdy beggar, and thereby secure an adequate supply of agricultural labor.[145] One section provided that any person under 30 not an apprentice could be made

[142] Nef, *Industry and Government in France and England, 1540-1640*, p. 20; Cole, *Colbert and a Century of French Mercantilism*, Vol. 1, p. 367.

[143] Heckscher, *Mercantilism*, Vol. 1, p. 151.

[144] Stella Kramer, *English Craft Gilds and the Government* (1905), pp. 61-62, 77-80.

[145] Heckscher, *Mercantilism*, Vol. 1, p. 228.

to work in agriculture by the year. The justices of the peace could compel women to work who were between the ages of 12 and 40. Any person under the age of 21, who was not an apprentice and who did not have a specified income, could be forced to become an apprentice in agriculture. Another section provided that any unmarried unemployed person below the age of 30, not worth 40 shillings a year, who had followed any one of a long list of callings for at least three years could be made to work at his calling. Other English laws forbade begging and directed local authorities to create workhouses for the unemployed. In France a comparable policy toward the unemployed beggar was followed and most severe penalties were imposed upon him. A convicted beggar could even be sent to the galleys for a period of years.[146] In some lines of activity, workers could be impressed to perform specific tasks. The holders of certain English mining monopolies could impress people to work in their mines; and the same was true in the case of the saltpeter monopolists.[147]

While the government believed that the individual had an obligation to work, it also considered that the employer had a comparable duty to make work for his employees. The Council and the Star Chamber in England took steps to compel employers to keep workers at their jobs even though they had no market for the goods produced. There were no acts of Parliament covering the problem; but the king used all of the powers at his command to compel the employment of workers.[148]

Partly to enforce the general obligation to work, the mobility of labor was restricted. Again the English Statute of Apprentices required that no stranger was to be employed unless he bore a statement from his local government authorities saying that his departure was lawful. In order to enforce a comparable policy, France in the eighteenth century required that each industrial worker must have his employment record entered

[146] Cole, *Colbert and a Century of French Mercantilism,* Vol. 1, p. 13.
[147] Lipson, *An Introduction to the Economic History of England,* Vol. 2, p. 124.
[148] Holdsworth, *A History of English Law,* Vol. 4, p. 380.

in a book and that industrial workers had to register with local authorities before they could be employed.[149] Workers could not leave their tasks at will. The Statute of Apprentices provided that in many significant lines of employment workers must be hired for a year or more. Heavy penalties were imposed upon those who left before their terms of employment were over, and workers were prohibited from quitting before their specific tasks were completed.

The English poor law also restricted the right of workers to move about at will. So-called settlement laws were enacted to prevent persons from becoming poor charges on a parish where they had not long resided. An act of 1531 provided that vagrants were to be whipped and returned to the places of their birth or the places where they had last resided for three years. A more restrictive system was introduced in 1662. The new law provided that within forty days of the arrival in a parish of a person who did not occupy property worth at least £10 a year, two justices could order him removed to the last parish in which he had been legally settled.[150] The sturdy beggars of France on occasion were removed to the place from which they came.[151]

The emigration of skilled workers was generally prohibited. The objective was to prevent rival countries from improving their capacity to produce handicraft or manufactured products. The Italian cities, France, the Netherlands, and England all took steps to prevent skilled workers from leaving the country.[152]

Many limitations were imposed on the right to work, some by local authorities and others by the guilds. Local restrictions were not unusual all during this period. Thus in Grimsby

[149] Renard and Weulersse, *Life and Work in Modern Europe*, pp. 195-98.

[150] Lipson, *An Introduction to the Economic History of England*, Vol. 3, p. 423; Holdsworth, *A History of English Law*, Vol. 6, pp. 351-52. In 1696 this was relaxed somewhat by the provision that he could not be removed if he had a certificate from his last place of settlement assuming responsibility for his relief.

[151] Cole, *Colbert and a Century of French Mercantilism*, p. 212.

[152] The same, Vol. 2, p. 139.

in 1583 no laborer was to work in the town until the authorities had admitted him "to work as a laborer."[153] And in 1686 Lincoln forbade a person to follow any occupation unless he was free of the city. English law even prohibited a person from following more than one trade at a time.

The guild system continued to restrict the freedom to work in a manner comparable to that already mentioned in Chapter II. The restriction of the right to work at a given craft to members of only a specific guild, high admission fees, onerous apprenticeship requirements, and preferential admission requirements for relatives of members still were very customary. The English Parliament attempted to regulate some of these restrictive practices; for example, excessive admission fees were forbidden. But in the case of apprenticeship the practice of the guilds was adopted for the nation as a whole by the Statute of Apprentices of 1563 which imposed a detailed system of apprenticeship on the whole nation. As was said before, the parents of apprentices had to have certain amounts of property. A definite ratio between the number of journeymen and of apprentices was provided. And most important, it imposed on the entire country a seven-year period of apprenticeship. This was a great victory for the guilds which had long wanted such a national program. The apprenticeship provisions of this law were not repealed until 1813-14.[154]

The actual workingmen had no right to form their own organizations or to engage in concerted action to improve their working conditions. The journeymen were members of guilds which were dominated by the masters. Although the guilds generally set the terms of employment, the journeymen had no voice in the process. Separate associations of journeymen were frequently forbidden. An English law of 1547 prohibited

[153] Lipson, *An Introduction to the Economic History of England,* Vol. 3, p. 344.

[154] Kramer, *The English Craft Gilds and the Government,* pp. 78-80, 102-06; Margaret R. Gay, "Aspects of Elizabethan Apprenticeship," *Facts and Factors in Economic History* (1932), p. 134; T. K. Denny, "The Repeal of the Appenticeship Clauses of the Statute of Apprentices," *Economic History Review,* Vol. 3 (1931), p. 67.

workers from associating together "to do their works but at a certain price and rate." Early in the eighteenth century Parliament made illegal all combinations of workers to improve their conditions of employment, to advance their wages, or to reduce the hours of work. These laws applied to those employed in the manufacturing of the following commodities: wool, silk, mohair, flax, linen, fur, hemp, iron, leather, cotton, and hats. From the sixteenth century on France likewise forbade workingmen from associating for the purpose of improving their terms of employment, and the public officials did everything in their power to prevent workers from engaging in collective action to improve their working conditions.[155]

Wages and hours of work also were regulated. As indicated earlier, the fixing of maximum wages was general after the Black Death in the mid-fourteenth century. Municipal regulation of wages was common in both England and France. In 1445 the English Parliament enacted a law providing for a fixed statutory maximum wage rate, and this law was extended several times. The Statute of Apprentices of 1563 established a variable maximum wage rate to be fixed by the justices of the peace. This was to fluctuate with the cost of living; that is, the price of food.[156] Much heavier penalties were imposed upon workers who took pay above the maximum than upon employers who offered it. Wage assessments by the justices apparently were made throughout the seventeenth and at least well into the eighteenth centuries, and the act was not repealed until 1814. A comparable policy of fixing wages under national laws was adopted in France toward the end of the sixteenth century.[157] In a few lines of work in England the law fixed minimum, not maximum wages. In 1604 Parliament pro-

[155] Lipson, *An Introduction to the Economic History of England,* Vol. 3, pp. 388, 407; Renard and Weulersse, *Life and Work in Modern Europe,* p. 201.

[156] Lipson, *An Introduction to the Economic History of England,* Vol. 3, p. 252; R. H. Tawney, "The Assessment of Wages in England by the Justices of the Peace," *Vierteljahrschrift für Sozial- und Wirtschaftgeschichte* (1913), pp. 312-33; R. Keith Kelsall, *Wage Regulation under the Statute of Artificers* (1938), passim.

[157] Renard and Weulersse, *Life and Work in Modern Europe,* p. 195.

vided for minimum wages in the woolen industry, and later minimum wages were provided for the producers of other textiles.[158] Not infrequently the hours of work were fixed. Where this was done, the hours prescribed were generally the minimum period of work required rather than the maximum permitted.[159]

VI. CONCLUSIONS

The absolute monarchies sought to develop state power as an end in itself. All activities of the individual were subordinate to the aggrandizement of the power of the state. After the Reformation, the state looked "upon religion as an instrument to use rather than as an end to serve."[160] The church became an instrument of the state. Comparably, economic activities were made subservient to political objectives. No phase of individual conduct was considered too minute for the state to control if some group could persuade the king or his advisers that it was allegedly in the public interest.

Since the state viewed its power primarily in material terms, economic activities were of pre-eminent importance to it. Power as a means of physical domination was its objective, and for this it required material wealth. This thirst for power was coupled with a relatively static idea of society. No one envisaged the possibility of an absolute increase in physical goods. Increasing the power of any one state meant the reduction of the power and wealth of other states. Commercial and political rivalries between nations were the inevitable outcome. With this great emphasis placed upon trade and commerce, the merchant and manufacturer became of great importance to the body politic.[161]

In the entire process of control little concern was shown for the individual. This was a logical outcome of the prevalent view of the place of the individual in society. Social organization

[158] Lipson, *An Introduction to the Economic History of England,* Vol. 3, pp. 255, 263.

[159] This is illustrated by sec. 9 of the Statute of Apprentices of 1563.

[160] Harold J. Laski, *The Rise of Liberalism* (1936), p. 84.

[161] Heckscher, *Mercantilism,* Vol. 2, pp. 280-83.

was imperative mainly because the individual, with his thirst for power, if left in a state of nature was disruptive of the peace. He was a disturbing element and therefore needed to be controlled. As Sir Thomas Gresham said in 1560: "As the merchants be one of the best members in our common weal, so they be the very worst if their doings be not looked unto in time; and forced to keep good order."[162] Another writer stated merely that "private advantages are often impediments of public profit."[163] There was no assumption that private interest and public interest ever coincided. The very nature of the individual as an animal craving for power produced disruptions that required state action. Thus Mandeville said: "Private Vices by the dextrous Management of a skilful Politician may be turned into Public Benefits." The absolute monarch did not believe that there was any limit to his wisdom and authority in guiding society, for under the theory of the divine right of kings, did he not derive his authority from God? A most extreme form of this belief in the supreme competence of the state is epitomized in a statement of the court chamber of Baden that: "Our princely court chamber is the natural ward of our subjects. It is in its hands to guide them away from error and lead them on to the right path and to teach them, even against their own wills, how they are to institute their own households."[164]

With the individual viewed as a disruptive force, it is not surprising that little concern was shown for him. No form of mistreatment was too extreme if it served the purpose of the state. Even the very process of justice was to be used in order to get victims for the power of the state. Colbert insisted that the judges should "condemn as many criminals as possible to the galleys." One subordinate wrote to Colbert that this was desirable "in order to maintain this corps which is necessary to the state."[165] The prevalent attitude toward the working

[162] The same, p. 320.
[163] Laski, *The Rise of Liberalism,* p. 163.
[164] Heckscher, *Mercantilism,* Vol. 2, pp. 293, 320.
[165] The same, pp. 298, 299.

classes shows this same complete disregard of the individual. The mercantilist believed that the "majority must be kept in poverty that the whole might be rich." The belief in the disruptive nature of the individual was the basis of this attitude toward poverty, for as one writer said: "The lowest orders should endure a state bordering on want in order that a necessity may exist for their labor."[166]

This all-embracing mania for regulating the individual terminated primarily because the absolute monarchies were unable to secure revenues adequate to meet their needs. The program of economic regulation was largely undertaken in order to provide a healthy economy out of which the state would be able to get revenue adequate for its needs. But, it was the very failure of the state to get the revenue necessary for the purposes of statecraft that produced the revolutions that caused the downfall of the absolute monarchs.[167] It was just this need for money that caused the English king to take steps that were a significant element in bringing about the two revolutions in the seventeenth century, and out of these came the constitutional limited monarchy. It was the bankruptcy of the French crown that led it to call the Estates General in 1789, and from this came the Revolution.

Throughout these centuries the demand of religious groups for freedom from the state—in fact it frequently was a claim to dominate the state—was the only continuing force for limiting the power of government. Most of the literature of the period that questioned state authority approached the problem from the standpoint of the claims of the religious sects. "It is not too much to say that political liberty would not nowadays exist but for that claim to ecclesiastical independence."[168]

In England most of the basic personal and political freedoms were won by revolution—freedom of speech, freedom from

[166] Furniss, *The Position of the Laborer in a System of Nationalism,* pp. 8, 118.

[167] A. D. Lindsay, *The Modern Democratic State* (1943), Vol. 1, p. 75.

[168] Figgis, *Studies of Political Thought from Gerson to Grotius 1414-1625,* p. 116.

arbitrary arrest, limited freedom of religion, an independent judiciary, and triennial parliaments with control over finance and the army resulted from the revolutions in the seventeenth century.[169] The economic controls were not removed for more than another century. The revolution in France was even more sweeping in freeing the individual from controls; feudalism, and the guilds were destroyed in the process, and the Church was shorn of its temporal power. Basic political freedoms came almost overnight. "The French Revolution . . . was a supreme attempt to realize the principle of individualism in the domain of actual institutions."[170]

The economic controls in England were finally eradicated largely as a result of another force—liberal utilitarianism. Many of the restrictive laws—such as the Statute of Apprentices, and the laws regulating types and quality of goods—largely went unenforced in the late eighteenth century. Ultimately, they came to be regarded as undesirable restraints on freedom. The merchants and manufacturers who were dear to the heart of the mercantilist always were anxious for freedom for themselves.[171] But it took the liberal utilitarians like Bentham, Smith, Ricardo, and the elder Mill to persuade the community that the public interest would be promoted if producers were allowed to pursue their own private interests. As a result of the conversion the vast mass of legislation relative to wages, guilds, and production methods was stricken from the statute book in the first four decades of the nineteenth century.[172]

[169] Laski, *The Rise of Liberalism,* p. 110.

[170] R. R. Palmer, "Man and Citizens; Application of Individualism in the French Revolution," *Essays in Political Theory Presented to George H. Sabine* (1948), p. 131.

[171] H. M. Robertson, *Aspects of the Rise of Economic Individualism* (1933), p. 206.

[172] J. H. Claphan, *An Economic History of Modern Britain* (1930), Vol. 1, pp. 334-49.

CHAPTER IV

COMMUNISM

This chapter on contemporary communism commences our detailed examination of the position of individuals in modern totalitarian society. The introduction gives certain general background information required for a correct interpretation of the analysis of specific areas of freedom. Just as it was advisable to preface our treatment of feudalism with material to recall to the contemporary reader important elements of the world of that day, it is necessary to clarify certain major aspects of Russian communist society which differ from their ostensible counterparts in the western world, and which are hidden from the ordinary observer by distance, propaganda, and censorship. Sections following the introduction analyze the conditions of freedom in the political, social and religious, economic, and intellectual fields.

I. INTRODUCTION

This chapter deals with communism as it appears in the theory and practice of power, society, and economics in the Soviet Union. Although communism has an involved and varied development far antedating the Soviet Union, it is only in its Russian-shaped form that it is now historically significant, a world challenge to freedom in society. There is no communism in the world today which is not dominated or shaped by the Russian pattern. Even the Titoist secession does not challenge the political, economic, or conspiratorial gospel at any theoretically important point other than the *rate* and *technique* of collectivization and industrialization of a predominantly peasant country. Tito's methods and models are those of the Kremlin.

Russian communism combines Eastern and Western characteristics. Its intellectual and economic roots are in the West, but its growth has been equally determined by the absolutism, the political and religious idolatry, the scorn for individual human life, the bloodiness, and intrigue of the East.

THEORETICAL POSTULATES

Communism postulates three historical epochs which are important for assessing the reality of communist government. First is the era of the bourgeois capitalist, merging into imperialism; second, the period of the dictatorship of the proletariat, in which the old oppressing order is smashed by proletarian revolution, the proletariat expropriates the means of production, and the transition is accomplished to socialism and to the final era, communism. Classical Maxism spent a great deal of time on the philosophical, economic, and sociological analysis of the first period; spent comparatively little time in dealing with society under the dictatorship of the proletariat, and spent no time at all in talking about society under communism. This latter, when it occurred among lesser lights, was immediately decried as utopianism, particularly by Lenin. Marx thought the dictatorship of the proletariat would be quick and relatively automatic in action. Although Lenin, the arch-conspirator of the revolution, spent much time in developing the strategy, the tactics, the ethics, and the organizational requirements for seizing power, even he did not realize until after the November Revolution that the problems of government during the dictatorship of the proletariat could not be automatically handled by any literate body of persons, and that the period of the dictatorship of the proletariat would be a comparatively long one. It remained for Stalin to blast the Marxist prediction that the state would wither away on the arrival of the classless society. This he did in two ways: first, by the Stalinist revolution in the interest of stability and conservatism, marked by the Constitution of 1936; second, by the bald pronouncement in 1939 that the power of the dictatorship of the proletariat would endure and intensify so long as Russia was threatened by capitalism anywhere in the world.

Since capitalism has shown far greater stability and vitality than the Marxists dreamed, Stalin's decision means that Russia will stay indefinitely in a period of great and increasing state power. Capitalist durability plus socialist economics have fastened a totalitarian system on Russia and its satellites for as long a period as it is worth-while considering.

How do the Communists themselves define power under the dictatorship of the proletariat? According to Lenin, this dictatorship is the "universal power" of the popular majority of workers and peasants, and as the "special form of leadership of the remaining masses of toilers by the proletariat." "The dictatorship of the proletariat is authority unlimited by any statutes whatever." It is power wielded solely on behalf of the proletariat.[1] This Leninist view has been later amplified in the following words of Vyshinsky:

> ... the dictatorship of the proletariat, creating its own laws, makes use of them, demands that they be observed, and punishes breach of them. Dictatorship of the proletariat does not signify anarchy and disorder but, on the contrary, strict order and firm authority which operates upon strict principles, set out in the fundamental law of the proletarian state—the Soviet Constitution.[2]

But the dictatorship of the proletariat embraces elements far transcending economics and politics, and it is in this sense that communism becomes fully totalitarian. In the words of Monsignor Sheen:

> Basically, comunism is . . . a complete philosophy of life, . . . an integral comprehension of the world, different from all other secular systems in that it seeks not only to dominate the periphery of life but to control man's inner life as well. Communism has a theory and a practice; it wishes to be not only a state but a church judging the consciences of men; it is a doctrine of salvation and as such claims the whole man, body and soul, and in this sense is totalitarian.[3]

At the same time that Communists assert the dictatorship

[1] See Andrei Y. Vyshinsky, *The Law of the Soviet State* (1948), pp. 41, 43.

[2] The same, p. 48. Vyshinsky fails to make clear that the communist state does not consider itself bound by the principles enunciated in the Constitution, which was a sort of epitome of current practice and "ground won," but no barrier to any practices they thought necessary to meet any new situation.

[3] Fulton J. Sheen, *Communism and the Conscience of the West* (1948) p. 58.

of the proletariat is unlimited, they unblushingly claim that it is the most democratic political system in the world. Lenin said their form of society was "a million times more democratic" than bourgeois society;[4] and Stalin claimed that the USSR "is the most democratic of all state organizations possible while classes continue to exist."[5] They base this argument on the allegation that their system is operated *in behalf of* the great majority of people—the proletariat. At the same time, they pour contempt on any machinery which would give the proletariat any genuine power of control over the selection, the decisions, or the actions of the revolutionary elite. Lenin unhesitatingly repudiated the decision of the Russian electorate in the only elections Russia ever had after November 1917—in the winter of 1917-18—when voters could choose between Communists and candidates of other parties. For example, Lenin says "The Soviet Socialist Democracy is in no way inconsistent with the rule and dictatorship of one person: that the will of a class is at times best realized by a dictator who sometimes will accomplish more by himself and is frequently more needed. . . ."[6]

Communism, whether in the period of seizure of power, of the dictatorship of the proletariat, or of the present "classless" society, claims freedom for the working class only. As Lenin put it: ". . . Every freedom is a fraud if it contradicts the interests of the emancipation of labor from the oppression of capital."[7] In the Soviet Constitution and in other forms of Soviet propaganda, this often appears as freedom from real or alleged repressions under capitalism or the Tsarist regime. The Communist does not mind if he introduces parallel and more severe repressions of persons outside the working class and its self-chosen elite. The historical sins of the exploiting classes are so great that they have no claim against communist society, or rights in it. Only through the mercy or the needs of

[4] Quoted in David Shub, *Lenin, A Biography* (1948), p. 390.
[5] Joseph Stalin, *Foundations of Leninism* (1934), p. 57.
[6] Quoted in Shub, *Lenin, A Biography*, p. 389.
[7] Quoted in the same, p. 390.

the new society can they be utilized as engineers or technicians, and then usually in constant threat to life, movement, or livelihood. The proletariat expropriates their property, basing the claim that such action is legitimate on the view that the former exploiters acquired it unjustly.

The abolition of exploitation in the communist society of today is understandable only in strictly Marxian terms. According to Marxian economics, exploitation consisted in the appropriation of the surplus value created by the worker (over and above his pay) by the capitalist. Hence, once the capitalist class is gone, and the value of all production returns to the individual directly, or indirectly through the mediation of the state or its organs, "exploitation" is no more.

The confusion of terms is worse confounded by the ideological struggles within socialism from the time of Marx. The Communists call themselves Socialists, and their country the land of socialism, because they have not yet applied the system they insist is characteristic of communism—distribution according to need, not to product. Other Socialists, coming out of the same ideological stream, make the most strenuous efforts to divorce themselves from that stream of communism which followed Lenin and Stalin in affirming the necessity of violence. We do not pay attention here to the revisionists, the reformists, the utopians, the social democrats, the bolsheviks versus the mensheviks, the Stalinists or Trotskyites; we speak of Communism as the ideology and practice of power in Russia and Russian satellites.

THE ACTUAL COURSE OF EVENTS

Communism in Russia has gone through several major periods of development since the emergence of what is now the Communist Party of the Soviet Union (bolsheviks). They can roughly be divided as follows: (1) party formation and struggles leading to the seizure of power in November 1917; (2) war communism, 1917-21; (3) NEP, 1922-28; (4) the Five-Year Plans, 1928-41; (5) World War II, and (6) from V-J Day to the present.

All of these periods are in one way or another apposite to our purpose. During the period of party formation and emergence, Lenin forged the theory and practice of a revolutionary party seizing power, which is important as a guide to the beliefs and actions of communist parties which would seize power and wield it in other countries. During the period of war communism, the landlords and capitalists, and most other property owners were expropriated, banished, or liquidated. All competing political parties were smashed and the Communists emerged as a monopoly party in a special sense: as a leader and controller of all elements of society, which would brook no competition or challenge from any man or any group. During the period of the New Economic Policy, it appeared to many observers that the socialist experiment had failed, and that older economic laws were asserting themselves. The return to the forms and incentives of private enterprise and ownership seemed to foreshadow a direction of development antithetical to the doctrinaire predictions of the Communists. These hopes were false and short-lived. With the first Five Year Plan, and the decision to proceed with rapid industrialization and rapid collectivization of agriculture, Stalin commenced his own conservative revolution. At the same time, Stalin consolidated his hold on the party, eliminated all factions which might in any way challenge his monolithic control, and thus demonstrated the fallacy of any claims to freedom or democracy within the party. During the Five Year Plans private enterprise was almost wholly eliminated as a significant element in Russian economy. In the process, millions were subjected to planned starvation, and the communist contempt and disregard for any human life or interest which stood in the way of the doctrine and programs of the party was blazoned for the world to see.

By the end of the second Five Year Plan, Stalin had told his country that life was better; he heralded rest and leisure, and new prospects for the consumer. During the third Five Year Plan, however, two main streams blocked this rosy hope: the continuance of the Stalinist conservative revolution in government, law, the family, and economic relations on the one hand; on the other, feverish preparation for the war indicated both by the communist obsession that capitalism *must* try to smash communism by violence, and by the rise of Hitlerian aggression. These were the years of the purges, in which Stalin eliminated any possible threat to his leadership, any possible source of treason on behalf of the capitalist enemy, and any belief that any man in any walk of life could pursue his calling without the detailed supervision of the party, the government, or the secret police.

The war years have least to teach us of all the periods; the requirements of survival or victory produce surprisingly similar controls in many forms of society. Yet during these years, we now know that Stalin made the decision that he could master the military threat of Germany without outside aid, and that he could safely return at an early date to the path of world revolution and destruction of the society of his war allies. The Red Army brought with it the conditions for forcing communist regimes on the Eastern satellites, despite the preference of majorities in all those countries.

The present period, which commenced openly with Stalin's pre-election speech of February 1946, has witnessed the return to world revolutionary agitation and action through the Cominform; a new impetus to the Stalinist conservative revolution in Russian society, and a new eruption of communist regimes founded on internal and external preponderance of communist violence.

We have taken illustrations from all of these periods in the analysis which follows, designed to show the full reality of communist control over individual freedoms.

Two other major conditions affect the freedom of the individual throughout Russian society in important ways. These are the use of violence, and the status and functions of the Communist party. They are sketched generally here, because they operate in every sphere of human life. There is nothing excluded from their purview.

THE ROLE OF VIOLENCE

It is well known that the Communist is ordinarily distinguished from other socialists because he believes that his revolution can be carried out only by violence. This means not only violence in the period when the capitalist is overthrown; it also means violence in the indeterminate period of transition from socialism to communism. According to Lenin, violence will be required even under communism, to prevent individuals from indulging in antisocial excesses. But in this latter period, there is no need for special machinery (the Marxist-defined state) to suppress anyone, since there is no *class* to be suppressed. Hence what violence is needed will be applied automatically by the "armed people."[8]

For the follower of Lenin and Stalin, no humanitarian consideration for the lives or dignity of any individual could ever override the ethical values of a successful achievement of communism. Hence communist philosophy, ethics, and above all practice assume, glorify, and utilize violence to a degree never elsewhere exemplified in history. The forms of this violence are legion, shading from the subtlest hints of threat or coercion to the most coldblooded and ruthless extermination of great groups of people who resist the will of the dictator.[9] Stalin, in seizing and consolidating power, has so fastened upon Russia the lessons of his training and experience as a conspiratorial revolutionary, that the institutionalized forms of coercion found in party, secret police, and elsewhere in the government will long outlast the exigencies and fears which gave them birth.

[8] See Lenin, *State and Revolution* (1932), pp. 74-75, and the quotations from Lenin's *Selected Works* given in Shub, *Lenin, A Biography,* p. 389. It is interesting that Lenin was so used to the idea of violence that he assumed that the people would remain armed even in communist utopia, where there certainly would be no economic incentives for aggression or defense.

[9] It might be argued that the term "violence" is not correctly applied to this situation; that the government, as rightful user of societal force, should not be called a user of violent means. However, the objective here is not to mince words, but to use terms which in general signify the virulence and unconstrained quality of communist means of ensuring compliance with their dictates or destruction of persistent obstacles.

THE ROLE OF THE PARTY

Power in the Soviet Union—and the ways in which it affects individuals—cannot be understood without comprehending the nature and dominant role of the Communist party. The party is not a political party in the Western sense of an organization designed to represent one or more interests in society as leader or participant in a government administered in the interest of society as a whole, until turned out of office by constitutional means. Western parties tolerate and often depend on the existence of other competing parties. The Communist party is conceived to be the "vanguard" of the dominant class, both in the period before seizure of power, and in the period of the dictatorship of the proletariat and transition from socialism to communism. As such, it tolerates no rival; it destroys those it can, and wages unremitting struggle against all others. Although Communist parties outside Russia may on Moscow's orders collaborate with other parties, this is done only as Moscow deems it necessary for the interest of world revolution. In every case where the Communist party has seized power, it has destroyed every other political party within the country.

The Communist party is not a mass group. It is a dedicated elite, more like the priesthood of a religion embracing both temporal and spiritual worlds than a group devoted only to political ends.

The party enjoys, by virtue of superior revolutionary and conspiratorial power and by law, the position of leader and director of all phases of political, economic, social, and cultural activity within Russia. The party is the disciplined instrument for co-ordinating and directing all non-party groups and functions within the state—government or otherwise. The role of the party as a revolutionary elite was defined by Lenin as early as 1903, in his classic treatise: *What is to be Done?*[10] Further

[10] In this pamphlet Lenin argued that the professional revolutionary was indispensable to the creation of communist society. The masses by themselves could generate only a "trade-union" consciousness (that is, could ameliorate their wages and working conditions slightly through peaceful organization and evolution), but only a revolutionary intellectual elite could produce socialist doctrine and lead the masses to communism.

restatement and elaboration of this role are to be found in Stalin's *Foundations of Leninism,* and the position of the party is outlined in Article 126 of the Constitution of 1936. In Stalin's words, "the fact that not a single important political or organizational question is decided by our Soviet and other mass organizations without directions from the Party must be regarded as the highest expression of the leading role of the Party."[11]

As summarized by Vyshinsky, "The political basis of the USSR comprises . . . the leading and directing role of the Communist Party in all fields of economic, social, and cultural activity. . . . A series of decisions *of the Bolshevik party* firmly established the organization forms whereby the party's guidance of state organs is effectuated."[12] Tightness of control is not mitigated by the administrative principle that "The party must develop its decisions through Soviet organs. . . . The party seeks to *guide*—not to replace—the activity of the Soviets."[13]

In practice, the party controls all state activity in three major ways:

1. By putting its candidates "into the basic posts of state work . . . at our elections for Soviets";
2. By checking ("verifying") the work of government organs "correcting unavoidable mistakes and shortcomings, helping them develop the decisions of the government and trying to guarantee them support of the masses—and not a single important decision is taken by them without corresponding directions of the party."
3. By giving general guiding directions defining the character and direction of the work of organs of authority—"whether along the line of industry and agriculture or that of building trade and culture."[14]

Moreover, the party is looked on as the organization for coordination and unified direction of every form of association

[11] J. Stalin, *Problems of Leninism,* quoted in Julian Towster, *Political Power in the U.S.S.R.* (1948), p. 119. The book by Stalin is cited in various ways in the notes which follow, depending on the translation used.

[12] Vyshinsky, *The Law of the Soviet State,* p. 159. Emphasis supplied.

[13] The same, p. 159, quoting a resolution of the 8th Congress of the Communist party.

[14] The same, p. 160, relying on Stalin, *Questions of Leninism.*

not affiliated to the party: "trade unions, co-operative societies, factory and shop organisations, parliamentary fractions, non-Party women's associations, the press, cultural and educational organisations, youth leagues, military revolutionary organisations (in times of direct revolutionary action), soviets of deputies as the state form of organisation. . . ."[15]

Communists say the party is not an end in itself, but a *weapon* of the proletariat. To serve as such, it must have "cohesion and iron discipline." This "presupposes conscious and voluntary submission, for only conscious discipline can be truly iron discipline. But after a discussion has been closed, after criticism has run its course and a decision has been made, unity of will and unity of action of all Party members become indispensable conditions without which Party unity and iron discipline in the Party are inconceivable."[16]

"True Bolshevik courage," said Stalin, "consists in being strong enough to master and overcome one's self and subordinate one's will to the will of the collective, the will of the higher Party body."[17]

II. POLITICAL FREEDOM

The political freedom of the individual in a state consists of his relation to governmental authority. In the Soviet state, it must also include his relation to the party, since the party occupies the dominant position of both *de facto* and *de jure* political power. The state of political freedom cannot be expressed in a phrase; it can only be estimated as a result of examining the formal and practical powers of government (including party) over the individual, the potentialities of the individual, singly or in masses, to control his government, and

[15] Stalin, *Foundations of Leninism,* p. 114.

[16] The same, pp. 118-19. This statement presupposes the existence of at least some degree of argument and criticism prior to decision, a condition which certainly characterized the party during Lenin's life. However, there has been a progressive tendency to reduce argument and criticism during the Stalinist period. A Communist who supports a losing argument may find himself outcast, his family punished, and in danger of his life no matter how loyally he may execute the decision he opposed.

[17] Quoted in A. M. Schlesinger, Jr., *The Vital Center* (1949), p. 56.

the position of the individual before the organs of state: administrative, legal, and judicial.

Limitations on the Power of the State

There are no limitations, legal or customary, on the power of the state in Soviet Russia other than the decisions of the Communist party. The only limitations are those of expediency. In the view of Soviet authorities as well as of Western observers, the development of power in the Soviet Union presents something of a paradox. The Marxian critique of political power, including its notion of the bourgeois state, rests on the view that political power is in itself the fundament of injustice; the long-term Marxian perspective finds utopia in the withering away of the state and the replacement of the government of men by the administration of things. Leninism and Stalinism, however, were impelled by the force of events and by their own power drives to the view that a non-bourgeois but nevertheless powerful state is required during the transition between capitalism and communism, during which the power of the state is *intensified* as a means first of destroying the power of the bourgeois world within or without to recapture power, and second as a means of hastening the transition to communism. Current Stalinist doctrine has amended Marx by asserting the necessity of a state even under communism, so long as there is threat of capitalist encirclement.

Hence, there is no practical limitation on the power of the state. Anything which is deemed necessary by the ruling elite for the survival of socialism in one country, can be brought within the powers of the communist apparatus. So long as capitalist threat is enhanced by nuclear weapons, it can safely be predicted that the communist ruling elites will not cease to arrogate wide spheres for their state authority.

Current communist theory leaves to the individual no grounds for arguing against unlimited state power. Since classes and exploitation are by definition abolished, and productive instruments are owned by everyone, there is nothing left for the individual to urge as a claim against the state; such a claim would only be against his own interest, or for something he himself owned, as a member of a class and society. There might be questions of administrative expediency involved, but these can be handled by decisions within government and party. There is no question of injustice.

Adjudication may be allowed in which individuals or groups urge customary rights or ask for redress from incorrect government decisions in the courts, but there is far less basis in Soviet law than in bourgeois law for suits against the sovereign, and far more difficulties arising from the extent of the economic and social role played by the socialist state. Matters of tort in Western countries become criminal acts against the state in Russia. Matters which would call for equity or civil procedures as between private parties in bourgeois states, became issues between individuals and the state, or between state organs, in Russia.

In particular, the role of the constitution as a guarantor of rights and as an effective limit on the sphere and mode of action of government, are vastly different in Soviet society from that in Western states. Both constitutional and other forms of lawmaking and administration are much more flexible in Russia than in non-totalitarian states.

Soviet legal practice makes clear that an individual cannot urge a constitutional provision as a means of setting aside a government decision or action. Some explanation of the nature of the Soviet constitution is required to show this. In Soviet practice a constitution is not merely a framework for government and a statement of the forms and procedures of government so arranged as to control governmenal activity in the interest of society or individuals. It is only a legal expression "of the actual correlation of social forces in the state."[18] If the party thinks there is a difference between the formal constitution and current political requirements, the constitution is treated as a fiction. Innovations are never subject to attack as unconstitutional, particularly since the party sponsors them.

[18] Towster, *Political Power in the U.S.S.R.*, pp. 18 ff.

The text of the constitution may be amended a day or so in advance by government decree, or changes may come only after innovations have proved themselves in practice. Although the constitution is called the fundamental law, and Union Republic constitutions may not conflict with it (just as Union Republic laws will be superseded by All-Union legislation if the two conflict), the flexibility of legal enunciation and the placing of *de facto* power in the party in Russia is such that the constitution is no safe guide to practice.[19] For example, the constitutional declaration (not guarantee) that the seven-hour day is won for the overwhelming majority of the working class (Article 119), was no barrier to the extension of hours during the war, nor any standard for postwar working arrangements. Nor was any constitutional revision thought necessary.

Even taking the constitution in its most favorable light, it fails to offer the formality of certain safeguards (common in non-totalitarian societies) against the abuse of political power. There is no constitutional limitation of the power which may be exercised by the Soviet government. There is no reservation of powers to regional or local government which cannot be contravened by the central government. There is no prohibition against governmental or party interference with freedom of speech or assembly. And certain safeguards appearing in the constitution are notoriously ignored in practice. For example, the constitution states (Article 128) that the citizen's home shall be "inviolable," yet that forms no barrier against search and seizure by control authorities. Finally, although Soviet citizenship is put on a very wide basis, and the discriminations as to civil rights and electoral functions found in the two earlier Russian constitutions are gone, much remains in the 1936 constitution which puts the "toilers and their organizations" in preferred status. The document leaves no doubt as to the interest of which class is paramount.

[19] For example, the electoral procedures prescribed for the nationwide election of Feb. 10, 1946, called for constitutional amendments. These were accomplished simply by government decree. See John N. Hazard, "Political, Administrative, and Judicial Structure in the U.S.S.R. Since the War," *The Annals* (May, 1949), Vol. 263, pp. 9-19.

Communists claim that from the standpoint of the individual, however, the constitution is not a completely meaningless document. As a statement of ground consolidated (although prewar), it does stand as a recognition of goals and practices which affect, even more broadly than do some Western constitutions, the economic, social, and religious as well as political life of the people. Stalin and Molotov claim that this constitution, as an important advance over bourgeois constitutions, is not only a statement of rights; but that it specifies duties and "guarantees," by the provision of certain "material means," the opportunity to the Soviet citizen to enjoy certain rights which he enjoys in formal ways only in bourgeois society.[20] Thus, freedom of the press is said to be "guaranteed" by the constitutional provision to supply approved groups with the necessary printing equipment and materials to enable them to express themselves. (The constitution is silent on those methods whereby the role of the press is defined, and the content of it kept constantly in line with party prescriptions.) The economic nature of socialist society is cited as the "guarantee" of "real" liberty to the Soviet citizen, who is freed from fears of unemployment, medical expenses, and the like.

The constitution, in short, states some legal norms, but by no means all. The real source is the party, "since the program and periodic directives of the Communist Party constitute continuous criteria for the functions of the entire body politic."[21]

When excessive security-mindedness, conspiratorial training and experience, and power hunger on the part of the ruling elite are combined with the absence of doctrinal, constitutional, and customary limitations on state power, the result is inevitable: the police state. In Russia the role and operations of a political police are well founded in history, commencing with the Tsarist Okhrana (a comparatively minute body of some one thousand skilled operators), passing to the Bolshevist Cheka (All-

[20] See, for example, J. V. Stalin, "On the Draft Constitution of the U.S.S.R.," *Report* delivered at the Extraordinary Eighth Congress of Soviets of the U.S.S.R., Nov. 25, 1936 (Moscow, 1936), pp. 17-22.

[21] Towster, *Political Power in the U.S.S.R.*, p. 21; who quotes one Soviet authority as stating the party to be the *sole* source.

Russian Extraordinary Commission) of the period of war communism, then to the OGPU (Unified State Political Administration) from 1922 to 1934, then to the NKVD (People's Commissariat of Internal Affairs) from 1934 to 1946, finally culminating in the MVD (Ministry of Internal Affairs) and its counterpart the MGB (Ministry of State Security). Lenin called the Cheka the "ever-present weapon" of the Bolshevist government against "innumerable attempts against Soviet authority." Even he found it necessary to curtail its powers, confining them to the political sphere, in calling for its reorganization in 1922.[22] The powers of the NKVD were similarly cut for a brief period after its creation, but since the assassination of Kirov (1934) the role and powers of the political police have steadily increased.[23] The individual could never look to any Soviet court for protection from NKVD action. Even if an individual might conceivably make a case that a particular NKVD action was outside its formal authority, the powers of NKVD were so large that it could take new action immediately to achieve its initial purpose.

Although the organs of police control are formally those of government, in reality they are completely dominated by the party. Party members man all key posts and key enforcement cadres of the Ministry. The espionage functions of NKVD and party are similarly entwined. According to Dallin,

> Every member of the Communist party, no matter where he may be working, is obliged to keep the NKVD informed of everything he sees and hears that may be of interest. That this is no mere "moral

[22] Vyshinsky, *The Law of the Soviet State,* p. 399.

[23] Vyshinsky, the same, pp. 411 ff. Vyshinsky says, in part: "To apply measures of administrative repression (exile, deportation, confinement in correctional-labor camps, or expulsion from the USSR), a Special Council, acting on the basis of a regulation affirmed by the Central Executive Committee of the USSR, was organized under the People's Commissariat for Internal Affairs. [This commissariat] is charged with: assuring revolutionary order and state security, guarding social (socialist) property, guarding the borders, and recording acts of civil status. In 1934-36 the scale of work of this commissariat was broadened in connection with the transfer to its jurisdiction (Oct. 27, 1934) of houses of incarceration, of solitary confinement, and the like and of central administration of paved and unpaved roads; . . ." See also David J. Dallin, *The Real Soviet Russia* (1944), pp. 240 ff.

obligation" has been demonstrated by the fate of hundreds of Communists who for reasons of carelessness or because of humane considerations had failed to report on their relatives. But in addition to the general obligation impressed upon the millions of party members, thousands of special Communist informers have the direct task of gathering information on various aspects of social life and informing the NKVD; these operatives are present in every institution, office, plant, scientific society.[24]

At one time the political police had its own "judicial collegium" and was completely independent of the courts; after 1934, however, "matters investigated by the People's Commissariat of Internal Affairs were cognizable by court organs."[25] This meant in practice that the courts could be used in certain types of cases to carry out NKVD wishes.

The individual as such has no defense against the administrative actions of the political police; only party position or connections can give him a certain degree of insurance—a degree suggested by the former party positions of many of those purged during the 1930's. What is the consequence? Without the surveillance or permission of the political police, the Soviet citizen cannot change his residence, cannot travel from one locality to another within or without his country; he cannot work in a factory apart from the supervision of militarized guards of industrial establishments; he cannot be married or divorced, or register the birth or death of members of his family. If he transgresses, or is thought to have done so, he is sent to a "camp of correctional labor" or prison or other penal institution run by these same police. As part of its forces to accomplish these and other objects, the MVD operates state and local archives, militarized fire departments, internal security troops, convoy troops, and police, and its economic activities (discharged in the main by forced labor) include highways of national importance and "special construction projects."

The Individual versus the State

If, then, the individual Soviet citizen is at the mercy of the

[24] Dallin, *The Real Soviet Russia,* p. 242.
[25] Vyshinsky, *The Law of the Soviet State,* p. 411.

policy of his state, what opportunities does he have to shape that policy, and to participate in the work of party or government? To answer this question it is necessary to examine somewhat more closely the structure and functioning of the party, and of the administrative organs of government.

THE INDIVIDUAL AND THE PARTY

What is the role of the individual in the party? What chance does he have under Soviet "democratic centralism" of contributing to the formation of policy and to exercise initiative in its execution?

We have already noted the dominance of party over government, and the operating concept of the party as the guiding force in all organizations. Because of this, Russia with equal reason has been called a party state and a no-party state. The latter designation is probably the more apt, since the Communist party is not a political party in the sense found in any non-totalitarian country. It is a dedicated elite which monopolizes the formulation and supervises the execution of basic policy in all fields of endeavor. As such, it is more nearly a religious order than a political organism. The Soviet interpretation of Russian law and practice[26] arrogate to the Communist party a monopoly of leadership and control of the all-pervasive government machine. Nor is it a party which seeks to maximize its membership[27] and thus to assure control of government through

[26] 1936 Constitution, Art. 126; Stalin, *Questions of Leninism,* quoted in Vyshinsky, *The Law of the Soviet State,* p. 627. To the Western mind the wording of the Constitution is ambiguous; to the Russian mind and practice no ambiguity is present. By July 1918 all non-Bolshevik parties (Left Social Revolutionaries, Mensheviks, and the moderate parties) had been effectively excluded from a politically significant role in government. This monopoly was won and is assured by party action, and is enshrined (except for the wording of Articles 126 and 141 of the 1936 Constitution) by *party* resolutions. See Towster, *Political Power in the U.S.S.R.,* pp. 122-24.

[27] By the 1905 revolution, the party had some 8,400 members; by seizure of power in 1917, 23,600; in 1940, 3,400,000. During the war it grew considerably, having some 6 million members in 1946. (The same, p. 344.) These figures include candidates, possibly one-half of the total. Para-party organizations such as the Komsomol (Young Communists) and the Pioneers are much larger. The same, pp. 140, 143.

electoral processes. Prior to 1939, workers and Red Army men enjoyed priority in consideration for membership. At the Eighteenth Party Congress, however, qualifications were broadened to facilitate the entry of intellectuals and white-collar workers.[28]

It is a group in which membership can be won only by fitness demonstrated by investigation and by candidacy; in which membership can be retained only by sustained demonstration in word and action of efficiency, discipline, and loyalty to the orders of the hierarchy. The party periodically prevents stagnation in its ranks by stringent purges. The competition of other parties is partly replaced as incentive and discipline by the ever-present possibility of dismissal, correction, or liquidation. The resultant premium on conformity and alacrity to obey authority is one of the heaviest burdens to be shouldered by any who would be so hardy as to try to shape, let alone challenge the dictates of higher authority.[29]

A further burden is constituted by the principles of party unity, centralism, discipline, and the prohibition of factions or groupings. Party unity is a sacrosanct principle, hallowed by Marx's intepretation of the experience of the Paris Commune, and the tactics prescribed by Lenin and Stalin for the seizure and the consolidation of power. Since bourgeois parties are claimed to be the representatives of factions among the bourgeois classes, they are logical in bourgeois society. In communism, however, there is no room for factional political groupings in a state organized on the basis of a single class. Factional activity was specifically prohibited by a resolution of the Tenth Party Congress (1921) which has been enforced with great

[28] Merle Fainsod, "Postwar Role of the Communist Party," *The Annals*, Vol. 263 (May 1949), p. 21.

[29] Postwar tightening up in standards for membership was signalized by Malenkov's report to the organizing committee of the Cominform in September 1947. Malenkov said in part that: "The party at present puts its emphasis not upon forcing further growth of its ranks but upon the development of political education of members and candidates. . . . Quality is more important than quantity." (Quoted by Fainsod, the same, p. 26.) When Malenkov spoke the party had already reduced its war-swollen ranks by several million.

stringency ever since. The counterbalance to this, at least in theory, is the possibility of discussion prior to decision, and the practice of "Bolshevik self-criticism." The first of these has been progressively de-emphasized in favor of the attempt on the part of subordinates to guess correctly what their leader's wish will be, and to resolve all doubts on the side of orthodoxy and caution. Self-criticism, however celebrated in communist propaganda, is even more restricted. It is not an opportunity to criticize policy (unless that has been done by authority) but to criticize performance which fails to put policy into effect with sufficient speed and thoroughness.[30] At bottom, self-criticism is an instrument of government, not a right of the individual citizen.

Critical discussion is taken within the party as a sign of disloyalty or weakness. "Intra-party democracy" has nothing to do with the determination of policy, only with its dissemination to the party masses and through them to the public.[31] There may have been some real intra-party discussion under Lenin's leadership; it disappeared completely under the threats and repressions instituted by Stalin once he had consolidated his victory over Trotsky.[32]

The party is organized as a hierarchy, a pyramid resting on cells found in geographic subdivisions and in local productive organizations. The tiers rise through territorial and economic hierarchies to culminate in the central, All-Union party organs. These are threefold: (1) the executive bodies: the Central Committee and its main components, the Political Bureau (Polit-

[30] The real freedom to engage in self-criticism varies somewhat with the class origin of the critic: a worker is on safer ground than an intellectual or an expert. A pontiff, or high party functionary, may criticize a peer or a lesser person very severely; in such cases one suspects that the critic is not acting without advance assurance of the most authoritative backing. *Communism in Action* H. Doc. 754, 79 Cong. 2 sess., p. 137.

[31] The limits of discussion are strictly stated in party rules. See Towster, *Political Power in the U.S.S.R.*, pp. 127-28. "And the Party itself, through its leading organ—the Central Committee—is the one that provides guidance with regard to the timeliness, propriety, tenor, and extent of complaints and accusations, and the concrete goals sought through self-criticism." The same, p. 129.

[32] See Boris Souvarine, *Stalin* (1939), especially Chap. 8.

buro), the Organization Bureau (Orgburo), and the Secretariat; (2) the representative bodies: the party congresses and conferences; and (3) the lesser bodies: bureaus and secretariats of formations at lower levels. In practice, the executive bodies rule the representative bodies, although they are theoretically responsible to them.[33] The party auxiliaries (the Young Communists and the Pioneers) carry out various tasks set by the party, as links between the party and the people. They are organized in parallel fashion to the party itself.

The distribution of power is officially stated to be governed by the following formulation of "democratic centralism":

(a) The application of the elective principle to all leading bodies of the Party, from the lowest to the highest.

(b) The periodical accountability of the Party bodies to their respective Party organizations.

(c) Strict Party discipline and subordination of the minority to the majority.

(d) The absolutely binding character of the decisions of the higher bodies upon the lower bodies.[34]

A western observer might conclude that this formula meant that higher bodies are responsible to the more numerous lower bodies which elect them. Nothing could be further from the truth. Decisions of the higher bodies—in reality, the decisions of the Secretary General of the party—are always binding on lower bodies. They form the rules enforced by strict party discipline. The subordination of the minority to the majority (point c) means that no factions (that is, groups which differ from the established line) may attempt to get their views accepted by the majority—the complete reversal of the functions of factions

[33] Stalin consolidated his dictatorial power by fusing party and policy and execution in the Secretariat, and establishing the Secretariat's dominance over the Politburo and the Orgburo. (Souvarine, *Stalin,* pp. 405 ff.) Subsequently the distribution of power between these agencies was unimportant, as all three served as instruments to carry out the dictator's will. The distribution becomes important once more as a factor in the struggle for succession to Stalin's position.

[34] Towster, *Political Power in the U.S.S.R.,* quoting Rule 18 of the 1939 and 1934 rules of the Communist party. Similar prescriptions are found in rules of the party published in 1919, 1922, and 1925.

within Western parties, or parties within the state. The decisions of the higher organs are always assumed to reflect the opinions of the majority, and may not be challenged on democratic grounds.

The essence of accountability of party bodies to their respective party organizations does not partake of the Western notion of representation. This "accountability" means in practice that party members of a local factory Soviet are responsible for convincing the other members of the correctness of party decisions, for applying them concretely and correctly to the particular conditions in the factory, and for seeing to it that decisions from above are promptly and intelligently executed by those below. The members of the Soviet have the rights of election and recall, but the standard they apply to their elected representatives is not loyalty to the demands or interests of the local organization. There is never any question of recalling a representative because he failed to uphold the local interest against the central authority. The grounds for recall, in those cases where recall has been exercised, are failure to act with sufficient zeal and alacrity in carrying out directives from above.

The elective principle gains in clarity if not in democratic reality when it is pointed out that several tiers, and hence several levels of choice separate the party member in the local cell from the choice of those officials who exercise the directive force sanctioned by point (d).[35]

What is the upshot for an individual who would make his opinion felt in party policy? The possible effects on policy are at best minute. Only as a member of a passively resistant group could he hope to slow the pace of a plan he disapproved, or alter somewhat the direction of the socialist state. If he aspires to party membership, he must undergo training, candidacy, and the most rigorous inspection. Any independence of view would disqualify him. As a member of the party "masses," he has to prove himself further by outstanding service in party work; never by challenging, but only by applying party policy. Any

[35] The same, p. 136 and pp. 136-37n.

possible deviations—especially in the direction of political initiative—risk sanctions imposed by the MVD, aganst which party membership is not only no protection, but a cause for more severe punishment than a non-party member would suffer for any given shortcoming.[36] As a young man, he may enjoy the prospect of rapid advancement; if he likes movement and travel, the pattern of the party work of the past has called for a great deal of turnover in party assignments, functionally and territorially. But wherever he goes, conformity is borne in upon him. Only if he reaches the "highest level" can it be thought he may have any significant influence on policy; and even at the level of the Politburo, the possibility of differences of opinion on such fundamentals as the rate of capitalist collapse must be kept within limits, at least those necessary to reassure the leader of continued loyalty. Such partial freedom is available for a few score out of two hundred million.

THE INDIVIDUAL AND GOVERNMENT

What are the political and civil rights of the inhabitant of the Soviet Union, with respect to governmental (non-party) authorities? We do not consider here rights in the economic field; that will be treated separately later. We discuss here the rights of the inhabitant to participate in political processes, and to shape and control them by such devices as elections, legislation, and expression of opinion. (General freedoms of speech and opinion are considered in more detail below.)

Citizenship. The Constitution of 1936 marks a significant stage in the legal recognition of the rights of citizenship and the equality of all citizens before the law. Prior to this, Soviet constitutions recognized the class nature of society. It was not until the formal victory of the proletarian class was announced—or in other words, until all other classes had been liquidated—that citizenship and the rights of citizenship were extended to all irrespective of class origin, and the preferred position of the proletariat disappeared from formal law. The provisions of the

[36] Harold J. Berman, "The Challenge of Soviet Law," 62 *Harvard Law Review* 260-61 (December 1948).

1936 Constitution were extended and clarified by a new Law of Citizenship of the USSR, adopted on August 19, 1938.[37] This law in some respects was not as liberal as previous Soviet practice.[38] The new law made clear, however, that Soviet citizenship is open to all irrespective of nationality, race, or sex. A citizen may withdaw from citizenship only by the action of the Presidium of the Supreme Soviet of USSR. He may be deprived of citizenship either by decree of the Presidium or by a legal court sentence. In consequence, the law has had to provide for a new category of persons without citizenship, who enjoy all privileges of citizenship except political rights and obligations. These privileges under the 1936 Constitution are formally at least considerable, especially in the economic and social spheres (right to rest and leisure, right to medical care, unemployment insurance, etc.).

Elections. The franchise is open to all citizens (except the mentally deficient and those debarred by court action) 18 years of age and older. Each voter votes directly for members of government organs at all levels up to the Supreme Soviet. Since the 1936 Constitution, the final vote is by secret ballot. The rights of nomination, however, are restricted by the Constitution (Article 141) to approved organizations and in practice nominees are selected by the party. The standard slate is that of "Communists and non-party Bolsheviks,"[39] which nominates only one candidate per vacancy. This slate is "ratified" by public

[37] Vyshinsky, *The Law of the Soviet State,* pp. 291 ff.

[38] Under regulations of 1931, everyone "found" within Soviet borders was a Soviet citizen unless it was proved he was citizen of a foreign power. Under the new law, Soviet citizens are all those who were citizens of Russia on Nov. 7, 1917 and have not subsequently lost citizenship, and those who have taken positive action to acquire citizenship under Soviet law. This latter requirement, says Vyshinsky, was necessitated by the practice of foreign powers in taking advantage of previous flexibility to infiltrate their "spies and diversionists" into the socialist state. The same, p. 292.

[39] In Vyshinsky's words: "The experience of the 1937 elections to the USSR Supreme Soviet showed that the non-Party masses of our country have nominated candidates to the Supreme Soviet in a bloc with the Communists. This bloc is guaranteed by the correctness of the policy of the Party and the unlimited confidence of the entire toiling population of the country which the Party enjoys." *The Law of the Soviet State,* pp. 711-12.

voting. The ratified slate is the only one on the final secret ballot.[40] There is no opposition, hence no competitive candidate. The voter can back the slate or spoil his ballot. Multi-candidate elections, promised by Stalin in 1937, are as yet unknown in Russia. The role of the individual in this process is explicitly circumscribed. "Candidates are . . . nominated not by individual persons but by collectives, general assemblies, wherein each citizen of the country may, according to his dwelling place or place of work, be present." The role of elections is to draw the individual into "this responsible political work,"[41] that is, into the claque celebrating the policy and the personnel backed by the party. Any citizen 23 years of age or more, may be a candidate for any elective All-Union office. Outside of the All-Union, Republic, and local Soviets, the only elective offices are those of the judges of "People's Courts."

All the Soviet constitutions have emphasized the rights of recall; and this instrument has been used extensively throughout the Soviet period. Initially it was used by the "masses" (that is, the party) to get rid of the non-Bolshevik members of the central government. Prior to the elections of 1937, the recall was still fairly extensively used to effect desired turnover in government "organs of authority." It was a much more important instrument at the lower levels than at the level of the Supreme Soviet. In the elections of 1937, the bloc of communist and non-party candidates was so highly publicized that it is doubtful whether subsequent large-scale use of the recall would have been politically wise. It would only have shown the party had picked poor henchmen. The device of recall, which constitutionally may be exercised by a constituency at any time, is described by Communists as part of "a mighty instrument for further educating and organizing the masses politically, for further strengthening the bond between the state mechanism and the masses, and for improving the state mechanism and grubbing out the remnants of bureaucratism."[42] In plain words, the recall

[40] Hazard, *The Annals,* p. 10.
[41] Vyshinsky, *The Law of the Soviet State,* p. 710.
[42] The same, pp. 719-22.

is a control measure used by the party to eliminate bad choices and keep the rest in line.

Influence over legislation. Formally speaking, "the legislative authority of the USSR is exercised solely by the Supreme Soviet of the USSR" (1936 Constitution, Article 32). "In the person of the Supreme Soviet . . . the genuine will of the Soviet people is manifested. . . . Laws of the Supreme Soviet . . . are of binding force in all the territory of the USSR. Soviet laws are near and dear to each Soviet person, because they are created by the will of the people and subserve the people's happiness and welfare."[43]

So much for the formality. In reality, legislation in the USSR is always under the control of the party—so much so that many important legal enactments, including amendments to the constitution, are issued over the joint signatures of government and party authorities.[44] But even within the formal government structure, the *de facto* role of the Supreme Soviet is far less important than the acts of its nominally subordinate bodies, the Presidium and the Council of People's Commissars (now Ministers) of the USSR, and the People's Commissariats (now Ministries).[45] These latter bodies have power to act for the Supreme Soviet when it is not in session (which is more frequently than not the case); there are no reported instances in which the Supreme Soviet has attempted to overturn acts of the Presidium or the Council of Ministers. Hence, in practice, the Supreme Soviet plays a ceremonial role in part of Russian lawmaking. The edicts and decrees of the smaller bodies have the force of law. The function of the Supreme Soviet is to act as a sounding board, and a channel for transmission of party views to the electorate. It is a link in the machine for the organization of consent.[46]

[43] The same, p. 311.

[44] Vladimir Gsovski, *Soviet Civil Law,* Vol. 1 (1948), p. 76. The chairman of the Council of Ministers and the secretary-general of the party sign as authoritative representatives of the two groups.

[45] Under the 1936 Constitution, the authority of these subordinate organizations, now known as ministers and ministries, as specifically outlined (Art. 14), is superior to that of the Supreme Soviet.

[46] See Hazard, *The Annals,* p. 13.

The job of the Republic or local Soviet is no more concerned than its All-Union counterpart with the formulation of policy. Their task is to conduct agitation for the current party line, to stimulate fulfillment of public programs, and to overcome shortcomings. The party is concerned with revitalizing these organs particularly at the local level, as a sort of morale, expediting, and inspecting agency.

Without the unifying influence of the party, the loose and overlapping government structure would quickly become hopelessly entangled in its own complexities. The formal legislative organs have no scope for initiative. The citizen must look to the party for any change in policy.

What of the possibilities of public opinion? Some exist, but not in the same form and not nearly to the same degree as in countries enjoying organs of press and channels of communication free from government control. The press in Russia is a channel for the indoctrination and education of the people, not a means whereby public opinion reveals itself or a place wherein the free citizen can air his criticism of government policy and action. Such criticism as appears there, is only that authorized or voiced by the party pundits.

In Russia the party watches public opinion as it manifests itself to the MVD, and to the party and its affiliates. Party propaganda agencies, as in all totalitarian states, play a special role in the estimation of public opinion on all topics, because intelligence on such matters is so directly related to the functions of propaganda and agitation.[47] In consequence, the individual influences the political judgment of his masters in his

[47] In Soviet theory and practice, a very important distinction is drawn between the two. Propaganda spreads belief; agitation manipulates opinion and action within the framework of established belief. In Russia, as in other totalitarian states, there is great emphasis on direct contact between the agitator and the groups he wishes to influence. It is out of this face-to-face relationship, with the opportunities it offers to the agitator to see how particular ideas and notions go down, that the main data for public opinion reports are secured. Russian agitators and propagandists are both missionaries; the idea of cynical manipulation of opinion is discredited, at least in domestic operations. The agitator must be passionately convinced of the truth and correctness of his positions, and his emotion must be used to disseminate correct views.

role as an object of observation, not as a vocal initiator and disseminator of ideas and plans.

INDIVIDUAL AND LAW

What is the position of the individual before Soviet law, and what can the individual expect the law to do for him as a regulator of the demands of party and state? It can correctly be inferred from the foregoing explanation of the genesis of Soviet law, that the Soviet individual could not and to a large extent cannot look forward to stability of the law. Furthermore, he cannot wisely expect the Communists ever to let a written legal principle or prescription stand in the way of anything which may be officially conceived to be in the interest of party or state. Conspiratorial power does not let itself be limited by anything except the expediencies as gauged at any moment.

It appears that something of a revolution has taken place in the Soviet concept of law, and in the basic party evaluation of how law should serve the interests of the dictatorship of the proletariat. Stalin's long-range policies, as symbolized by the rise to power of such lawyers as Vyshinsky and by the critical changes in the policy of the Soviet state subsequent to the great purges, have overturned some of the early doctrinaire theories of law and administration. Stalin's decision that the Soviet State would not and could not wither away even though formal "communism" had been established in Russia, called for measures to stabilize the state in all its totalitarian ramifications. Thus, the *expediencies* of state power came to include a conservative and stabilizing element, and the Soviet citizen, in however small fashion, could look with greater trust upon law and the law-court. In the communist double talk, it was necessary to increase legal "culture"—that is, the technical competence of the practitioners of the law, including advocates and judges; and the internal consistency and logic of the legal structure as a whole.

In the Soviet scheme of things law as such occupied a humble place at the outset. In Marxian theory existing law at the time of the revolution was bourgeois law, an instrument to protect and preserve the injustice and exploitation of the landlord and capitalist. In the early years of the revolutionary period, law was administered by workers' tribunals, using their "revolutionary conscience" as a guide. This was altogether in line with communist theory concerning the nature of law and ideology as a reflection of the class position of those on whose behalf law was being administered; it ignored the amount of specialized study and intelligence necessary if law were really to be formulated and applied in the interest of the workers.

Two other aspects of early revolutionary law were important; the doctrine of analogy, and the principle embodied in the first article of the Civil Code to the effect that no law could be applied against the interest of the revolution.[48] The first doctrine is found in other totalitarian societies, and asserts that if an act endangering the state is done which falls under the provisions of no existing law, it shall be judged and punished according to the most nearly applicable provision of existing law. As such, it is the antithesis of a major principle of Anglo-Saxon law to the effect that there can be no just punishment for a crime not defined by existing law. The second doctrine is merely the statement that revolutionary power will not be bound by precedent or tradition, even those it creates itself.

Once the Communists had imposed their dominance and elaborated police-state methods to take care of current disobedience or deviation, the legal doctrines of analogy and the provisions of Article 1 of the Civil Code, no longer necessary and possibly detrimental to Soviet interests, fell into disuse.

As a result of this Stalinist revolution, the position of law and its significance for the individual has markedly improved. More attention is paid to the development of judicial "culture" and more educational time and effort is devoted to the training of judges and lawyers, although present standards in this regard are far below Western counterparts.[49] Another aspect of this revo-

[48] The Code reads: "Civil rights shall be protected by law except in instances when they are realized in contradiction with their social-economic purpose." Quoted in Berman, *62 Harvard Law Review* 232-33.

[49] Hazard in *The Annals,* pp. 17-18, indicates shortcomings and countermeasures.

lution is the improvement in the impartiality and independence of the courts which was categorically denied under earlier Soviet legal theory.[50]

Independence of the judiciary was at the outset unthinkable; the election, recall, and easy dismissal of judges, coupled with their insignificant training, made them easy for the party to control. The 1936 Constitution and the Judiciary Act of 1938 tried to marry the notions of the court as servant of the proletariat with the independence of judges called for by the Constitution. This was done by defining the area of independence, not by asserting that the court was now free of class responsibility. To do the latter would only open the way for "counter-revolutionary activity." The court was declared to be independent only from "local influences." As late as 1941, it was authoritatively re-emphasized that "Neither court nor criminal procedure is or could be outside politics. This means that the contents and form of judicial activities cannot avoid being subordinated to political class aims and strivings."[51] And the propagandist use of judicial proceedings was made clear in 1947 by the comment of the Minister of Justice: "The judge must know how to conduct the court proceedings and how to write the

[50] As stated by Krylenko in 1923: "No court was ever above class interests, and if there were such a court, we would not care for it. . . . The court is, and still remains, the only thing it can be by its nature as an organ of the government power—a weapon for the safeguarding of the interests of a given ruling class. . . . A club is a primitive weapon, a rifle is a more efficient one, the most efficient is the court. . . . For us there is no difference between a court of law and summary justice. A court is merely a better organized form which warrants a minimum of possible mistakes and better evidence of the fact of the crime.

"The court is an organ of State administration and as such does not differ in its nature from any other organs of administration which are designed, as the court is, to carry out one and the same governmental policy . . . our judge is above all a politician, a worker in the political field . . . and therefore he must know what the government wants and guide his work accordingly . . . therefore, the court must be organized so that there is the possibility of directing the judgment in conformity with the aims of State policy pursued by the government. We look at the court as a class institution . . . completely under the control of the vanguard of the working class. . . ." Quoted in Gsovski, *Soviet Civil Law,* pp. 241-42.

[51] Vyshinsky, *The Theory of Evidence in the Soviet Law* (1941,) quoted by Gsovski, the same, p. 255.

judgment in a manner which shows with the utmost clarity the political significance of the case so that the defendant and those present in the court room see clearly the policy of the government in the court action."[52]

Certain distinctions remain in the content of Soviet law, however, which sharply limit and condition the administration of justice. In criminal actions there is a sharp distinction between crimes involving only private relations, and cases involving offenses against "socialist property," political matters, or the safety of the state. If there is any question whether a political element enters into a judicial proceeding, it will be dealt with as a political matter according to procedures lacking the safeguards specified in the Constitution, often by special tribunals. The Constitution (Article 131) and a law of August 7, 1932, make clear the sacrosanct nature of socialist property, and impose special sanctions to preserve it. According to this law,

> Socialist property (state, kolkhoz, and co-operative) is the basis of the Soviet social order, sanctified and inviolable. Persons making an attempt upon it must be deemed enemies of the people, wherefore a decisive struggle with pillagers of social property is the very first obligation of organs of Soviet authority. . . . The supreme measure of social defense shall be applied by the court to put down pillaging (thievery) of kolkhoz and cooperative property; guilty persons shall be shot and all their property confiscated, although if there are extenuating circumstances, the sentence may be commuted to imprisonment for not less than ten years and to confiscation of all property.[53]

Where socialist property or the safety of the state is not involved, Soviet justice characteristically tempers sentence and correction to the presumed individual circumstances of the transgressor, looking on rehabilitation as a useful member of society as a more important object than the exaction of revenge or the possible deterrent influence.[54]

Communist apologists claim that certain constitutional and procedural safeguards exist against arbitrary or unfair law-

[52] "Socialist Legality No. 2" (1947), quoted in Gsovski, the same, p. 255.
[53] Vyshinsky, *The Law of the Soviet State,* p. 647.
[54] Berman, *62 Harvard Law Review,* 260-61.

enforcement procedure which may be of significance to the individual in private and nonpolitical cases. The Constitution requires all cases to be heard in public, unless otherwise provided by law (Article 111) and the accused is guaranteed the "right to defence." Article 127 guarantees "inviolability of the person" and provides that no person shall be arrested except by court order or with the sanction of a state attorney. Trials must be in the local language and interpreters furnished where needed. The prosecutor general must see that officials as well as citizens observe the law. Article 128 guarantees "the inviolability of homes" and "privacy of correspondence."

The reality is completely distinct from claims based on impotent formal enactments. Cases can be heard in public or not, depending on the desire of the party to publicize cases of the punishment and shame of transgressors—particularly in cases such as "crimes against Socialist property." The guarantees of inviolability of homes or of correspondence have never deterred either state or party organs from carrying out whatever searches, seizures, or other control measures they see fit to apply. According to Hazard, the guarantee of inviolability prevents "an individual without training or experience from making an unauthorized arrest or search."[55] Vyshinsky points out[56] that searches, arrests, and seizures can be rightfully carried out only with the prior written permission of the state prosecutor. This limitation is supposed to apply to "investigating organs" as well. One can only inquire in what court of the USSR a citizen could successfully challenge an act of the MVD as being *ultra vires* or unconstitutional.

The power of the courts in Russia, and in consequence their ability to protect the individual, is limited in several important ways. From the standpoint of jurisdiction, many disputes do not come within the purview of the courts.[57] The system of courts

[55] John N. Hazard, "Law, the Individual and Property in the U.S.S.R.," *American Sociological Review,* Vol. 9 (June 1944), p. 253, quoted in *Communism in Action,* p. 138.

[56] *The Law of the Soviet State,* pp. 632-33.

[57] A list of common examples, but not an exclusive one, is as follows: disputes involving tenure of agricultural land, membership in a collective farm, dismissals from executive posts and the application of disciplinary

itself is centralized in the Supreme Court, with the significant exception that other courts may not interfere with the imposition of punishments by the Ministry of the Interior.[58] This means that peoples' courts, military tribunals (including courts martial), and the courts of regions and republics are ultimately responsible to the Supreme Court. This court, however broad its powers over lower courts,[59] cannot finally interpret the law. This function is reserved under the Constitution to the Presidium of the Supreme Soviet (although interpretations requested of the court by the Presidium appear close to authoritative judicial interpretations in other countries).[60] Nor may an individual party appeal to this court. This right is reserved to the attorney general or the president of the court.

In civil cases the individual party enjoys the right of appeal to a court of higher instance, which can review the case as to law and facts, and overturn the initial decision if it is not "well founded." Further appeals are possible by applying to those qualified government officers who enjoy *ex officio* rights to carry the case further.[61] A more effective instrument of redress for failure of a government agency to observe legal requirements in procedure, or for exceeding authority, is application to the system of government attorneys. Under the 1936 Constitution, the hierarchy of government attorneys extends from the attorney general of the USSR down to the locality. This hierarchy is assigned the broad task of supervision over law enforcement. As such, it exercises the "general supervisory power" over observance of law by the administration and over administration of justice, especially by the local authorities.[62]

---

codes in certain industries, refusal of management to allow transfer of employees, evictions and certain other housing matters, and some phases of domestic relations (naming of children, appeals from acts of guardians, etc.). Gsovski, *Soviet Civil Law,* p. 837.

[58] The same, pp. 845-46.

[59] The court in plenary session may issue binding directives to lower courts.

[60] Gsovski, *Soviet Civil Law,* pp. 836-45.

[61] The same, pp. 869-70, 876 ff, especially pp. 908-09.

[62] The same, pp. 846-51. Gsovski comments: "As did the autocratic emperors of Russia, the Soviet rulers sincerely wish to check the abuses of local administrators and insure 'the observance of law'. However, while under a constitutional regime the remedy is sought in an independent

Fundamental to the Soviet doctrine of individual rights is the view that freedom depends on economic security. This is commonly illustrated by Stalin's statement (1937) in an interview by the American journalist Roy Howard:

> Implicit in your question is the innuendo that socialist society negates individual freedom. That is not so. . . . We have not built this society in order to cramp individual freedom. We built it in order that human personality feel itself actually free. We built it for the sake of genuine personal freedom, freedom without quotation marks. What can be the "personal freedom" of an unemployed person who goes hungry and finds no use for his toil? Only where exploitation is annihilated, where there is no oppression of some by others, no unemployment, no beggary, and no trembling for fear that a man may on the morrow lose his work, his habitation, and his bread—only there is true freedom found.[63]

The Marxian corollary to the first proposition is that there is no true civil freedom, especially for the worker, in bourgeois society. The civil rights of bourgeois law and practice are dismissed as a sham for the masses, valid only for the ruling class. In Russia the contrary is claimed—there can be civil freedom only where the success of socialism has abolished "exploitation."[64]

A second fundamental Soviet conception is that rights are inseparable from obligations. The classic doctrine was expressed by Engels, in his comment that the bourgeois formula of equal rights for all, must be replaced for socialism by the formula: "For the equal rights and *equal obligations of all.*"[65] This addendum serves as the basis for those obligations laid on Soviet citizens in the Stalin Constitution and by Soviet practice. These include the duty to work (Article 12 of the Constitution: "He

---

judiciary and the combined result of public opinion, free press, and free elections, the Soviet rulers rely, as the emperors did, upon a highly centralized bureaucratic machinery assigned to perform this task." The same, p. 851.

[63] Quoted in Vyshinsky, *The Law of the Soviet State,* p. 539. See also the section on USSR in the United Nations, *Yearbook on Human Rights for 1946* (1947), pp. 308-17.

[64] See Vyshinsky, *The Law of the Soviet State,* pp. 552 ff.

[65] Marx and Engels, quoted by Vyshinsky, the same, p. 636.

who does not work does not eat");[66] and the duties "to observe the USSR Constitution, fulfill the laws, uphold labor discipline, maintain an honorable attitude toward social duty, and honor the rules of socialist community life." (1936 Constitution, Article 130.) Further duties are to "safeguard and strengthen socialist property" (Article 131), to defend the fatherland and to render universal military service (Articles 133 and 132). Vyshinsky points out that a Soviet citizen may or may not take advantage of his constitutional rights, as he chooses; but if he fails to discharge his constitutional obligations, he is in all cases legally responsible.[67]

Another consequence of the Marxian notions concerning bourgeois law, which is sometimes forgotten but of first importance in estimating the probable effects of a seizure of power by Communists, is the discontinuity of law. As pre-revolutionary law is of necessity bourgeois law, it is inconceivable to a revolutionary that it could be carried over formally into the new regime. So with the Soviet Civil Code of 1922, which flatly denies all continuity of rights and of law effective prior to November 7, 1917, canceling automatically all pre-revolutionary rights and depriving them of legal protection.

There is no such thing as initiative or referendum in the Western sense in the Russian polity; nor are the formal lawmaking bodies considered to be sources for legislative initiative. The dominant and initiatory role of the party on the one hand, and the conscious use of the Soviets as barometers of public attitude on the other,[68] explain the fact that no legislation of any

[66] This finds its ethical justification in the Marxian comment on Communist utopia—a state in which labor ceases to be a mere means and becomes a *prime necessity* to the individual. Marx, *Critique of the Gotha Programme* (Rev. Ed. 1933), p. 14.

[67] Vyshinsky, *The Law of the Soviet State,* p. 639.

[68] Note Stalin's statement of Apr. 23, 1923: "In our Soviet country we must evolve a system of goverment that will permit us with certainty to anticipate all changes, to perceive everything that is going on among the peasants, the nationals, the non-Russian nations, and the Russians; the system of supreme organs must possess a number of barometers which will anticipate every change, register and forestall . . . all possible storms and ill-fortune. That is the Soviet system of government." Quoted by Towster, *Political Power in the U.S.S.R.*, p. 186.

importance has come from the initiative of members of the Supreme Soviet. The most spectacular case of referral of important legislation to the people was in connection with the promulgation of the 1936 Constitution. The draft constitution, disseminated throughout Russia in millions of copies, was used as the basis of mass propaganda on behalf of the Soviet system, and to make clear the nature of the economic and social doctrine on which the constitution was founded. Soviet propagandists point out that discussion was heated, that millions of people sent in suggestions and comment, and that at the end, some 43 popularly suggested changes were made in the final text. The authorship of these changes is nowhere made specific, although they are used to point up the essentials involved, and as a means of discrediting undesired or irrelevant points of view.[69]

The only other important case in which legislation was submitted to prior popular discussion and plebiscite was in connection with the prohibition of abortion in 1936. The Communists took test votes in a number of factories and meetings, which showed a majority against the proposed law. Consequently, the promised plebiscite was called off and the law promulgated by decree.[70]

III. SOCIAL AND RELIGIOUS FREEDOMS

Closely complementing specifically political freedoms, shaping and informing political life, are the potential rewards of group life. The modern world is set off from its predecessors in important part by the wealth and richness of associations available to the individual, within which he finds much of the meaning and value of life. What is the state of freedom of association in the Soviet Union, in general, with respect to religion, and to the family?

[69] See J. V. Stalin, "On the Draft Constitution of the USSR," *Report* especially Chap. 5.

[70] Arthur Koestler, *The Yogi and the Commissar* (1945), p. 168. Says Koestler, "The dangerous counter-revolutionary experiment of public discussion has never since been repeated."

GENERAL FREEDOM OF ASSOCIATION

The stringently limited right of citizens to form associations and the duty and purpose of such associations in Russia are set forth by Article 126 of the 1936 Constitution:

> In conformity with the interests of the working people, and in order to develop the organizational initiative and political activity of the masses of the people, citizens of the USSR are ensured the right to unite in public organizations—trade unions, co-operative associations, youth organizations, sport and defense organizations, cultural, technical and scientific societies; and the most active and politically most conscious citizens in the ranks of the working class and other sections of the working people unite in the Communist Party of the Soviet Union (Bolsheviks), which is the vanguard of the working people in their struggle to strengthen and develop the socialist system and is the leading core of all organizations of the working people, both public and State.

The civil rights of such organizations are constitutionally ensured (Article 125) "by placing at the disposal of the working people and their organizations, printing presses, stocks of paper, public buildings, the streets, communications, facilities and other material requisites for the exercise of these rights."[71]

Yet such associations enjoy these truncated freedoms only under the license and supervision of the party and of the government. The position of trade unions and co-operatives is discussed below under economic freedoms. The position of other "voluntary" societies is clarified by the following. Under militant communism, all such societies were prohibited unless specifically ordered by the state. The federal law of January 6, 1930, restated the principle of state license, leaving details and administration to the individual republics, but subjected commercial concerns, trade unions, and religious associations to special regulations. The R.S.F.S.R. law is a model for those of other republics. It defines sharply the socialist purpose of all such associations, and requires that their constitutions must be confirmed by a government authority of appropriate geographical

[71] Quoted from United Nations, *Yearbook on Human Rights for 1946,* p. 316.

jurisdiction. Such authorities must ensure that the organization is "desirable," and that its purpose "conforms to the general purpose of the particular fields of socialist reconstruction."[72] This authority must also supervise and control approved associations, with power to eliminate members, expel officers, dissolve prematurely elected committees, etc., and finally to take any measures, including liquidation if the association deviates from its constitutional purpose.[73]

The unions of "creative professions"—artists, writers, musicians—are authorized to protect the material interests of their members, but are in fact "devices for control over the arts and a machinery for promotion of trends corresponding to current plans of the government."[74]

FREEDOM OF CONSCIENCE AND RELIGION

In Russia as in other modern totalitarian systems, the position of religion in society and rights and freedoms in the religious sphere are limited by the demands of the totalitarian political elite to dominate every phase of life. The Russian position is conditioned in part by history. The state and church have had a long history of joint domination over the souls and bodies of the Russian people, but the church has emphasized ritual rather than doctrine, and has subordinated its own claims to those of the state. On the other side has been the classical atheism of Marx and of subsequent orthodox communist doctrine, which has attacked the church as an institution positively interfering with the welfare and development of the individual. The mid-course between considerable freedom for the church to act as a servant of constituted temporal authority, and to enjoy ritualistic freedom within this role on the one hand, and the complete destruction of the church in the name of Marxist atheism on the other, has again been determined by the expediencies of practical power-seeking in Russia. The church has neither been wholly economically stifled nor been driven from the ideological

[72] Gsovski, *Soviet Civil Law,* pp. 408-09.
[73] The same, p. 410.
[74] The same, pp. 410-11.

field. The regime hopes that religion will die naturally under socialist economic and social conditions. Yet the communist leadership has never yet been able to dispense with the church as a mechanism of social control. This was dramatically illustrated by the rise in status of the church during the recent war, when Stalin drew on every conservative source of strength within Russia as means to survive the German onslaught.

In Russia there is sharp separation of church and state in formal law, but considerable fusion in recent practice. Soviet policy toward religion is a combination of Marxist struggle against religion, tempered by the expediences of fruitful collaboration in many phases of social reconstruction, and of avoiding the fanning of fanaticism by excessive repression. The basic law is Article 124 of the 1936 Constitution, which provides: "In order to ensure to citizens freedom of conscience, the church of the USSR is separated from the State, and the school from the church. Freedom of religious worship and freedom of anti-religious propaganda is recognized for all citizens."[75] According to Vyshinsky, true freedom of conscience requires that church and state be completely separated, that the state be neutral as between all religions, that there be no dominant church, that the state not intrude into religious convictions of communicants or internal church affairs, and "that every legal limitation and civil privilege whatsoever connected with religion be abolished."[76]

Militant atheism was organized by the Communists to conduct propaganda against religion, although the major strategy of the party was written into section 13 of its program, still the foundation of Soviet legislation on religion: "The All-Union Communist Party is guided by the conviction that only the planned development and awareness in all the social-economic activity of the masses will bring to pass the complete withering of religious prejudices."[77] The struggle with religion is carried on "not by administrative repressions, but by the socialist refashioning of the entire national economy which eradicates

[75] *United Nations Yearbook on Human Rights for 1946,* p. 315.
[76] Vyshinsky, *The Law of the Soviet State,* pp. 605-06.
[77] Quoted in the same, p. 607.

religion, by socialist reeducation of the toiling masses, by antireligious propaganda, by implanting scientific knowledge, and by expanding education."[78] Something of the repressions which were actually carried out is suggested by the following measures taken to ensure separation of church and state. According to a decree of the Council of People's Commissars (January 23, 1918),

> The keeping of records of civil status was transferred from ecclesiastical to civil authority. Religious organizations were deprived of their juristic personality and, in particular, of the right to possess property, and were put into the position of private societies enjoying neither advantages nor grants of any kind from the state. All the property of churches and religious societies was declared the property of the people. The gratuitous use of buildings and of the necessary objects of their cult was granted to the appropriate religious societies for the holding of divine services.
>
> The school was separated from the church and the teaching of religious beliefs in schools was forbidden. Citizens could, if they wished, teach and be taught religion privately.[79]

The Constitution of 1918 declared that the clergy were not workers, but servants of the capitalist class. They were therefore denied the rights of citizens: work, sometimes food. Families of priests were under great pressure, being subject to equal discrimination in finding work or pursuing education.[80]

No one could, however, decline to fulfill his civic obligations on the plea of religious conviction, with one exception: a people's court could replace one civil obligation by another. This meant in practice that a people's court could allow a conscientious objector to perform sanitary service in place of military service.[81]

The earlier constitutions (1918 in particular) gave equal freedom to religious and to antireligious propaganda ("without which freedom of conscience is impossible"). Although the 1936 Constitution pairs the grant of religious *worship* with antireligious *propaganda,* this distinction must not be taken too seri-

[78] The same, pp. 609-10.
[79] The same, pp. 607-08.
[80] M. Searle Bates, *Religious Liberty: An Inquiry* (1945), pp. 3, 5.
[81] The same, p. 608.

ously, since sects have apparently enjoyed some chance since the 1920's to proselytize and to get bibles and other literature printed with state approval. It is unclear to what extent this literature is censored by state agencies to eliminate or keep within predetermined bounds any religious attacks on the atheistic and materialistic dogmas of communism—the main sources of doctrinal differences between party and Christian church (at least the Russian Orthodox).[82] It is claimed that the state does not in fact interfere with doctrine or local administration of church organizations.[83]

With the onset of war, from 1941 at least, the party sought a real rapprochement with the church as a means of maximizing national morale; this movement gave the church more *de facto* bargaining power, and strengthened the views of those who did not wish to press antireligious propaganda on expedient grounds. The antireligious publications were stopped in October 1941. A significant conference was held in 1943 between Stalin and Molotov and three Orthodox bishops, at which official approval was given to the election of a patriarch, and the church accepted the creation of a State Bureau on Church Affairs.[84] Johnson says this Bureau does not control internal church matters, but acts as a necessary instrument to allow the church to function as a practical institution within a socialist state: it sees to the procurement of buildings, printing paper and facilities, materials for vestments and the like. It is also clear from Johnson's account that this Bureau was empowered to supervise "correct and timely execution of the laws and the decisions of the Government in respect to the Russian Orthodox Church," and to decide for the government questions of establishment of seminaries; church requests for needed materials are presented through this agency to the rationing authorities. A similarly constituted government bureau (Council for Affairs of the Religious Cults) deals with the affairs of other Christian sects and other religions on parallel grounds.[85]

[82] See the declaration of Metropolitan Sergei quoted in Bates, *Religious Liberty: An Inquiry*, p. 5.
[83] Hewlett Johnson, *Soviet Russia Since the War* (1947), pp. 117 ff.
[84] The same, p. 119.
[85] The same, pp. 120-24.

In conformity with established practice in dealing with non-government associations, the government does not permit the church to engage in activities or to found related associations not specifically approved. Much of the pastoral functions of churches was held to be irrelevant in a socialist society.

Article 17 of the law of April 8, 1929 forbids religious associations:

> (a) to establish mutual aid funds, co-operative and productive associations, and in general to use the property at their disposal for any other purpose than the satisfying of religious needs; (b) to give material aid to their members; to organize either special meetings for children, youth, women, for prayer and other purposes, or general meetings, groups, circles, departments, biblical, literary, handworking, labor, religious study, and so on, and also to organize excursions and children's playgrounds, to pen libraries and reading-rooms, to organize sanatoria and medical aid. Only such books as are necessary for the performance of services are permitted to be kept in the church buildings and house of prayer.[86]

One commentator suggests that a main reason for keeping the war-generated relations between the Orthodox church and the state in their present relatively happy state is "the intention to use the church in world affairs both as a rallying-point for other nations which adhere to the Greek Orthodox faith, and as a weapon against the Vatican."[87] Acceptance of this role by the church is facilitated by its centuries-old role as the official state religion, and by the fact that the state has once more provided it with an economic base.[88]

The religious communities of those areas into which Russia expanded during the prologue and aftermath of the last war tasted fully Russian oppression. In those areas Russia occupied as a result of the 1939 Hitler pact, the Communists wiped out schools and theological seminaries, replaced Christian by communist teachers in remaining institutions, banished and persecuted the clergy of all sects. The clergy in these areas lost civic rights, which had been restored to Russian clergy in 1936 after

[86] Quoted in Bates, *Religious Liberty: An Inquiry,* p. 4.

[87] Vera Micheles Dean, *The United States and Russia* (1947), p. 73.

[88] Edmund Stevens, *Russia Is No Riddle* (1945), pp. 21, 77, quoted in *Communism in Action,* p. 132.

they had been tamed or crushed; church property was confiscated outright or subjected to unbearable taxes. Roman Catholics and the Ukrainian Evangelical church took the most severe blows, though every sect suffered.[89]

The present party attitude seems to be one of careful waiting. The party genuinely believes that the conditions of life under communism will lead to a natural withering away of "religious prejudices," and the party need not risk current defeats by pressing for an inevitable consequence. Yet the party repeats from time to time its attitude decrying religion and "religious prejudices"; sees to it that the church is kept within the sphere of *worship* alone, set for it by the party; supports propaganda for "scientism" designed to undercut religious foundations, and reiterates its devotion to antireligious principles.[90]

THE FAMILY

The institution of the family, like so many institutions threatened with serious change under communist ideology,[91] has undergone various developments during the Soviet period, conforming to the efforts of the party to establish the classless society; and has benefited by the Stalinist stabilization policies of

[89] Bates, *Religious Liberty: An Inquiry*, pp. 8-9.

[90] The defunct League of Militant Atheists seems to have been incorporated into the more general All-Union Society for the Dissemination of Political and Natural Science. The party is dissatisfied with pro-scientific propaganda. An editorial in *Pravda* (June 28, 1948) complained that "the insufficiently aggressive character of scientific propaganda is manifested from time to time in the failure to emphasize the struggle against religious prejudices . . . freedom of conscience . . . certainly does not signify that our political and scientific organizations are neutral in their attitude toward religion." Quoted in Alex Inkeles: "Family and Church in the Postwar U.S.S.R.," *The Annals*, Vol. 263 (May 1949), p. 43n.

[91] Said Lenin: "It is impossible to be a democrat and a socialist without immediately demanding complete freedom of divorce, because the absence of such freedom is the utmost oppression of the subdued sex, woman—although it does not take brains to gather that the recognition of freedom to leave one's husband is not an invitation for all wives to leave their husbands." (Quoted in Gsovski, *Soviet Civil Law*, p. 126.)

And Brandenburgsky: "If at present [1927] we maintain the duty of mutual support within the family, because the State cannot yet . . . replace the family in this respect. . . . The family creating a series of rights and duties between spouses, parents and children, will certainly dissappear in the course of time and will be replaced by governmental organization of public education and social security." Quoted in the same, p. 127.

the mid-thirties. The Revolution moved against the specifically bourgeois features of the family—the authoritarian position of the father, and the rights of the family or head of family to benefit economically from the labor of its members. Children were "liberated" from family control as to education, livelihood, and choice of career, to have these things decided for them by the authoritarian state. Wherever family influences got in the way of the establishment of socialism, the family was bitterly attacked. Under the guise of establishing the true equality of women, numerous "reforms" were instituted. Divorce became easy to the point of farce. Financial responsibility for spouses, present or previous, was correspondingly light and flexible. The resultant chaos in domestic relations was found to have no place in the stabilized state, and most of the reforms were rescinded, although the new regulations gave some effect to the principle of equality between the sexes and between legitimate or illegitimate offspring.[92]

As a blow at the church, earliest Soviet legislation recognized only civil marriage, although religious marriage could be legalized as *de facto* marriage and give rise to property rights, prevent other marriages, etc. The codes also prohibited marriage with insane persons, incest, etc. The codes required mutual consent and attainment of marriageable age. Race was never a barrier, but nationality (citizenship) may be; since February 15, 1947, marriages between Soviet nationals and aliens have been forbidden.[93] The earlier codes did not punish abortion, bigamy, incest, adultery, or homosexuality. Nor could a citizen refuse to give testimony against another on grounds of close relationship.[94]

[92] Until 1944, for example, the established principle was that there was no connection between family relationship and marital relationship. Family relationship was determined by birth. Children had no rights to the property of parents, or vice versa. The parental obligation to support the child was recognized only insofar as the state failed to provide. The obligation to support marital or family relatives was conditional, even after 1944, upon the inability of the indigent member to support himself, either because of destitution or physical disability. The same, pp. 112-13.

[93] The same, p. 116.

[94] The same, pp. 118-19.

The "tightening" process began in 1935 and culminated in an Edict of the Presidium in July 1944. Parental responsibility for the conduct of the child was vastly increased, and liability for the torts or crimes of minors established. Divorce became more difficult and expensive in 1936; abortion was made a punishable offense in the same year, as homosexuality had been in 1934. After the decree of July 8, 1944, the parental responsibility for children born in or out of wedlock was more sharply fixed, but natural fathers were freed from responsibility for children born out of registry. The mothers were given a small grant-in-aid. Divorce became much more difficult, being granted by the courts (not registering organs only), and only for grounds the court deems justifiable.[95]

The present policy seems to be to re-establish the family as a strong institution as an element of stability in the state, and to indulge in both honorific and pecuniary stimulation of motherhood.[96] Yet Gsovski concludes: "The recent soviet legislation, though inconsistent with earlier soviet laws, shows a consistency of the soviet policy of interference of the State with the family life of the citizen."[97]

IV. ECONOMIC FREEDOMS

The issue of economic freedom, as considered here, is not that of a standard of life, but of the freedom enjoyed by the indi-

[95] The same, pp. 122-23. According to Koestler, divorce was purposely made so expensive, time-consuming and difficult that it was in effect restricted to the elite. *The Yogi and the Commissar,* pp. 168-69.

[96] The decree of the Presidium of the Supreme Council of July 8, 1944 is entitled "On increasing state aid to expectant mothers, mothers of large families and unmarried mothers, and protection of motherhood and childhood, the institution of the honorary title of Mother Heroine and the establisment of the Order of the Glory of Motherhood and the Motherhood Medal." The decree is said, in part, to encourage large families, and to contribute to the "consolidation of the family." The aid involved consists in subsidies related to size of family, the provision of facilities for expectant mothers and mothers (maternity leave, exemptions from overtime and night work, additional food rations) and reduced fees at kindergartens and nurseries for members of large families. (See *United Nations Yearbook on Human Rights for 1946,* pp. 313-14.)

[97] *Soviet Civil Law,* p. 135. He cites the prohibition against marriage with aliens, the withdrawal of divorce as a right, and the impossibility of regularizing *de facto* religious marriages under the Edict.

vidual in the economic sphere. What are his choices of economic action? It is obvious that entrepreneurial freedoms are foreclosed in a socialist society, which not only owns the instruments of production, but holds that all private rights are conditioned upon their use in a manner designed to further socialist objectives. But even in the socialist state, there are theoretical possibilities for choice of a career or skill to be followed, and room for the exercise of initiative, even if only the initiative of the bureaucrat to find means to implement the directive, or to shape the directive by his reports and recommendations. Such possibilities are enhanced by the needs of the state, and the bargaining power of the unusual individual whose skills or capacities are at a premium.

Now that it is clear that the period of the dictatorship of the proletariat may last indefinitely, and that stability and fighting effectiveness are the chief desiderata, the present state of economic affairs in the USSR is a much more reliable pattern of what may be expected when doctrinaire socialism on a large scale is combined with a sense of global mission in a world of violence and power politics. The socialist system of economy, after the strategic retreat of the NEP, is now firmly entrenched. The Russians are gradually learning that the mere seizure of ownership of the instruments of production left open major issues of social and economic policy as to how these instruments are to be used. The major societal strategies are to improve production techniques and fighting efficiency, both for survival in a hostile world and for ultimate world victory. A small but minor role of private property seems well established, particularly in agriculture and small commerce. But equally well established, and of critical importance for the functioning of society as a whole, is the method of state planning of the national economic life. This system, however undesirable or cumbersome from the standpoint of a free society, has nevertheless proved in war its power to endure. It will not collapse of its own weight, as was frequently predicted by many observers in the early years of the Revolution. It may prove to be of superior survival value in harnessing all national forces for monolithic military, political, and economic action.

PROPERTY RIGHTS

The issue of property rights is fundamental in evaluating socialist society, not because of its central position in Marxist doctrine, but because of the way it affects concrete economic operations. Classically, Marxism was founded on expropriating the capitalist, because of what ownership implied in bourgeois society as to *control over economic action.* The assumption was that the owner controlled significant economic operations by virtue of his *ownership.* Hence it was necessary for revolutionaries operating in the name of the dispossessed classes to seize ownership as a means of ensuring economic processes in the interest of the worker. The Marxist, unlike the pure historical Communist, stopped short of socializing the ownership of all forms of property, but insisted on socializing the ownership of any form of property which might affect adversely the interest of the worker if left in private hands. Hence the tremendous limitations on the concept and functions of ownership in the USSR.

Yet one of the major lessons taught by the modern totalitarian state is that ownership is not crucial either to control or to the sustained enjoyment of the major values offered by modern society.

In Russia this has operated in double-edged fashion. In the first place, once political and economic control had been wrested from those who wielded it by hereditary or traditional right, controls over political and economic processes were monopolized and operated by other means than by formal ownership, means which have tended themselves to be stabilized. In the second place, once it became clear that an ownership as such was not crucial to control, it was possible for the elite to permit a mild reintroduction of various forms of ownership and such concomitants as inheritance, as part of the system of incentives whereby the Communists drive the masses to sustained effort.

What the Communists did was to diminish sharply the scope of the rights of ownership. Since nothing could rise above the interest of the communist state in communist theory, the Communists abolished the notion that property carried with it any form of rights which could be legitimately urged as superior to the demands or interest of the state. Gradually, through NEP, through state lotteries, through Stalin prizes, through special subventions and salaries and gifts to favored persons in the Soviet state, there appeared a sizable sphere for ownership within the Soviet system. Yet currency devaluations, expropriations of bank accounts, and comparable moves indicate clearly that no such rights can ever be put in the balance against state interests.

Soviet spokesmen make clear that neither Marx nor Engels espoused the full communistic principle that the individual has no rights of possession in any property whatsoever. Soviet practice has worked out compromises between the communist demand that *all* instruments of production be socially owned, and the practical requirements of leaving considerable property rights in the individual, as a necessary economic incentive. Communism does not proclaim poverty as an ideal. Russia's bleak poverty since 1917 has been due to economic conditions and to politico-military decisions. These include the economic backwardness of pre-revolutionary Russia, the lack of productivity of an unskilled peasant people particularly in industrial areas, and the decisions (1) to concentrate on the rapid creation of heavy industry (first Five Year Plan), (2) forcibly to liquidate the kulaks and carry out socialization of agriculture at great cost in agricultural productivity, and (3) to prepare for and to conduct total war. Current shortages are partly due to the necessities of repairing war damage and to the efforts to prepare for new wars.

The essential propositions governing property are written into the 1936 Constitution. There are two forms of socialized property: state property and co-operative and collective farm property. The first is defined to include "The land, its mineral wealth, waters, forests, mills, factories, mines, rail, water and air transport, banks, communications, large State-organized agricultural enterprises . . . municipal enterprises and the bulk of the dwelling-houses in the cities and industrial localities. . . ." (Article 6), and are said to belong to "the whole people." Collective and co-operative property consists of public enterprises in collective farms and co-operative organizations, their livestock, implements, products of the collective farms and co-operative organizations, and their common buildings (Article 7). The use of land occupied by collective farms is guaranteed to them in perpetuity (Article 8).[98] "Personal property" consists of property held either by individuals or by households. The former includes the "right of citizens to their income and savings from work, in their dwelling-houses and subsidiary home enterprises, in articles of domestic economy and use, and articles of personal use and convenience, as well as the right of citizens to inherit personal property" (Article 10). Article 7 also assures to every household in a collective farm, for its personal use, "a small plot of household land [not exceeding one hectare: 2.47 acres] attached to the dwelling, and, as its personal property, a subsidiary husbandry on the plot, a dwelling-house, livestock, poultry [all strictly limited in number] and minor agricultural implements in accordance with the rules of the agricultural *artel*."[99]

The situation with respect to private property and economic activity of individual peasants and craftsmen has a similar function, even though the significance of these forces by 1936 was negligible in relation to the total economy. Its propaganda purpose is to show "the transfer of such small private economy into

[98] This means, in practice, that any peasant who has given up his land to a collective in order to become a member, may not withdraw it if he withdraws from the collective for any purpose.

[99] This regulation was "created under the immediate guidance of Stalin, accepted at the Second All-Russian Congress of Kolkhoz Shock Workers, and confirmed by the Council of People's Commissar's of the USSR and the Central Committee of the All-Union Communist Party (of Bolsheviks) February 17, 1935." (Vyshinsky, *The Law of the Soviet State*, p. 189.) It is the fundamental basis for regulating kolkhoz activity. It both protects the kolkhozes from unwarranted interference in their internal management and affairs, while authorizing the Village Soviets (the lowest government unit) to suspend unlawful enactments of the kolkhozes, and authorizing the district executive committees to abrogate them. The same, p. 190.

large-scale socialist economy is by the voluntary choice of the petty producers themselves, convinced of the advantages of socialized economy aided by the state in every way, under the guidance of the worker class."[100] The continued existence of such subsidiary economy is always conditioned on the principle that there be no "exploitation (that is, employment) of man by man. This principle is enforced by legislation against speculation, against contracts for "exploiting" other persons, and legislation limiting the extent of individual property, and ensuring that it is not used for "nonlabor purposes" and has a "consumer" or "use" character.[101]

The right of inheritance was included in the Constitution as an "incitement" to labor, and is not designed as an instrument for preserving and strengthening capitalist private property.[102]

The possessor of personal savings, income, etc., over and above current needs cannot invest them productively (in the capitalist sense), but he can invest them in state bonds, put them in savings banks, and in other ways build up for himself income beyond that of his current wage or salary. Greater ratio differences in incomes between workers and specialists exist in the USSR than in many capitalist countries, giving rise to economic inequities of a special socialist character. However, it is unlikely that any significant portion of the population could use savings or investments to free itself from the constitutionally imposed duty to work as a prelude to the right to eat. Moreover, such savings are always threatened by currency conversions, capital levies, or other fiscal measures adopted to curb inflation, take away war profits, or for whatever purpose or reason pleases the ruling clique.

STATE PLANNING

True entrepreneurial freedom is impossible under Russian state planning. So comprehensive is state control over all essential economic decisions, that only a small degree of technical

[100] The same, p. 193.
[101] The same, pp. 196-97.
[102] The same, p. 198.

and managerial scope remains to be exercised by individuals working in the gargantuan process. These economic decisions are related to the major political objectives of the regime by party decisions at the very top. The instruments of government, whether acting as economic operating agencies or as technical control agencies, are all closely controlled within the fields relevant to the major objectives. The five-year plans, and the technical organization for state planning, the *Gosplan,* are only the detailed forms for expression and execution of the thinking and the decisions of the party leadership. The party leaders decide such basic questions as the planned rate of capital formation; the planned distribution of effort among production for military purposes, for other productive organization, or for consumers' interests; the planned emphasis on alternative fields of scientific research and development, and even of cultural activity. In Russia the question decided about any potential economic activity is never whether it would be profitable; it is always in terms of its potential contribution to the central purposes adopted by the state. "Planned profit" exists in Russian economics, but never as an indicator of the desirability of an enterprise or program.[103]

Scope for the manager in Russian economics is limited not only by the detail of state plans and the hierarchy of control; it is also limited by the direct and local pressures of party, labor union, and government. On balance, however, this scope has increased, as a managerial class has arisen which is not suspected because of nonproletarian origin, which is often fused with government and party, and which is recognized as more valuable to the communist system than the toothless labor union. Stringent state control has freed the manager from many of the onerous burdens of controlling his labor force on the one hand,

[103] Extended and informative discussions of the process of state planning in Russia can be found in Bienstock, Schwarz, and Yugow, *Management in Russian Industry and Agriculture* (1944); Alexander Baykov, *The Development of the Soviet Economic System* (1946), and in Towster. Pro-Soviet accounts are legion: noteworthy are the books of Maurice Dobb, and the publications of Soviet propaganda agencies which accompany the announcement of each five-year plan.

and on the other hand freedom to distribute a manager's fund built up out of "planned profits" has given him some power to control labor by offering special incentives.

The position of the manager in the late 1930's has been summarized as follows:

> Under Soviet conditions of economy, functions pertaining to management have acquired highly characteristic forms . . . [The day-to-day tasks of a single Soviet manager] . . . are profoundly affected by the Plan (whether fulfilled or not) and by the almost complete absence of free markets. . . .
>
> Both the quantities and prices of industrial goods are fixed by authorities. The manager, head of the lowest unit of industrial administration, participates in the working out of details, not of general outlines of a Five Year Plan or its currently revised short-term versions. And, although over-fulfillment of the allotted quota is encouraged and rewarded, production of a plant must, on the whole, appear rigid as compared with the extremely flexible output of a capitalist enterprise, sensitive to minute changes in profit expectation. The plant's capacity is fixed by outside authorities. In theory at least, construction funds at the manager's disposal are limited to repairs and, under certain conditions, to workers' housing construction. To sell parts of a plant or equipment is strictly illegal. The most important materials are allocated from above. . . .
>
> The Soviet manager is unable to manipulate freely the size of his plant or his inventories. Nor can he take advantage of market situations, current or prospective, by bargaining with sources of supplies or with customers for better prices, or by winning customers through low prices, and sources of supplies through high ones. To be sure, with supply chronically lagging behind demand, it would in any case be pointless for a manager to reduce prices in order to win customers. On the other hand, to win preference from a source of supplies by bidding up prices for raw materials would not be pointless.—But it is forbidden.
>
> . . . .
>
> The manager's energies are thus directed into the one remaining channel: reduction of real units costs of production. . . .[104]

The situation is not greatly different in agriculture, although government surveillance is exercised not only by higher government agencies, but by the machine and tractor stations as well.

[104] Jacob Marschak, in Introduction to Bienstock, Schwarz, and Yugow, *Management in Russian Industry and Agriculture,* pp. xviii-xix.

Party supervision seems to be somewhat less important at the local levels than in industry, chiefly because the party is not large enough or widely enough distributed fully to cover all collectives or individual households. Management authority is vested in the chairman of each collective, delegated to foremen (brigadiers) in charge of particular agricultural operations, subject to the over-all decisions in some areas of the collective as a whole. The economic autonomy of the collective is limited somewhat by the position of the peasant household within it, even as a subsidiary form of economy. The collective as a unit decides the distribution of time between collective and household activities, sets the work day, and so forth; but the same members who act as collective are also members of the households, and do not wish to deprive themselves unduly of the rights to grow and market produce on their own account. According to Berman, the collective may not "illegally" use household land for collective purposes; the aggrieved peasant household can sue for and get damages in the courts.[105]

Despite these economic rights of the collective, control by the state is considerable. The state determines what proportion of the output of each collective must be delivered to the state in kind. The excess is distributed among the members of the collective on a work-day basis, with special attention to incentive values, and to the rewarding of the local elites—managers, brigadiers, shock workers, etc. Prices at which deliveries to the state must be made are set from above. Surpluses, if any, may be sold in free markets for prices usually far above the state level. The

[105] Berman, *62 Harvard Law Review* 263. With respect to the rights of the peasant household, Berman says: "Situated on the collective farm, the peasant household holds its land in perpetuity, and exercises a customary ownership, limited by ancient usages, over its dwelling house and farm buildings, livestock and poultry, agricultural implements, fodder and seed, crops, and furniture. The management, use, and disposal of the household property are in the members as a whole . . . a majority vote of the adult members is decisive. Members may voluntarily leave the association and thereupon claim an appropriate share of the joint property, though when a member leaves to join another household (as through marriage) he is not entitled to such a share but acquires full rights in the new household." The same, p. 262.

collective must contract with other state agencies, especially the machine and tractor stations (MTS), for the performance of certain services. The MTS enjoy a privileged position since they may own certain types of heavy equipment—tractors, threshers, etc.—which the collectives or peasant households may not own. Similarly, the collectives must buy seed, fertilizer, and other specialized requirements not produced on the farms themselves, from the appropriate government agencies at fixed prices.

LABOR

Labor in the Soviet Union is in the position of a woman raped in the name of her self-fulfillment.

The communist revolution was carried out in the name of the working class. Yet from the beginnings of Leninist theory, the working class was only a means to an end. This class by itself could develop no more than a "trade-union consciousness," that is, it could never do more than try to reduce hours, increase wages, and improve working conditions. It had to have professional revolutionary leadership—which could come only from the intellectual, not the laboring classes. And in the sphere of practical application, labor in the Soviet Union has lost its autonomy, its rights, and its weapons.

The right to organize is possible only within the limits set by the communist state, and under the detailed supervision of party functionaries. There is no right to found any organization, labor union or other, in the Soviet Union which is not authorized and supervised by the party.

The right to strike is abolished. Any attempt to strike, or to foment a strike, is subject to capital punishment as treason.

The right to collective bargaining is also abolished. The labor union can participate only in a technical, advisory capacity as one of the factors manipulated by the party in the determination and promulgation of wages, hours, and working conditions. The labor representative in a factory can intercede only to ask for a fulfillment of contractual provisions dictated from above—and even then cannot take steps if such an action would contravene a current demand of the party for all-out production.

The labor union has turned into a sort of combined welfare and production-incentive organization whose function is to spur the workers to fulfill the production demands of the state, or to propagandize or educate them with current dogma.

During the prerevolutionary period, the role prescribed by communism for labor, and especially for the trade unions, is to heighten proletarian dissatisfaction, and to exacerbate the postulated tensions between labor and capital to the point where successful revolution is possible.[106] Accordingly "bourgeois" freedoms for labor to organize, and to have its own political parties, enjoy freedom of speech and assembly, and so forth, are valuable as a means to the revolution. Once the revolution has taken place, however, the role becomes different. In the early Russian post-revolutionary experience, the trade unions were used as a means to eliminate bourgeois and capitalistic elements in society, as a means of checking on nonproletarian managers, technicians, engineers, and so forth, and against the "bureaucratism" of the state. The right to strike was permissible and valuable so long as a sizable sector of the economy was in private hands, and labor action could be a useful instrument of control and discipline of the non-state sector. But even before the state had effectively taken over the economy, both the value of the strike to the state, and hence its permissibility, disappeared. During NEP, Lenin put main emphasis on productivity and enjoined "industrial peace." At this time the Russian unions lost their character as instruments of industrial struggle.

By 1928 Stalin had officially formulated the new role for the trade unions: "The trade unions are called upon to play a decisive role in the task of building Socialist industry by stimulating labor productivity, labor discipline and Socialist competi-

[106] In Lenin's classic formula, revolution can take place *only* when the *"lower classes" do not want* the old way and when the "upper classes" *cannot carry on in the old way.* Quoted by Historicus, *Foreign Affairs,* Vol. 27, No. 2, January 1949, p. 188, from Stalin, *Problems of Leninism,* (11th ed., 1945), p. 19. Furthermore, in Leninist dogma the masses by themselves cannot generate more than a "trade-union" (reformist) consciousness; the party must act through them to bring the proletariat to a *revolutionary* consciousness.

tion, and extirpating all remnants of guild isolation and 'trade unionism.' "[107]

The official dogma of the party is contained in a declaration adopted by the 16th Party Congress in 1930. This declaration spelled out Stalin's formula, calling bluntly for a complete reorganization of the trade unions, both as to personnel and policy. The objective was summarized:

> It is necessary to concentrate on production. . . . Socialist competition and the shock brigades must become the primary concern of all the constructive activities of the unions. . . . The chief concern of all union organizations must be the promotion of outstanding workers to the position of factory directors, officials of departments and their assistants. . . . The trade unions must make it their particular business to draw women into production.
>
> The Congress pledges the party organizations and the trade union bodies to increase the propaganda of Leninism in the entire system of the cultural-political work of the unions, to impregnate it with communist dogma, to remove completely all nonpolitical and narrow cultural elements.[108]

The Soviet trade union now acts as an instrument of the state subordinate to party, to government agency, and to manager, designed to increase production, to direct, train, and discipline the workers, and to administer certain amenities and welfare arrangements.[109]

[107] Manya Gordon, *Workers Before and After Lenin* (1941), p. 99. Gordon points out how Stalin liquidated representatives of the earlier "bourgeois" trade unionism, and comments: "Henceforth the trade unions were compelled to drive the workers, to organize 'shock brigades' and 'Socialist competition' and bring to trial workers who lagged behind in their quantitative 'norms' or in quality. As a result, the trade unions in Soviet Russia are today a misnomer, and have nothing basically in common with similar organizations in other countries. They are merely a whip over the workers. . . ." The same, p. 100.

[108] Quoted in the same, pp. 100-01.

[109] See Bienstock, Schwarz, and Yugow, *Management in Russian Industry and Agriculture,* Chap. 3. The official delimitation of the role of industrial unions in plants was defined by a resolution of the Communist party adopted in 1929, which established "one-man control"—that is, the control of the plant manager, dominant in his plant, irrespective of the party or trade-union position of any subordinate within it. "The trade-union organ (workers' plant committee) 'represents the day-to-day needs of labor in the field of culture and living conditions as well as in economic life,' and

The trade unions lost any effective power in the hiring process, vested in management from the time of dissolution of the Commissariat for Labor (1933). Procurement of man power was vested in 1938 in central and republican interdepartmental commissions. Not the state, but the system of collective labor contracts withered away between 1933 and 1935. As a result, the unions lost all power to affect the fixing of wages or of labor conditions.[110]

The new labor union leadership was hand-picked for its subservience to the new party line. Gordon quotes one leader (Weinberg) as saying in 1933:

---

is at the same time 'the energetic organizer of the productive initiative of the working masses.'" It can participate in discussions, receive reports, and so forth, but may not intervene in any way which would circumscribe one-man control. The same, p. 36.

[110] The actual process of fixing wage rates and piece rates is described by Schwarz as follows:

"Fixing of wage rates in the Soviet Union has been, almost from the beginning, a dual process: (a) the setting-up of a schedule of relative wage rates, expressed as multiples of the wage rate of the lowest-paid category of workers; and (b) the fixing of this lowest wage rate generally on a monthly, sometimes on a weekly or daily basis. . . . The old schedules of relative wage rates were taken over; the fixing of wage rates of the lowest category (which determines all others) became, in fact, a function of the various organs of industrial management (plant manager or higher bodies), who had to keep within the payroll allowances fixed by the Plan. Occasionally they also revised the schedules of relative rates; since 1938 these schedules have been set up by the People's Commissariats and approved by the Economsoviet.

"Piece rates—the prevailing form of pay—are usually fixed in Russia separately for each plant. The piece rates are determined by two factors: a monthly wage rate fixed as described above, and the performance norm fixed, as a rule, for the individual plant. The piece rate equals time rate divided by performance norm.

"Participation in determining the performance norm had, for years, been one of the most important tasks of labor's representatives within the plant. . . .

"During the thirties, however, the Piece-Rates Committees gradually lost power to pure organs of the plant administration, the bureaus for wages and norms. Since 1933 these bureaus have had exclusive jurisdiction in fixing performance norms. Only when these are obviously "wrong" may the Piece-Rates Committee, on the initiative of its labor members, suggest revision. The labor members of the Piece-Rates Committee have, in addition, the task of popularizing among workers the norms and rates fixed by management, and holding labor up to fulfilment of the norms." The same, pp. 41-42.

. . . The proper determination of wages and the regulation of labor demand that the industrial heads and the technical directors be immediately charged with responsibility in this matter. . . . [The workers] must not defend themselves against their government. That is absolutely wrong. That is supplanting the administrative organs. That is Left opportunistic perversion, the annihilation of individual authority and interference in the administrative departments. It is imperative that it be liquidated.[111]

This shift in the power of labor unions to deal with the fixing of wage rates is both logically consistent and inevitable in a centrally planned economic system. As to consistency, the Soviet apologist points out that the interest of the worker in a socialist state would not be pitted against that of an employing capitalist, but against the community. As to necessity, it is not possible for a planned society to leave to the chance of bargaining such a crucial element as the determination of rates which in effect fix levels of consumption, production, and division of national product between consumers' goods and other types of output.[112] Determination of these matters are policy decisions, which once made, determine the wage fund available for labor; the only remaining question, or eligible topic for bargaining, is the way the fund is to be distributed among classes of workers. The trade union is no longer an instrument to increase economic rewards to workers at the expense of capitalists.

The possibility of reviving collective agreements was considered in 1937, and it was officially decided that:

Collective agreement as a special form of legal regulation of labor relations of manual and clerical employees has outlived itself. Detailed regulation of all sides of these relations by mandatory acts of governmental power does not leave any room for any contractual agreement concerning one labor condition or another.[113]

Yet in March 1947 the Russians turned again to collective agreements as means "to achieve and exceed the production plan,

[111] Quoted in the same, pp. 104-05. Gordon points out this policy was *in contravention* to Soviet labor law in effect in that time.

[112] See Maurice Dobb, *Soviet Economy and the War* (1943), p. 75.

[113] Gsovski, *Soviet Civil Law,* p. 797, quoting Aleksandrov and Genkin, *Soviet Labor Law* (in Russian, 1946), p. 106.

to secure further growth of the productivity of labor, improvement of the organization of labor, and the increase of responsibility of management and trade organizations for the material condition of living of the employees and cultural services rendered to them."[114] Certain important topics were specifically excluded from bargaining, however, and the scope of agreements carefully indicated. Only rates approved by the government may be included in the agreements. Such agreements must be negotiated on the principle that "the interests of the workers are the same as the interests of production in a socialist state" and that the agreements must only give juridical expression to this unity.[115] In other words, the workers' representative can never argue that a wage increase is justified because those he represents want it or need it; he can only argue that it would benefit the state as a whole. In practice, he cannot even do as much as that. The central policies leave him only the job of getting his workers to accept what they must with the best grace possible.

LABOR CONTROLS AND DISCIPLINE

The broad trend in Soviet labor legislation since 1929 has been to increase the powers of management (that is, the state) over the individual employee or his union. Employment in the Soviet Union comes into being not as a contract between employer and employee, but as an administrative act of the management. Once on the job, an employee may not quit it without special authorization from management; although management can fire for cause at any time. Some classes of employees may be transferred against their will. By the Edict of June 26, 1940, workers were frozen to their jobs, and could leave only on pain of imprisonment. War laws drafting labor have not been repealed, and have been included in postwar compilations as of continuing effect. The worker is often assigned to his job in the

[114] Gsovski, the same, p. 798, quoting a decree of the Presidium of the Central Council of Trade-Unions, issued with approval of the Council of Ministers.

[115] The same, pp. 798-99.

first instance: graduates of higher educational institutions, including technical schools, are assigned by the ministry in charge of the school for initial work periods of three or five years. In 1940 a system of drafts of youth for industrial training was instituted; after training the draftee is assigned to a four-year tour of duty in industry or railroading. Failure to report for appointment is a court offense. The managerial right of dismissal gains suasion because of the perquisites which go with employment: housing especially. A dismissed employee may be removed from his dwelling by "administrative action," if he enjoys quarters by reason of his job.[116]

What remedies does the worker have against decisions of management? Arbitral boards were established in the early period to handle such affairs. The courts have some powers to remedy arbitrary action. But the arbitral boards no longer will deal with matters arising out of the establishment or change of labor conditions. Disputes boards will deal with disputes between individual employees and management concerning application of existing regulations, and may make "final" awards. These awards may be overturned *ex officio* by higher officials, in which case the aggrieved party may appeal to a court in some cases; in others, he may not appeal to a court, but must go to higher administrative authority. In those industries where "disciplinary codes" apply, the employee may not appeal to the court nor to a conciliation board, but only to his own superiors.[117]

Gsovski concludes his survey of recent labor law changes in the following words:

> The abolition of private ownership of the instruments of production and their transformation to socialist ownership has not been followed by an increase of rights of labor in labor law. On the contrary, in comparison with the legislation of the New Economic Policy period, when private enterprise was tolerated, the legal status of labor has changed for the worse. All the channels through which labor can plead its case in the capitalist world—legislation, courts,

[116] The same, pp. 801-03.
[117] The same, pp. 803-05.

administrative agencies and trade-unions—are in the Soviet Union the agencies of the principal employer of industrial labor—the government. another feature of the present soviet labor law is the numerous penal provisions. The labor law is to a large extent criminal law.[118]

Minimum wages are now considered obsolete in the Soviet Union, since wage rates and piece rates are now set by "higher authority." Wages paid in a given establishment are controlled in two ways: by the setting of rates, including piece rates, for industrial groups and worker categories as a whole, and by requiring that wages paid in an individual establishment do not exceed a total set by higher organs. Since these totals are set by worker categories, they influence the organization and functional structure of the plants. For particular specialists it is possible to pay "personal salaries" outside scales so fixed. Minimum wages are not guaranteed; to attain scheduled rates, the worker must attain a standard of output, which is in most cases set without reference to trade-union wishes.[119] In case of labor stoppages due to the employees' fault, no wages are payable; part wages may be paid if stoppages are due to other causes. Similar arrangements govern the reduction or withholding of pay for spoilage, except during training periods. Damage to products or property caused by employees must be compensated by the employer, over and above any monetary disciplinary measures imposed.

Warning, demotion, dismissal, or compulsory labor with reduced wages await the transgressor of factory rules. Managers risk similar penalties for failure to impose labor discipline on their workers.[120] Labor discipline by these and comparable measures is brought together in a directive of the Council of People's Commissars of January 18, 1941. For special categories, such as railway workers, a specially strict regime is imposed comparable to full military discipline.[121]

[118] The same, p. 805.
[119] Acts of June 4, 1938 and Jan. 14, 1939, quoted in the same, p. 812.
[120] Such sanctions may be imposed for as little cause as one instance of twenty minutes tardiness. The same, pp. 816-17.
[121] The same, pp. 818-20.

Hours and leave are established by edicts of the Council of People's Ministers; they are relatively liberal, even taking into account the pressures for long hours imposed by war, and the fact that they may be altered at any time. The eight-hour day appears to be the present standard,[122] with two weeks' annual leave for workers remaining eleven months in one establishment. Leave canceled during the war was subject to special compensation.

Control over hiring is maintained by a labor-book system, introduced in 1938. This book is prepared and kept by the establishment employing a worker, showing name, age, education, profession, labor record, work changes with reasons therefor, and rewards. It is given to the employee only when he leaves an establishment; without it he cannot be hired. The employee may exercise some initiative in seeking new employment, although the incentives system as such is designed to stabilize employment, and during critical periods, important categories of workers are frozen at their jobs.[123] An edict of October 19, 1940, gives ministers the right to transfer technical personnel and skilled laborers from one establishment to another, regardless of the employees' desires.[124]

FORCED LABOR

An inevitable feature of a society preoccupied with internal revolution, and the double problem of defense from expected foreign aggression and the achievement of world revolution, seems to be a system of economic exploitation of those who have transgressed the directives of the new society. Such transgression can be met by liquidation, but for a society as backward in

[122] Sec. 119, Labor Code, enacted Feb. 25, 1947.

[123] Act of Dec. 28, 1938, sec. 3. Edict of June 26, 1940 prohibits employees from resigning or changing employment without express permission of management. In cases of health, or enrollment in an institution of higher education or vocational training, permission may not be denied. Leaving jobs without authority is punishable, both as to the employee and to the manager guilty of unauthorized hiring. In the case of defense industries, sanctions are severe: imprisonment of five to eight years for unauthorized quitting. Gsovski, *Soviet Civil Law,* pp. 828-39.

[124] The same, p. 830.

productivity and technical organization as Russia, liquidation is expensive and foolish. Hence the growth during the 1930's of the labor camps and other institutions of forced labor thrown up during the early years of revolutionary struggle.

Estimates as to number of inmates vary—from the estimate of 6 millions made by Eugene Lyons in 1933, to the more recent and larger estimates of from 10 to 18 millions population during the 1940's.[125] Since Moscow savagely denies the evil intent of these camps,[126] and no official statistics appear concerning this type of labor, it is impossible to do more than take the best available informed estimates.

The degree of compulsion and regimentation also varies: some workers undergoing compulsory discipline are not confined, but work at their previous jobs at reduced wages, under special supervision. Other large groups are housed in barracks, and used in large state construction or other enterprises along with "free" labor. Still other groups, probably the largest category, are housed in the correctional camps at or near the site of their work, apart from the "free" population. Such enterprises are those of state mines, forestry, canal and highway construction, etc., including those in which conditions of work are most disagreeable, and economic conditions are such that the enterprises would find it difficult if not impossible to attract and retain without compulsion enough labor to permit continued operation. Conditions of work are affected by a number of considerations: revenge and punishment for severe offenders; correction and rehabilitation for less severe offenders who seem worth-while or safe to salvage; the balance between clothing and diet furnished and the value of output.

The sources of forced labor include political offenders, suspect engineers, intellectuals, and officials, kulaks and other recalcitrant peasants, deviating Communists, and members of

[125] See *Communism in Action*, pp. 56-57.

[126] For example, the statements of Russian delegate Tsarapkin to the Economic and Social Council in February 1949 in response to the charges made by the American Federation of Labor on this head. See article by Edwin L. James, "On Educational Value of the Russian Camps," in *New York Times*, Feb. 20, 1949, p. E-3.

national communities (for example, Volga Germans) whose loyalty is in doubt. The flow from these sources is large enough to provide the MVD with a surplus of labor to be farmed out to enterprises not under its direct administration. It is not clear whether the MVD trumps up charges against particular types of specialists whose skills are in special demand.[127] Prisoners are sometimes paid, but never at rates comparable to those for similar work outside. Yet the enterprises as a whole, and their components and individual workers are assigned comparable production norms. The result, according to Dallin, is great profit to some of these enterprises, and opportunity for the state to work with a minimum of capital investment and equipment.[128]

V. INTELLECTUAL FREEDOMS

Closely connected to the political and economic freedoms are the intellectual freedoms in modern society: the freedoms to educate and to be educated; to choose, to be trained for, and to pursue a skill of mind or hand; the freedom to shape individuality, and to prepare for participation in the life of society. Within any society there are limits to these freedoms; they are not absolute. They are conditioned by survival of the society itself, and in particular by survival and life on such terms that the precious freedoms can themselves exist and flourish. In Russia, however, these freedoms are conditioned not alone by the presumed requisites for the survival of communism in a hostile world; they are much more sharply conditioned by the nature of communist theory and communist society, and the dogmatism with which the Marxian all-inclusive "science" is brought to bear by power-specialists on the whole of life in Russia.

The "science" of Marxism is a curious combination, made up of elements of Western bourgeois philosophy, economics, and sociology of the mid-nineteenth century, which has come to

[127] *Communism in Action*, pp. 54-57.
[128] David J. Dallin and Boris I. Nicolaevsky, *Forced Labor in Soviet Russia* (1947), pp. 88-89.

possess for its adherents aspects of revealed truth, and a special quality of orthodoxy and authority because of the use made of it by the revolutionary Communists. It is not science in the sense known among the educated population of the Western world—a body of theory, observations, and generalizations or hypotheses which is capable of growth and change in any direction in which sound reasoning and correct and ever more precise and extensive observation takes it, untrammeled by any unchanging propositions except the correctness of its inner logic and method.

In communist practice, Marxist "science" has been turned into an instrument of totalitarian control, wielded for the current purpose of the ruling class. Marxism purports to be all-inclusive, covering all fields of philosophy, social behavior, science as commonly understood, and culture. It is materialist in the sense that material things are taken as fundamental. Systems of ideas, of law, religion, art, music, and literature are seen as "superstructures" erected on and governed by the economic relations of a society—the way in which economic production is carried on. In strict Marxian terms no system of ideas as such can be controlling on the "real" world; all ideas only reflect material reality. Yet in communist practice, the currently approved set of ideas—or interpretation of the effects material conditions are having on society—is taken as binding on every sphere of human activity.

Thus Marxism both potentially, and in Russian reality, is the deadliest instrument in the hands of a totalitarian elite against any intellectual freedom.

There have been changes in Marxism, due to the expansions and refinements of Lenin and Stalin; but these changes have been and can be made only by the rulers, and are made in such a way as to protect the authority of Marxism as the ultimate criterion for settling arguments. The party, and in particular its leaders, as the guardians of official interpretation and exegesis, use Marxism against any development in any field of science or the arts which they feel is contrary to the interests of the communist state or its rulers.

In some fields, the social sciences in particular, the Marxian orthodoxy always acted as a highly restrictive matrix. The writings of social scientists who wished to play it safe, were studded with references to the prophets of Marxism—Marx, Engels, Lenin, and Stalin—while showing a minimum of reference to the works pertinent to current technical research.[129] Until the latter part of the 1930's, there were areas of intellectual endeavor which were as a matter of practicality left largely alone by the Marxists; most of physics, biology, and other experimental science fell in this category. The arts would come under periodic stimulation or control, but had many opportunities for flowering.

But recent developments in the fields of music and genetics have demonstrated that it was only a matter of time before the rulers extended their domination over every sphere.

The reasons for this complete extension are difficult to fathom. It is hard to see, for example, why the communist leaders would adopt a doctrine in the field of genetics which is counter to the preponderance of Russian and of world scientific opinion, in favor of one which promises early gains and apparent compatibility with "materialism," but which may set back agricultural and economic progress by many decades. The reasons seem to include the following factors: a hag-riding security consciousness; the presumed urgency of a number of propaganda points; the necessity of gearing every function and resource within the state to the accomplishment of communist programs, and finally, the compulsive demand of the totalitarian leader to demonstrate dramatically his power over every phase of every form of activity within the society he controls.

Security consciousness leads the Russian leaders, trained almost from infancy in the skills of underground warfare against the established regime, to fear any group or function in society, however innocent on the surface, as a possible cover for dissi-

[129] Counts cites a Soviet psychology textbook published in 1946 which quotes no one but Marx, Engels, Lenin, and Stalin, except for a few references to the author's own works; and the names of the prophets are always printed in larger type than those of the author.

dence or counter-revolution. These leaders know what they would do if they had the problem of attacking their own regime; they leave no possibility unscanned or unscathed which might harbor discontent or revolt.

Soviet propaganda, whether at the level of Marxian dialectics or at the level of daily mass agitation and reiteration of dogma, insists with utmost parochialism on arrogating all intellectual progress first to Russia, then to communism. Any theory widespread in the bourgeois West is suspect for no other reason. The great sin for the contemporary Soviet scholar, writer, or artist, is to utilize Western theories, ideas, or forms, simply because they are Western. Hence there is a premium on the acceptance of any theory however shaky intellectually, if it denies Western views and seems to comport with the economic necessities and political dogma of the Communists.

Soviet propaganda must constantly echo and re-echo that Soviet science serves Russian progress and ministers to the needs of the Russian people; that Western science does no such thing; that only under communist conditions can science really be free to perform progressive societal functions.

The party finally demands conformity simply because it must have conformity. Any deviation, however unimportant to the progress of the regime or to the safety of the state, is condemned because it is deviation, and hence a challenge to the authority of Soviet power. No successful challenge in any area can be permitted; censorship and propaganda try to shield from the Russian citizen those instances in which Soviet power cannot rule everything, within or without the communist sphere.

Apparently the urgency of world struggle is so severe, in the communist view, that the party cannot allow anything to go on not demonstrably necessary for immediate results. The communists have apparently decided to forego the possibilities of major advances, possible only on the basis of a science freed from the trammels of proving itself today or tomorrow, in favor of the technical gains possible within the limits of known scientific knowledge. Furthermore, they have decided to forego even some of those gains if they depend on scientific principles or practices conspicuously identified with Western views. This may not be a crippling decision for a society which is so backward technologically that it has a long way to go before it has fully applied known science to its current processes, but it is hardly compatible with the Soviet emphasis on using every possible means to perfect its fighting effectiveness for a struggle with capitalist enemies which it considers inevitable. There remains the possibility that Soviet scientists may be permitted clandestinely to utilize theories and processes which the Soviet regime feels it must disavow to maintain propagandistic consistency for the public. It is much more probable, however, that the Soviet attacks represent deliberate and unrestrained intrusion into the sphere of proper scientific independence, and that the Politburo insists in controlling in the last analysis, the content as well as the conduct of science. The criterion of scientific value is not logically defensible, experimentally verifiable truth; it is public necessity as formulated by the party.

The Communists claim to have freed the life of the mind from the trammels of bourgeois society and from the limits imposed by bourgeois systems of production and consequent class domination and social relations. Communism has admittedly made vast strides against prerevolutionary Russian illiteracy, and has done much to bring out politically innocuous cultural richness in the multinational pattern of Russian society. The educational system was vastly expanded. After the liquidation of undesired classes at least a minimum of educational opportunity is open to all, and there is a chance through state support and scholarships for the student of ability who has influential backing to pursue his studies through the university.

Yet these strides have been taken, so to speak, for clearly defined and limited purposes, and the whole system operates within rigid regulation. Russia needed a new "intelligentsia"—managers, army officers, bureaucrats, teachers—who were politically safe if not technically competent; through her new educational system she has largely staffed herself with them, although Soviet "self-criticism" reveals that the levels of technical competence leave much to be desired. Education for literacy is always combined with indoctrination in correct political beliefs and attitudes, summed up in the slogan for Soviet school children: "I want to be like Stalin." The new attention to primitive peoples and their national cultures is similarly regulated by the slogan—"nationalist in form and socialist in content." Let the folk dances, the folk music, the folk poetry flourish, so long as there is no anti-communist dogma in them, and particularly if some Chechen-Ingush bard finds it in his poetic soul to compose new folk odes to Stalin. But folk practices of property ownership must come under socialist criticism, and nomadic tribes are apt to find themselves reorganized into collectives, overfulfilling norms for the production of karakul hides or yogurt. Finally, the new literacy allows the Soviet citizen to exercise his freedom to read what the Soviet propagandist is allowed to circulate, and to write what is permitted or encouraged by the state.

EDUCATIONAL FREEDOMS

Education, as other elements of communist society, went through an important transition during the period of consolidation of socialism in one country. During the 1920's, rights of education were restricted, especially for those of non-proletarian origin. With the inauguration of the first Five Year Plan, however, important changes were introduced: education was closely tied into the preparation of the country for industrialization. Previous "progressive" theories and practices were abandoned; the authority of the teacher and school administration over the pupil was sharply reasserted and increased. The content of curricula, teaching methods, and prescribed achievement were stiffened.

The 1936 Constitution called for universal education, and reaffirmed communist views concerning separation of church and school. Article 121 gives citizens of the USSR the right to education, ensuring it by

> . . . universal, compulsory elementary education; by education including higher education, being free of charge; by the system of

State stipends for the overwhelming majority of students in the universities and colleges; by instruction in schools being conducted in the native language, and by the organization in the factories, State farms, machine and tractor stations and collective farms of free vocational technical and agronomic training for the working people.

Article 124, in order to ensure "freedom of conscience," provides that "the church in the USSR is separated from the State, and the school from the church." The material support of education in the USSR is said to be more generous than in any other country in history.[130]

Control and administration of education is highly centralized in the USSR. The over-all directives are issued by the All-Union Council of Ministers. Uniformity is highly valued, so the Soviet student can move from school to school with a minimum of administrative and technical friction, but even more to see that no significant variation in doctrine or technique is allowed to creep into the educational apparatus. The party exercises watchful control, and any shortcomings in the educational sphere are sure to be the subject for party strictures, *mea culpas* from repentant administrators or teachers, and promises to strive to overcome shortcomings in the shortest possible time, so the goals of the current Five Year Plan may be achieved and its norms overfulfilled.[131]

This party and governmental supervision is coupled with a further aspect of Soviet emphasis: the concept that the entire machinery of the state, political, military, and economic, is in a sense an educational institution. Machine tractor stations and factories figure in the Soviet constitution as in Soviet practice as educational organs.

Education is a totalitarian instrument in Soviet Russia in more senses than one: totalitarian not only as an instrument for the achievement of national economic or social goals, but as a means for inculcating a basic morality which governs action in

[130] George S. Counts, "Remaking the Russian Mind," *Asia and the Americas* (October 1945), p. 479.

[131] See *Bulletin of Atomic Scientists* (May 1949), pp. 140, 156.

all spheres of life, and to which all types of educational efforts are devoted. Physical education is not confined to the development of bodily skills, but includes "the cultivation of communist morality and the traits of Bolshevik character in the pupils," and stresses militarily valuable aspects.[132] History is taught because of its "exceptional significance for the education of the growing generation in communism."[133] Aesthetics is similarly bent to inculcate communism, and to nurture hatred toward present enemies of communism and those vestiges of the past which impede its fruition. Examples used in teaching mathematics are chosen, for example, in such fashion as to "teach pupils to save state pennies in industry and daily life, or which instruct in the application of mathematical knowledge to military affairs."[134]

Given such sharply defined objectives and comprehensive application of them, it is easy to see why curricula and their contents are rigidly prescribed, and the freedom of the student to seek subject and content is restricted. It is too much to say that no anti-communist views are allowed in Soviet schools; they are: but only in prescribed form, and in conjunction with overbalancing counterassertions of communist orthodoxy.[135] Deviation from prescribed texts and courses runs the risk of punishment for counter-revolutionary activity; it is useless to look for much leeway within which the Soviet teacher can exercise initiative.[136]

Some educational specialization is of course open to the Soviet teacher or scientist, because of his special capacities and

[132] See the translation made by George S. Counts and Nucia P. Lodge of excerpts from the Russian text on pedogogy written by B. P. Yesipov and N. K. Goncharov under the title *I Want to be Like Stalin,* (1947), pp. 7 ff.

[133] The same. The quotations are from the translated original.

[134] The same.

[135] Vyshinsky's work on *The Law of the Soviet State,* for example, is full of "bourgeois" and anti-communist dogma and information (although it is hardly accurate or representative of the reality of non-communist thought and environment), included as a means of pointing contrasts held favorable to the Soviet side, and as a means of inoculating the Russian student against the virus of a non-communist point of view.

[136] See the same, pp. 13-20.

the need of the state for competent technicians. But, according to Stalin,

> There is one branch of science whose knowledge must be compulsory for all Bolsheviks of all branches of science—this is the Marxist-Leninist science of society, of the laws of development of society, of the laws of development of the proletarian revolution, of the victory of communism. For it is imposible to consider him a genuine Leninist, who calls himself a Leninist, but who is cloistered, let us say, in mathematics, botany, or chemistry, and who sees nothing beyond his specialty.[137]

The results of this great intellectual endeavor of indoctrination have been great and striking. They are signalized by Stalin's announcement at the 18th Party Congress of the creation of a new Soviet intelligentsia, "intimately bound up with the people and, for the most part, ready to serve them faithfully and loyally."[138] It must be noted that the other noneducational factor (unless taken in the sense of a tremendous example) in this creation of a new and trustworthy intelligentsia, was threat and violence to the old intelligentsia, culminating in the great purges of 1935-38.[139]

RESEARCH

Freedom of research in the totalitarian state is limited not only by ideological censorship, but by controls over the provision of essential materials, equipment, skilled and unskilled assistance, and over the work and leisure time of the potential researcher himself. Science in the Soviet Union is avowedly and indissolubly connected with and controlled by politics.[140] In a state where all instruments of production are owned and

[137] Quoted in Counts and Lodge, *"I Want to be Like Stalin,"* p. 12.

[138] Stalin, Report to the 18th Party Congress, p. 76, cited in Towster, *Political Power in the U.S.S.R.*, p. 44.

[139] See Bienstock, Schwarz, and Yugow, *Management in Russian Industry and Agriculture,* pp. 104-09, 120.

[140] See "A Reply to Professor H. J. Muller," by the Presidium of the Academy of Sciences of the USSR, in *Pravda,* Dec. 14, 1948 (translated in *Soviet Press Translations,* Jan. 15, 1949, pp. 47-48), which says in part: "We, the Soviet scientists, are convinced that the entire experience of history teaches that there does not exist and cannot exist in the world a science divorced from politics. The fundamental question is with what kind of politics science is connected, whose interests it serves—the interests of the people or the interests of the exploiters."

managed by the state, it is unthinkable to carry on any research beyond that which an individual, working without specialized or extensive resources, can perform. Since exploitation is defined as economic control of one individual over another, research is limited to the scope of voluntary collaboration under ever-present and all-surrounding restrictions. In a state which has resources small compared to its requirements; which is obsessed with the achievement of specified national economic and military goals; which is equipped with an all-pervasive control and surveillance mechanism, it is obvious that all research of any significance will be controlled by the state, and will be bent to politically established time schedules and urgencies. This in practice means emphasis on technological application rather than fundamental research, unless research of the latter sort is so obviously connected to national survival as to warrant a large outlay of resources and skilled personnel—as, for example, the case of nuclear energy. And even here it is suspected that more emphasis goes to immediate defense, offense, or industrial applications than to further fundamental inquiry.

Both from the ideological and the economic points of view, research in the Soviet Union comes under political domination —in particular that of the party leadership and bureaucracy. The tragedy of Soviet research is not so much that it is directed into channels considered urgent by the state; it is that scientific conclusions are dictated not by the conclusions and reasons of trained observers considering relevant evidence, but by political leaders applying conclusions from Marxist-Stalinist principles.[141] The effect on scientific inquiry is stultifying, making sycophants out of potentially independent intellects. This is particularly true in the fields of history[142] and politics, where the task of the

[141] See H. J. Muller, "Back to Barbarism, Scientifically," *Saturday Review of Literature*, Vol. 31, Dec. 11, 1948, p. 9. See also the series of articles in the May 1949 issue of the *Bulletin of Atomic Scientists*, Vol. 5, No. 5.

[142] The most striking evidence of this is found in official complaints over shortcomings in Soviet historical research. Soviet historians do not touch the Soviet period (they do not dare to); and membership in the Historical Institute of the Academy of Sciences has become an "anteroom," where scholars do not stay. See D. Erde, "The Academy of Sciences Ignores the History of the USSR," in *Literaturnaya Gazeta*, Oct. 2, 1948 (translated and reprinted) in *Soviet Press Translations*, Nov. 15, 1948, pp. 611-12.

scholar is to find and apply texts from authority to cover the current line as laid down by the party, and to explain away, to blanket, or to suppress earlier statements of doctrine which are no longer expedient or flattering, fashionable or safe. The major work is done by the political leaders: Stalin himself wrote the *Short History of the CPSU (b)*,[143] and recast the major lines of Russian history to eliminate early communist errors, to suppress the deeds of early heroes who fell afoul of Stalin in later years, and to re-establish connections with Russian sources of traditional patriotism and love of motherland. Of the subordinates, those survive who correctly interpret the trends and make the right choices. Those who are wrong, and persist in their error, are dropped; those who are willing to make their intellectual peace with the regime are publicly shamed, demoted, switched to other work, or kept from the limelight for a time. This latter alternative has become increasingly used, as it conserves specialists, and makes it possible for the elite to signalize changes in line by putting forward or retracting exponents of differing views.

The dramatic controversy in Soviet genetics which came to a head in July and August of 1948 after festering for some years, illustrates more clearly than any abstractions the nature of Soviet control over scientific activity.[144] The role of biology is important to the party because "Biology is immediately bound up with the solution of the historic problem of creating an abundance of products in our country."[145] For some years Soviet

[143] Issued first in 1938 as a fundamental directive text outlining the accepted version of the establishment of communism in Russia and the whole related series of developments in Russia and abroad; issued postwar as a reiteration of orthodox doctrine in editions of millions of copies. See Historicus, *Foreign Affairs*, pp. 176 ff.

[144] For the Soviet report, see the authoritative article by I. Laptev in *Pravda*, Sept. 11, 1948: "The Triumph of Mitchurin Biological Science," as translated in *Soviet Press Translations*, Dec. 15, 1948, pp. 686-94. For an account by an American geneticist of world reputation, who had worked closely with Soviet geneticists in Russia and here, see H. J. Muller, "The Destruction of Science in the USSR," *Saturday Review of Literature*, Vol. 31, No. 49, Dec. 4, 1948, pp. 13 ff; and his "Back to Barbarism—Scientifically," in the following issue, pp. 8-10.

[145] Laptev, *Soviet Press Translations*, Dec. 15, 1948, p. 687.

geneticists had been arguing the relative merits of generally accepted theories of heredity (those stemming from Mendel and Morgan) and those advanced first by a Soviet plant breeder, I. V. Michurin (now dead) and later by T. D. Lysenko. The scientific merits of the argument (set forth succinctly by Muller) do not interest us here so much as the role assigned to biology in the Soviet system, and the fact that in the last analysis, a scientific argument is decided in the Soviet Union not on the basis of scientifically relevant and acceptable data and reasoning, but by decision of the Communist party. The argument did not take the form of the correctness of conclusions from fully reported data, experimental procedures, observations, and reasoning. The controversy was officially viewed as an "intense ideological struggle . . . between materialism and idealism on questions pertaining to knowledge and the changing world," taking place between "the progressive and materialistic [trends], as represented by the *Michurin* school . . . and the reactionary, idealistic, represented by the *Weismann* (Mendel-Morgan) school. . . ."

At the meeting's sessions, Laptev reports, holders of the Weismann-Morgan views attempted to defend them against the arguments and "facts" advanced by the supporters of the Michurin school. These were overborne by "rebuttal"; three of the Weismannites recanted, and at the conclusion of the session, Lysenko pointed out that the Central Committee of the Communist Party had read and approved his report. "This statement evoked a storm of applause which became an ovation. All rose to their feet, greeting with enormous enthusiasm the great friend and coryphaeus of science, our leader and teacher, Comrade Stalin."[146] The example from Soviet genetics is only illustrative of methods of control already extended to most areas of Soviet science, and a forerunner of sharper controls over fields now comparatively free.[147]

[146] The same, p. 694.

[147] For example, a letter to Stalin from the Presidium of the Academy of Medical Sciences of the USSR, appearing in *Pravda* on Sept. 15, 1948, says in part:

MUSIC, LITERATURE, AND THE ARTS

Soviet control over the arts, as control over other phases of intellectual life, has gone through several developmental periods, in which censorship and controls of varying scope and rigor have been exercised. During the great patriotic war, when all efforts in all fields were bent to survival, it was demonstrated how much could be done to control all aspects of the fields of literature and art. After the war, the degree of control rose higher, if anything, because of the urgent efforts of the party to reaffirm doctrinal unity and faith and to extirpate the infection carried to those large numbers of Russians who were exposed directly to capitalist society. Postwar orthodoxy was signalized by the drive commenced by Zhdanov in August of 1946[148] to impose new and sharper discipline over the entire field of the arts. Zhdanov undertook to enforce with fresh fanaticism the communist tenet that it is not enough for artistic expression to be ideologically neutral, to be permitted. Art must serve a positive, creative purpose in the scheme of state development: it must advance communist doctrine, build fervor for communist programs, attack all bourgeois "slanders." But art must give no expression whatsoever to any phase of the people's weariness or discontent with their leaders or their lot.[149]

No artist is too great or secure in his own field to escape the party lash: the cases of discipline administered to Prokofiev,

---

"We promise you, our dear leader, to rectify in the shortest possible time the mistakes we have permitted to occur, and to reconstruct our scientific work in the spirit of the directives issued by the great Party of Lenin and Stalin. We promise you to master fully the great Mitchurin teaching and to utilize it for the further development of Soviet medicine." *Soviet Press Translations,* Jan. 15, 1949, pp. 48-49.

[148] See "Purge of the Arts set in Leningrad," *New York Times,* Aug. 23, 1946.

[149] See Sam Welles, *Profile of Europe* (1948), p. 75. Zhdanov's directive speech reads in part: "Imperialists and their ideological lackeys, their literatures and journalists, their politicians and diplomats, seek by all means to slander our country, to present it in a false light, to slander socialism.

"Under these conditions, the task of Soviet literature is not only to reply blow for blow to all this foul slander and attacks on our Soviet culture, on socialism, but boldly to flay and attack bourgeois culture." Quoted by Edmund Stevens in *Christian Science Monitor,* May 6, 1947.

Shostakovich, and Khachaturyan in music are matters of world knowledge, and were accepted at least to the point where these artists confessed error, admitted rightful subordination to the dictates of the party, and promised better performance in future.[150] The Soviet writers Zotschenko and Akhmatova, although not so well known to the outside world as their musical co-culprits, were viciously condemned by the Central Committee, and their works taken as examples to point up the campaign of the party to stiffen control over Soviet arts.[151]

The official role of Soviet literature, according to an authoritative *Pravda* article of August 21, 1946, is as follows: Soviet literature "cannot have any other interests outside those of the people and the State. The tasks of Soviet literature consist of helping the State to properly educate youth, to respond to the needs of youth, to train a new generation, vigorous and confident in its cause, unafraid of obstacles and prepared to surmount all obstacles." With this directive the party declared war on "art for art's sake." Whatever evanescent freedoms may have been won for the arts by being freed through communist revolution from bourgeois or aristocratic trammels, or by service to

[150] During 1945, musical artists were operating under a decree of the Politburo directing Soviet composers to "purify music along the lines of simple rhythm to which workers can beat time and hum as they try to accelerate production." Shostakovich, in replying to a Party criticism, said, "I know the Party is right, that the Party wishes me well and that I must search and find concrete creative roads which will lead me toward a realistic Soviet people's art." Kenneth Campbell, "Shostakovich in Soviet Delegation to Attend Arts Conference Here," quoted in *New York Times,* Feb. 21, 1948, pp. 1, 6.

[151] See Drew Middleton: "Russian Magazine Ordered to Close," *New York Times,* Aug. 22, 1946. Middleton quotes from an article appearing first in *Culture and Life* (published by the Propaganda and Agitation Committee of the Central Committee of the Party) on Aug. 20, and reprinted in *Pravda* the next day. "Our journals, be they scientific or artistic, cannot be nonpolitical and stand aside from politics." A literary magazine *Zvezda* (Star), published in Leningrad, was severely castigated and given a new editor, because of its "gross errors" in publishing works of the now-proscribed Zotschenko, and including in its pages "many ideal-less and ideologically harmful articles." Both writers were criticized for the harmful effects of their "decadent, hooligan" works on Soviet youth. Both *Zvezda* and *Leningrad* were critized for "worship of everything foreign," for disseminating ideological confusion, and cultivating "a spirit of worship of modern bourgeois culture alien to the Soviet people."

the state as evoker of loyalty, patriotism, and superhuman national efforts during the war, are now overmastered by the decision of the party. The party sets the line, and determines what art must celebrate or criticize, when, and for how long.[152]

VI. FREEDOM OF SPEECH AND THE PRESS

It is only a short step, or no step at all from Soviet control over education, art, music, and literature to all-out control of speech and press in the Soviet Union. What special and very limited freedom exists in these fields rests on Marxist, Leninist, and materialist grounds: it consists in the freedom of approved individuals or organizations in the socialist state from the domination of capitalists and the bourgeoisie, coupled with the state provision to approved organizations only of the material means of publication or expression.[153] But most emphatically it is not a genuine freedom for any individual or organization to publish what he pleases short of criminal libel or public indecency. Nor is it free of state control both of the content of

[152] The pattern of party control of the arts during the revolutionary period as a whole is set forth in George Reavey, *Soviet Literature Today* (1947). Reavey points out the periods in which control has been manifest and direct (exercised through the Union of Proletarian Writers), and those in which it has been comparatively relaxed. The present note combines emphasis on Soviet Humanism and Socialist Realism, which together state the tasks of Soviet art. "Socialist Realism, being the fundamental method of Soviet artistic literature and literary criticism, demands of the artists a truthful, historico-concrete portrayal of *reality in its revolutionary development*. In this connection, the truthfulness and the historical concreteness of the artistic portrayal must take into account the problem of *ideological transformation* and *education of the workers* in the spirit of Socialism." (Pp. 19-20.) Modernism is ruled out by the principle that "art must be comprehensible to the people" (p. 22, citing Ioganson), and by rejecting "any art that is abstract, mechanical or experimental for its own sake, and which does not throw into prominence the human passions and the social background." P. 23.

[153] Article 125 of the 1936 Constitution reads: "In conformity with the interests of the working people, and in order to strengthen the socialist system, the citizens of the USSR are guaranteed by law: (a) Freedom of speech; (b) Freedom of the press; (c) Freedom of Assembly, including the holding of mass meetings; (d) Freedom of street processions and demonstrations. These civil rights are ensured by placing at the disposal of the working people and their organizations, printing presses, stocks of paper, public buildings, the streets, communications, facilities and other material requisites for the exercise of these rights."

publications and of the provision and manner of use of the material requisites therefor.

Party directives and surveillance ensure control of content; Soviet accounting and control of economic activity assure control of the availability and use of printing presses, stocks of paper, and the other "material requisites."

There are two agencies by which party control of the content of all publications is exercised, formal and informal; of these the informal is the more effective and severe. Formally, the law establishes a main office for literary and publication business, the *Glavlit,* to carry out "all kinds of political and ideological, military, and economic control of printed matters, manuscripts, photographs, pictures, etc., destined for publication or circulation and of radio messages, lectures and exhibitions."[154] This office exercises formal control by pre- and post-publication censorship, in order to limit works to those which actively contribute to current government purposes. Some evidence exists, however, to suggest that the *Glavlit* is more like a proofreader than a censor, because of the tremendous power of the informal directive system, and of the indirect controls over persons engaged in publishing activities of any sort.

In the Soviet totalitarian system, no writer can ever safely take his eyes off Stalin. His views set the sacrosanct limits to the treatment of anything to which they may conceivably apply. No writer can transgress them save at his professional and personal peril. Stalin's words are dutifully and immediately echoed and reiterated by every organ throughout the land, and used as final authority on every conceivable topic. Immediately below Stalin are a number of pundits, such as Molotov and Zhdanov (before his death), whose words are of almost equal authority, and whose pronouncements are always scanned for the correct interpretation of what Stalin has said. Comparable in influence are the authoritative publications, *Pravda* ("Truth"—organ of the Communist party) and *Izvestia* ("News"—organ of the All-Union Government). Several party organizations have their

[154] RSFSR Laws 1932, text 288, sec. 3, subsec. 6, quoted in Gsovski, *Soviet Civil Law,* p. 65.

own journals such as *Culture and Life* (organ of the Propaganda and Agitation Committee of the Central Committee of the Communist party) which are particularly important in setting the directive line for all publications. The regional party and government papers (such as Leningrad's *Pravda* and *Izvestia*) perform intermediate directive functions, applying centrally stated dogma to local situations. Other specialized journals take up items of particular relevance to special groups, such as *Trud* (for the trade unions), the service papers (*Krasnaya Zvezda*—Red Star, the Army journal; *Krasny Flot*—Red Fleet; etc.), and the Literary Gazette *(Literaturnaya Gazeta)*. In the field of books, authoritative doctrine is stated in the *Short History of the CPSU (b)*, Stalin's *Problems of Leninism*, the authoritative state-edited editions of the works of Marx, Engels, and Lenin; and reprints from time to time of especially important directive statements of the party leadership to party congresses.[155]

Soviet authors of all types of writing—scientific, technical, literary, educational—pay the closest attention to these basic dogmas, and lighten the load of the *Glavlit* by seeing to it that

[155] Especially in the field of books, the directive role of this literature is described by Historicus, "Stalin on Revolution," *Foreign Affairs*, January 1949, pp. 175-214, especially pp. 175-77. With respect to the *Short History*, S. Petrov, in *Izvestia*. Oct. 1, 1948, says: "The appearance of J. V. Stalin's classic work, A Short History of the ACP (b)* was an event of universal and historic significance. . . . The book provides a scientific history of Bolshevism and sets forth and generalizes the enormous experience of the All-Union Communist Party (Bolsheviks), the equal of which no other party in the world has ever possessed. . . . [the Short History] sets forth the history of the Bolshevik Party in the light of the development of the fundamental theses of Marxist-Leninist doctrine and educates our cadres in the ideas of Marxism-Leninism. . . . [it] sets forth the theory of Marxism-Leninism as the only well-balanced doctrine which embraces in full the philosophy, history and political economy, as well as the ideological, organizational, tactical, and theoretical principles of the proletarian party. *(Soviet Press Translations*, Feb. 15, 1949, pp. 115-16.) [*The abbreviation ACP (b), All-Union Communist Party (bolsheviks) is often used in English translations as an equivalent for the abbreviation CPSU (b): Communist party of the Soviet Union (bolsheviks). Official Soviet publications in English use both forms; they are interchangeable.]

For a thumbnail sketch of the current Soviet press, see Robert Kleiman, "Role of the Russian Press," in *World Report*, Oct. 21, 1947, pp. 22-23; based on ten weeks' first-hand observation.

nothing is submitted which the author himself has not done his best to keep in line with accepted doctrine. In the Soviet system, survival depends on ideological correctness. The author can lose position, career, safety and comfort, or life if he gives his competitors grounds to charge him with deviation. Hence he lashes out only when he is absolutely sure of his ground, and writes nothing outside of current orthodoxy.

The controls over access to equipment and materials complete the machinery of direction. Facilities for printing are in fact confined to the party, to the government, and to publicly created and controlled organizations. Printing offices of any kind, including mimeographing or hectographing processes "may be opened only by government agencies, cooperatives, and public organizations"; and only such organizations may trade in printing equipment.[156] All agencies, including government agencies, except the Communist party, *Izvestia,* and the Academy of Sciences, are controlled by the *Glavlit* and must account strictly for all paper and typemetal used.[157] These controls over publications are the counterbalance to the formal rights of copyright and compensation assured by Soviet law to authors. An author may not publish his own work nor may he employ a private publisher to do it for him. He is forced to turn to the state-licensed enterprise,[158] which may contract to publish his work, and always pays at least a minimum honorarium; but the government may order publication without the author's consent.[159]

Soviet censorship extends to foreign writers in the USSR, especially to correspondents of foreign publications. Says Welles:

[156] Law of 1932, quoted in Gsovski, *Soviet Civil Law,* pp. 64-65.

[157] The same, pp. 65-66. The excepted agencies maintain internal controls of equal or greater severity.

[158] The same, p. 614. Gsovski quotes a Soviet textbook of 1944 as follows: "An author in the U.S.S.R. does not have any monopoly in his work and does not need it; if the work deserves wide circulation the socialist society will be also interested therein. As any other toiler, the author has the right to remuneration in accordance with the quality and quantity of his labor, if the product of his labor is used by society." The same, p. 615.

[159] The same, pp. 615-16.

> The Kremlin has a standing rule against the sending of any information from Russia which it thinks might hurt Russian interests in any way. . . . Anyone reading a news despatch or hearing a radio item datelined "Russia" should always remember that the censor may have cut its guts out—or that the correspondent, knowing it would be cut there, eliminated some material before he sent it to the censor.[160]

This freedom to write and transmit news is reinforced by Soviet restrictions on the movement and travel of foreign correspondents within the USSR, and in general on their access to news sources. In practice, foreign correspondents are limited to "approved areas" or to guided tours. Soviet citizens are so afraid of reprisal that the foreign correspondent has great difficulty in developing news sources independent of official channels.[161] Soviet isolation from abroad, and choking and channeling communication to or from Russia, seems indispensable to the Russian rulers as a means of safeguarding socialism from bourgeois error or imperialist attack.

Freedom of assembly, or "freedom of the streets," is a hangover in Soviet law and propaganda from the days when the Marxist parties were struggling for power; they merely assert the rights of these parties to bourgeois freedoms denied them by Tsarist suppression. They do not establish the right of any group not approved by the Communists to use public buildings for protest meetings, to demonstrate in the streets, or in any other way to exercise by right the forms of political assembly and action the Communists used on their road to power.

VII. SUMMARY

In the preceding sections we have examined in some detail the position of the individual in Soviet Russia, with respect to his status and scope in the political, social and religious, economic and intellectual fields. In the political fields, we found that the individual as such can wield insignificant influence. Either as a citizen, or as a member of the ruling party, his

[160] Welles, *Profile of Europe,* p. 86.
[161] See Robert Magidoff, *In Anger and Pity* (1949).

political freedom is overwhelmed by the hierarchical and authoritarian organization of government and party. He can express his opinion only at the risk of safety and career—not only his own, but those of his family as well. He is the victim of a system in which directives come from the top, and the role of the individual is at best that of an enthusiastic executor of orders from above. He has no choice among political parties, nor is he free to found one of his own. The fate of the traitor awaits any who would try. He can vote in public to ratify the slate of political officers chosen for him by the party. Afterward he can vote in secret, either to confirm the party's choice, or to spoil his ballot. He can recall public officers, only if he and his fellows think the officer in question has not displayed enough alacrity in carrying out the orders of the regime. The persons he elects most directly, the members of the Supreme Soviet, are in fact without effective powers to control the collegial presidency (the Presidium) or the real center of administrative power (the Council of Ministers). The individual has no power to control the membership or the hierarchical construction of the ruling elite, the Communist party. Only as a member of a passive and disgruntled mass can he hope to slow down, or possibly to shift the course of state.

Despite classic Marxist views on the injustice of political power and on the automatic withering away of the state, the individual in Russia lives under a state power as total as that of Czarist Russia or of modern dictatorships. State power is always superior to individual judgment and individual dignity. Hence, state power is so organized that no over-all checks limit it on behalf of the individual and no internal checks keep organs of government within their proper sphere. The state is bound by no rule of law, which would assure to the individual that state power will be kept in previously stated channels and exercised according to previously authorized methods. The Soviet Constitution is not a constitution in a Western sense, but a record of the state of political affairs achieved by the communist revolution. As such, it is never a barrier to government action, hence never a protection of the economic, social, or political position of the individual. Now that all classes inimical to the proletariat have been liquidated, class distinctions have all but disappeared from the law, with one exception: a party member, because of his position in the vanguard, can expect more severe punishment than would be meted out to an ordinary worker or peasant for a given crime. However, prior to this liquidation, courts were used as the instruments of revolutionary class justice. Courts in Russia are never instruments for preserving the constitutional freedoms of the individual, or the position of the individual against the government. Courts are political instrumentalities of the government used to accomplish those purposes of state for which the ruling elite deems them most appropriate.

In the social and religious spheres, we found the individual completely regulated according to the principle that no organization may exist in the communist state which is not authorized and supervised by the regime. There is no freedom to organize voluntary groups for any purpose whatsoever—sport, travel, or any other purpose however innocuous by the standards of the free society. On the contrary, every voluntary group is used in one way or another for the purposes of the state. Leisure time is appropriated for purposes of state propaganda. Vacations are awarded as part of the system of incentives and rewards designed to call forth maximum disciplined economic effort.

The Constitution of 1936 guarantees to the individual the right of religious worship, and to the state the right of antireligious propaganda. The individual or his religious group may not engage in proselytizing, or in any activity, charitable or educational, which is outside the immediate realm of worship, according to strict Soviet law. In practice, religion enjoys more freedom than this in Russia, because of the expedient interest of the state in utilizing religion for internal stability and foreign aggression. Yet all organized religious groups are supervised by state officials, and church organizations depend for their material necessities upon the state.

All these policies exemplify an underlying strategy of all modern totalitarian systems: to deny the individual any chance to use any part of his time or any organizational device as a withdrawal from the state, or potential revolt against it.

In the economic sphere, the freedoms of the individual are completely hedged in by the invariant state ownership, control, or operation of all significant forms of economic activity, and by total state control over the individual movements and group life of every person. No individual may employ ("exploit") another. Some forms of property have been allowed to the individual, and particularly in connection with agriculture. Some rights of inheritance have grown up during the Soviet period after the economic base of the old propertied classes had been smashed. However, the state insists that to eat, one must work, and the most coveted economic rewards are reserved for those who hold important positions. The ousted incumbent loses the perquisites with his job, and in most cases the perquisites are equally or more important than prestige or money income. The regime does not hesitate to threaten the loss of job and position both as a spur to vigorous action and as an instrument ensuring rigid compliance with orders.

The manager can work only for one employer: the state. The workers, in most occupations, are tied to their jobs. Neither worker nor manager can move without permission of state authorities.

The worker enjoys none of the freedoms of organization, striking, or collective bargaining allowed in free societies. Not only is there no freedom to organize labor groups independently of the state, or to use the strike or other weapons of industrial struggle against the state; such action is treason, and punished by death. As to collective bargaining, the trade union has no influence whatsoever on the major economic decisions which govern wage rates, working hours, and working conditions. As a sort of incentive and morale group, the trade union can work with local managers to improve working conditions and factory amenities within the limits set by government directives.

Finally, the economic sphere in Russia exhibits the characteristic feature of the police state: forced labor. Dissidents of all lands and classes being punished with less than death for all sorts of transgressions against the regime, are drained of labor and often of life for roads, canals, reclamation, fortification, and many other enterprises the state wishes to conduct with maximum security and minimum material cost. The human costs are negligible because the dissident's life is forfeit anyway.

The basic economic decisions governing the functions of the manager, the workers, and the consumer are made centrally by the top policy deciding organs of the Communist party. Now and for the foreseeable future, these decisions are not made in the interest of the manager, the worker, or least of all of the consumer as such; they are made according to the judgment of the politburo to meet politico-military requirements.

In the intellectual sphere we have grouped education, scientific inquiry, art and culture, and freedom of speech and the press. Here as elsewhere in totalitarian Russia we find the individual has little scope for choice or unchanneled initiative. The whole educational system operates under detailed state management, as dictated by the Communist party. Not only the normal fields of propagandist penetration are taken over for the transmission of indoctrination desired by the state, but all other fields are penetrated to assure conformity to currently interpreted Marxist orthodoxy. But the state does not stop with the content of courses; it directs individuals into lines of training and determines their careers. As to scientific research, the individual researcher is limited in two ways. First, he is completely dependent on the state for the material means of research. Any inquiry requiring more than the simplest materials or beyond the capacity of an individual worker, runs inevitably into state control. Since the state dominates the leisure time of every worker, it is hardly feasible for a scientific worker in his spare time to look into matters which are not part of his state-delimited job. Research as a whole is directed according to state-determined priorities, toward state-evaluated projects. There is no freedom to undertake research for purely scientific purposes. All outlays of materials or personal time must serve ends which directly and immediately further the current program of the regime.

In the spheres of art and culture, just as in the spheres of science, there is no freedom for the artist to indulge in art for art's sake. All forms of art—music, painting, sculpture, architecture, and so forth—must be constantly bent to the achievement of the current urgencies of the regime. Progress or modernism in any of these forms is condemned and criticized from two points of view: the artistically conservative standards insisted upon by the party, and state security. Artists and musicians must be allowed no freedom of independent expression outside the areas approved by the party; they might be cover organizations for dissidence, and might by their example of independence encourage dissatisfaction and potential rebellion among other groups. "Westernism" is both an affront and threat to the state.

Finally, in the spheres of freedom of speech and publication, there is claimed to exist a formal freedom recognized in Russia's constitution; in reality, there is no freedom of speech or publication whatsoever. Every form of public assembly, every form of public utterance is controlled by the regime. The informer, the secret police, the government official, the party member all work to guarantee purity in those spheres which are not sanitated in advance by government operation or censorship. The sanctions of loss of job, public defamation, pain to family, forced labor or exile, or death await the deviant.

Remaining supporters of Russian communism try to establish essential differences between Russia and other modern totalitarian systems, in that communism is fundamentally democratic, serving the interest of the whole people. Yet our foregoing analysis shows that the dictatorship of the proletariat leaves no part of human action outside its control; there is no prospect, moreover, that this dictatorship will disappear. We shall see from our examination of the impact of other major totalitarian states on individuals that there is no fundamental difference in the purposes or extent of control. Details may vary, but the scope of state action in all these systems is the same: it is unlimited. The position of individuals under each may vary with economic class, racial or national origin. But the facts will indicate that no individual as such in any of these systems can set up his judgment or his dignity against the purposes of the collectivity as articulated by the worshipped leader.

CHAPTER V

FASCISM IN ITALY

This chapter covers modern totalitarianism as it appeared in Italy following the communist seizure of power by five years, and antedating the Nazi seizure by eleven. The Fascist period is useful to our over-all purposes both in its theoretical and in its practical aspects. The fascist theory represents the clearest and most straightforward denial of the liberal and individualist position, and makes most baldly its claims for the supremacy of the state over the individual.

The fact that Italian practice revealed a somewhat less violent, ruthless, and thoroughgoing application of this supremacy to all phases of the nation's life, and the fact that fascism enjoyed a very large measure of public acceptance in Italy, do not vitiate the essential virulence of the theory or alter the tendency of totalitarian control. The Italian theories served as a prototype for the German Nazis, and it remained for the Germans to work them out and apply them with unremitting energy and completeness. Certain vagueness in the languages of the Communist and of the Nazi may obscure the essential values given to state supremacy: the Communist speaks of his state as a class instrument, now operating as an instrument of the proletariat; the Nazi in speaking of the state usually means the administrative apparatus of government. But the Fascist speaks for all of them when he refers to the state as an all-encompassing entity, an absolute before which all individuals are subordinate and relative, and an institution whose interests and claims always override those of any constituent body, natural or artificial.

I. INTRODUCTION

Fascist theory may be modified by certain aspects of fascist history and practice. The object of the Fascist—in particular, Mussolini—was power. The biography of Mussolini demonstrates clearly that for him all ideology was useful mainly as an instrument for propaganda in the struggle to seize and hold power; his speeches unblushingly point to the fact that the early program and policies of the Fascist party were not definite and clear, but were formulated during the struggle as instruments of action.[1] The most sophisticated of the intellectual apologists for fascism, Giovanni Gentile, asserted at the philosophical level that truth is defined only by action; Mussolini both affirmed the proposition and acted on it. Yet the ideology thus shaped by action and the conditions of successful political struggle left no scope to the individual or the component group within the state. The Communists, in their effort to distinguish their own totalitarianism from fascist collectivism, claim that fascism is the political form assumed by decadent monopoly capitalism. A review of the history of fascist control shows that the capitalist, equally with the other classes in society, was dominated by the politician exercising controls to maximize the power of the state for war.

It is essential also to grasp this fundament of fascist theory—the complete, conscious rejection of individualism and liberalism, and the complete, conscious assertion of the supremacy of the state. From this principle all other essential elements of fascism follow. From a pragmatic point of view, the only consistent modifier as to rate and thoroughness of application was Mussolini's judgment as to how fast he could go, and what he could do while retaining and increasing his power.

Two classic fascist formulas gave the limits within which the individual could expect to play a role in politics, or in any other phase of life. The Charter of Labor stated:

> The Italian nation is an organism having ends, life, and means of action superior to those of the separate individuals or groups of individuals that compose it. It is a moral, political, and economic unity integrated in the Fascist State.[2]

[1] See Gaudens Megaro, *Mussolini in the Making* (1938). See also Mussolini, "Political and Social Doctrine," *Fascism* (1935), *pp.* 15-31.

[2] Art. 1 of the Charter of Labor, promulgated by the Grand Council on Apr. 21, 1927.

The Scala formula, issued by Mussolini, read: "Everything in the State, nothing against the State, nothing outside the State."[3] In the words of one of its major philosophers,

> . . . For Fascism, society is the end, individuals the means, and its whole life consists in using individuals as instruments for its social ends. The state therefore guards and protects the welfare and development of individuals not for their exclusive interest, but because of the identity of the needs of individuals with those of society as a whole. . . .[4]

Fascism explicitly rejected the welfare state, although certain concessions to individual well-being are found in its structure. Rather it appealed to the person to "live dangerously" and to find in devotion and sacrifice spiritual rewards which transcend the material benefits offered by the liberal or socialist systems.[5]

II. POLITICAL FREEDOMS

Fascism was explicitly antidemocratic, antimajoritarian, and antiparliamentarian. Fascism did not claim to abolish individual rights, but to leave the individual only those freedoms which were good for him—and in any case of doubt, it would be the state, not the individual that would decide the limiting points.[6] As to the political capacity of the masses, and as basis

[3] Mussolini, *Fascism* (1935), p. 40.

[4] Alfredo Rocco, "The Political Doctrine of Fascism," Carnegie Endowment for International Peace, *International Conciliation* (1926), p. 403.

[5] The same, p. 8 and following. Note: "Fascism sees in the world not only those superficial, material aspects in which man appears as an individual, standing by himself, self-centered, subject to natural law which instinctively urges him toward a life of selfish momentary pleasure; it sees not only the individual but the nation and the country; individuals and generations bound together by a moral law, with common traditions and a mission which suppressing the instinct for life closed in a brief circle of pleasure, builds up a higher life, founded on duty, a life free from the limitations of time and space, in which the individual, by self-sacrifice, the renunciation of self-interest, by death itself, can achieve that purely spiritual existence in which his value as a man consists."

[6] Said Mussolini: "Far from crushing the individual, the Fascist State multiplies his energies . . . The Fascist State organises the nation, but it leaves the individual adequate elbow room. It has curtailed useless or harmful liberties while preserving those which are essential. In such matters, the individual cannot be the judge, but the State only." *Fascism*, pp. 29-30.

for its expression of a form of leadership-principle, Fascist doctrine claimed:

> Fascism is . . . opposed to that form of democracy which equates a nation to the majority, lowering it to the level of the largest number; but it is the purest form of democracy if the nation be considered—as it should be—from the point of view of quality rather than quantity, as an idea, the mightiest because the most ethical, the most coherent, the truest, expressing itself in a people as the conscience and will of the few, if not, indeed, of one, and ending to express itself in the conscience and the will of the mass, of the whole group ethnically moulded by natural and historical conditions into a nation, advancing, as one conscience and one will, along the self-same line of development and spiritual formation. Not a race, nor a geographically defined region, but a people, historically perpetuating itself; a multitude unified by an idea and imbued with the will to live, the will to power, self-consciousness, personality.[7]

And further,

> Fascism denies that numbers, as such, can be the determining factor in human society; it denies the right of numbers to govern by means of periodical consultations; it asserts the irremediable and fertile and beneficent inequality of men who cannot be levelled by any such mechanical and extrinsic device as universal suffrage.[8]

From this position it was only a short step in theory to the abolition of opposing political parties and the parliamentary institutions through which parties might function to determine questions of public interest and of public policy. By 1926 the Chamber of Deputies had been turned into a fascist claque, and all opposing parties had been crushed. The Fascist party emerged as a totalitarian party, its central leadership and governing policy bodies were fused organically with the institutions of the state, and the world was treated to a demonstration of the role of party in a totalitarian community.

In the developed fascist state, it was impossible for the individual to express his political interests and preferences outside the framework of the corporative state or the Fascist party.

[7] The same, pp. 11-12.
[8] The same, p. 21.

Fascist theory assigned a subordinate place and value to the individual in the total scheme of the state, as we have seen. Fascist practice made it impossible for the individual to express his own political beliefs, or to organize into a political party those who agreed with him. Fascism explicitly rejected, as a device for the formulation of state policy, the clash of political opinion and organization found in the liberal state. Fascism enforced its rejection first by violent intervention into the political deliberations of opposing groups of all shades of opinion, left or right or center. Fascism consolidated this position by altering the fundamental nature of representative political institutions and eliminating all political organizations outside the one party.

In its early years, the Fascist party was fashioned as a tool for the seizure of power. Its first tasks were those of violence —the capturing of the streets and the disruption of the assemblies, deliberations, and demonstrations of opposing parties, which in essence amounted to forcible prevention of rational and deliberative processes for the functioning of political life. The party was organized on formally democratic lines in its early years, but, like all other important institutions, was reshaped on an authoritarian and hierarchical basis after the seizure of power.[9] Like its Communist and Nazi counterparts, the Fascist party proper was not an inclusive group. Membership in the later years was restricted to males who had grown up through the *Balilla* and *Avanguardisti* youth-movements, and occasional purges were used to rid the party of those whose efficiency and loyalty were no longer of desirable standard. The Fascist party appeared less as a managerial elite than does the Communist party in Russia today; it was closer to the phases of Nazi party activity which had to do with the enforcement of the leader's will. Yet the fascist leaders like the communists, were woven into the leading organs of government and those control instrumentalities, the syndicates and corporations through which the state shaped the national life. As the domi-

[9] See the Statute of the National Fascist Party, reprinted in Mussolini, *Fascism,* pp. 198-217.

nant institution controlling national activities, the party became the arena within which both legitimate and illegitimate interests pressed their claims. It served both for testing the temper of the masses and for manipulating them in the state's interest. It offered a career to the energetic, the active, the power-hungry, and the sadistic. For the latter in particular it offered many opportunities to visit violence on unarmed opponents.[10] The party demanded strict discipline, unswerving and prompt obedience to the will of the leader—a complete submergence of individuality so far as judging ends or means was concerned.

Fusion of top party organs with the state was accomplished by laws on the Grand Council of Fascism in 1928 and 1929, and by the Statute on the National Fascist Party.[11] Fusion was similarly guaranteed by the provisions of later statutes setting up the corporative state, by reserving top positions of leadership and control in the corporative structure to party officers or members.[12] The laws on the Grand Council define this organ as "the supreme organ which co-ordinates and integrates all the activities of the Regime. . . ." (Article 1), provide that its President shall be the Head of the Government,[13] and that its secretary shall be the General Secretary of the National Fascist Party. (Articles 2 and 3.)

The Statute of the National Fascist Party, issued November 12, 1932, wrote into public law the nature of the party; its organs and hierarchy, national and provincial; its procedure for inducting new members, disciplinary regulations, and major administrative arrangements. This statute did not outlaw other

[10] See Emil Lederer, *The State of the Masses* (1940), pp. 90-91, and elsewhere.

[11] The laws on the Grand Council of Fascism dated December 9, 1928, as modified by the law of December 14, 1929 are reprinted in *Fascism,* pp. 194-97.

[12] For example, Art. 2 of the law of January 13, 1934, on the information and functions of corporations, reads: "Corporations are presided over by a Minister or by an Under-Secretary of State, or by the Secretary of the Fascist Party, to be appointed by decree of the Head of the Government, who is President of the National Council of Corporations." *Fascism,* p. 173.

[13] The Prime Minister Head of the Government is an office regulated by a law of December 24, 1925, in which the executive power is completely concentrated (Art. 1), and which exercises complete control over the procedures of legislation.

political parties, but by the time it was issued, the other parties had been smashed for six years; the issue was academic.[14] The task of the statute was not to regulate party life, but the life of the party. The statute specifies by law the loyalty oath which all Fascists must take upon induction into the party[15] and provides the major sanctions for good behavior as a party member. In addition to an elaborate system of party courts, there was a clear hierarchy of penalties ranging from reprimand through fine and suspension to expulsion. An Italian expelled from the party was excluded from any participation in public life. The statute makes clear the nature and tasks of the party in its first article: "The National Fascist Party is a civil militia, under the orders of the DUCE, in the service of the Fascist State."[16]

Initially, membership in the party was open to anyone who would take on the responsibilities of party membership, but after the seizure and consolidation of power, party membership was restricted to males who had come up through the young fascist organizations. Yet party participation in one form or another was open to all, either in the all-inclusive *Dopolavoro* (after-work) leisure-time organization, or in connection with the fascist youth organizations, or in one or another of the fascist auxiliary formations.

[14] Final dissolution of non-fascist political parties in Italy was accomplished according to the terms of a law of November 6, 1926 dealing with measures of "public security." This law empowered prefects (provincial administrators) to dissolve all associations whose activities were "contrary to the national order of the State." (Art. 215). On Nov. 11, 1926, the government issued a communique stating that "All political parties, all anti-Fascist political organizations, and others of a suspected character have been dissolved." The effect of the law was further ensured by the operation of another law of Nov. 25, 1926, which prohibited persons from re-establishing under other names, organizations dissolved as measures of public security, and which penalized membership in such illegally re-established organizations, on pain of imprisonment up to five years. Gaetano Salvemini, *Under the Axe of Fascism* (1936), p. 10.

[15] Art. 14 of the statute reads in part: "The Young Fascists who enter the National Fascist Party take the oath before the Political Secretary of the Fascio di Combattimento in the following form: 'In the name of God and of Italy I swear to carry out without discussion the orders of the DUCE and to serve the Cause of the Fascist Revolution with all my might and if necessary with my life.'" Entire paragraph underscored in original. *Fascism*, p. 208.

[16] The same, p. 198.

POWERS OF GOVERNMENT

The individual in Italy, just as the individual in Germany or Russia, could not under fascism depend on any legal or customary limitations on the powers of government, substantive or procedural, to protect him in any area from arbitrary or unjustified state action. Whatever tradition had developed in Italy to limit the powers of government by constitutional, legal, or customary means was specifically overturned by the political and legal philosophy of the fascist regime. To a regime which baldly put everything in the state and made everything subordinate to the state, the continuance of a realm in which the individual would be free from state intervention was illogical, unnecessary, and unthinkable. This viewpoint was gradually applied to Italy's political institutions. Something like a rule of law was maintained for a time. The courts were not reshaped as they were in Germany or smashed as they were in Russia, and executive decree powers were at first limited to areas authorized by existing law. Yet it was not long before parliament had been altered to fit the fascist concept, and the institutions of government and the administration of justice reshaped to give quick and efficient expression to the fascist will. Regional representation, opposition and majority parties, cabinet responsibility and other old political forms were permitted initially, but by 1928 the powers and constitution of both houses of the legislature had been greatly curtailed, regional constituencies had been abolished, and the structure of the Chamber of Deputies remodeled on a national list plan contrived to ensure fascist dominance. Parliament as such finally disappeared with the emergence of the "corporate state" in 1934. Even the preceding parliament, composed of delegates appointed by the Fascist party and ratified in plebiscitary fashion by the electorate, was replaced by representatives of the new corporations, and degenerated into a sounding-board for the regime.

The new concept of the rule of law was conscientiously applied by the fascist courts—in which the ideas of procedural guarantees to ensure justice to the individual were subordinated to the new task for the law: to serve as an instrument ensuring execution of the will of the state. Under the new concepts, the individual had no realm of rights which the state was bound to respect, or freedoms which transcended the requirements of public administration.[17] Not only was this the case in the realm of behavior covered by existing law, but the fascist state also had its secret police, the OVRA,[18] specifically designed to sanction the will of the party in matters not covered by law. Thus the fascist state left no gaps in its procedure for ensuring compliance.[19] This did not mean that the individual had no rights of appeal to higher authorities in the fascist state. It did mean that in every case of an appeal, the root question was never the protection of the individual's right *against the state,* but only a correct determination of the interest of the state in the particular instance—which might redound to the advantage of one or another party in, say, a labor dispute.

It does not appear that the role of violence was nearly so great in Fascist Italy as it was in Nazi Germany or as in Russia —once power had been seized and consolidated. The Italians exiled politically dangerous persons to penal island colonies, where they could think, talk, enjoy the scenery, but not infect others.[20] The Fascists hounded nonconformists from the universities and many other avenues of public life, but the areas of required conformity were not nearly so all-embracing in practice as they were in Germany or as they have become in Russia. The relatively high degree of acceptance of fascism by Italians in all walks of life seems to have kept the over-all employment of violence within limits. The period between 1926 and 1936, with the commencement of the Ethiopian venture, seems to have been one of comparative acceptance of the

[17] See Lederer, *The State of the Masses,* p. 95; E. B. Ashton, *The Fascist: His State and His Mind,* p. 139, who says: "Fascist law is a *means of regulating* the people's function of serving the state," and ". . . . in no conceivable Fascist structure can a citizen ever *count* on any of his personal interests to carry weight against communical purpose."

[18] The OVRA, or *Opera Vigilanza Repressione Anti-Fascista* was created by Mussolini and consisted of Fascist party militia, party adherents, and regular police.

[19] Ashton, *The Fascist,* pp. 128-29.

[20] One stark account of life under these conditions and escape from it, is Francisco Nitti, *Escape* (1930).

regime and public tranquillity. At that point, anti-fascist Italians claim that the international war adventure demonstrated the ultimate tendency of the regime so clearly that a genuine underground movement grew up, which did not subside for the duration of the fascist regime.[21]

III. SOCIAL AND RELIGIOUS FREEDOMS

The ambition, if not the success of Italian fascism was to make every group in the nation subordinate to the state. Lederer points out[22] that the essence of fascism is to destroy all groups within the state other than those subordinated to the party. This was more nearly achieved by the Germans than by the Italians, who were unable completely to wipe out group life in Italy, and less successful than their northern neighbors in bringing all group life into the web of the Fascist party. The Fascists had in effect to compromise with catholicism, together with its components of Catholic Action and Catholic Youth organizations, although the Fascists never forewent their hope of bending the church to the party's domination, and restricting religion to what fascism laid out as the proper sphere of the church. The Fascists did not formally outlaw professional, artistic, or other economic groupings, but early in the regime did deprive all such associations not approved by the state of legal authority or representative quality, and extended over businessmen, workers, and professional persons the authority of approved associations, whether the individuals were members or not. The Fascists left at least an outward shell of freedom to *de facto* associations, while robbing them of any genuine scope. Fascism respected the family somewhat more in practice than did the Germans, but also utilized the family as an educational device and as a necessary element in population policy.

[21] See G. A. Borgese: "Commemoration of Fascism" in the *Atlantic Monthly* (February 1945), pp. 68-74. Borgese elsewhere has pointed out the deep historical roots which nourished fascism and were responsible for its widespread acceptance: the failure and weakness of liberalism in Italy, the historical analogies to the Catholic Church, complete with its authoritarian, disciplinarian, and Roman imperial tradition. See his chapter "The Origins of Fascism" in F. Gross, ed., *European Ideologies* (1948), pp. 684 ff.

[22] Lederer, *The State of the Masses*.

Fascism succeeded in consolidating power in part because of its success in harnessing the bogey if not reality of the class struggle. This was the essence of fascist syndicalism, which is treated in its economic aspects below. From the standpoint of the freedom of the individual to form groups, the basic policy was expressed in the law of April 3, 1926, concerning the legal regulation of the collective relations of labor.[23] The pertinent passages from Article 5 follow:

> The legally recognized associations are incorporated bodies legally representing the whole body of employers, workers, employees, artists, and professional men of the class for which they are formed, *whether they be registered members thereof or not* . . .
>
> The legally recognized associations are entitled to levy annual dues on all employers, workers, employees, artists, and professional men whom they represent, *whether they be registered members or not* . . .
>
> Only legally recognized associations can appoint representatives of employers or workers to sit on all councils, guilds . . . or other bodies on which such representation is provided for by law.

In addition, only registered members were allowed to participate formally in association activities, elections, and so forth.

Some groups which were foolhardy enough to try to take advantage of this formal loophole to form *de facto* associations, quickly discovered that they had no genuine freedom whatsoever. To maintain legal existence, they had to have their charters approved by the state, and had to file lists of their officers and members with local authorities. This meant in practice that their purposes, acts, and corporate life were under constant surveillance, and any anti-fascist or nonconformist act, fancied or real, rendered their officers and memberships subject to violent reprisals by fascist action squads, often in conjunction with police measures. Any independent action displeasing to the regime would be instantly annulled, and violence was not long in visiting part or all of the members. As a further control measure, the regime established the legal power to turn any association over to a state-appointed commissioner, who could

[23] Quoted in *Fascism,* pp. 75-90.

run its affairs, dissolve it if necessary, and dispose of its assets according to the "moral purposes" for which the association was formed. This in practice usually meant that the assets were turned over to the Fascist party.[24]

The Fascist was not tainted so much as the Nazi with the doctrine of race hatred or in particular, anti-Semitism. This was due chiefly to the absence of anti-Semitism from the Italian heritage, and to the small number of Jews in Italy. Only late in the regime did Mussolini engage in anti-Semitic statements, partly as an expedient of domestic politics (the creation of a symbolic scapegoat) and partly as an accommodation to the ideology of his northern neighbor. Nor did racialist pronouncements come early or in large measure from fascist intellectuals. The spirit of the regime was on balance best expressed by Mussolini's comment to Emil Ludwig: "Race: it is a feeling and not a reality; 95% a feeling."[25] The reason for this tolerance had nothing to do with principle—except the principle that it was not profitable politics in the Italian state.

The fascist attack on the family was much more gentle than the nazi or the early communist. The Fascist left much educational influence to the church, allowed the family as the source of man power, and decried birth control. Nominally candidates for the Italian youth organizations were supposed to have their parents' consent, although it does not appear that was particularly important as a deterrent to a willing youth. The Fascists regarded the family as a breeding organization, to provide the population needed for national strength and imperialist expansion. This population policy embodied one of the main welfare aspects of the fascist policy, in its initial impact on the individual. Characteristically, the Fascists set up an all-inclusive National Organization for Maternity and Child Welfare[26] with "powers of control over all public and

[24] Cases cited in Salvemini, *Under the Axe of Fascism*, pp. 25-41.
[25] Emil Ludwig, *Talks with Mussolini* (1932), p. 75, quoted in *Fascism*, p. 41.
[26] By the law of Dec. 10, 1925.

private institutions for maternity and child welfare," and authorized it to found, subsidize, and "co-ordinate all public and private institutions for assistance to mothers and children, directing their activity in view of filling the most pressing local needs, and if necessary, revising their constitution and regulations, in so far as this is allowed for by existing laws."[27]

The main influence was exercised in the fields of education and of youth organizations. Education will be discussed below. From the standpoint of the youth, family, and leisure-time occupations, the main fascist impact was through the youth organizations for children, boys and girls, through adolescence, and through the leisure-time organization, *Dopolavoro*.

Fascism, like its compeer totalitarians, could not allow any unsupervised part of the life or time of the individual, from childhood to the grave. Its youth programs were as much a preventive attack on the possibility of independence and ultimately the rise of new centers of political power, as they were an effort to shape the individual's inmost conscience to the fascist pattern. Fascism commenced its program for boys at the ages of 6 to 18 in the *Balilla,* and from 18 to 21 in the *Avanguardisti*. Both organs were supervised by the *Balilla* Organization, itself a part of the Ministry of Education,[28] together with parallel organizations for girls, the *Piccole Italiani* and the *Giovinale Italiani*. These organizations for boys were paramilitary in nature, and were supplemented in 1937 by the Italian Youth of the Littorio, under the motto "Believe, Obey, Fight." In 1938 they boasted some 7,600,000 members, although membership was not compulsory. The officially stated purpose of the *Avanguardisti* and *Balilla* was "to give moral and physical training to the young, in order to make them worthy of the new standard of Italian life."[29] The *Balilla* institutions were ordered to:

[27] The same, arts. 5 and 6. It is hardly worth pointing out that under the fascist system, the limitation expressed by the final clause was nugatory, since the regime could change the law at any time.

[28] By virtue of Art. 2 of the decree of Nov. 14, 1929. *Fascism*, p. 276.

[29] The same, Art. 1.

1) teach the young the spirit of discipline and of military training, and give them:
2) premilitary training;
3) physical training through gymnastics and sports;
4) spiritual and cultural training;
5) professional and vocational training;
6) religious teaching.[30]

At the conclusion of youth training, selected youths were inducted into the Young Fascists as candidates for the Fascist party. The successful ones from this group were taken into the party by annual mass ceremonies, called the Fascist Levy, in which they took the oath of loyalty to Mussolini and to fascism. After the consolidation of the regime, this avenue was the only way open for entry into the party, and preferment in the party was reserved either for special classes of old Fascists, or for those coming through the training program.

Equally if not more symptomatic of the fascist attack on privacy and free leisure was the *Dopolavoro* organization. This was established by a royal decree-law of May 1, 1925.[31] Its aim was to consolidate within one fascist-dominated organization the welter of leisure-time groups, under varying sponsorship, which had grown up all over Italy. Its objects as stated in its fundamental statute were:

a) the healthy and profitable occupation of the worker's leisure hours, through institutions for developing the worker's physical, intellectual and moral capacity;
b) to promote the development of these institutions by furnishing them with the necessary support, . . .
c) the grouping together of all such associations, in order to equip them materially and for purposes of propaganda, as well as in view of other common aims and interests;
d) to make known by publications and other means the advantages of these institutions, and such provisions as are made to raise the standard of the working classes . . .[32]

Dopolavoro was the Italian equivalent of the German *Kraft durch Freude,* and sought by parallel means to see that the

[30] The same, Art. 10.
[31] *Fascism,* pp. 245-51.
[32] The same, Art. 1.

leisure time of all Italian workers was channeled in ways and for purposes of interest to the state.

Fascism recognized that the leisure time of workers would not alone measure the problem of dominating the leisure of all within the fascist state. Hence the establishment, for purposes of control and propaganda, of a Fascist Institute of Culture, equally under party domination, for those intellectuals and professionals who would not ordinarily come within the "welfare" provisions of the after-work groups. The intellectual status, if not respectability, of this institution was greatly buffered by the fact that its director was the world-famous philosopher Giovanni Gentile, who came early to support fascism by virtue of his neo-Hegelian position, and who was welcomed by Mussolini as a persuasive advocate, no matter what line of argument he chose to advance.[33]

In the field of religious freedom fascism turned the clock back. Part of the development of Italian unification had been the rise of secularism in Italy, leading to a struggle between the Catholic church and the state, and consequent increase in real freedom for those other religious groups not comprehended within the great Roman Catholic majority. Fascism recognized the Catholic church as the official state religion, and gave that hierarchy special opportunities in the fields of education and public life. But this was conditional—the Fascists used the church as a means to the consolidation of power, and never relaxed their efforts to assert the supremacy of the temporal power as expressed in the total fascist state. Fascism was willing, however grudgingly, to make its compact with both political and spiritual catholicism, but it was never willing to allow catholicism or any other institution within Italy to set its own limits, or to move unhindered to the nurture of possible foci of political infection.

In terms of theory, the fascist position with respect to religion was logically consistent with its basic view of the state—nothing outside the state, nothing superior to the state. Fascist theoreticians carried their characteristic attack on historical

[33] William M. McGovern, *From Luther to Hitler* (1941), pp. 553-54.

liberalism into the field of religious affairs. They rejected the liberal impartiality towards varying religions and the agnosticism which "first invoked a state indifferent to the various gods, then conceived of a God indifferent to the various religions." Fascism, on the other hand, claimed that as the state had a life and reality of its own, it had a religious belief of its own.[34]

Although the Fascist was willing to admit considerable freedom for the church to operate within the religious sphere, he tried to reserve for himself the decision as to the limits of that sphere, and to see to it that the church did not successfully compete with the movement for the fundamental loyalty of the Italian people.[35] Since fascism classically adjusted itself as it developed to Italian political reality, it had to reckon from the beginning with the traditional and deep-seated catholicism of the nation. Hence Mussolini's reversal of his socialist atheism, and his negotiation of a concordat with the Pope (1929). Fascist group policy was relaxed to permit a revival of Catholic Action and Catholic student organizations in the universities. Mussolini reintroduced religious teaching into the schools and gave the Catholic hierarchy large freedom in the religious aspects of the *Balilla* program.[36] He curbed anticlericalism within the party, assigned chaplains to the military forces and to the fascist militia, gave back to the church some of the property taken by the pre-fascist government, put down Freemasonry, appointed a state commission to revise ecclesiastical law along lines desired by the church, and commenced negotiations in

[34] M. Searle Bates: *Religious Liberty: An Inquiry* (1945) p. 43, quoting Giurati, editor of the parliamentary debates on the Concordat.

[35] Mussolini told his Chamber of Deputies on May 13, 1929: "The Fascist State claims its ethical character: it is Catholic but above all it is Fascist, in fact it is exclusively and essentially Fascist. Catholicism completes Fascism. . . ." *Fascism,* p. 39.

[36] Art. 36 of the decree of Jan. 9, 1927 on the *Balilla* specified that "the religious teaching and assistance is entrusted to a central Inspector selected among priests of the Roman Catholic Church. Each *coorte* shall be provided with a Catholic priest, entitled Chaplain of the National Balilla Organization, who shall attend to the religious life of the members." Art. 38 provides "Religious instruction shall consist in the teaching of Catholic ethics, Christian doctrine, the Old Testament and the Gospel. . . . The form of worship is that practiced by the Roman Catholic Church."

1926 leading to the Lateran Accord of 1929.[37] Yet, according to Borgese, "Nothing was so alien to the Fascist mind as the genuine Christianity of Manzoni."[38]

Under the Concordat, the Fascist state exercised important powers over the appointment of officials of the hierarchy and over the administration of Catholic church affairs. The state could veto the appointments of bishops and parish clergy, and for "grave reasons" could force the removal of parish priests. The state controlled the management of the great preponderance of church property in the country. These powers of veto and management, whether exercised directly or as a threat in reserve, guaranteed the good behavior of the vast majority of the clergy. The dissident always knew he risked his career if he opposed the state.[39]

The position of non-Italian Catholic minorities illustrates the efforts of the Fascists to put nationalism above religious belief. German-Austrian minorities in the Tyrol, and Slav minorities beyond Trieste, although Catholic, were subjected to nationalist controls. Hymns or sermons in Croatian and Slovenian were prohibited. Officials refused to register babies named for the Slav saints Cyril or Methodius. This was done on the ground that use of a non-Italian tongue was proof of disloyalty, and the fact that one was used in a religious ceremony did not alter the case. In the fascist view even the simplest religious ceremony took on political significance.

The position of non-Catholic minorities was formally regulated on a reasonably fair basis by the Law of Admitted Cults (1929), but in practice such minorities were denied the right freely to proselytize for their faith. The law permitted parents to ask that their children be exempted from religious teaching in the schools, but any parents who tried to do so ran the risk of pressures from Roman Catholic officials and hierarchy. The "admitted cults" consisted of those non-Catholic religious

[37] U. S. Library of Congress, Legislative Reference Service, *Fascism in Action,* H. Doc. 401, 80 Cong. 1 sess., pp. 192-93.
[38] G. A. Borgese, *Goliath* (1937), p. 293.
[39] Bates, *Religious Liberty: An Inquiry,* p. 44.

groups already existing in Italy. The Salvation Army and the Pentecostalists were excluded on the grounds that their activities threatened public health by encouraging neuropathic manifestations.[40]

Thus fascism violated the liberal tradition of state neutrality with respect to the church. Discord persisted to the end of the regime, because of the sustained effort of fascism to assert the spiritual primacy of the state.[41]

IV. ECONOMIC FREEDOMS

The classic communist characterization of fascism holds that it is a form for the domination of the masses by the monopoly capitalists. Closer examination reveals that whatever is plausible in this allegation is disproved by the actual history of the development of fascism, and by its impact on capitalism. The dominant aspect of fascism was its drive for power, and its attempts to subordinate every element in the state—economic, political, and social—to its control. At the outset fascism turned to a regulation of the labor struggle, and developed the syndicates as characteristic state institutions to control the working relationship. Later, after the consolidation of political power, Mussolini set up the framework for the regulation of production which took the form of the "corporative state." Two years after, with the commencement of the Ethiopian venture, Mussolini clearly announced that the regulation of all phases of the economy of the state were to prepare and to strengthen the nation for war.[42] In this latter effort, Mussolini bent all interests and classes to his will—capitalist, worker, and professional alike.

Mussolini affirmed the principle of private property, not from any grounds of ethical or economic doctrine, but purely and simply as the most effective incentive for maximum production from the relatively undeveloped Italian economy. Any such early declarations did not prevent the party from shaking down

[40] Bates, *Religious Liberty: An Inquiry*, pp. 48-49.

[41] Legislative Reference Service, *Fascism in Action*, H. Doc. 401, relying on Daniel Binchy, *Church and State in Fascist Italy* (1941).

[42] Speech to the General Assembly of National Council of Corporations on Mar. 23, 1936.

the private capitalist, threatening policy shift to the left if compliance was not forthcoming. Mussolini was no more wedded to the principle of private property than was Lenin. On October 7, 1933 Mussolini pointed out that he had accomplished the necessary political reforms, and his hands were then free to modify the economic system. He moved seriously thenceforth to erect the corporative state. Shortly thereafter he asserted:

> The Fascist State lays claim to rule in the economic field no less than in others; it makes its action felt throughout the length and breadth of the country by means of its corporative, social, and educational institutions, and all the political, economic, and spiritual forces of the nation, organized in their respective associations, circulate within the State.[43]

Mussolini defined his notion of private property and private enterprise within the corporative system as follows:

> Guild or corporative economy respects the principle of private property. Private property completes human personality. It is a right, and if it be a right it is also a duty. So true is this that property should be considered in its social function, not therefore as passive ownership but as active ownership, which does not merely enjoy the fruits of wealth but develops, increases, and multiplies them. Corporative economy respects private enterprise. The Labor Charter specifically states that it is only when private enterprise is deficient, lacking, or inadequate that the State intervenes.[44]

Yet Mussolini preceded these words with the statement:

> If liberal economy is the economy of individuals in a state of more or less complete liberty, Fascist guild economy is that of individuals, and also of associated groups, and also of the State.

And followed them with these:

> Corporative economy introduces order in the economic field. If there be one phenomenon which requires regulating and which should be directed toward certain fixed objectives, it is precisely the economic phenomenon for it concerns the whole nation.
>
> Not only must industrial economy be regulated, but agricultural

[43] *Fascism,* p. 29.

[44] Speech in the Senate on the bill establishing the corporations, Jan. 13, 1934, in *Fascism,* p. 70.

economy, commercial economy, banking and even artizan (sic) activities. How should this regulation be carried out in practice? Through the self-discipline of the categories concerned. It is only in the second resort, when the categories fail to agree and to secure the due balance of forces, that the Government may intervene; and it has the sovereign right to do so, in this field as in others, for the Government represents the other term of the equation: the consumer, the anonymous mass. . . .

. . . even if there were to be a general economic revival tomorrow and we were to return to the easy business conditions prevailing in 1914 . . . then more than ever regulation would be necessary, for men have short memories and they would be induced to commit once more the same foolish acts, they would repeat the same follies.[45]

The corporations as contemplated by this law were organs of the state, under party and government control, including in their membership both business and labor representatives for twenty-two "categories" or economic activities into which the entire economy of the nation was divided. The corporations were in the main devices to regulate production.[46]

In conformity with the statement of Mussolini, it was for the members of the corporation in the first instance to draw up agreements among themselves for the regulation of economic matters under their control—price and wage policy in particular. But such agreements were valid only upon the approval of the National Council of Corporations (Article 9), an agency dominated by the minister for corporations, the head of the government—or in other words, the Duce of the Fascist party. Once approved, however, such agreements on regulations, plans, and salary scales became compulsory and a part of the law of the land when published by decree of the head of the government. Infringement of their provisions was punished according to the procedure legally established for enforcing collective labor con-

[45] The same, pp. 69-71.

[46] Art. 8 of the law of Jan. 13, 1934, on the formation and functions of corporations, empowers each corporation to draw up the rules authorized by a previous law "to regulate economic relations and the unitary discipline of production." Art. 10 says "The Corporation is given faculty of fixing salary scales for the work and economic services of producers carrying out their activity in the field under the jurisdiction of the Corporation."

tracts. (Article 11.) The corporations were empowered to give advice to the government on matters requested by the appropriate officials, and it appears that such a consultative function was not completely ignored. The corporations came to play the dominant role in setting policy for the field of labor regulations. It was also required (Article 13) to compose the Board of Conciliation necessary under specified procedure for the requirement of conciliating labor disputes.

It is often argued that the corporative system, in essence, was only a device whereby the big capitalists used state power to ensure their economic interests. This viewpoint is not completely without foundation, especially if the observer confines his judgment to the early years of the regime. The Fascists moved first to regiment labor, and did little or nothing to hamper the activities or interfere with the initiative of the larger capitalists. *Laissez-faire* died early in fascism, since the state took steps, as did most Western countries, to see to it that the economic effects of depression were not allowed to work themselves out inexorably upon firms unable to compete in difficult times. It could hardly be argued, however, that the fascist moves to bail out weak firms and to bolster the national economy were directed against the employers as a class. On the other hand, the corporative state, largely myth, ambiguity, and propaganda prior to 1934, contained within itself the seeds of full-scale regimentation of all elements in the economy. These seeds germinated and the results flourished in the years which saw national regimentation first for the Ethiopian venture and as a reply to international sanctions, and later as the economy was bent to prepare for war and to wage it.

In the earlier years the big capitalist could usually count on a sympathetic hearing and a favorable decision from the party. The federations of employers enjoyed considerable autonomy in selecting their officers, and getting them approved by the party. Party-capitalist fusion was furthered by the entrance of many big capitalists into the higher ranks of the party. But the hegemony of the capitalist was offset, says Salvemini, by at least three competing bureaucracies: those of the regular civil service, the army, and the Fascist party. Mussolini, as top manipulator, found it to his interest and profit to play these classes off against one another. The civil servant found it to his profit, immediately or in a near future, to shake down business firms for bribes or for jobs as the price of favorable decisions. The party found it necessary to set the price of government supervision in return for the boon of compulsory unification for firms in particular economic lines. The collaboration of the army was valuable to firms interested in the components of arms and other military materiel.[47]

As a result, even as early as 1935, Salvemini noted the growing distrust of the capitalist for the fascist system.

> Why? Certainly not because Mussolini did not try to compensate the big business men for the losses they suffered through revaluation of the lira, and to help them to battle the world depression. The reason is that they feel they are no longer the masters of the government as they were in the early years of the regime. A machine has been formed which eludes their control. . . .[48]

The fundamental drive of the Fascist was for power. Hence the corporative system turned into a device whereby the Fascist in the last analysis controlled prices, entry into business, exit from business, the conditions of labor relations, the supply and distribution of raw materials, money and credit, foreign trade, foreign exchange—not as a means whereby the big capitalist could eat the little business man by natural law, but as a means of maximizing economic activity in the interest of national military and diplomatic strength.

PRICE CONTROL

Price control came relatively slowly in fascist Italy. It appeared at first on a local basis, extending only to wheat, wheat flour, and to meat. A decree law of December 16, 1926 gave the communes power to fix retail prices for the principal kinds of food. Local fascist officials sometimes took a hand in price fixing or enforcement. On the whole, price fixing on this basis

[47] Salvemini, *Under the Axe of Fascism,* pp. 383-92.
[48] The same, p. 391.

was unsatisfactory, and the price powers of the communes were abolished in 1930. However, price control over wheat, wheat flour, and meat was continued, with a centralized price fixing mechanism carried out by local authorities. As part of the "battle for grain," central government regulations not only set prices, but set quality classifications and regulated stringently the proportions of hard to soft wheat in various classes of flour, and total proportions of domestic to imported grain. Price control for most commodities was hardly needed from 1927 to 1934; the depression took care of that. But with returning prosperity from 1934 on, the problem of price control again became acute.

The first steps taken to meet the new conditions were programs of exhortation and propaganda, carried out by the party designed to keep purchasing power stable and to lower costs of production and prices as a stimulus to exports. On June 16, 1934 the secretary of the Fascist party ordered provincial party officials to regulate prices of 21 basic commodities by issuing compulsory price lists.[49] These lists were supplemented by so-called "indicative" lists, issued by local authorities to fix prices on a semivoluntary basis for additional commodities. From the middle of 1934 to October of 1935, price control was conducted loosely on a local basis, with no central supervision other than that exercised by the party and by the Fascist Confederation of Merchants.[50] The result was big interprovincial differences in prices, and a striking rise of prices during the first nine months of 1935.

With the prospect of international sanctions, and faced by the economic requirements of the Ethiopian adventure, the Fascists had to take much sterner measures. They established a "Permanent Price Committee" as an organ of the party, with representatives from the interested government departments, including syndical federations. They centralized price control

[49] These "intersyndical" lists covered bread, wheat flour, corn flour, rice, dried beans, food pastes, potatoes, beef, fresh pork, sausage, dried cod fish, eggs, lard, salt pork, cheese, butter, olive oil, sugar, roasted coffee, milk, and charcoal.

[50] Henry Siefke Miller, *Price Control in Fascist Italy* (1938), pp. 23 ff.

further, giving main attention to commodities widely consumed, and to those necessary for the national interest. Luxuries they left alone. Wheat prices were controlled by the establishment in 1936 of compulsory wheat pools, and an elaborate system for equalizing the cost of domestic and imported grain. The fascist pooling system had been extended by 1939 to ten other commodities.

With the growth of the corporative system as the main agency for over-all economic control, price fixing was ultimately vested therein on April 28, 1937, and the "permanent" party committee abolished. Under this system, as we have seen, the economic participants were used as preliminary negotiators and as specialist advisers, but the final approval and control was reserved to the government, party, and the Duce. The criteria for these controls were not economic, but political. An authoritative Italian economist commented:

> The purpose of [economic] intervention is essentially political. The complete coordinated program of objectives for prices, profits, purchasing power, etc., must come only from the head of the government, because he alone has the possibility of evaluating the political utility involved, and the technical organs can do nothing other than move in the direction of these aims. . . . The techniques should indicate the most scientific means to reach the political ends. . . .[51]

The Fascists were not blind to the fact that price control is not an end in itself, nor is it possible of achievement without other controls over other phases of the economy. Summarizes Miller:

> Price control cannot stand alone, but must be linked with the control of wages, money and profits. In Italy we find all of these. Wages are now controlled by the guilds, and wage adjustments are theoretically arranged by mutual agreement between the workers' syndicates and the employers' organizations. . . . Profits are limited through heavy taxes. . . . Mussolini remarked in a speech at Rome on October 28, 1937, "In Fascist Italy capital is subject to the orders of the state."[52]

[51] Professor Filippo Carli, quoted in the same pp. 64-65.
[52] Miller, *Price Control in Fascist Italy,* pp. 137 ff.

CONTROLS OVER LABOR

There was no right to organize and to strike and the terms of employment (wages, etc.) were fixed by public act. The characteristic fascist institution for the control of labor was the syndical system, set up by the law of April 3, 1926 on Syndicates and Collective Relations of Labor[53] and set into the economic and political system as a whole by the Charter of Labor promulgated on April 21, 1927.[54] Fascism characteristically did much by propaganda to glorify labor, and by certain welfare institutions (*Dopolavoro,* aid for mothers and children, and compulsory insurance to protect against old age, tuberculosis, and involuntary unemployment) to improve the standard of life of labor, and thus to improve the importance of labor in the scheme of things.[55] The price was twofold—controls on wages in the first instance, but more important, revocation of all the rights of labor—freedom to organize, to bargain collectively, and to enhance its positions by such weapons as the strike. The neo-liberal right to work was replaced by the duty to work.

Lock-outs and strikes were prohibited by Article 18 of the law of April 3, 1926. The prohibition was sanctioned by severe penalties against both employers and employees breaking the statute, with particularly severe penalties for strikes against the state, strikes of public employees, or labor action taken in an attempt to coerce the will or influence the decisions of a department, organ, or official of the state. (Articles 18-22.) The beginnings of the corporative state adumbrated in the labor charter put certain duties on employers as part of the attempt to unite the forces of production and integrate economic interests. The charter declared the interests of production were national interests, and recognized the syndicates (often confusingly called corporations) as instruments of the state. The charter also declared that "The corporative state regards private initiative in the field of production as the most effective

[53] Reprinted in *Fascism,* pp. 75-90.
[54] The same, pp. 133-43.
[55] Salvemini points out that fascism really did little more than to maintain standards of social welfare established in Italy long before the fascist advent, *Under the Axe of Fascism,* pp. 284-339.

and useful instrument of the national interest" (Article 7), but made it clear that the organizer of an enterprise is responsible *to the state* for its management. Two things are noteworthy: the senior responsibility of the manager, not the worker; and the fact that the responsibility of the manager was not to the shareholder or the owner, but to the state.[56] This latter responsibility was particularized as follows:

> . . . The occupational associations of employers are obliged to promote in every way the increase and perfection of their products and the reduction of costs. The representatives of those who practice a liberal profession or art and the public associations co-operate in protecting the interests of art, science, and literature, in perfecting their production, and in pursuing the moral ends of the corporative order.

Membership in syndical associations was voluntary for citizens or for corporations or companies whose directors and administrators "have always been of good political and moral conduct from a national standpoint." (Royal Decree of July 1, 1926, Article 1.) But, as has been explained, the Fascists gave an effective monopoly of legal status and powers of negotiation and representation to those groups, one per "category," recognized by the state. Associations (or "federations") could be grouped into confederations, representing related economic activities. If a confederation was recognized for a group or all classes or employers or workers, no federation could be recognized which was not affiliated to that confederation. The right of membership in international labor associations was also destroyed for recognized groups.[57]

[56] In the words of the charter, "Since the private organization of production is a function of national interest, the organizer of an enterprise is responsible to the State for its management. From the co-operation of the productive forces it follows that they have mutual rights and duties. The employee, whether a technical expert, clerk, or laborer, is an active co-operator in the economic enterprise, the direction of which belongs to the employer who is responsible for it." (Art. 7.)

[57] Art. 6 of the law of Apr. 3, 1926, said in part: "In no case can associations be recognized which, without the preliminary consent of the Government, have contracted any ties of discipline or dependence with associations of an international character."

As organs of the state, it was logical that the forms and powers over appointments to syndical offices, the syndical statutes, and the like, should have been reserved to the state.[58] Major officers were appointed by royal decrees, and lesser ones by ministerial decree; appointments were always from above, and the leadership principle was applied to each segment of each association: the president or secretary of each one had to be responsible for its work.

Salvemini describes power relationships within the syndicalist system as follows:

From the very beginning the officials of the confederations were invested with full authority in the negotiation of labour agreements, which should have been the essential function of the local, provincial and national organizations subject to the confederations. The lower organizations were without importance and atrophied from the moment of their birth. In reading that the confederations were gaining in strength, one must interpret these words to mean that the officials of the confederations were gaining unlimited power over the officials of the lower organizations. . . .

. . . the pre-Fascist organizations operated according to the will of their members. In the Fascist organizations the will of the members is suppressed. The members are passive and inert material. All action is the province of the officials, and these are accountable

[58] Art. 13 of the decree of July 1, 1926 stated that syndical associations must be politically, economically, and socially acceptable to the state. Art. 15 stated "The Government always has power to demand, and if necessary to decree *ex officio,* a revision of the statutes of legally recognized associations."

Art. 8 of the law of Apr. 3, 1926, provided for government supervision of syndical associations at all levels. "The competent Minister, acting jointly with the Minister of the Interior, can dissolve the Boards of Directors of the associations and concentrate all authority in the hands of the President or Secretary for a period not to exceed one year. He can also, in graver cases, entrust the special administration to a commissioner of his choice." Supervision of subordinate associations could be delegated wholly or in part to federations or confederations.

Art. 9 of the same law authorized revocation of official recognition of a syndical association at the discretion of the state—"when grave reasons exist, and in all cases when the conditions laid down . . . for recognition cease to exist."

Arts. 29-31 of the decree specified the right of the state to examine syndical records, to inspection, and the right to annul decisions of such organizations as not consonant with law, regulations, or the statutes or "essential aims" of the associations.

not to the members, but to the leaders of the party and to the governmental bureaucracy.[59]

The syndical associations required compulsory dues payments from all persons for whom they were legal representatives, whether members of the associations or not. Part of the proceeds was diverted by law to the support of the para-fascist organizations.[60]

The Fascists did not abolish their own form of what they chose to call "collective bargaining," or the formal right of the employee to make his own terms with his employer if he could better the terms of the collective contract. But under fascism, the only valid collective contracts were those drawn up by the recognized syndicates, under the control of the state and party; once published, they were compulsory for "all employers, workers, artists, and professional men belonging to the category to which said contract refers."[61] Such contracts, to be valid, had to be written and officially published. Once so validated, both employers and workers were civilly responsible to both employers and employees associations for failure to abide by contract provisions. Such bargaining was prohibited for state employees (that is, for labor relations "already subject to conditions issued by public authorities"). Article 54 of the Royal Decree of July 1, 1926 provided that: "Private labour contracts stipulated between individual employers and workers who are subject to collective contracts, must conform with the conditions laid down in the latter," but private contract conditions prevailed if they were more favorable to workers than those of the collective contract.

The major state agency for ensuring compliance with collective contracts was a system of labor courts, available only to aggrieved associations, not to individuals as such. These courts were integrated with the normal judicial system, being estab-

[59] *Under the Axe of Fascism,* pp. 63-64.

[60] Art. 18 of the decree of July 1, 1926, provides "The following contributions are furthermore an obligatory item: contributions to the 'Dopolavoro' organizations, the Maternity and Child Welfare organization, the *'Balilla'* organization, the School Patrons (Patronato). . . ."

[61] Art. 10 of the law of Apr. 3, 1926.

lished as special sections of the sixteen courts of appeals. The labor law required that conciliation efforts must precede resort to the labor courts, and the president of the court had to make a final effort at conciliation before consummating judicial procedure. Appeals from the labor courts could be taken on certain grounds to the Court of Cassation. Decisions of labor courts could be enforced by special procedures, to permit quick action. Judgments of the labor courts were not only binding on the parties actually represented in each case, but were valid for all concerned within the district of the association suing.

For the individual, the most important recourse in the case of an individual labor controversy was to a special section of the local courts. It appears that such cases were numerous, and one observer comments that the decisions were fair and took into account the legitimate demands of the worker. Yet in the opinion of the same author, it remained highly doubtful if the degree of labor peace and justice arising from a "judge-made wage" was sufficient to offset the worker's loss of freedom to bargain by threat of the strike.[62]

THE CORPORATIONS

The syndical system thus set up was integrated into the new corporative system in 1934, and the corporations became the genuine units for collective economic control, taking precedence over the older syndicates.[63]

In terms of fascist policy and timing, this decision meant that it was now considered feasible and necessary to regulate economic production as a whole, not merely the sector of labor regulations and some phases of prices. Earlier powers granted to the projected corporations were brought into actuality, and the powers of the law of 1934 put into effect. These powers in-

[62] William G. Welk, *Fascist Economic Policy* (1938), pp. 82-86.

[63] Art. 7 of the law on corporations in 1934 had provided that syndical associations united in one of the new corporations should become autonomous in the syndical field. In other words, although such a syndical association could retain membership in a confederation, it was not bound by the labor agreements of the confederation; it could not freely conclude collective labor contracts or other agreements with the several federations of workers or employers.

cluded the power to compel firms to join industrial trade associations, and to control the activities of all such associations.[64] The state controlled entry into any line of economic activity.[65] The state could punish unauthorized entry into a field, as well as direct contraction or expansion of business. The ambit of control of any authorized association was complete for all activities within its authorized categories of activities, as new entry into a field, or expansion of existing functions, were made automatically subject to existing regulations.[66]

According to Mussolini, this system was not supposed to work by the imposition of all decisions and provisions of all initiative and impetus from above.[67] Mussolini criticized early Rooseveltian New Deal policies as erring too far in these directions. The state in Italy had plenary powers of control and direction, but corporations were supposed to draw up in the first instance, and in the light of their technical and special knowledge, the main lines of economic regulation: prices, wages, distribution policies, standards for quality and quantity of production, and fair trade practices.

In practice, however, the party exercised full-scale control. One analyst describes it as follows:

> Like all the other organs of the state, the corporations are, in practice, under the complete control of the Fascist party. The membership of each corporation is composed exclusively of party members sworn to absolute obedience to the leader and to the party hierarchy. Since all the corporations are presided over by the Minister of Corporations, who has the power to determine their agenda, and all their decisions and recommendations must be approved by the Central Corporate Committee before they become effective, there is ample certainty that no discussion will ever arise within a corporation that is not welcomed by the party and the government, and that no decision will ever be taken which the government does not approve. . . . Despite the independent normative powers conferred upon the corporations by law, they are, in

[64] Decree of June 16, 1932.
[65] The same, Art. 8.
[66] Law of Jan. 12, 1933.
[67] Speech of Mussolini on May 15, 1937, to Third General Assembly of the corporations.

actual fact, little more than advisory organs whose recommendations may or may not be accepted by a central government with which all final decisions ultimately rest.[68]

FOREIGN TRADE

In the fields of control over foreign trade, fascist Italy was slow to apply as extensive controls as those current in other European states during the 1920's. It maintained a low-tariff policy until forced by international economic competition and the failure of international negotiations looking to freer trade, to adopt retaliatory measures. By 1934 Italy was well on the way to protectionism, and the fascist control mechanisms facilitated the administration of an autarkic policy. Hence by the imposition of sanctions on Italy in 1936, it had both policy and machinery to enable it to cope with its new economic stringency. After the conclusion of the Ethiopian affair, Italy was completely ready to carry out the economic controls in the field of international currency and trade matters necessary to preparation for war and its final conduct.[69]

CONTROL IN THE FIELD OF AGRICULTURE

The machinery for control in the field of agriculture was contained within the corporative machinery, as agricultural elements were included within the corporations in Group I.[70] The fascist program in this field was dominated by three interrelated objectives: autarky as a preparation for foreign war, stimulated by the experience with sanctions; land reclamation; and the "battle for grain." Land reclamation by the state—which had antedated Mussolini by many years—was one of the great propaganda programs of the regime, and a favorite example of the type of economic activity impossible to the private economy, but required in the interest of maximum state

[68] The same, pp. 144-45.

[69] Welk, *Fascist Economic Policy*, pp. 171 ff. and pp. 205 ff.

[70] These corporations are for the following categories: grains; vegetable, flower, and fruit growing; viticulture and wine production; edible oils; sugar beets and sugar; animal husbandry and fishing; wood and wood products, and the corporation of textile products.

productivity and power. The battle of grain was designed to free Italy, a country in which wheat was one of the most important dietary components, from dependence on imports. The battle was "won," and self-sufficiency in wheat attained except for years of unusually bad harvests, at the cost of much higher prices for grain and grain products. The fascist government launched great programs of agricultural education, designed to improve production, conserve forests, etc. But it does not appear that the Fascists tied the peasant to his land, or circumscribed his activities in as many ways as did the Germans or Russians.

THE POSITION OF THE CONSUMER

In the structure of the corporative state, the position of the consumer did not come in for attention at all—except insofar as the party and government claimed that their participation in corporative activities expressed the consumer's interest. The position of the consumer is well illustrated by the example of the battle for grain—higher prices were not too high a price to pay for the military security of independence from external sources of supply for a fundamental product. From another point of view, it could be argued that large-scale consumers (or purchasers) were constantly active in the corporative process, in the course of bargaining with suppliers over price scales, codes of fair competition, quality and quantity standards, etc. But the final, individual consumer of an end product had no mechanism outside of the party or government hierarchy through which he could affect the economic process. Consumers' choices in this sense were a negligible and neglected factor.

V. INTELLECTUAL FREEDOMS

Intellectual freedoms under fascism were brought under theoretical total control, but in practice the degree of regimentation and unification was somewhat less thorough and universal than in Germany or in Russia. Fascism moved in 1922 to tighten up state control over education, and steadily extended its apparatus for control of the media of mass communication. As we have seen, fascism also created organizations for laborers, for intellectuals, and for youth which served as major channels for party propaganda.

EDUCATION

Fascist control over the educational system was not so sweeping or deep-reaching as in Germany or in Russia, although it far transcended the bounds of control normal to a liberal society, and was only partly ameliorated by admitted administrative improvements. The pace of educational reforms and of imposition of fascist control was more leisurely than in Germany, and was carried out, according to one authority, in large part by liberal scholars.[71] These initial "reforms" had three aims: to achieve more centralization of state control over the Italian school system (in which state control was the established norm); to tighten up educational standards by imposing severe entrance and leaving examinations for secondary schools; and to check "over-production of intellectuals."

Doctrinal controls, enforced by fascist loyalty oaths and party membership as prerequisites to holding a teaching post, were not introduced until 1928. The fascist loyalty oath required all teachers to swear "to exercise the office of teacher . . . with the purpose of forming citizens industrious, honest, and devoted to the Fatherland and the Fascist regime."[72] This oath was introduced at the instance of Giovanni Gentile, the Minister of Education, as a means of punishing opponents to his authoritarian reforms.[73]

Shortly thereafter a unified organization for teachers was set up within the syndicalist-corporative system. The state imposed its will on textbooks for the school system. In primary schools existing texts were banned and only new texts provided by the state were permitted. In secondary schools teachers could choose

[71] Article by I. L. Kandel in Legislative Reference Service, *Fascism in Action,* H. Doc. 401, pp. 28-29.

[72] McGovern, *From Luther to Hitler,* p. 569.

[73] Borgese, *Goliath,* pp. 302-04. This author states that Mussolini hesitated for two years to impose this oath, fearing widespread and vocal opposition from Italian intellectuals. Mussolini overestimated his opposition; all but 31 professors signed without protest.

books only from approved lists furnished by the state. Kandel notes that fascist conformity was chiefly important in the field of history; in other areas, the state claimed power to exercise control, but did not as a rule exercise it. Fascist theory, as we have seen, was primarily a justification for fascist action; it was not erected into a universal philosophic system, and consequently the content of much of the curriculum was not of interest to it. The Fascists saw to it that a good proportion of school activities were devoted to inculcation of loyalty to the Duce, to the party, and to the nation.[74] The fascist ambitions to impose larger controls were not absent; in 1939 they promulgated an Educational Charter to integrate education more completely with fascism. The onset of war rendered this abortive.

PROPAGANDA AND CENSORSHIP

Fascist propaganda took the three classic forms: organizational work, positive exploitation of mass media, and censorship. Propaganda for Fascists was more like agitation, in the Leninist sense. That is to say, it was less devoted to the dissemination of doctrine and basic viewpoint than it was to the stirring up of the masses on immediate causes and issues. Propaganda in the former sense was hardly possible to the Fascists during the early period of seizure and consolidation of power, because they had no clear, firm, and stable doctrine to disseminate. Their doctrine was in process of becoming, and as a rationalization for violence always followed the fact.

Yet the Fascists, like any other totalitarians, could not endure contrary voices or criticism in those fields they held to be important. Hence they kept up the violence characteristic of the early days, when newspaper or other opponents were dosed, slugged, or killed, and gradually rooted out all opposition in the fields of mass communications—newspapers, publications, motion pictures, radio.[75]

[74] H. W. Schneider, *Making Fascists* (1929); Borgese, *Goliath*.

[75] Arnold Zurcher, "State Propaganda in Italy," in Harwood L. Childs, ed. *Propaganda and Dictatorship* (1935), pp. 35-57; also his chapter, "The Conscription of Liberty," in James Shotwell, ed., *Governments of Continental Europe*, (1940), pp. 702-24.

Organizational propaganda was a major function of *Dopolavoro* and the fascist youth organizations. It goes without saying that the party as such was a major organizational instrument for spreading official view and doctrine.[76]

Control over mass communications commenced with control over the press, and then expanded to control over publications, motion pictures, and radio—the latter two came under fascist domination as they achieved importance as propaganda channels. Controls over the press commenced at first with powers of local officials to confiscate issues displeasing to the party.[77] In 1925 a system of licensing was introduced, and it was forbidden to publish a newspaper without prior permission from the Ministry of Justice, and responsible editors or owners were required to post bond or pledge printing equipment as surety for any fines or penalties imposed for infringement of regulations.[78] As a result, many journals were discontinued (for example, the official communist, socialist, and republican newspapers) and others with great liberal traditions made their peace with the regime after dismissing oppositionist editors.

Professional regimentation supplemented censorship. The free press associations were dissolved by October 26, 1925, and by the end of the year, journalism was declared a quasi-public profession which could be engaged in only by those whose

[76] The Royal Decree of Jan. 9, 1927, dealing with youth organizations, says: "Art. 30.—The National Balilla Institution shall also train the conscience and minds of these boys, since they are destined to become the Fascist men of the future, from whose ranks national leaders will be selected.

"Art. 31.—In order to achieve this end the National Institution may found schools for cultural training and centres of study and propaganda. The doctrine of Fascism, its logical development and its historical significance, shall be taught in these schools." *Fascism,* p. 274.

The party embodied as a major department a unit for press and propaganda under the direct control of the secretary of the party (Statute of the National Fascist Party, Art. 7). Each party member, under the immediate observation of his party superiors, was supposed to exemplify in his every act, fascist spirit and discipline. The same, Art. 13.

[77] The official formula was newspapers containing "false, tendentious or misleading information, or information calculated to inspire class hatred or bring the government into contempt." Zurcher, in Childs, ed., *Propaganda and Dictatorship,* p. 36, citing a decree law of July 15, 1923.

[78] The same, citing a law of Dec. 31, 1925.

names appeared on government-approved registers. This gave the party new means of control, because a recalcitrant journalist could be prevented from practicing his profession by dropping his name from the list, or could be punished by reclassifying him to a junior status. The Fascists formed their own press associations to control the lists; this power went to the later-formed syndicalist associations, which formed a part of the Corporation of Professions and Arts.

Mussolini regarded the editorship of major journals as appointments within his personal prerogative. He could and did dismiss or shift editors by his own fiat and often without prior notice to anyone.[79] This control over professional participation and economic life was the ultimate sanction underlying the issuance of press directives from central authority. Such directives might be general, calling on editors to give prominence to a particular phase of the news; or they might be in detailed form, specifying position in the paper, length and tone of treatment, and desired or undesired words or phrases. Such directives were sent either directly, or indirectly through local enforcement officials. The government exercised a meticulous post-publication check, and all journals were required to deposit perfect copies with enforcement officials for scrutiny.

Journalistic controls extended to the ostensibly private world press agency, Stefani, and control over the movements and copy of foreign journalists working in Italy.

Parallel controls were exercised over publishers of periodicals and books. Control over periodicals was similar to control over the daily press. Control over books, however, was technically less rigid. Publishers were not required to submit manuscripts in advance, but they could expect quick reprisal if they published anything displeasing to the regime, and were accordingly willing to accede to the government's "invitation" to submit manuscripts dealing with social, historical, or political topics to the government in advance of publication.

Control over the motion pictures and radio was carried out

[79] Salvemini, *Under the Axe of Fascism,* p. 83.

through the operations of government-dominated "institutes" or organizations. Motion pictures came under the government monopoly, LUCE (*L'Unione Cinematografica Educativa*) a producer chiefly of documentaries dealing with national and international events, fascist activities, Italian foreign enterprise, and a variety of agricultural, industrial, military, cultural, and hygienic subjects. LUCE productions had to be shown as parts of cinema bills in theaters throughout the country. Productions of other agencies were subject to government scrutiny as a prerequisite to showing.

Radio was always a government-controlled activity in Italy, and the Fascists created an organization, *Ente Italiano per le Audizioni Radiofoniche* (familiarly known as *Ente*), to take over from an earlier government concession, and gave it a twenty-five year monopoly. All radio programs were checked in advance by a National Board of Review and Supervision, appointed by the minister of communications to represent the fascist confederations and syndicates in appropriate fields. *Ente* was used throughout as an instrument for domestic and foreign propaganda on behalf of the party and nation.

Other main channels of communications were equally controlled by the government and party, in part through the medium afforded by the corporations. The pertinent groups were the Corporation of the Professions and Arts and the Corporation of the Theater and of Public Entertainment. These latter groups functioned in parallel fashion to Goebbels' propaganda ministry and the organizations of theater, film, and music entertainers in Germany.

The machinery for control was supplemented by restrictions on the sources of public information, and especially severe sanctions against publication or dissemination of information affecting state security.

It was further supplemented by the use of the National Fascist Institute of Culture, the Italian Royal Academy, and other devices for the honoring and gratification of sympathetic foreigners, and the parading of historical Italian culture to put the party in the best light. The slogan of the Italian Academy was "not science for the sake of science and art for art's sake; but science and art together consciously, intentionally and directly working for the progress of the nation."[80]

Controls over nonparty organizations went hand in hand with the assault on public opinion through organs of all forms of public communications which were directly owned or managed by the leaders of the party. Just as Goebbels had his authoritative *Das Reich* and the Communists their *Bolshevik,* Mussolini had his *Gerarchia,* as an official channel for his views on economic and political topics. Just as the Nazis had their *Voelkische Beobachter* and the Communists their *Pravda,* Mussolini had his *Popolo d'Italia* and *Regime Fascista.* The publications of the Fascist Institute of Culture consisted chiefly of rehashes and reissues of the latest authoritative pronouncements with tame exegesis and commentary.

VI. CONCLUSION

The essence ot fascism, as with the other modern totalitarian systems, was the struggle of a man and a clique for total power. The history of fascism does not reveal that this power was totally achieved or totally exercised, although the leaders of the party never gave up their efforts to impose their domination on every sector of national life, and to destroy any person or group who opposed them. The points at which fascism failed to exemplify total state domination were points at which they had to make accommodations with social and historical forces as a means of gaining and maintaining power. The position of religion and the state, and especially that of the Catholic church, was the most striking illustration. But the extent of fascist political infection was not fully realized until after Mussolini's defeat, when the struggles of Italians to regain democratic political life after the fascist destruction of political groups, testified to the thoroughness with which the Fascists smashed centers not only for opposing political organization, but for generating competing political belief. It took a national military disaster to break the hold of the party.

[80] Quoted in McGovern, *From Luther to Hitler,* p. 570.

The compromises and particular political paths of fascism illustrate a major modifying element for fascist total domination—the necessity of accommodation to indigenous political belief and tradition as the emotional foundations on which fascism as a mass-state had to rest. The attack of fascism on the liberal position was especially shocking to the traditional liberals and democrats, because it proceeded from an explicit denial of the values of the liberal position. But the denial and the practice built upon total deification of the state were possible for fascism only because of the failure of the liberal state, and the weakness of the liberal tradition, in Italy.

In the final analysis, a survey of the whole fascist period shows that the tendency toward genuine, total control never abated—against political opposition, against the church, against centers of intellectual and educational dissidence. The corporative state might rely on technical advice and discussion in the first instance, but it was crystal clear from Italian practice that the claim of the state to over-all control of these economic organs was not left to atrophy. Neither capitalist nor worker could count on immunity from the demands of the regime, made in the name of the nation, and enforced by state and party suasion.

Founded on the unprincipled seizure of power, dramatized for the nation by the demonstration of power, fascism foundered on the failure of power.

CHAPTER VI

NATIONAL SOCIALISM

Naziism, historically, was the third of the modern totalitarian movements to seize power. Communism seized it in the name of a class; fascism seized it in the name of the nation; naziism seized it in the name of a race. All three had deep roots in European thought and patterns of action. Communism in particular specialized in the critique of the existing economic and political order, and developed a rich literature specifying the ethics and the pragmatics of the seizure and exercise of power by a revolutionary elite, taking necessary steps on the violent road toward the establishment of a moral utopia—a utopia which communist theorists wasted little time in trying to describe. The Fascists developed their political rationale as they went along, as justifications of their moves to seize and consolidate power. But the Fascists did more: they elaborated the theory and practice of totalitarianism in behalf of a restricted entity—a nation or race, no matter which—that were carried to ultimate conclusions by the Germans. This chapter shows in some detail how the Germans applied fascist patterns to their own problems, adding the elements of racialist and eugenic beliefs to the fascist ideological arsenal.

I. INTRODUCTION

The leading ideas of national socialism, which underlie its politics, its economics, and its history, are the ideas of *Volk* (folk, or people; the German race, and racialism), of leader, and of movement. The idea of the equality and dignity of the individual, fundamental to the Western notion of human freedom, is specifically and consciously repudiated by the Nazi, who bases his political values on the supremacy of the German (Nordic) race, who looks to his Führer for expression of the true will of that race, and who finds in the hierarchy of the movement the dynamic force of the state, which includes the hierarchically organized party and society.

The position of the individual is determined not by his existence as a competent and law-abiding person, but by his racial origin and sex; these in turn determine his status and possible role in society, according to an elaborate system of privileges, rights, duties, obligations, and disabilities.

National socialism is antidemocratic. Like communism, it used democratic or liberal freedoms to seize power, but once having done so, repudiated democratic forms. Said Goebbels in 1934:

> We National Socialists have never maintained that we were representatives of a democratic viewpoint, but we have openly declared that we only made use of democratic means in order to gain power, and that after the seizure of power we would ruthlessly deny to our opponents all those means which they had granted to us during the time of our opposition.[1]

In particular, national socialism denies the elective principle, as a logical consequence of Nazi estimates of the role of the people in the political process. Said Hitler:

> . . . the people must possess some means for giving expression to their thoughts or their wishes. Examining this problem more closely, we see that the people themselves have originally no convictions of their own. Their convictions are formed, of course, just as everywhere else. The decisive question is, who enlightens the people, who educates them?[2]

The thought was completed by Neesse:

> The people, however, is never politically active as a whole, but only through those who embody its will. The true will of a people can never be determined by a majority vote. It can only display itself in men or movements, and history will decide whether these men or movements could rightly claim to be the representatives of the people's will.[3]

The elective principle was found neither in party nor in gov-

[1] Josef Goebbels, *Wesen und Gestalt des Nationalsozialismus* (1935) pp. 12-13, quoted in U. S. Department of State, *National Socialism* (1943), p. 4.

[2] Adolf Hitler, Speech of Dec. 10, 1940 in Berlin (Rheinmetall-Borsig Works), quoted in *My New Order* (edited by Raoul de Roussy de Sales, 1941), p. 879.

[3] Gottfried Neesse, *Die Nationalsozialistische Deutsche Abeiterpartei—Versuch einer Rechtsdeutung* (1935), p. 59, quoted in U. S. Department of State, *National Socialism,* p. 26.

ernment, not even to the extent found in the hierarchical election formalities of the Communists. Such elections as took place during the nazi regime were either plebiscites or ratifications, giving the voter no significant area of choice. He could vote *Ja* or spoil his ballot. And voting *Ja* was persuaded if not ensured by the ridicule or violence or both imposed by the party or its correlated organizations. Elections to the Reichstag or to municipal councillorships had little meaning. The Reichstag lost all power as a law-giving or government-controlling body, turning into a speech-chamber for the Führer. Municipal corporations were brought under the jurisdiction of the Ministry of the Interior; however efficient, they had small scope for the exercise of administrative, let alone political initiative.

Nazi Germany was classically totalitarian, in the sense that no area of human activity was left outside the sphere of control of the state. Like the Communists, the Nazis had to take time to impose their controls thoroughly and completely on all levels of society. Some agencies, like the church, proved particularly difficult to "co-ordinate"; and to the end, the Nazis had to combat the ultimate defensive tactic of the individual: privatization and withdrawal from participation in state-party activities. But labor unions, political parties, youth organizations, all fell under the onslaught of the nazi application of German thoroughness and organization.

The principle of leadership was applied not only to the political sphere, and at the level of the leader, Hitler; it was applied throughout the nazi organization of all German society. The roles of leader and follower were spelled out for each relationship; from above came orders, from below, execution.[4] Originally developed in the party, the nazi principle of authoritarian

[4] Said Hitler in the Berlin *Sportpalast* on Apr. 8, 1933:

"When our opponents say: 'It is easy for you: you are a dictator'—We answer them, 'No, gentlemen, you are wrong; there is no single dictator, but ten thousand, each in his own place.' And even the highest authority in the hierarchy has itself only one wish, never to transgress against the supreme authority to which it, too, is responsible. We have in our movement developed this loyalty in following the leader, this blind obedience of which all the others know nothing and which gave to us the power to surmount everything." U. S. Department of State, *National Socialism,* p. 40.

leadership was first applied to the spheres of civil service, labor service, and the military (where it had, indeed, little to add),[5] and then to the spheres of "private" economy.[6]

The nazi system was totalitarian, but not universal in the world community. Since it conducted revolution in behalf of a mystic but restricted racial elite, it was quite truthfully and obviously not an article for export. German national socialism was not a *world* revolutionary doctrine in the same sense as communism, for it offered international salvation only to Germandom abroad, and provided no means whereby the oppressed of other lands (who were not German nationals) could so identify themselves with national socialism as to bid for preferment within its society. It was *national* socialism not alone in its appeal to the principle of nationality, and its affirmation of the legitimacy of German national aspirations. Although the pattern of national socialism might be repeated elsewhere, it would take the form of an affirmation of the particular national aspirations and adapt itself to the local conditions of the state in which it appeared. All national socialism had to export ideologically was its model of hierarchy and discrimination.

II. FREEDOM IN THE POLITICAL SPHERE

For the Nazi, freedom in the political sphere had meaning chiefly for the nation, the state, and little if any positive meaning for the individual. The Nazi could understand freedom for Germany from the threat of bolshevism and the controls and oppressions of world Jewry and the imperialist democracies—Great Britain, France, and the United States. He could understand freedom for his movement to organize, to agitate, to propagandize, and to seize political power, and then to exercise the

[5] See Ernst Rudolf Huber, *Verfassungsrecht des grossdeutschen Reiches* in U. S. Department of State, *National Socialism,* p. 41 as follows:

"The ranks of the public services are regarded as forces organized on the living principle of leadership and following: The authority of command exercised in the labor service, the military service, and the civil service is Führer-authority. . . . there can be no political leadership which does not have recourse to command and force as the means for the accomplishment of its ends."

[6] See below, pp. 282 ff.

most valuable freedom: the freedom to suppress all other political competitors. But freedom for the individual was conceived as a negative thing: freedom from the "capitalists" or from the same forms of Judo-democratic or bolshevist oppression as hedged in the German nation, but rarely if ever freedom *for* anything except to be a German, and to play the sacrificial role of the individual in a community where the state counted for everything, and the individual nothing. It was a Hegelian freedom: the freedom for one to do what he must. Individual freedom was always a limited notion in fascist theory. Joad says that it was equally true of naziism and of fascism that "only so much liberty shall be allowed to the individual as is compatible with the convenience of the State."[7] Freedom for the individual is not a final or even an intermediate goal of the nazi system. Finally, Hitler affirmed the essentially Marxist proposition that freedom is meaningless apart from wealth and power.[8]

The logical corollary of this view of freedom is that the individual possesses no basic rights which he can urge against the state.[9]

[7] C. E. M. Joad: *Guide to the Philosophy of Morals and Politics* (1938), p. 622. Joad quotes Mussolini as saying that the individual in the fascist state is "deprived of all useless and possibly harmful freedom, but retains what is essential: the deciding power in this question cannot be the individual, but the State alone."

[8] ". . . we were further persuaded that economic prosperity is inescapable from political freedom . . . freedom can be only a consequence of power and that the source of power is the will. Consequently the will to power must be strengthened in a people with passionate ardor. And thus we realized fifthly that

"5. We as National Socialists and members of the German Workers Party—a Party pledged to work—must be on principle the most fanatical Nationalists. We realized that the State can be for our people a paradise only if the people can hold sway therein freely as in a paradise: we realized that a slave state will never be a paradise, but only—always and for all time—a hell or a colony.

"6. And then sixthly we grasped the fact that power in the last resort is possible only where there is strength, and . . . that truth is valueless so long as there is lacking the indomitable will to turn this realization into action!" Hitler's speech of Apr. 12, 1922, at Munich, quoted in *My New Order*, pp. 24-25.

[9] Huber, *Verfassungsrecht des grossdeutschen Reiches* (1939) says: "Not until the nationalistic political philosophy had become dominant could the liberalistic idea of basic rights be really overcome. The concept of personal liberties of the individual as opposed to the authority of the state had to disappear; it is not to be reconciled with the principle of the

Whatever rights the person enjoys, he enjoys as a member of the folk-community, and his rights are always subordinate to the duties imposed by that community. Rights do not exist for the individual, but for the community. The legal result is "the organic fixation of the individual in the living order."[10]

PARTY AND GOVERNMENT

The nazi state was a one-party state—a logical outgrowth of the nazi emphasis on unity, which pervaded all spheres. Political truth was not supposed to come out of the clash of parties; the will of the people is voiced through the leader, and it is the function of the one party to see that all organs of national life give expression to that will. There is no room for other parties than the party of the leader; no function of political balancing or of giving expression to groups within the state. The nazi result was made possible in part because of Germany's historical experience with parties: German parties had characteristically represented particular interests, and had not tried to formulate platforms which conceived the interest of the nation as a whole, if only for the purpose of assuring a majority at the polls. German parties represented religious groups, economic groups, and other special groups of many sorts. During the Weimar period, these groups, encouraged by the provisions of the Weimar constitution for proportional representation, multiplied to the point where clear party majorities were unthinkable as means of controlling national legislation.

The laws promulgated in 1933 changed all that. The first prohibited the formation of new political parties on July 14,

---

nationalistic Reich. There are no personal liberties of the individual which fall outside of the realm of the state and which must be respected by the state. The member of the people, organically connected with the whole community, has replaced the isolated individual; he is included in the totality of the political people and is drawn into the collective action. There can no longer be any question of a private sphere, free of state influence, which is sacred and untouchable before the political unity. The constitution of the nationalistic Reich is therefore not based upon a system of inborn and inalienable rights of the individual." Quoted in U. S. Department of State, *National Socialism*, p. 50.

[10] The same, quoting Huber, pp. 365-66.

1933.[11] The second, promulgated December 1, 1933, said in part (Section 1 (1)): "After the victory of the National Socialist revolution the National Socialist German Workers' party has become the bearer of the German government and is inseparably connected with the state." This law specified the official connection at the cabinet level between party and state, defined the party as a "corporation of public law," set forth its main constitutional and disciplinary authority, and established a special legal position for members of the party and its related organizations.[12]

From the time of seizure of power in January 1933, the Nazi party carried out a program of establishing the dominance of the party over all elements of the state; the civil service, the judiciary, and the army. For the greater part of the nazi period, it could be said that the party was moving toward, but had not yet achieved complete fusion with the state.[13]

The Nazi party, like the Communist, was an elite party, not

[11] It provides as follows: "1. The National Socialist German Workers' party is the only political party in Germany. 2. Whoever undertakes to maintain the organization of another political party, or to form a new political party, is to be punished with imprisonment in a penitentiary up to 3 years or with confinement in a jail from 6 months to 3 years unless the act is punishable by a higher penalty under other provisions."

[12] The law, sec. 3 (1) stated that "Members of the National Socialist German Workers' party and of the S.A. (including affiliated organizations) have, as the leading and moving power of the National Socialist State, increased duties toward the leader, the people, and the state."

[13] See Franz Neumann, *Behemoth: The Structure and Practice of National Socialism* (1944), pp. 50-51, 66-68.

In 1933 and 1934, for example, party members were not allowed to "interfere with the bureaucracy" and in particular told to keep their hands off business and administration. In the early years, party members had to resign their party active memberships when serving in the army, since they were subject to a different "disciplinary authority." But such strategies in winning the support of heavy industry, and in keeping party functionaries at lower levels from upsetting necessary agencies, were dropped as party dominance became clear in the latter years before the war. The fusion of party with state was accomplished only by the liquidation or discipline of those radical elements in the party who wished to supersede state organs, not to use them for the imposition of the program of the party on the nation. Such conflicts had to do with the personal spoils and privileges of the lesser party members; for those at the top, it was necessary to maintain both party and state agencies; the one for specialized violence and discipline, the other for executive action.

a mass party; neither strove for a membership to include everyone who wanted to join, but both sought for membership of those who would carry out, with unfailing enthusiasm and energy, the party program. The test of ideological loyalty was not widely important in the Nazi party; the sole test was clear: unquestioning acceptance and execution of the will of the leader, whatever that might be. The Nazi party, of course, accepted only those who were racially "pure."

Both parties were hierarchically organized, although the Nazi dispensed with the communist formalities of democratic "election" of leaders at all levels. And the Nazi party in particular developed a bureaucracy rivaling that of the state in size and complexity.

POWERS OF GOVERNMENT

Nazi theorists of the early years of power paid much attention to developing a theory that the nazi state is not totalitarian; that there are areas where the state may not enter. Thus the party demanded all control in the *political* arena, but claimed that the state had no business in the economic realm. However, this claim was to prove abortive, just as was the appearance to which it gave rise of an area where the powers of the state and its henchmen would not go.

The Nazis destroyed the German constitution, with whatever guarantees it provided for limitation on the powers of government, and direction of state power into certain procedural and topical channels. They replaced it with fluid notions of their own. Constitutionalism did not mean nearly so much to the German individual as a guarantee of his rights, and a control over the scope of government and its forms of action, as it did to his English or American contemporary. Yet it meant something, and even this something was destroyed by the nazi revolt against the rule of law, and against the role of a constitution in that role. The nazi constitution was radically different. As stated by a foremost German juridical authority in 1939,

> The new constitution of the German Reich . . . is not a constitution in the formal sense such as was typical of the nineteenth cen-

tury. The new Reich has no written constitutional declaration, but its constitution exists in the unwritten basic political order of the Reich. One recognizes it in the spiritual powers which fill our people, in the real authority in which our political life is grounded, and in the basic laws regarding the structure of the state which have been proclaimed so far. The advantage of such an unwritten constitution over the formal constitution is that the basic principles do not become rigid but remain in a constant, living, movement. Not dead institutions but living principles determine the nature of the new constitutional order.[14]

Harder to destroy was the deep-rooted German tradition of a *Rechtsstaat,* which allowed to the state absolute power, but required that the executive agents of the state must apply legally sanctioned principles.

The solution of the Nazis was to revise the procedure of lawmaking, to maintain scrupulously the appearance of constitutionality and legality, and to provide through such doctrines as legal analogy for cases which could not be dealt with satisfactorily under law already published. Part of this process included the destruction of the independent judiciary, the inanition of the Reichstag as a lawgiving organ, and the centralization of all political power in the federal government.

Finally, during the period when the individual might yet assert his rights and position against the state by praying for a correct application to his case of existing law, the individual faced the purely expedient judgment of the party, which might take from him by ridicule or violence what the state might allow him under existing statutes.[15]

The position of the individual against the state in Nazi Germany was regulated by expediency and bargaining, in which

[14] Ernst Rudolf Huber, *Verfassungsrecht des grossdeutschen Reiches* quoted in U. S. Department of State, *National Socialism* (1943), p. 23.

[15] The end of Weimar constitutionalism was largely accomplished by the "Law to Combat the National Crisis" (of Mar. 24, 1933) which gave effective lawmaking power, including power to alter the constitution, to the Cabinet, and was sealed by the law of Aug. 1, 1934, fusing the offices of President and Reich Chancellor. Federal centralism was established by the laws of Jan. 30, 1934 (Law for the New Structure of the Reich, which states in Article 1: "The State legislatures are abolished"), the related Decree of Feb. 2, 1934, and the Law Relating to National Governors of Jan. 30, 1935.

the needs of the party and the state were balanced against whatever demands for freedom of action the individual might try to secure. There was no doctrine of reserved powers, which would keep the state from any area of political control, either as the proper province of lesser polities or of the people. Nothing in nazi theory, as it developed under the stress of preparation for the wars required by nazi national expansionism, gave any individual protection from the extension of political power or its classic expression in violence. The racialist and hierarchical theory of society meant that the individual as such was nothing; only particular classes of individuals could look for certain forms of advantage, while others could expect disabilities with equal certainty. Withdrawal from participation in state functions, slow-down or nonparticipation, and privatization of interest were the only avenues open, and then only partially open, to the individual as a defense against the constant efforts of the state to shape his entire waking life.

What procedures available in Western democracies for the control of governments by individuals were available to the German citizen? Few or none. At best, the device of election to public office was an avenue for the expression of discontent, rather than an opportunity to choose from genuine alternatives of policy. Public opinion was the object of constant observation and solicitude by party agencies, including the party press, but there was no effective free channel whereby the individual could make himself heard as one of the voices which the Führer might take to be that of the *Volk*. The channels of communication were closed, in particular, to any dissenting group. The will of the people was not necessarily what the people thought; the Nazis expressly rejected majorities as ways of deciding political questions.[16]

Although national socialism claimed to rest on the will of the

[16] Said Hitler in 1922: "Democracy is fundamentally not German; it is Jewish. . . . This Jewish democracy with its majority decisions has always been without exception only a means towards the destruction of any existing Aryan leadership." (*My New Order,* p. 22.) In 1933: "We must now get rid of the last remains of democracy, especially of the methods of voting and of the decisions by the majority. . . ." Speech to Reich Commissioners, Berlin, July 6, 1933.

people, or more exactly *Volk,* that will did not express itself in legislation formulated by elective, representative legislative organs, applied by executive agencies subject to its prescriptions and controlled by an independent judiciary. Law in the national socialist state is the product of the will of the people expressed by the leader, who directly embodies that will. He is not responsible to the people, but only to history. Historical developments alone show whether his expressions and actions are correct, and entitle him to his position of leader.[17]

Formally speaking, the German citizen could affect political decisions by elections to public office, and by expressing himself on whatever matters might be referred to the people by the National Cabinet.[18] Elections to the Reichstag became meaningless with the disappearance of any power from the Reichstag as an institution. The plebiscites were held to get the approval of the people on overwhelmingly popular deeds of the government; two of the four were coupled with elections. The suffrage was naturally wide, subject to certain restrictions: Jews could not vote, nor could women be candidates. But all Germans not thus disqualified, twenty years of age or older, whether living in Germany or not, could vote.[19] The suffrage administration was very flexible, subject to the regulations of the Minister of the Interior.[20] The percentages of turnout, and approval for

[17] Says Huber (quoted in U. S. Department of State, *National Socialism,* p. 36): "It would be impossible for a law to be introduced and acted upon in the Reichstag which had not originated with the *Fuehrer* or, at least, received his approval. The procedure is similar to that of the plebiscite: The lawgiving power does not rest in the Reichstag; it merely proclaims through its decision its agreement with the will of the *Fuehrer,* who is the lawgiver of the German people."

[18] The last relatively free election was that of March 7, 1933, which confirmed the position of the Nazi party in the Reichstag, 44 per cent of the popular vote, a small parliamentary majority; see Fritz Morstein Marx ed., *Foreign Governments* (1949) p. 333. Under Hitler there were only three Reichstag elections, and four plebiscites. The same, p. 337.

[19] Marx, ed., *Foreign Governments,* p. 337.

[20] "Suffrage Law for Reichstag Elections," Mar. 7, 1936. The law made the following eligible: German nationals considered Reich citizens under the Reich Citizenship Law, and German nationals of German or related blood. The Minister of the Interior could change the requirements of the national law governing eligibility and the distribution of seats to the

the proposals of the party, are too well known to require recapitulation here. Although a "Law Concerning Referenda" was promulgated on July 14, 1933, it is clear that the only avenues which the German citizen had for affecting the political decisions of the government, were bureaucratic avenues—government or party. The individual organized in a nongovernmental group, such as a religious body, might be effective in the total process of struggle and bargaining which marked the nazi strides to power, but as an individual his wishes counted for little more than a weight to be moved by the apparatus.

The political status of the individual in Germany was rigidly regulated according to the racialist and "folkish" views of the party. Citizenship was regulated by a law of September 16, 1935 and a decree of November 14, 1935. The law specified that "only such persons as are of German or kindred stock and who have proved by their conduct that they are willing and fit loyally to serve the German people and Reich are citizens of the Reich."[21] Citizenship was important, despite the limited political powers of the individual as such, because "Reich citizens shall be the sole possessors of complete political rights according to the provisions of the law."[22] Non-citizens could not hold public office, which in Germany debarred them from wide sectors of the Economy. Under the decree of November 14, 1935, it was technically possible for a part Jew to hold citizenship, if he had been endowed with "temporary Reich citizenship" by the Minister of the Interior in agreement with the Deputy Fuehrer. Yet a full Jew "cannot be a Reich citizen. He is not allowed to vote in political affairs; he cannot hold a public office."[23]

The essence of these and many other technical restrictions on political and civil liberties, was to create a situation in which

---

candidates on the election lists, and shorten the time interval provided in the national election law. The law characteristically authorized punishment for those who voted without being eligible.

[21] Sec. 2 (1).

[22] Sec. 2 (3).

[23] Sec. 4 (1). Sec. 4 (2) provided for the retirement of all Jews from public office by specified dates.

almost any member of society could be threatened in one way or another with loss of job, of property, or of other vital interests. Since these and other legal enactments were characteristically subject to amendment by the administering authority, the possibilities for administrative or party blackmail were multiplied.

THE INDIVIDUAL AND THE COURTS

In pre-Nazi Germany, the courts were by no means either incorruptible, insensitive to the class position of prisoners in the dock, or forgetful of the political implications of judicial choices. Yet most individuals had access to judicial remedies against arbitrary action by government. Under the Nazis, however, the earlier shortcomings were intensified; the legal position of the individual deteriorated, and the courts were turned into one more instrument of the movement. Nazi changes in the nature of law, the nature of the state, and the role of the party, were coupled with the shackling of the independent judiciary. Law had become the will of the *Volk* as expressed by the Führer, liable to change with the Führer's whim, or any other authoritative view of current requirements. For the Nazis, law became "what is useful for the German nation." State and party were largely fused, and the state bureaucracy brought under the surveillance and policy control of the party. Under the Nazis all government courts were brought under the control of the Federal Ministry of Justice,[24] and a triple system of courts grew up: the previously established judicial system, the nazi additions thereto, exemplified by the People's Courts, and the special judicial organs set up by the party to administer

[24] Centralization of the administration of justice was signalized by the law of Jan. 31, 1935, which reads in part: "Since the administration of justice in the states has been placed in the hands of the National Minister of Justice, the Reich hereby takes over, as possessor of full judicial power, the entire judicial system with all of its privileges, rights and duties, and with all of its officials and offices. Consequently, the Cabinet has decided upon the following law which is hereby proclaimed:

"1. On the first of April, 1935, the state authorities of justice will become Reich authorities, the state officials of justice Reich officials, and the employees and workers of the state authorities will enter the service of the Reich."

party discipline in those cases where the party did not wish to avail itself to the public courts. In the non-party courts, some cases were decided on a basis of justice or equity, except where Jews or party members were involved. But in these as in other courts, a doctrine of analogy was devised and applied to execute the party will, whether justified by expressed law or not. Under this doctrine an individual could be punished for an act not covered by an existing statute, under the terms of the nearest applicable statute, if the individual had committed an act violating "the healthy sentiment of the people." Nor did the service of sentence passed by an ordinary court suffice to discharge a transgressor's debt to the state: a decree of the Ministry of Justice provided that "persons inimical to the State, after having served their sentence or after acquittal (sic) by the court, be placed in the hands of the secret police for reforming them further in concentration camps."[25]

Under the Weimar republic, there had been a federal supreme court which could judge the constitutionality of state laws; this disappeared with the Nazi seizure of power. And at the same time, there disappeared the practice of judicial review of administrative decisions, either as a procedural or legal matter. Most of the decrees regulating business, for example, provided that the application of their provisions were not subject to court review.[26] Since courts were now only an instrument of a unitary state, subject to a central will, and the individual possessed no constitutional right against the government there was no logic remaining in any system whereby the courts, as one agency of government, should check the correctness of the procedures of others in the interest of individual rights. Such a concept was completely alien to naziism. The courts were used as an instrument of the state against any person or group transgressing state commands.

The individual was supposed to have the right of representa-

[25] See Marx ed., pp. 337-38, and Neumann, *Behemoth*, pp. 20-22. See also Ernst Fraenkel, *The Dual State* (1941).

[26] Ludwig Hamburger, *How Nazi Germany Has Controlled Business* (1943), p. 99.

tion by counsel, but this was largely negated by *in camera* proceedings, and by the dangers involved for the counsel themselves, who ran risk of loss of livelihood or physical harm if they put up a vigorous defense for a racially or politically suspect prisoner. The whole subject of evidence was recast to give effect to nazi and racialist doctrines.

The dominance of the judge over proceedings, well established in the pre-nazi period, took on new meaning with the "purification" of the judiciary, the bringing of all judges within the jurisdiction of the Federal Ministry of Justice, and the reduction to impotence of the role of the jury. Independence of tenure and long preparatory training were abolished, and the judges opened up to powerful political and other pressures, whereas previously they were able to exercise some choice as to when and in what conditions they wished to temper application of the law in view of political or other special conditions. The individual lost in effect whatever rights he might theoretically enjoy under prescribed judicial procedure.

The dominance of political control was especially marked in the special courts set up by the Nazis, such as the Courts for the Protection of Social Honor organized by the Act for the Organization of National Labor.[27]

In the special nazi courts and to a high degree in other courts, the individual could not count on procedural guarantees which would give him a chance adequately to defend himself.

The most notorious violations of accepted Western standards of the administration of justice and penal law were those concerning cruel and unusual punishments. The whole system of concentration camps, exposed in their full horror by the liberating Allied armies and by the subsequent trials of war criminals and those accused of crimes against humanity, is the

[27] See Wallace R. Deuel, *People Under Hitler* (1942), pp. 326-31. Deuel describes cases in which Junkers or businessmen were severely punished by these Courts for unsubstantiated threats, accusations against, or abuse of workers. These courts were staffed by political appointees, and usually operated according to the suggestions of Labor Trustees, who were also Party appointees.

first example. Its details have been given world publicity, and need not detain us here. The second, less thoroughly dramatized for the civilized world, was the practice of castration and sterilization as judicially determined penalties—both outcomes of nazi racialism and pseudo-genetics.

Castration as a measure against criminality, and sterilization as a measure against the transmission of certain hereditary diseases, were introduced by law in 1933, and the laws subsequently revised and tightened.[28] "Habitual Criminals" were defined as "persons over twenty-one years old who have been twice sentenced to prison terms of six months each for sex crimes, or to persons sentenced for murder or manslaughter committed to incite or satisfy sexual lust."[29] Sterilization was prescribed in cases of hereditary imbecility, schizophrenia, manic depressive psychoses, hereditary epilepsy, Huntington's chorea, hereditary blindness, hereditary deafness, and extreme physical malformation. The castration penalty was ordered by the ordinary criminal courts. Sterilization was ordered by special courts, composed of a judge, a medical officer, and a medical practitioner. Decision of a lower sterilization court could be appealed to a higher sterilization court, similarly composed, whose decision was final. Cases could be brought before such courts by the patient, the medical officer, or the director of an institution in which the patient was confined.[30]

Castration was numerically far less significant in Germany than sterilization; Deuel estimates that before the war, some 375,000 persons were sterilized, as compared to 2,000 castrated. In determining whether or not to sterilize, it was frequently argued that special gifts—artistic or other—should be preserved to the nation, even at the cost of perpetuating a modicum of hereditary disease. But such arguments were not allowed, since

[28] Statute against Habitual Criminals, Nov. 24, 1933; Statute to Prevent Hereditarily Diseased Offspring, July 14, 1933, amended June 26, 1935 and Feb. 4, 1936.

[29] Neumann, *Behemoth,* p. 111.

[30] The same, pp. 111-12.

the Nazis held that blood purity was primary, and the nation would not suffer if all the artists were sterilized.[31]

The legal and medical standards for determining the presence and severity of a disease rendering a person liable to compulsory sterilization, were admittedly fluid. The result was to put a terrible weapon in the hands of the party, to be exercised as a means of punishing or reducing overt hostility to the regime or for other purposes not stated in the law. This was slightly mitigated by the efforts of the regime to protect sterilized persons from ridicule by conducting proceedings in secret.[32]

Possibly more important in total impact than either was the undetermined number killed by the SS because of "unfitness"; Deuel estimates that some 100,000 defectives were killed during 1939 and 1940, and William Shirer estimates that some 50,000 more were killed during the course of the war.[33] In such cases, the sentence of a court was not thought necessary.

THE SECRET POLICE

Far more important to the concrete, day-to-day freedom and security of the individual than the loss of freedoms and rights before the bar of justice or as a citizen against the bureaucracy was the position of the individual before the government or party organs of arbitrary and terrible violence: the political police, the SS, and the concentration camps. The political police, or Gestapo (*Geheime Staatspolizei:* secret state police) was created as an organ of the Prussian Ministry of the Interior,[34] and ultimately incorporated into the Reich Security

[31] Deuel, *People Under Hitler,* p. 223.

[32] The same, pp. 228-29. He strikes a trial balance here of the impact of sterilization on some groups in German society, pointing out that while the majority are horrified by the prospect, others accept it on explanation that sexual activity is not estopped (sterilization does not mean castration), that few die from the operation, and that no emotional disturbances ensue. Others positively welcome sterilization as eliminating barriers to a libidinous life.

[33] The same, p. 220; Neumann, *Behemoth,* citing Shirer, on p. 112.

[34] By laws of Apr. 26, 1933, Nov. 30, 1933, and parts of the decree of Mar. 8, 1934, rescinded by the Law Concerning the Secret State Police of Feb. 12, 1936. This law provided in part that the duty of the Gestapo was to expose and oppose all collective forces dangerous to the state, to

Police (*Sicherheits polizei*). The SS (*Schutzstaffel:* Elite Guards or defense group) was a party organ created in 1925 to serve as a special protective body for party purposes, which ultimately turned into a paramilitary organ of protective police, a source of personnel for the Gestapo, and a source of elite military formations (the so-called *Waffen* or armed SS). The SS enjoyed special status by government decree and by court decisions.[35] In the field of police, SS leadership was fused with that of the ordinary police, and SS formations exercised similar functions to those of the ordinary police (as well as numerous special ones); in practice this meant that police actions were freed from any procedural restrictions, and not reviewable in the courts.

Concentration camps were started with the Hindenburg decree of February 28, 1933, suspending civil liberties (the so-called Reichstag fire decree). They were turned over to the Gestapo by section 7 of the Prussian decree, cited above, establishing the Gestapo as an organ of the public prosecutor's office. The individual had no redress against a decision of the Gestapo to send him to a concentration camp—which the Gestapo could do, for whatever reasons pleased it, and for whatever length of time it deemed necessary.[36] Once in the con-

---

collect and evaluate results of these "findings," to inform the government and to keep the "remaining authorities" informed about "all evidence." The law made the Minister President chief of the Gestapo, and gave this organ the prerogatives of the state police authorities. Gestapo officers were appointed and removed by agreement of its chief with the Minister of the Interior. The law specifically provided "7. The orders and business of the Secret State Police are not subject to review in the administrative courts." *Source Book on European Governments* (1937), pp. IV-70-71.

[35] The decree of Nov. 9, 1935 required and authorized every SS man to defend his honor with his weapon (characteristically his dagger). Sec. 53 of the penal code as interpreted by the courts prohibited the ordinary man from using a weapon except in self-defense, but allowed an SS-man to use his weapon even if he could ward off attack by other means. Finally, a "ruling" of May 26, 1939, defined the relations of the SS to the ordinary police.

[36] See Neumann, *Behemoth,* pp. 452-53. He says that "at first some judges tried to restrain the discretionary power of the police. . . . Needless to say, the absolute and arbitrary power of the Gestapo over all personal liberties is not disputed by any court today [1944]."

centration camp, the individual had no redress whatsoever against the decisions or the measures taken by the camp authorities. The SS could both incarcerate and execute without a judicial determination. Initially for "political prisoners" the concentration camps came during the later years of the regime, especially in the war, to be respositories for all sorts of persons deemed inimical to the regime or to society—from gypsies to hardened criminals, from nonconformist liberals to Communists.[37]

The control of the SS, especially under the leadership of Himmler, was ramified throughout the nazi system, because many high SS officers, as the most Nordic and "best" Germans, simultaneously held high administrative and judicial offices and could wield the entire power of the bureaucratic apparatus against an individual, if necessary.

The powers of the office of public prosecutor were also of first significance in estimating the status of the individual before the law. In most of the great variety of special courts created to serve the needs of nazi-sponsored or government groups, the individual had no right to choose his counsel, to present evidence, to obtain a public hearing, or to appeal to higher authority. The public prosecutor could bring a case in any of the special courts, at his discretion. A decree issued immediately after the outbreak of war empowered the prosecutor to bring any criminal case immediately before a special division of the Supreme Court, and to reopen within a year's time any case in which the leadership was dissatisfied with a decision. The prosecutor actually determined the final judgment, usually capital punishment.[38]

[37] A graphic survey of life in concentration camps is given in Eugen Kogon, *Der SS Staat* (1947).

[38] Neumann, *Behemoth*, pp. 456-57. He describes the wartime developments as follows:

"Lay judges have completely disappeared from the field of criminal justice, except in the people's courts. The so-called juries, consisting of three judges and six jurymen, no longer exist. The rights of defense counsel have been virtually abolished and criminal law has been brutalized. . . . Many new crimes have been created, with capital punishment the rule. Every attempt at, or preparation for, a political crime is punishable by death. By decree of 1 September 1939, intentional listening to

III. SOCIAL AND RELIGIOUS FREEDOMS

The state of social and religious freedoms in Nazi Germany was determined by the nazi demand for totalitarian control of all phases of human life including the intellectual and spiritual. The Nazi was not content with outward conformity or negative civic virtue; he strove for inner, enthusiastic acceptance of the creed and program of the regime. Obsessed with the ideal of unity, he attempted by propaganda both to achieve it and to demonstrate it, and by all other means available to the unlimited state to ensure it. The concepts of race and *Volk* were brought to bear on every sort of association. The ideal of the leader was at bottom a religious ideal, in which no Saviour or other God could be allowed to interfere effectively with the relation of the German follower and his leader. Hence the formal tolerance of Christianity or other religious creeds was belied by the ideal and the strivings of the nazi movement to replace all spiritual loyalties with those to the people and its historically if not divinely appointed leader.

In Germany there was no freedom to form private associations outside of the ambit of the state, or free from the surveillance and control of the party. Essentially, the history of the nazification of society consists of the abolition or confiscation of property, destruction of the leadership, or the *Gleichschaltung* (co-ordination) of all forms of association—social, economic, or religious—within the nazi social structure. The church showed the greatest powers of resistance, but was forced to undergo organizational overhauling, numerous disabilities and strictures, as well as the competition of the nazi-supported German Christian movement. The family suffered even more from Nazi pressures.

SOCIAL FREEDOMS

This section deals with the family, and with the position of noneconomic and nonreligious forms of private association. The

---

foreign radio broadcasts is punishable by imprisonment or death. . . . No distinction is drawn between the perpetrator and the accessory, between the attempt and the consummated act. Retroactivity and the abolition of the territorial principle are now universal."

family was of first importance to the Nazis as the foundation of education, of civic attitudes, and loyalties; as the source of new Germans; and as a form of association in which the individual might conceivably withdraw from the sphere of the state. Hence education and propaganda were devoted to reducing the influence of the family in undesired directions, reshaping family influences to reinforce nazi ideas and to carry out nazi plans, and as a source of control. And the family was obviously of first importance to the carrying out of racialist and population policies.

The family. The basic statutes affecting the family included the Law for the Protection of German Blood and German Honor, of September 15, 1935, and an appurtenant decree, of November 14, 1935. The law stated in part:

> Clearly realizing that the purity of the German blood is the prerequisite for perpetuating the German people, and inspired by an inflexible determination to secure the existence of the German nation for all time to come, The Reichstag has unanimously passed the following law which is hereby proclaimed:
>
> 2. (1) Marriages between Jews and citizens of German or kindred stock shall be prohibited. Marriages concluded despite the law shall be considered void even when they were concluded abroad in circumvention of this law. . . .
>
> Non-marital sexual intercourse between Jews and citizens of German or kindred stock shall be prohibited.[39]

The decree also prohibited marriages between Jews and Jewish intermixures who have only one Jewish grandparent, and allowed Jewish intermixtures with two Jewish grandparents to marry Germans or one-Jew-grandparent intermixtures only with the permission of the Minister of the Interior and the Deputy Leader. The decree further prohibited marriage between Jewish intermixtures each of which had only one Jewish grandparent, as well as sexual intercourse between Jews and Jews with only one Jewish grandparent.[40]

Contamination could arise from other than Semitic sources

[39] *Source Book,* p. IV-80.
[40] The same, pp. IV-80-81, citing secs. 2, 3, 4, and 11 of the decree.

(for example, gypsies and the feeble-minded): consequently, the aforementioned decree also prohibited marriage "if children may be expected who may endanger the purity of the German blood," and required that engaged couples must prove their physical fitness for marriage prior to the ceremony.

The crime of race-betrayal (*Rassenschande*) was of consequence to the Nazis whether consummated within or without Germany; nazi sanctions were applied to Germans living anywhere that the party power could reach them, as well as to foreigners domiciled in the Reich.

The other side of the coin of racialism was the great emphasis on eugenic marriage and procreation, particularly marked in members of the party or of its paramilitary formations. SS-men required a special permit for marriage, and the racial antecedents of the prospective bride were carefully scrutinized. The qualifications of others were also examined, under the provisions of a Law to Protect the Hereditary Health of the German People (*Ehegesundheitsgesetz*) passed on October 18, 1935.[41] This law forbade persons to marry who were suffering from a contagious disease which might harm either the marriage partner or progeny; those under guardianship or temporary trusteeship; those suffering from a mental disorder "which causes marriage to appear undesirable from the viewpoint of the community of the people," and persons suffering from hereditary diseases in the meaning of the law for sterilization. And the courts added a fifth category: no sterile person might marry a fertile one capable of begetting or bearing healthy children.[42]

Divorce under the Nazis was chiefly important during the

[41] Neumann, *Behemoth,* p. 488, note 48. According to Deuel, this law was administered by the public health offices. Couples applying for the certificate of physical fitness had to show they did not fall into any of four categories of physical, mental, or moral diseases, and were examined in addition with respect to the following: "Bony structure, distribution of fat, muscular development, bearing and other general physical characteristics; sex life and sex organs; number of times failed in school, and other aspects of mental development; ages at which learned to walk and talk; childhood and other diseases; character development; use of alcohol and tobacco; ability to beget children; adaptation to environment." *People Under Hitler,* p. 231.

[42] The same, p. 233.

early period after they took power when it was used as an instrument to bring about marriage relations in conformity with the racial laws. Divorce for the gentile partner in a mixed marriage contracted before the promulgation of laws prohibiting such marriages, was made easy. In some cases, the Nazis forced the gentile partner to divorce the Jewish spouse, without regard to the wishes of either.

These controls on marriage are more than overbalanced by nazi emphasis on population increases of racially desirable sorts. To bear children was not a right but a duty for the racially fit. Thus both marriages and births increased during the 1930's, due to state financial subsidies, to propaganda incitement, and to such measures as conferring special privileges and recognition on parents of large families, restrictions on the manufacture and advertisement of contraceptives and on the dissemination of birth control information, and the enforcement of prohibitions against abortion.[43]

The drives to increase population had an inevitable effect on the position of children some aspects of which were not wholly without merit: the social and legal distinctions between legitimate and illegitimate progeny were minimized. During the thirties German youth were encouraged to "have fun by having a baby for Hitler." Particularly during the war were German women urged to do their duty by the Fatherland, taking advantage of home leaves of eugenically satisfactory males to arrange for procreation of more Germans than would be possible otherwise. The position of such progeny had to be protected.

The position of the family in the hierarchy of social institutions was subordinated to those associations connected with the party and the state.[44] Thus, however much the family might have been extolled as a device for breeding and nurturing children, its claim on the time and energies of the individual were subordinated to those of the movement. Within the family, the authoritarian leadership ideas of the movement strength-

[43] The same, pp. 241 ff.
[44] See Neumann, *Behemoth*, pp. 365-67, and especially pp. 400-01.

ened the position of the father, and strictly confined and regulated that of the mother and of the children. German women were confined, in nazi ideology and social policy, to the area of *Kinder* and *Kueche,* if not *Kirche,* until the stress of war on the national economy forced the Nazis to comb out all sources of labor power and draw on German womanhood for national economic production.

Private associations. The essence of nazi policy toward all associations is explained by one authority as follows:

> National Socialism has no faith in society and particularly not in its good will. It does not trust the various organizations to adjust their conflicts in such a way as to leave National Socialism's power undisturbed. It fears even the semi-autonomous bodies within its own framework as potential nuclei of discontent and resistance. That is why National Socialism takes all organizations under its wing and turns them into official administrative agencies. The pluralistic principle is replaced by a monistic, total, authoritarian organization. This is the first principle of National Socialist social organization.[45]

The second principle, according to Neumann, is the "atomization of the individual," achieved by breaking down all possibly competing associations (family, church), and by increasing the size of those permitted and controlled associations to the point where the individual counts for nothing within them.[46]

And a third principle consists in the fostering of elites within the major social groups, as means of differentiation between leaders and followers necessary to maintain leadership over the masses as a whole. Propaganda and terror are finally applied as means of keeping the masses from thinking, and possibly upsetting the whole structure.[47]

In consequence, although the Nazis may have left much of the legal road open to the formation of private associations, in practice no association of any importance whatsoever could escape nazi pressure. Only the most strongly rooted in tradition

[45] The same, p. 400.
[46] The same, pp. 400-01.
[47] The same, pp. 401-02.

and such agencies as the family or the church were able to survive to any degree.

RELIGIOUS FREEDOM

Doctrinally the Nazi party professed to be Christian. Point 24 of the party program reads:

> We demand liberty for all religious denominations in the State, so far as they are not a danger to it and do not militate against the moral feelings of the German race.
>
> The Party, as such, stands for positive Christianity, but does not bind itself in the matter of creed to any particular confession. It combats the Jewish-materialist spirit [i.e., Communism] within us and without us, and is convinced that our nation can only achieve permanent health from within on the principle:
>
> THE COMMON INTEREST BEFORE SELF.[48]

When the party seized power, it announced that "In gaining our victory over bolshevism we overcame at the same time the enemy that combated Christianity and the Christian churches and threatened to destroy them."[49] Yet even before the seizure of power, nazi propaganda attacked the church as a competing institution, and the nazi struggle to capture Christianity for the movement, and to weaken, disperse, and destroy the Christian

[48] The party program was adopted at Munich, Feb. 24, 1920. Text from U. S. Department of State, *National Socialism,* pp. 224-25, following German edition of 1932.

[49] From Evangelical Church Letter to Chancellor Hitler of June 1936, Carnegie Endowment for International Peace, *International Conciliation* No. 324 (1936), p. 557.

Note also Hitler's statement on Mar. 23, 1933: "The government, being resolved to undertake the political and moral purification of our public life, is creating and securing the conditions for a really profound revival of religious life. The advantages of a personal and political nature that might arise from compromising with atheistic organizations would not outweigh the consequences which would become apparent in the destruction of general moral basic values.

"The National Government regards the two Christian confessions as the weightiest factors for the maintenance of our nationality." *Source Book,* pp. IV-128-29.

Nazi attacks on religious freedom are powerfully summarized in the German Evangelical Church Manifesto of Aug. 23, 1936. In *International Conciliation,* No. 324, pp. 568-73.

confessions was intensified. Although the party arranged a concordat with the Catholic church, it violated its agreements in every point;[50] and the party forced the reorganization of the confessional churches, to make their structure more easily amenable to state discipline and control. The party professed to have no interest in questions of doctrine as such, and claimed only to try to put the churches in their "proper" sphere. The party also took over the functions of charity by creating such organs as the Winter Help, and moved against the church-sponsored youth organizations as competitors to the Hitler Youth, the *Bund Deutscher Maedel,* and other nazi organizations.

The party harbored a vigorous atheistic or agnostic wing, which was more than articulate in all channels of propaganda, attempting to persuade Germans away from their earlier religious affiliations and capture their full emotional loyalties for the movement. At the same time, the churches were not allowed to engage in counterpropaganda to defend themselves publicly from nazi attacks. The Nazis deliberately scheduled parades, demonstrations, and other party-sponsored gatherings at times which would prevent or deter church attendance.

The party defined "positive Christianity" in an arbitrary way. Dr. Goebbels called it "merely humanitarian service," and coupled his remarks with attacks on the church for their theological hairsplitting and their lack of attention to Christian charity. For Rosenberg, however, "positive Christianity"

[50] The concordat was concluded July 20, 1933. It provided considerable formal liberty for the Catholic Church, but provided ample room for state supervision as well. The liberties were quickly overrun in practice, the opportunities for state supervision exploited from the beginning. The agreement provided for complete freedom of correspondence between the German church and the Vatican; the right to publish pastoral letters and church decrees; religious instruction in primary and secondary schools to be conducted in accord with Catholic principles; organization and maintenance by the state of confessional schools in those districts where parents ask for them and there are enough pupils, and finally, for the state protection of nonpolitical Catholic organizations. On the other hand, Catholic priests in Germany must be German citizens; the state must approve the election of archbishops, bishops, etc. and bishops must take an oath of allegiance to the state before entering upon their functions. M. Searle Bates, *Religious Liberty; An Inquiry* (1945), pp. 22-23.

appeared as the mystic doctrine of the blood, something quite other than the traditional faith.[51]

Finally, membership in party organizations was made difficult if not impossible for members of traditional churches. SA and SS men could be "positive Christians," but to be an SA man and to belong to the confessional front of "negative Christians" was declared to be in absolute contradiction.[52]

The party moved against the organization of the church, especially the Protestant church, declaring that it was unthinkable for such sectarianism to exist in a unified Germany. The party installed state commissars to run church organizational affairs in the main states, forced new church elections, brought church finances within state supervision, conducted vigorous propaganda against the church in behalf of "German Christianity" (for example, a speech broadcast by Hitler on July 22, 1933), curbed the freedom of the churches to conduct pastoral work among their congregations or to publish and to express their doctrines, and finally passed a law on September 24, 1935, establishing a German Evangelical Church. These actions directed against organization, finance, and functioning were paralleled by individual acts of repression, defamation, imprisonment, and violence against churchmen of all degrees. The nazi strategy was to intimidate and interfere with the clergy in every way short of rendering them martyrs.[53] The Nazis moved strongly against church controls over education, even over the education of theologians.[54]

The essence of the matter is found in a quotation from Dr.

[51] Rosenberg is quoted in the evangelical letter as follows: "We recognize today that the central ideas of the Roman and of the Protestant Churches are negative Christianity, and do not, therefore, accord with our soul, and we see that they stand in the way of the organized forces of the nations following nordic-racial principles, that they have to make room for these forces, and that they must allow themselves to be transformed within the meaning of Germanic Christianity." Carnegie Endowment for International Peace, *International Conciliation,* No. 324, p. 558.

[52] The same.

[53] The same, pp. 559 ff.

[54] Said the letter: "The education of the coming race of theologians in the universities is entrusted more and more to professors and lecturers who have proved themselves to be teachers of false doctrine; the destruction of the theological faculties in Prussia throws a strong light on this

Ley, the Labor Front Leader: "The party claims the totality of the soul of the German people. It can and will not suffer that another party or point of view dominates in Germany. We believe that the German people can become eternal only through National Socialism, and therefore we require the last German, whether Protestant or Catholic."[55] Consequently, in Nazi Germany, there was no freedom of conscience guaranteed by separation of church from state and recognition of a sphere of church rights. There was an attempt at the closest fusion of church and state, with domination over the conscience of the individual as prescribed by the latter. This culminated in the ultimate blasphemy charged by many church leaders, that the party often revered the Führer in a manner rightly due to God alone.[56]

IV. FREEDOM OF THE MIND

In the sphere of the freedoms of the mind—of education, of research, of teaching, or writing and publication in any medium whatsoever—the nazi drive to total control knew no restraints. The first article of the first decree issued by the Nazis to destroy the constitutional basis of the old Germany in effect abolished all constitutional bars to government restrictions on "personal liberty, on the right of free expression of opinion, including freedom of the press, on the right of assembly and the right of association, and violations of the privacy of postal, telegraphic, and telephonic communications, and warrants for house-searches, orders for confiscations as well as restrictions on

---

picture. The Ministry for Science and for the Education of the People has demanded the reinstatement of teachers of false doctrine as members of the examining boards of the universities." The same, p. 563.

[55] The same.

[56] The letter quoted Goebbels, who said on Apr. 19, 1936:

"When the Fuehrer addressed his last appeal to the people on March 28, it was as if a profound agitation went through the whole nation; one felt that Germany was transformed into one single House of God, in which its intercessor stood before the throne of the Almighty to bear witness. . . . It seemed to us that this cry to heaven of a people for freedom and peace could not die away unheard. That was religion in its profoundest and most mystical sense. A nation then acknowledged God through its spokesman, and laid its destiny and its life with full confidence in His hand." The same, p. 567.

property. . . ."[57] This decree in effect opened the way to official domination of the life of the mind, or, in other words, to the achievement of the nazi ideal of a complete and enthusiastic conformity to the views and feelings of the movement. As Goebbels put it,

> . . . National Socialism does not strive for the totality of the state but for the totality of the idea: that is, a complete prevalence of that way of looking at things for which we have been fighting during the last decade and which we have brought to victory. It is to be applied in the entire public life of the nation. . . . In Germany there can no longer be any regulation of relations which is not consistent with the National Socialist point of view.[58]

The nazi movement was mystic, irrational, and anti-rational, yet demanding of complete conformity to official doctrine as currently stated. Consequently, it did not hesitate to move along the twin paths of propaganda and censorship to propagate and ensure monopoly of communications for those ideas on which it was founded: racialism, hierarchy, and the leadership principle, and the notion of the *Volk*. The main governmental agencies which moved to bring all dissemination of ideas under central domination were the Ministry for People's Enlightenment and Propaganda, set up in 1933, and a Reich Ministry of Education, created in 1934. But over and above these units, primarily dedicated to the task of shaping the national mind, all other units and powers of government played greater or lesser roles in ensuring conformity to the official line, and in denying livelihood and means of operation to dissident or deviationist elements. The loss of freedoms in the intellectual sphere was not so much a loss of formal rights, as it was the result of a concerted, systematic, and all-encompassing attack on the problem of controlling the life of the mind. The party youth organizations, granted monopoly positions after the attainment of power, spent at least half their efforts on political indoctrination (the rest

[57] U. S. Department of State, *National Socialism,* pp. 47-48, citing Art. 1 of the Decree of the Reich President for the Protection of the People and State, Feb. 28, 1933.

[58] The same, p. 172, citing Joseph Goebbels: *Wesen und Gestalt des Nationalsozialismus* (1935).

going to more direct forms of military preparation). Special party schools for leaders (Adolf Hitler Schools, *Ordensburgen,* and *Napoli*) were specially devoted to training future fanatic leaders. The whole economic control apparatus could be, and was used to control those phases of intellectual expression which did not have to turn to government agencies for dissemination. The Nazis monopolized the radio, and established far-reaching controls over press and publications. Censorship was built into the structure of the Ministry of Propaganda, only occasionally appearing as a separate unit, but pervading the spirit and operation of all phases of the ministry's work. The ministry, under Hitler and Goebbels, dominated all forms of public and current expression, save those operated by other official agencies, or coming under the control of the Ministry of Education.[59]

EDUCATIONAL FREEDOMS

The Nazis took a deliberate and eclectic view of educational "reform." They did not move rapidly, but moved on a broad front to capture every channel whereby the mind of the German, adult or adolescent or younger, was formed. Their attack in the educational sector moved to bring three main influences under strict control: the schools, the Hitler Youth, and the family. These institutions where both objects and channels for the operations of the Ministry of Education and the Ministry of Propaganda, as well as of other government and party agencies for educating the German people, and in particular, German youth. The objective of education was more the building of "character" than the transmitting of information or skills.[60] Labor service was made a prerequisite for higher edu-

[59] See, for example, the breakdown of units in the Ministry of Propaganda given in U. S. Library of Congress, Legislative Reference Service, *Fascism in Action,* H. Doc. 401, 80 Cong., 1 sess., at p. 33. A general study of the Propaganda Ministry is Derrick Sington and Arthur Weidenfeld, *The Goebbels Experiment* (1943).

[60] "The schools should teach not only how to think, but also how to act." Germany altered curriculum to give more emphasis to subjects closely allied to nazi ideology (like heredity and ethnography) and to physical education. "The importance of physical exercise and gymnastics, for the development of will-power and healthy thinking are recognized in the form of three

cation, and the educational system was used as a device for selecting and training leaders for all walks of life. Intellectual fitness is not the sole criterion for such selection.[61] The organization and curriculum for higher training for women were adjusted in terms of national socialist ideology. Agrarian institutes were energized and shaped as instruments of the ideology, ostensibly to make good the previous slighting of the peasant in the educational world.

The Nazis moved powerfully against traditional academic freedom. They attacked the schools and universities first by abolishing security of tenure and opening educational administration up to the political dictates of the party—as to personnel, curriculum, and doctrine. Jews and other ideologically disbarred persons were hounded from faculty, administration, and student bodies. The curricula were reshaped to give first prominence to studies dear to the nazi heart: ethnography, anthropology, and a folkish reinterpretation of history; the content of these disciplines was severely regulated in terms of the current nazi ideology. Even in those courses where the content was not inherently of interest to the ideology, the Propaganda and Education ministries saw to it that problems and examples were so constructed as to disseminate a nazi lesson.[62]

Constant pressure was brought to bear to see to it that research in universities and in higher technical institutes was concentrated on topics of importance to the war-making capacity or the political ideology of the nation. The researcher lost in effect all freedom to choose his line of research, except within the limits of areas sanctioned or emphasized by the state. If he tried to publish individually conducted or subsidized research, he would have to run the gamut of the censorship of the state,

---

compulsory gymnastic classes each week. According to the text of the above order, stress is not so much to be laid on mere instruction or occupying the mind of the student, but upon positive character-building." From report of German Delegation at the 4th International Education Conference, Geneva, August 1935. *Source Book,* pp. IV-111. The order referred to is one issued by Rust, Minister of Education, on Jan. 15, 1935.

[61] Decree of Mar. 27, 1935. The same.

[62] For example: a primary problem in arithmetic: two good Hitler Youth plus two good Storm Troop leaders equals four good Nazis.

particularly if he were operating in a field of interest to the party.

FREEDOM OF THE PRESS

As we have pointed out, one of the first official acts of the Nazis on taking power was to abrogate the freedoms of the press established by the Weimar constitution. Yet the Nazis claimed to have made their press free in a new sense—free from "capitalist domination." Or, in other words, they claimed to have freed the editor and worker from the domination of the business office, the owner, and the capitalist forces of pre-Nazi society.[63] On the other hand, the editor (*Schriftleiter*) and the working journalist were no longer allowed to remain anonymous, but were made responsible to "the people, to their conscience, and to the Nazi State."[64] The Nazis used little if any *pre*-censorship, but watched the entire field of press and publications with an argus eye. Sanctions of every nature were brought to bear by the totalitarian system on any writer or publisher who offended seriously or repeatedly.

The nazi attitude toward the press was similar to the communist: the press, for these totalitarians, is not an organ for expression of individual opinion and for criticism of the state and its institutions. Under national socialism, the task of the press is "to bring the individual to a comprehension of the vital principles of the community."[65] The objective of press control was not uniformity in manner of expression and treatment. It was conformity to the essence of prescribed journalistic lines—which were indicated to every paper in Germany by directives issued by the Propaganda Ministry. These directives were usually generalized in form, containing some specific prohibitions, but for the most part consisting of instructions to play particular

[63] This point of view is officially set forth by Otto Dietrich, "Liberty of the Press and Press Peace" (*Völkerbund,* Geneva, July 1938, pp. 261-67), an address to the foreign press and diplomatic corps given in Berlin on Mar. 5, 1938.

[64] *Schriftleitergesetz,* Jan. 1, 1934.

[65] Dietrich, "Liberty of the Press and Press Peace," in *Völkerbund,* Vol. 7 (July 1938), p. 262.

topics prominently, to play down others. Often editorial location was suggested, and from time to time, particular phrases or slogans were prescribed. But the task of the editor was to bring efficiency, imagination, and inventiveness to his job of expressing the party line. Nazi censorship feared blank spaces; it was considered preferable to postcensor news and punish those responsible for deviations. The Nazis claimed to have used state power to secure the editor and journalist from "undue influences"—but did not hesitate to use both economic and political sanctions, including disbarment from the writing profession, to ensure conformity. The editor who transgressed might find himself without help or without newsprint. The writer who transgressed might be reprimanded, fined, suspended, or ejected from membership in his prefessional organization—in short, prevented from getting employment as a writer. Sanctions were less severe for foreign correspondents. Their material was always censored—although they could always send one last despatch. But those who did not co-operate by telling "the truth" about Germany were expelled from the country.[66]

In the field of publications, the Nazis did not restrict their censorship to current production; as early as 1934, a commission was set up to give effect to decrees "protecting National Socialist literature" by examining existing publications, and issuing lists of "unobjectionable" ones which would be allowed to circulate. Prohibition of circulation of proscribed books was dramatized by the infamous nazi book-burnings—ceremonial immolations of the works of decadent, Jewish, or plainly anti-nazi works, many of world stature.

FREEDOM OF THE ARTS

The fine arts, creative, or performing, were treated by the Nazis chiefly as a means of communication, hence a channel for propaganda, and thus appropriately brought within the power

[66] According to Dietrich, the task of a foreign correspondent was "to give his countrymen an unprejudiced and true picture of a foreign country and people. . . . We will not contest their right of objective criticism if they are dominated by a desire to serve truth." The same, p. 266.

of the Propaganda Ministry. The Nazis took over the existing organizations in the artistic fields, brought them into a Culture Chamber (*Kulturkammer*) and ran them as a branch of the national propaganda effort. Two major influences were thus brought to bear—the lower-middle class artistic standards of Hitler, as expanded and refined somewhat in the nazi ideology; and the expedient interest of using creative art as a means of political education and the building of conformity. The sanction here as in the writing professions was the same: conformity on pain of ejection from the professional organization, thus from the practice of the profession, if there were serious deviation—with the ultimate sanction of party violence through concentration camps. True, an artist could create what he liked in the privacy of his atelier, but he could not exhibit or sell his work openly if it were to run afoul of the nazi censor. If he were to try to sell his wares abroad, he would still be subject to penalties if his work attracted more than a modicum of attention. Furthermore, a prominent artist or musician had to maintain at least neutrality vis-a-vis the party, if he were to continue to practice his art unmolested. It would not do for a first-class musician to use his prestige to denigrate the party.

V. ECONOMIC FREEDOMS

For the Nazis, it was never an issue *whether* to control economic life; the only question was *how*. The objectives of this control were socialist chiefly for purposes of propaganda; the history of the nazi regime shows that the real objectives were the gearing of the total economy for war, and for the dual purposes of expropriating certain elements in society (the Jews) and enriching the nazi elite. The economy as a whole was thus organized for international looting, while internally the possibilities for blackmail, extortion, and legalized stealing were manifolded by the structure of racialist regulations compounded with the large scope offered to violence in the name of the party.

The methods of control of business offered the party a choice among nationalization, commandeering, or regulation. The party chose the latter.[67] By this means the Nazis left the *principle* of private ownership intact, but robbed it of its substance. Rights of private ownership no longer conferred on the individual the power to make the significant decisions about an economic enterprise. These were made by the state. The system was rounded out by the application of the leader-follower principle to the administration of business enterprise, making of the manager a leader in his factory, but subjecting the manager to the directives of leaders higher in the scale.[68]

Proceeding together with the erection of a vast system of regulation of the economic life of the nation was the nazi propaganda which offered economic hopes and rewards, both material and psychic, to large segments of the German people. Thus the party program (point 3) demanded territory (colonies) for the nourishment of the people and settlement of superfluous population; called (point 7) for the state "to promote the industry and livelihood of citizens of the State, for the abolition of unearned incomes" (point 11), for the "ruthless confiscation of all war gains" (point 12), and finally, a series of points of particular appeal to the German proletarian or lower-middle class citizen: the nationalization of all trusts (point 13), the sharing of "profits from the wholesale trade" (point 14), "immediate communalisation of wholesale business premises, and their lease at a cheap rate to small traders" (point 16), and

[67] See Hamburger, *How Nazi Germany Has Controlled Business.* pp. 10-11.

[68] The Nazis paid special attention, at least during the early years of consolidation of power, to the maintenance of good relations with a sizable sector of the large industrialist group. Obviously, it was necessary to say the threats of expropriation or of nationalization were not meant for them; the Nazis, on the contrary, held out a twofold hope: a guarantee of orders and economic support from the state if need be, and a chance to participate in the spoils of party expropriations directed against Jews. The same was true with respect to the Junkers. In their case, it was necessary for Hitler to explain that point 17 of the party program, calling for the confiscation without compensation of land for communal purposes, "merely refers to possible legal powers to confiscate, if necessary, land illegally acquired, or not administered in accordance with national welfare. . . . It is directed in the first instance against the Jewish companies which speculate in land." U. S. Department of State, *National Socialism,* p. 223.

"land reform, abolition of interest on land loans, and prevention of all speculation in land" (point 17). These latter points were grouped under the general rubric: "abolition of the thraldom of interest."[69]

Economic controls did not spring full-blown from an economic plan worked out in advance of the seizure of power. They were improvised after January 1933. The Germans were told in 1936 that they had for the preceding four years been living under a "plan," and a second "four-year plan" was announced. But the former was a fiction, and the latter a device to sell Germans measures required to complete German militarization.[70] Agriculture was most rapidly brought under central control; in other fields, controls were developed and extended both over the economy as a whole, and in particular sectors. Prior to 1936 the two most important control mechanisms were the Reich Ministry of Economy and the Reichsbank. The former controlled the production and flow of essential commodities, supervised allocation of foreign exchange, and controlled subsidizing and licensing of exports. The Reichsbank controlled the flow of money and capital. Other important areas remained outside the control of these two groups: production, importation, distribution, and pricing of farm products; wages; prices of non-agricultural domestic products. These were controlled by special agencies. Other institutions, particularly party subsidiaries, affected the economy in important ways. During this period the nazi pattern of control was foreshadowed through the manipulation of a loose, complex, regulatory framework.

In 1936, however, the institutional arrangements for economic control were tightened up. Hitler invested Goering with dictatorial legislative and executive powers over the whole economic life of the country on October 18, 1936; these powers were renewed in 1940. There appeared an Economic High Command which brought together the heads of the various govern-

[69] The same. Wholesalers, department stores, and moneylenders were usual objects of nazi attack; they symbolized economic oppression or injustice for many of Germany's little men.

[70] Hamburger, *How Nazi Germany Has Controlled Business*, pp. 12-13.

ment departments, the economic services of the armed forces, a representative of the deputy leader of the party. But more important than the role of the council on which these groups were represented was the power of Goering to direct the economic activities of the entire government and party structure. This power he exercised through the office of the Four-Year Plan, at first with dubious efficiency, but later with powerful effect. Under this new office, certain of the operating offices came to have particular influence, especially the Reichsbank and the previous Ministry of Economy taken together, and the Ministry for Arms and Ammunition. Between them, in collaboration or competition, these agencies dominated the great preponderance of German economic life.

What was the extent of nazi controls over German business? The following were regulated in detail: entry into business; supply of capital; supply of materials; supply of labor; prices, profits, allocation of profits and other funds; and termination of business. From life to death, no business decision could be made apart from the regulations or requirements of the state; business nowhere escaped the Nazi net.

These controls over business were exceeded by the extent of nazi controls over labor. With the creation of the Labor Front and the application to economic life of the leadership principle, the role of labor as an independent factor in the productive process was effectually abolished. Business independence was hampered by control over the business leader; and the laborer, through his labor trustee, had certain remedies which might be effective if the party wished to crack down on a particular employer. Any independence from the state and party were gone by 1936.

Controls over business and labor were matched by those over the consumer, many of which grew inevitably out of the control of production and pricing, the rest coming from rationing.

CONTROLS OVER BUSINESS

The communist charge that naziism is only the form of political control in behalf of the monopoly capitalist is hardly borne out by the extent and nature of controls the party exercised over all business in Nazi Germany.

Control of entry. Control of entry into business was not merely a restriction against entry; it included power to force enterprises to enter and conduct operations which they would not otherwise have done. Pre-nazi restrictions on entry had been great in Germany, as they had been found in other Western countries; but they were designed to protect and serve the public, not to enforce government policies. Under the Nazis, the government policies so furthered included the protection of existing shopkeepers, the restriction or elimination of Jews from economic life, as well as such matters as the control over investment in new business in such fashion as to safeguard priorities on rearmament. Licensing as a method of control increased to the point where it became the rule, rather than the exception, that a license was required for entry into almost any business or occupation.[71] The *right* to a license did not exist; an applicant might meet all promulgated government requirements and be denied a license if the government so decided.[72]

Compulsory expansion of plants occurred too frequently to be specified. Compulsory extension of activities to new fields was hardly less frequent. It could take the form either of new investment, a favorite method of nazi shakedown (forcing firms to contribute toward the establishment of the Hermann Goering works, for example); or of commencing new activity. This was especially frequent in production of ersatz products; but the requirement of entry was offset by the provision of government subsidies, information, and advice. German firms were often required to create subsidiaries to exploit conquered territories.

Hamburger concluded:

> It is not left to the citizen to decide whether or not he wants to go into or to expand his business. This vital step is a matter of

[71] Hamburger lists as illustrative the following: (1) opening of new advertising firms; (2) establishment of new credit institutions; (3) opening of new or reopening, expansion, or conversion of old textile plants; (4) entry into or expansion of farming activities, including timber cutting; and (5) plying of crafts or trades. *How Nazi Germany Has Controlled Business,* p. 22.

[72] The same.

government decision. For the former right to enter business as one chose the Nazis have substituted a duty to enter business as the government directs. Entry into business or its expansion can be made a matter of conscription.[73]

Control of supply of capital. Although the supply of liquid capital was relatively small in the early nazi years, the party did not overlook it as an essential element in totalitarian control. Under a cabinet decision of May 31, 1933, a committee headed by the president of the Reichsbank was given wide powers to allocate capital. This committee utilized an embargo against the flotation of private securities, whether of new companies or of established concerns in search of new funds. The purposes of control were to withhold investments from consumers' goods industries and to direct the bulk of available liquid capital into rearmament. One result of this was to force private investors to buy government bonds; once the proceeds were in the treasury, they were allocated to the proper rearmament functions. The other was to put an important new weapon in party hands: the arbitrary decision to lift the capital embargo in whatever cases the party saw fit. This was done notably in the cases of a few essential industries: ore and coal mining, iron smelting and manufacuring, production of ersatz materials, especially gasoline; and power and chemicals.

Finally, the party restricted investment in mortgages.

As early as 1935, the government controlled at least two thirds of the capital market; it is assumed that it controlled all of it just prior to the war.

Control of supply of materials. Even more important to the tasks of rearmament were the controls over supply of materials, of foreign or of domestic origin. The control pattern started with imports: initially of certain agricultural products, and later of all imports. The devices included permits and the allocation of foreign exchange; a decree of June 24, 1934 prohibited all unauthorized imports. These restrictions created distortions in the domestic economy, calling for new regulations, which

[73] The same, p. 24.

were issued under the basic legislation of March 22 and September 4, 1934. At first, these extended only to some raw materials, but were later extended to the entire economy, requiring an elaborate network of 31 control boards, covering every commodity. This network was so complex, and the operations of each board differed so markedly from the others, that nobody had a complete picture of the entire pattern of regulation.

It is clear, however, that controls extended to the listing and use of inventories; the possession and use of maximum or minimum stocks; and a developing arsenal of regulatory methods. At the outset, a flexible rationing system seemed enough. This developed into a system of priorities. This in turn developed into the unified allotment of all materials needed for a particular contract or operation. During the war, this took the form of the most detailed regulation of all phases of armament production, from raw materials to end products. Under the aegis of the Armaments Ministry, two sets of committees were established, each with its own hierarchy. One dealt with end-products, the other with raw materials. All participating firms came under the detailed control of one or another set. The end-product regulating committees had "full control over production programs of firms under their jurisdiction, including the right to specify which firm [was] to specialize on a given final good, and even to prescribe the manufacturing processes applied."

Control over the purchase of consumers' goods by the final recipient was not instituted in direct form until 1939, when first a triple system of rationing cards, one each for consumers, retailers, and wholesalers) was introduced, to be followed by points-rationing in a form to become all too familiar throughout the world.

Control over physical materials was combined with price control to comprise unified, and on the whole, very effective control over the production, distribution, and use of commodities in accord with a unified policy. The Nazis controlled the supply of materials to every firm; and they controlled the flow of the more critical materials throughout their course from producer or importer of raw material to the consumer of the finished product.[74]

Control of labor. The problem of labor supply turned completely around from the pre-nazi through the nazi period. In the late Weimar and early nazi period, the main problem was to overcome unemployment. Later in the nazi period, the problem was more and more that of allocating a labor supply which was made scarce by the national rearmament effort, both in total figures and in specialization. The Nazis centralized labor administration under an Employment Service Board already set up in 1927, which operated through a nation-wide network of regional and local offices. This board controlled the supply of labor by virtue of its monopoly over employment service, vocational guidance, and the placing of apprentices.[75] The board was later incorporated in the Ministry of Labor, which together with the Labor Front, exercised complete control over the German worker in his work relationships. From the standpoint of the worker, this control paralleled that of the state over the manager; it denied and directed him, keeping him out of some forms of employment, and requiring him to work in others.

The basic control device was the workbook, required of every German laborer after September 1936. Each workbook was a complete record of the employment and experience of the individual worker; it gave the state the basic data concerning the national reservoir of skills, and provided the information on which it could be decided whether each worker was in an appropriate employment.

The control pattern over labor developed by degrees. At the outset, the Nazis were concerned with controls over certain types of hiring. The main initial problem was national unemployment, which the state sought to alleviate by grandiose public works and construction projects in preparation for rearmament. These attracted so many farm workers that measures had to be enacted partially to freeze farm workers to their jobs in

[74] The same, p. 37.
[75] Act of Nov. 5, 1935, the same, p. 38.

May 1934. Scarcities among skilled metal workers led to increased mobility, which was met by remedial decrees.[76] Parallel measures had to be taken in the building trades. Once full employment had been attained, labor controls were extended much farther over the economy. The pre-1939 controls were only partial, however: a farm worker could move to another farm job; metal workers or masons could move to other high-priority employment such as seaman, and the individual could still exercise his right to get out of the labor market by retiring, or trying to get into independent business.

On March 10, 1939 the state moved to control release from employment; in specified trades an employee could leave only with permission of the employment office designated to serve his employer. From this date forward workers in designated categories were tied to their jobs; on September 1, 1939 these controls were extended to all enterprises, businesses, or administrations, public or private, and to all workers, clerks, apprentices, or persons working without claiming wages or salary.[77] The only escape in this mesh was through mutual agreement of worker and employer to release the worker—which could be arranged if the worker behaved badly enough, or the employer's plant was stopped due to shortages, enemy action, or the like. Even this loophole was closed by Sauckel's decree of May 20, 1942.

The administrative controls were reinforced by control over wage rates, which reduced the incentive of workers to leave their jobs.

The Nazis completed the revolution in German labor by substituting compulsory for voluntary labor mobility, in the interest of maximum national productivity. Compulsory direction of the worker to his job commenced with a decree of November 7, 1936, which forced former metal workers to quit lower priority jobs and go back to metal-working. This was done on

[76] A decree of Dec. 29, 1934, made it illegal for any public or private agency to hire a skilled metal worker from outside the district of his original employment office without special permission.

[77] Hamburger, *How Nazi Germany Has Controlled Business*, p. 40.

the ground that the worker is most productive in the job for which he is specially trained. With the approach to war, controls were extended and tightened to make sure that skilled men were used only for skilled jobs, and that skilled workers were directed to the most appropriate tasks within an occupation. These controls were partly directed against employers, who wished to hoard skilled labor. At the outset, the government dealt only with classes of workers, by incentive means.[78] However, with the approach and the development of the war, controls became more rigid; classes of occupations were rigorously combed out to get man power for the armed forces or for high-priority occupations; and regulations extended to the individual workers. Leisured persons were forced to work at assigned occupations.

Control of prices. The Nazis did not bring price control to Germany: either by public decree or collective action, the pattern of controlled prices was already established, and formed a groundwork on which the nazi system was built.[79] The nazi system included at the outset control over the elements entering into cost: (rates and incomes); commodity price control, currency control, and import prices. During the first three years, the Nazis did not stabilize prices, but were able to keep increases well under control. From 1936 on, however, the situation was much more dangerous from the standpoint of potential inflation: the nation embarked on a full-scale militarization effort, unemployment had virtually disappeared, and the prospects of a repetition of the inflation of the twenties was everywhere feared. Hence the Nazis moved from cost control to the establishment of maximum figures by regulating prices of practically every commodity, wholesale and retail, new or second-hand; real

[78] For example, relief was denied to textile workers below 30 working part time in 1937 in order to get them to move to other occupations.

[79] Wages, considered as prices, were controlled by freely-negotiated collective agreements between employers and trades unions, with government arbitration in case of deadlock. Prices of services and commodities were commonly regulated by cartel agreements. Government controlled the price policies of the coal and potash cartels, in which membership was compulsory. Retail price maintenance agreements were also common. In the fields of public ownership, government agencies set rates.

estate prices, rentals, leases; compensation for all services; and rates for utilities, insurance premiums, commissions and fees of all sorts, and indirect municipal taxes. A few luxuries were exempted, as were shipping rates set by international agreement. Controls extended to security prices and to interest rates, the state executing mandatory conversions of private securities if need be.

Price control embodied two main elements: (1) price freezing as of a base date wherever applicable; and (2) price administration. The critical date for the freezing measure was October 17, 1936. "No person or firm was to sell or deliver any commodity or to sell or supply any service at a price higher than had been charged on the latter date."[80] If no price was established by a transaction on that date, the price was to be whatever it would have been had there been a transaction. For new commodities such as books, the maximum price for a comparable article was controlling. For other new commodities, such as synthetics, a decree of November 8, 1940, provided an elaborate machinery for determining what the price would have been had it been calculated as of 1936. Net prices rather than quotations were controlling. Real estate was valued by taking tax assessments as the maximum. Nonstandard goods such as building construction were covered by special regulation, and specialty items manufactured for government account were priced on a cost-plus basis (later on the standard of the cost of production of a "well run firm"). The objective was to freeze value relationships rather than nominal prices.

Price administration was vested in a commissioner for price formation. This official was responsible for all prices except wages, interest, and security prices. The labor trustees controlled wages, the Reichsbank interest rates, and the Ministry of Economy, security quotations. The objectives of policies within the control of the price commissioner included the promotion of broad economic policies (for example, stimulation of agricultural production); the expansion of domestic production of

[80] Hamburger, *How Nazi Germany Has Controlled Business,* p. 55.

war materials (for example, synthetic rubber), and the curbing or increase of consumption. Some price increases were ordered to offset rising costs, although a full offset was rarely sought, and price authorities strove for reduction in total unit costs by improvements in technical processes or administration. Price authorities also forced firms to absorb some additional costs out of profit margins. Price lowering was used for the same objectives and as a means of lowering government costs and to stimulate economic shifts (such as development of certain auxiliary farm activities, facilitated by cuts in prices of motors and other electrical equipment). The final objective of price lowerings came as a by-product of war, in which the businessman was made responsible for adjusting downward the prices of his product so as to keep his profit margins within allowed limits.[81] This led, of course, into the establishment of determination of "adequate" profits, hence profit control.

Certain other corollaries of price control affected the sphere of managerial decision. For example, entrepreneurs could reduce quality, and controls had to be imposed to control this. Or they could concentrate on higher-price or the more profitable items; hence requirements that a percentage of the output of a firm must be of lower-price or less profitable items. Finally, there was the field of distribution, in which the black-market or barter trade arose as main devices for circumventing price controls.

Even the sphere of cost accounting was thoroughly controlled. The government forced all enterprises to keep books, including small retailers and farmers; then it standardized accounts and accounting procedures throughout all branches of industry and trade.[82] These steps were taken to allow price authorities to ascertain and interpret readily the cost structures of thousands

[81] Decree of Dec. 8, 1940, enforcing an order of Sept. 4, 1939. In cases of excess profits, the commissioner did not always order price lowering; he might direct new investment for cost reductions, or use high prices to offset excess purchasing power, and recapture excess profit.

[82] Joint decree of Minister of Economy and price commissioner, Nov. 11, 1937, Hamburger, *How Nazi Germany Has Controlled Business*, p. 63.

of businesses, and helped to keep costs as low as possible.[83] Cost accounting was enlisted as a means for enforcing other controls. For example, wage rates as fixed by government were interpreted as maximum payments; under approved accounting procedures, the businessman had to take these government rates, multiplied by standard working hours, as the maximum allowable figure in determining wage costs. Remuneration of risk and interest outlays were similarly watched.

Control of the volume of profits. Although opposing propagandas have characteristically criticized the nazi system as one organized for the interest of the capitalist, and have pointed to the spectacular cases of growth in size of enterprise and of personal incomes enjoyed by top party members or industrial magnates, it is nevertheless true that the nazi system imposed stringent and broadly-applied controls on the volume of business profits. Since the planned-profit margins allowed to enterprise were so defined as to include taxes, the tax system was a potent weapon in controlling the significant element: net profits. Under the Nazis, taxes were systematically extended and rates increased over all types of business. This was especially marked during the war, when taxes were used to keep down consumer purchasing power. Taxation was also used directly to control excess profits, as part of the apparatus of price control. Finally, businesses were taxed to provide the government-directed subsidies to other business. Nonexporting industries and certain branches of commercial enterprises were so exploited; later certain branches of agriculture and agricultural industry were added. Funds so raised were used to subsidize exporting ventures, and during the war, to subsidize industries working at low capacity ratios or inactive due to shortages of labor, power, raw materials, etc. This process took place within economic activities, as well as across industry lines.[84]

Control of allocation of profits and other funds. Permitted

[83] The government thus regulated the permissible items in determining cost, and the main policies for valuation (for example, purchase price, not replacement determines inventory value).

[84] Intra-industry subsidies were ordered by the law of Feb. 10, 1940.

profits did not escape nazi control, which either prohibited certain uses, or directed other uses to be made of them. Dividend policy was rigidly controlled partly as a means of controlling consumer purchasing power and maintaining price control, and partly as a means of supporting government securities. Dividend rates were controlled in the sense that only a limited dividend could be paid in cash; the rest had to be paid in special forms dictated by the state (usually government-handled securities). This led to increased reinvestment of profits. Failure of compliance through "voluntary discipline" of business led to the imposition in 1941 of ceilings on total dividends which could be distributed in any form.[85]

Further controls took the form of directing the investment of undistributed profits or other funds; it was prohibited to use them for expansion of consumers' goods activities, or other functions not contributing to armament or the war. The nazi controls over establishment of new business or expansion of old ones effectively channeled investment of such funds.[86] These prohibitions and controls were supplemented if needed by direct order. Such orders took the form of directing a plowing back of funds; embargoes on the issuance of securities to prevent access to the capital market; and refusal of subsidies to firms which did not reinvest as ordered. More particularly, the government directed the uses within the enterprise to which such funds could be put.[87] Finally, the Nazis forced large-scale purchase of government bonds by business organizations.

[85] Decree of June 12, 1941. This did leave a loophole: companies could increase their capital stock, and "distribute" profits in the form of stock dividends. Smaller companies, percentage-wise, took main advantage of this. Some of the big ones, like I. G. Farben, only brought their stock up to the 1926-31 level; others, like Mannesmann, took no advantage of it at all. Hamburger, *How Nazi Germany Has Controlled Business*, p. 76.

[86] The program was supplemented during the war by requiring businesses to turn certain types of reserves over to the government, which established a blocked account for the duration, to be released for new capital purposes after the war. These accounts were not even "forced loans"; they paid no interest, and served merely to insulate markets from purchasing power.

[87] Says Hamburger: "Other techniques included prohibition or restricted licensing of plant expansion, and control of the supply of raw materials, equipment, electric current, and labor. For example, a firm intending to

These controls required a good deal of industry participation; the Nazis characteristically worked through the established business organizations in devising particular methods and putting them into operation. Both industry and government representatives discussed financial requirements and possible methods; the results were not always put into the form of specific orders, but the resulting "agreements" or understandings were put into effect by the business group involved.

Control of termination of business. As the Nazis controlled life, so they controlled the death of businesses. During the early period of the regime, closings were often forced as means of pressuring opponents or liquidating Jews. Once industry had been reorganized to eliminate what Nazis considered to be surplus enterprises, this earlier type of closing ceased, and those remaining gained a privileged position. Later, as rearmament progressed and the economy was directed more and more completely to war, businesses were closed to restrict consumer production and to concentrate resources for war production.[88] The threat of closure was a potent weapon throughout in enforcing compliance with government or party fiat. Techniques of closure varied widely, from withdrawal of licenses, drafting away of essential labor, imposition of especially onerous fiscal burdens, blocking critical supplies, and outright orders from government through the applicable trade association.

The worker, up to a point, had the freedom to quit to become a businessman, but in Nazi Germany, no plant was free to close and no businessman free to quit working without the government's permission. Some of the obligations to continue were enacted into law; but the overriding sanction was the nazi policy, which abolished the *right* to conduct a business, and replaced it by a duty.

---

build workers' dwellings or a new office building would not get the required authorizations to build, to buy bricks or other materials, or to hire construction workers unless it undertook to expand or improve production facilities." *How Nazi Germany Has Controlled Business,* p. 78.

[88] Wartime man power comb-outs affected such enterprises as banks, bank branches. insurance, newspapers, magazines, department stores, wholesale firms, and other financial and processing businesses.

THE POSITION OF LABOR

Labor, whether organized or unorganized, was regimented in Nazi Germany as was every other element of society. The nature and to some extent the purpose of this regimentation varied, but was controlled throughout by the drive of the Nazis first to seize power in Germany, and then to prepare Germany for expansion through war. The first moves of the Nazis were to destroy free trade unionism, and to incorporate labor organization into the structure of the nazi governing apparatus, and then to regulate all phases of labor relations in the national interest. The initial problem was to combat unemployment, by siphoning off large elements of the labor supply from the labor market—women, soldiers, etc.; and by engaging in large-scale programs to provide increased employment opportunities. After 1936, as the rearmament program got under way, unemployment disappeared and labor shortages extended from agriculture and a few critical industrial fields until by 1939, they appeared in practically all fields of production important to the state. As a consequence in part of these developments, the Nazis resorted first to the determination of minimum wages, and then to attempts to determine maximum wages; to controls over the hiring of workers and of release from employment; to controls over training and the choice of vocation; to a variety of methods to force independent workers, small businessmen, and artisans into the labor market, and finally to draconian measures to direct labor to particular employments and to freeze workers to occupations and to jobs.

As a result of these measures, the formal freedoms enjoyed by workers in free countries were without exception lost as practical alternatives to the German worker by 1939; so complete was regimentation that the government did not have to alter the system in any way to move from peace to war economy in September 1939. The worker lost his right to decide whether or not to join a labor union, or to pick among competing unions. He lost his right to participate through a union in collective bargaining in 1933. Although for a considerable period during the 1930's he could haggle with employers for wages or perquisites higher than those set by wage regulations, he had to submit to the programs of the government to control maximum wages and to curb spendable funds. He was ultimately frozen to his job. Although the Nazis never outlawed the right to strike, they made this right completely useless. If the individual struck, he was thrown out of the Labor Front, thereby preventing re-employment in any line whatsoever. There were no independent labor organizations to call for group stoppages. He lost his freedom to choose his occupation, and might be forced to move from employer, occupation, or job if the interest of the state required it. Ultimately he lost his freedom to choose not to work—women, children, the aged, the convict, and the Jew were ultimately forced into the labor market. Women were tempted or forced out of the labor market in 1933, only to be tempted and then forced back into it by 1939. Finally there were the specialized types of compulsion, not directed to the ordinary worker, expressing themselves in a widespread system of convict labor, concentration camp labor, and compulsory service in labor camps, in agricultural or domestic occupations.

The worker was not deprived of membership in a labor organization; he was forced to apply for membership in the Labor Front. If he was rejected, he could not be hired. If he was accepted, he could not look to the Labor Front to perform the services rendered by a free union, or even by a company union. The Labor Front was in the main an organization affiliated with the party, for spreading nazi philosophy among workers. In addition, it taxed workers (dues paying was automatic and compulsory) and provided certain benefits such as the *Kraft durch Freude* (KdF, Strength Through Joy) vacations, for which the workers paid whether they took the trips or not. It was supposed to negotiate settlements of disputes between "followers" (employees) and "leaders" (plant managers) arising out of the individual labor contracts regulating the individual's employment. As such, it represented both parties. Since there were no collective contracts, it obviously did nothing to negotiate them on behalf of the worker. Nor did it act at high policy levels as a spokesman or intercessor for the workers' interest in the formulation of wage or employment policies, or other economic policies affecting the work relationship.

These functions were carried out by other governmental or party agencies. The task of mitigating the power of employers against labor, so far as it was necessary to institutionalize it, was entrusted to labor trustees acting under the authority of the Ministry of Labor. The functions of employment service were given as a monopoly to the National Employment Service Board, and vocational guidance was also vested elsewhere. The worker had no voice in selecting the officers or leaders of the labor front; these were appointed from above according to the leadership principle. The Labor Front has been aptly termed a morale and compliance division; although it included some 25,000,000 members, it could not be said to have been a genuine expression of the workers' right to organize.

Nazi restrictions on labor mobility—the freedom of the workers to choose their jobs, their employers, and their place of work—began with restrictions on agricultural labor. These were necessitated by the consequences of the nazi peasant policy, tying land to the owning family and restricting inheritance to the eldest son, and nazi wage policy for agricultural employment, which combined to reduce incentive for farm workers to stay in the country at a time when nazi re-employment policy enticed them into urban employment or to public works. By 1935 the employment offices had to give special permission for the employment of former agricultural workers, and employers were told to discharge any workers engaged during the preceding three years in agricultural work. On the other hand, a system of farm "aids" was set up, whereby urban labor was conscripted for six-month tours of duty on farms, in return for room, board, and a tiny wage.

These dual moves provided the pattern for future nazi policy to deal with shortages in other fields. The first industrial field where they appeared was in that of skilled metal workers. Due to rearmament, new shortages appeared, and the government needed machinery to direct labor to areas of high priority and present or potential scarcity. This machinery was found in the National Employment Service Board. By November 5, 1935 this board was given a full monopoly of employment service, vocational guidance, and the placing of apprentices, replacing previous private agencies and whatever trade-union functions remained vestigially in the Labor Front. The main administrative device on which central control depended was the work book, required initially of every employee in particular trades, and ultimately of any employee in any line of work.

Rearmament dictated controls over training and choice of vocation, as well. Vocational training was made compulsory by the first decree under the Four-Year Plan; first exercising compulsion on plants to train given percentages of apprentices, and after 1938 giving employing authorities power to open or close an occupation to a potential apprentice, and compelling all young people to report to the employment office for disposition on completion of primary or secondary school. Control over the occupational future of each young person in Germany was complete by September 1, 1939. Such a state of affairs divested the person of responsibility for shaping his own future. Its purposes were not the development of the individual, but the service of the state. Employment urgencies led to highly specialized training, so apprentices to particular occupations did not get a well-rounded schooling, but quickly learned particular specialties.

Employment priorities robbed the worker of freedom to change his occupation, or to persist in one when he had been trained for another which was of higher priority. The Nazis proceeded on the principle that a worker was best at the trade for which he was originally trained. Although some cases would show this to be true, and some workers directed back to earlier occupations might welcome the return, it is certain that as early as 1937 "a substantial number of former metal workers and skilled members of the building crafts were sent back to their original occupations against their will and desire."[89] Further-

[89] Hamburger, *How Nazi Germany Has Mobilized and Controlled Labor* (1940), p. 20.

more, in allotted occupations, neither the employer nor the worker was free to decide the kind of work the worker was to do, and transfer within occupations was forced by the state. Broadly qualified workers were not allowed to be used as specialists. Finally, these regulations extended both to the repatriation and expatriation of German workers.

Under "expatriation," an employee could not be retained in his primary line of work if that line were itself of low priority, and the employee possessed age or other qualifications for work in other more urgent fields. Clerks and textile workers were the first classes to be raided.

The remobilization of women, youth, the aged, and Jews was attended with a high degree of regimentation and classification. Young women were directed to agricultural and household employments by requiring that they could not be employed in private or public businesses or agencies unless they had worked for one year in agricultural or household tasks; ultimately this "duty year" was required as prerequisite to employment in any trade whatsoever. The girls were no longer free to choose the employers for this preliminary year, but were forced to rural areas. Ultimately, as labor shortages became acute, women were subject to outright conscription and assignment to tasks. By similar stages, the Nazis not only legalized but made compulsory child labor and labor of the aged.

On June 22, 1938 the government finally achieved full-scale labor conscription with a compulsory service decree. Under this decree, the president of the National Employment Board, could assign persons subject to conscription—that is, any German national, whatever sex, economic status, or age—to work at any place he assigned them, for a specified period not greater than six months, or to take specified vocational training. Neither the employer nor employee could choose one another, or dicker over the terms and conditions of employment. Official notice to the employee was all that was necessary to conclude a labor contract, which could not be abrogated without consent of the employment office.

Despite these stringent conditions surrounding the work

relationship, the individual employee, particularly if he possessed a high-priority skill, enjoyed considerable bargaining power against the employer which the state was not always able to offset. Since employers in urgent occupations were usually under both political and economic pressure to meet commitments and expand production, they were forced to offer special inducements over and above established wage rates or other perquisites to attract and retain necessary workers. From 1934 on, when collective agreements no longer operated, the state imposed only minimum wage rates, and employers were free to pay more. From 1936, however, the state had to take steps to reduce undue labor mobility, and had to decide whether to adopt a maximum-wage policy or to restrict the rights of workers to leave their jobs. The regime tried a discreet but initially unsuccessful policy of fixing maximum wages. Only with the advent of war was it possible completely to tie all workers to their jobs, and to re-establish for employers in many fields the feudal right of requiring the worker to return to the place he had quitted. Workers who fell under the decree of March 10, 1939 were subject to criminal penalties if they quit work without permission of the employment authorities.

NAZI CONTROL OF AGRICULTURE

To the reader of national socialist propaganda, it would have appeared logical that the position of the agricultural individual in Nazi Germany would have been an unusually favored one. The German peasant was the foundation on which the ideology of blood and soil rested; he was hailed as the source for the vigorous and pure German race of the future, and accounted the fount and carrier of the most highly prized national virtues. These favors of attention were complemented by favors of policy, arising from the autarkic requirement of rendering Germany free from wartime peril of blockade or starvation. Yet favors for agriculture were restricted—not every man or woman of the soil could hope to benefit by them—and were balanced by a rigid determination of the status, control over the movement, and circumscription of the economic freedom of the peasant. The two major nazi implements for control in the field of agriculture were the Hereditary Farm Act, and the Reich Food Estate. The former established the conditions for creating and extending a peasant elite. The second established an over-all agency to control the production, distribution, and pricing of all agricultural goods—from the farm to the consumer. Lesser control items arose out of the program for rural resettlement and for control over the supply of labor; the latter has been sketched above.

The Hereditary Farm Act. The Hereditary Farm Act was announced on September 29, 1933 with great fanfare. It was supposed to establish an agricultural basis for the society of the nation, by tying peasant families to farmsteads large enough to be self-sufficing (from 20 to 300 acres approximately). To qualify as a peasant, however, the individual had to be a German citizen, to have had pure Germanic blood since 1800, to be a competent farmer (*Bauernfähig*), and to possess an honorable character. The act required, however, considerable shifting in holdings, and in those qualified to hold them. On the passage of the act, all farms of the specified size owned by a peasant automatically became hereditary farms. Others were created by attaching to them sufficient additional land from various sources (state property, large estates, other small holdings) to allow them to qualify. This led to expropriation of small holdings and to the withdrawal of old rights from poor peasants—such as the use of common lands for grazing.[90] Further, no such estate could be sold, mortgaged, or foreclosed. The act rigidly regulated inheritance on the principle that the entire landed estate must be inherited as a unity, ordinarily by the eldest son. This provision aggravated problems of agricultural labor by reducing or eliminating the economic interest of members of farm families other than eligible inheritors, thus contributing to movements from farm to city and reducing supplies of competent farm labor. As a source of pure German blood, the hereditary farmer could marry only persons of approved racial characteristics.

[90] Maxine Y. Sweezy, *The Structure of the Nazi Economy* (1941). p. 181.

Controls over land ownership perpetuated a long-established trend toward agricultural centralization, at the expense of the independent small farmer. By 1938 the hereditary farms comprised 37 per cent of the total area under cultivation, and the estates of the Junkers were not diminished; an elite class of some 700,000 hereditary peasants had been created.[91]

The Reich Food Estate. The Reich Food Estate was created in September 1933 as a self-administering statutory corporation, including all persons and organizations engaged in the production and distribution of agricultural commodities. It was tied into the government structure by the fact that the leader of the Estate was also the Reich Minister for Food and Agriculture. As a public corporation, it was authorized to regulate production, marketing, prices, and profits of German landowners, tenants, cultivators, agricultural workers, wholesale and retail traders in agricultural products and foodstuffs, agricultural co-operative societies and marketing associations.[92] Its theoretical control over the farmer and the farm was complete. Although it kept or caused to be kept elaborate records of acreages, production, and yields of farm products, and information on farming methods, and specified broad production goals, it relied on general rather than specific controls. The government did not dictate individual production quotas, although it requisitioned stated percentages of crops and tried to keep marketing within prescribed channels. Price control appeared both as to maxima and minima. Marketing controls extended to the propagandistic pushing of the use of domestically produced products in long supply as against imported grains or fats, where both self-sufficiency and foreign exchange positions might be threatened. Controls of the Food Estate extended to complete control over foreign trade in agricultural commodities.[93]

From the standpoint of individual freedoms, the central characteristics of this system were fixity of occupation, status,

[91] Neumann, *Behemoth,* pp. 395-96.

[92] Legislative Reference Service, *Fascism in Action,* H. Doc. 401, pp. 138-39.

[93] Sweezy, *The Structure of the Nazi Economy,* pp. 184 ff. describes these controls.

and residence for the farmer. For the agricultural marketer or processor, so-called "self-government under the supervision of the State in the interest of the community as a whole" appeared as compulsory membership in the appropriate branch or branches of the Food Estate, and the substitution of appointive for elective principles in the selection of officials. The farmer could look to the state for subsidies, price guarantees, help in getting labor, and fertilizer and equipment at reduced prices. In the other side of the balance was his semi-feudal attachment to his farm and to his occupation. To the great landed proprietor, the Nazis presented a certain amount of propaganda threat in the early days. But the Junkers were able to make their political power felt, and they enjoyed a continuation of subsidies (*Osthilfe*) and *de facto* freedom from any large-scale program of subdivision of their estates.

THE POSITION OF THE CONSUMER

The position of the consumer as such was determined in the nazi system by the priority on rearmament and militarization of the economy. This meant in practice that the planned allocation of the resources of the nation went first to other things; the consumer had no opportunity to affect central economic decisions by expressing his preference in a free and competing market. From the fiscal and financial point of view, the nazi system treated the consumption function as one to be rigidly controlled, to avoid inflation, and to maintain the necessary over-all economic stability to ensure a high level of national production. Although price policy might favor the consumer, restrictions on consumption were effectively maintained by control over national production and control of distribution through other means than price. The criteria for regulating foreign trade did not maximize the interest of the consumer by allowing the importation of commodities if they could be put down more cheaply in German markets than home produce. On the contrary, the policy objectives of foreign trade were to conserve and increase foreign exchange, to build up adequate stockpiles of strategic materiels, and to fit a pattern of production cut for rearmament and war. Only as the German could be considered a consumer of such products—and the analogy may not be completely without reason—could it be said that the German system had the interest of the consumer in view. For the Nazi, the consumption function was both a source of danger and an instrument of control.

VI. CONCLUSION

It is not, in all probability, true to say that naziism is the most rigorous of the three modern totalitarian examples in its regimentation of the individual, or in its repression of nonconformity in any portion of human society. Fascism was less rigorous in practice, although equally total and severe in theory. Communism was less rigorous in theory, if one takes into account the promised freedoms of the communist utopia. But an objective observer would be hard put to it to distinguish between the extent of nazi or current communist domination of the individual. While the Communist decries the Nazi's repression on grounds of race, the Communist is equally insensitive to his own repression of humans on grounds of class or questionable loyalty to the communist cause.

Whether the palm for totalitarian supremacy goes to the Nazi or to the Communist, it is abundantly clear that there is no group in society, no process, which the Nazis did not control or attempt wholly to regiment, in the name of the leader, the *Volk,* and the movement.

With the discussion of the nazi system, we have completed our survey of both modern and historical forms of totalitarian state control over the individual. We now examine briefly how certain voluntary societies have regimented the individual in America. We then summarize and appraise this phenomenon of totalitarian control as it is revealed both by its history and by its present practice.

CHAPTER VII

THE IDEALISTIC CONTROLLED COMMUNITIES IN AMERICA

Do voluntarily organized controlled societies treat their individual members differently than do comparable groups that are established by physical force? All of the totalitarian regimes that have been surveyed thus far were imposed by government authority on all persons residing in a given geographical area; the individuals involved had little choice concerning their inclusion in the authoritarian states. But on many occasions in the United States groups of individuals have voluntarily established controlled societies for the purpose of furthering some religious, social, or economic ideal. The people who entered these groups gave up their freedom voluntarily to achieve some transcendent religious or economic goal. How have such voluntarily organized experimental groups regulated their members? In an effort to answer this question the American experience with such idealistic associations will be briefly surveyed.

In the last 150 years well over one hundred different attempts were made to establish controlled societies in various parts of the United States. By far the larger part of these experiments were short-lived; and only a handful of them are now in existence. Despite the large number of these undertakings, there is but scant material on which to base an appraisal of them. The available literature leaves much to be desired. Many of the works that deal with these groups are of a romantic or antiquarian nature; the majority of them were written by persons who had little scholarly training and who were more interested in describing a noble experiment than in presenting a real scientific analysis.[1] In this field the able, analytical studies are few.[2]

[1] George B. Lockwood, *The New Harmony Communities* (1902); Clara E. Sears, *Bronson Alcott's Fruitlands* (1915); and Albert Shaw, *Icaria, A Study in Communistic History* (1884).

Nevertheless, there are two reasons why a review of our experience with these undertakings is desirable. First, many people have shown an interest in the experiments; but often those with only a superficial knowledge of the history of them argue that since many of the noble experiments were undertaken years ago it is desirable to organize more and larger similar communities today. Second, a study of these experiments will probably enable us to answer such questions as: Will the members of such communities voluntarily long suffer themselves to be regulated in almost unlimited ways even though the restraints involved are only incident to the attainment of some fundamental religious or social objective? It is generally agreed that most of these experiments were dismal failures. Was this because of the unwillingness of their members to voluntarily surrender their freedom over a long period? Certainly if the members became dissatisfied with regulations imposed on them in these small islands of control, they could freely escape into the vast sea of freedom that surrounded them in this country, for obviously no physical restraints could be imposed upon them. Were non-physical sanctions able to hold individuals in the groups, despite the allurements of the outside world? Did spiritual forces give more cohesion to these endeavors than was furnished by a common desire to attain a social or economic objective?

The majority of the undertakings were of a religious nature, and those so organized seemed to have been more successful than the ones created for other objectives. Among these religious groups were such experiments as Amana, Zoar, Icaria, Oneida, and the Hutarian communities. All of them were communistic in philosophy and structure. Only one of the major religious experiments was non-communistic in nature—that was the Mormon settlement in Utah. In addition a number of non-

---

[2] For example, B. M. Clark, "The Hutarian Communities," *Journal of Political Economy,* Vol. 32 (1924) p. 357; Frederick A. Bushee, "Communist Societies in the United States," *Political Science Quarterly,* Vol. 20 (1905) p. 625; Hamilton Gardner, "Cooperation Among the Mormons," *Quarterly Journal of Economics,* Vol. 31 (1917) p. 461.

religious experimental communities were established in this country in the second quarter of the nineteenth century. Robert Owen and Louis Fourier organized or inspired some of them, including the colonies at New Harmony, Brook Farm, and a number of others in Wisconsin, New Jersey, New York, and Ohio. Late in the nineteenth century another series of short-lived socialist communities emerged.

The analysis begins with a discussion of some of the more successful religious experiments and is followed by a description of a few of the less enduring religious groups. The second part summarizes the experience of such nonreligious associations as those inspired by Owen and Fourier; and in the last part of the chapter an analysis is made of the general problem of individual control in such voluntarily constituted organizations.

I. THE RELIGIOUS GROUPS

In this section the more successful religious groups—Amana, the Hutarians, and the Mormons—will be considered in some detail. Among the other numerous religious experiments only the Shakers have had a long life. The Zoar community in Ohio existed for almost 75 years, the Hopedale colony in Massachusetts, a mere handful of people, ran for about 15 years.[3] The rather spectacular Oneida community lasted for less than 40 years. The Shakers, the Oneida community, and the Zoar experiment will be briefly reviewed.

AMANA

This group operated as a communistic undertaking from 1854 to 1931, when it was reorganized as an agricultural co-operative association. For almost 80 years the Society of True Inspiration functioned as a theocracy; but now its religious aspects have been separated from its governmental and economic phases. The members of this religious sect came to the United States from Germany in 1842[4] and first settled near Buffalo, New

[3] Aden Ballou, *History of the Hopedale Community* (1897). See pp. 5-291.

[4] Bertha M. H. Shambaugh, *Amana, the Community of True Inspiration* (1908), p. 58.

York. Twelve years after their arrival in this country they migrated to Iowa. In the southeastern part of the state they bought at first 18,000 acres of good farm land and subsequently acquired much additional acreage. Only when this group moved to the frontier did it adopt communism as a part of its religion.

Although the government of the community was to a degree democratic in form, actual authority was highly centralized.[5] Most of the time supreme power over the group as a whole was vested in a board of 13 trustees, elected annually by majority vote. The re-election of the members of this board was customary despite the existence of a strong sentiment against personal ambition in government. As long as the founder of the society lived he had "to bear the bulk of the burden and care of the community."[6] Each of the seven villages into which the community was divided was run by a board consisting of from seven to nine elders appointed by the board of trustees previously mentioned. Each board of elders had general control over its own village. Within its authority were not only the ordinary concerns of town government but also the direction and management of all of the economic activities of the members under its jurisdiction. It allocated work, housing, and money. It ran the various industries in the village, named the foremen, and kept its own books. Thus the central board of trustees operating through the village boards effectively ran the whole community. On a few occasions some of the residents criticized the arrangement as being an aristocracy of the elders, but generally the religion of the group inspired a spirit of unquestioning obedience among its members. The leaders were careful to leave very few questions for decision by the full membership of the society, and as a studied practice mass meetings were kept at a minimum to reduce the possibility of dissension.[7] As a consequence of these factors, the potentiality of popular opposition was small.

Until 1931 economically and socially the community was

[5] The same, p. 103.
[6] The same, p. 107.
[7] The same, p. 110.

organized on a communistic basis; but its communism and the concomitant controls were only a subsidiary aspect of its religion. When a person joined the group he surrendered all of his property to the corporation. Remuneration of individuals was based upon their needs which were not in all cases considered to be identical. All received free lodging and board, and a specified allowance or credit at the community store. With this credit the member could buy such goods as he saw fit. The work required of each individual was allocated by the village board. The occupation to be followed by any person was determined by this board, as were the hours of work and the place of employment. The cultivation of its 26,000 acres of agricultural land was the main economic activity of Amana. Large numbers of cattle and hogs were raised, and in addition the society owned extensive woolen mills and calico printing works. Its enterprises even developed to the point where the labor of the members themselves was insufficient, and at times more than a hundred outside workers were employed.

Far-reaching controls were imposed on the individual members. For example, there was general disapproval of reading and the acquiring of detailed knowledge although "members were allowed" to buy books and periodicals.[8] A distinctive dress was required for women but not for men. Amusements such as dancing, cards, games, and music were not permitted. "Pleasures seem to have been discouraged in the community simply because they were pleasures."[9] The approval of the governing authority was required for all marriages. It was not considered to be desirable for members to vote in the elections for officers of the regular civil government.

Despite these far-reaching general restraints on the activities of the individual, apparently some freedom was left for personal development. The division of the community into seven villages permitted some diversity. The families lived in separate establishments, although they took their meals in common. Thus

[8] The same, p. 149.
[9] The same, p. 166.

Amana avoided a concentrated single household and its consequent rigidities which spelt havoc for a great number of other experimental communities.

Most of the growth of the community was due to the natural increase in its population. Few recruits were taken in from the outside and those thus admitted were carefully selected. Persons who sought admission to the society because of their interest in social experimentation were considered to be less acceptable than those who were attracted by religious motives.

For a decade before 1931 deficits had been accumulating, largely as the result of malingering.[10] The decline in religious zeal was a primary reason for the slackening in general interest and in economic activity. In an effort to remedy this situation, the community was reorganized in 1931 as an agricultural co-operative enterprise; and as a part of this change the religious phase of the undertaking was divorced from the economic aspect. In recent years the society has numbered about 887 members and has had assets of over 1.5 million dollars. As a co-operative it has made an annual profit of about $125,000.[11]

The long life of this group was probably due to the deep religious faith of its members. The religion instilled a sense of discipline, and new recruits were carefully selected to make certain that they were true believers in the faith. The government of this society was highly centralized and autocratic in power, and to preserve their hold on it, the leaders were careful to keep the meetings of the membership at a minimum so that criticism and discussion thereby were kept within bounds.

THE HUTARIAN COMMUNITIES

These Mennonite groups constitute probably the oldest religious communistic society not of a monastic nature.[12] Although the Hutarians had existed in central Europe since the sixteenth century, it was not until 1874 that they sent their first colony of

[10] Joseph W. Eaton, *Exploring Tomorrow's Agriculture* (1943), p. 152.
[11] N. A. Crawford, "Communism Goes Broke in Iowa," *American Magazine* (November 1946).
[12] Clark, *Journal of Political Economy,* Vol. 32, p. 357.

immigrants to the United States where the new settlers found homes in South Dakota. In 1916 the total membership was only 982 and by 1936, when the last census of religious bodies was taken, their number had declined to 501.

The Hutarian communities are completely communistic; private property in any form is unknown. When a member joins the society he surrenders all of his property, and the group assumes full responsibility for his welfare. Title to all property is vested in each specific community, and each community constitutes a separate financial entity. The communicants live in dormitories, eat together, and wear a prescribed uniform. There is a studied avoidance of ostentation—no lawns are permitted around the houses, all decorations are forbidden, and musical instruments are not allowed.

The direction of community government is concentrated in the hands of a few officials, although it is democratic in form. Supreme temporal authority in each village is vested in a chief officer, called a householder, and a council of five advisers. On the religious side all authority is entrusted to a minister. These various officers are chosen by an assembly composed of all of the male members of the church. Once elected the holders of office enjoy life tenure, subject to removal by a vote of the assembly. Only very important questions are referred to that body for consideration, and for deciding the most significant of such problems a unanimous vote is required. The householder, the chief officer in each group, has control over all of the work activities in the village. He assigns specific tasks to each person, and he makes certain that all members of the community carry on some menial work. The women are grouped into squads which change their work assignments every two weeks. The time of each individual is fully organized in the most minute detail.

Among the Hutarians agriculture is the primary occupation, and every community aims to be self-sustaining. No member of the organization can produce luxury goods or weapons of war, nor may he be an innkeeper or operate a store. Money cannot be loaned, insurance is not used, and speculation is forbidden. Money is used only in dealing with the outside world. Profits for individuals are not permitted—only for the group. Any profits from their activities are used for one purpose—to buy more land and found new communities.[13]

The longevity of this group is probably due to several reasons. One of the most important is the deep religious feeling of its members which has been strengthened by centuries of persecution in Europe. Outside harassment has tended to keep internal dissension at a minimum. Second, their language has separated them from the rest of the nation. The members generally have spoken German, although during most of their 400 years of existence they have been located in countries where that language was not generally used. Obviously, this has set them off from the rest of the society. Third, the use of distinctive uniforms has also served to distinguish them from other people. Fourth, their leaders have been definitely trained for their tasks. Consequently, the death of one significant leader does not hurt the community. Finally, the group appears to have had a definite talent for organization.[14]

THE MORMONS

The Church of Jesus Christ of Latter Day Saints constitutes the only large group, numbering 678,217 in 1936, that tried to carry on a controlled society in the United States. In Utah political control largely is in the hands of the Mormons for, at the time of the last religious census, they constituted 60 per cent of the population of the state.

The movement developed in the frontier society of western New York in the 1830's and underwent numerous vicissitudes until it finally became established in Utah. Because of local persecution the members first moved to Missouri, then to Illinois, and ultimately to Utah. Relatively early in the history of the movement polygamy was adopted as one of its tenets. Even

[13] The same, p. 367.
[14] The same, pp. 484-85.

before the migration to the far west in 1847, communism had been accepted as a basic ideal, although in first organizing their new community in the desert, they did not utilize the communist methodology. Instead, in Utah there was developed a theocracy that exercised widespread control over the individuals.[15] In the economic sphere it operated through co-operative associations and an extensive use of capitalistic institutions; the philosophy of co-operation was widely used to attain religious objectives.

When the Mormons first settled in their new home, the church itself constituted the only form of government, but when nonmembers of the church began to move in, the need for some form of civil government became evident. As a consequence, in 1848 by the establishment of the *de facto* State of Deseret, civil government was nominally separated from the theological organization of the church. Although legislative, executive, and judicial organs of government were created, actually the Mormon Church controlled all branches of the civil state.[16]

When Congress at last got around to organizing the Territory of Utah in 1850, Brigham Young, the first president of the church, was appointed governor, a post that he continued to hold until 1857. Since the Mormons acted as a group under theocratic direction, many of the non-Mormon territorial officials sent out from Washington found it almost impossible to co-operate with them,[17] and for a long period the church continued to dominate the politics of Utah both as a territory and as a state. Thus in 1903 Professor Richard T. Ely observed: "The whole population vote as directed. . . . The Mormon vote is cast as the interests of the church may demand."[18]

The geography of Utah encouraged centralized control by the church. Since the region was an inhospitable desert in-

[15] Hamilton Gardner. "Communism Among the Mormons," *Quarterly Journal of Economics,* Vol. 37 (1922), p. 134; L. R. Creer, *Utah and the Nation* (1929), p. 92.

[16] The same, pp. 66, 101.

[17] The same.

[18] Richard T. Ely, "Economic Aspects of Mormonism." *Harper's Magazine,* Vol. 106 (1903), p. 677; H. H. Bancroft, History of Utah (1889), p. 449.

habited by hostile Indians, the pioneers required guidance and assistance in order to survive. In laying out the new communities the church played a dominant role because of the need for defense and for water, and under its direction the towns were carefully planned and built.[19] Church officials directed and inspired the co-operative work that was involved in building the irrigation ditches needed to bring water to the crops. The preachers in their sermons frequently gave specific directions to the members of the congregation as to how much labor they were to contribute to such work during the ensuing week and as to exactly how the tasks were to be performed.[20] Practically all of the irrigation system developed in the first half century of settlement was constructed by such co-operative efforts under church direction and control. It is evident that the church through its activities and policies accomplished an almost superhuman task of developing the inhospitable desert.

Although communism was viewed as a religious ideal, and also as the ideal form of economic and social organization, it actually was not practiced. It never was developed supposedly because of "the hardness of men's hearts." The Mormons believed that the "second best state is one based upon a far-reaching recognition of common needs, involving a generous provision for all public purposes, and also for all classes in the community requiring help, especially the aged. Private property and private industry are maintained, but at every point in all activities the guidance of the church is supposed to be felt." In this society "industry and thrift are inculcated as cardinal duties," and the church made a "strong and vigorous attempt to maintain an approximation of equality of opportunity."[21]

The spiritual authorities exercised far-reaching control over what its members did with their lives, although they did not generally assign definite vocations to specific persons. Thus from the very first, Brigham Young did his best to prevent the settlers from engaging in mining, especially for gold. He real-

[19] Charles H. Brough, *Irrigation in Utah* (1898), p. 15.
[20] Ely, *Harper's,* p. 669. See also Brough, *Irrigation in Utah,* p. 12.
[21] Ely, *Harper's,* pp. 672-73.

ized that the survival of the Mormons in the hostile environment of the desert required the maintenance of group solidarity and the assignment of the highest priority to food production; the pursuit of mining obviously interfered with both.[22] A sympathetic biographer asserted that, "Brigham Young maintained that nothing should be done without his advice and permission. When a man decided to enter a certain business he was expected to consult Brigham Young before he took action."[23] Bancroft observes that "Labor was regarded as a duty no less than prayer or temple service."[24]

Frequently, the church ordered the establishment of new colonies in outlying areas and designated specific individuals to be members of such expeditions. As a result extensive settlements were developed in the bordering states of Idaho, Arizona, Colorado, and Wyoming. The Perpetual Immigration Fund constituted another important device for exerting economic control over the settlers. By advances from this fund large numbers of immigrants were brought from Europe before 1883. Loans covering the cost of transportation were made from it, and until these advances were repaid the church was in a position to exercise far-reaching authority over the lives of the new arrivals.[25]

The church also influenced the commercial life of the community.[26] With the opening of the railroad in 1869, the need for controlling the distribution of commodities became evident to the clerical authorities. An extensive system of co-operative stores was organized under the church which operated primarily through the Zion Cooperative Mercantile Institution. Branches or affiliated retail establishments were developed in most of the small communities. Originally, only tithe-paying members of

[22] M. R. Werner, *Brigham Young* (1925), p. 255.
[23] The same, p. 424.
[24] Bancroft, *History of Utah,* p. 296.
[25] Stewart E. White, *The Forty-niners* (1918), p. 82; Werner, *Brigham Young,* p. 271.
[26] Hamilton Gardner, "Cooperation Among the Mormons," *Quarterly Journal of Economics,* Vol. 31, p. 461.

the church could subscribe to the stock of the co-operatives,[27] and nonchurch merchants frequently were boycotted.[28] Although many of the local co-operatives have declined, even today the ZCMI is a significant mercantile establishment, and it probably still is under at least indirect ecclesiastical control.

The church has been a significant stockholder in numerous corporations engaged in manufacturing and other activities.[29] For instance, the processing of sugar beets was long carried on by such enterprises. The construction of the secondary network of railroads was first undertaken by the great leaders of the church. The major hotel and the leading newspaper in Salt Lake City were long under church control. A large part of the revenues of the church have been derived from investments in such enterprises.

The Mormon church has exercised far-reaching power over the intellectual activities of the people of Utah. For example, among the early objectives of the first university in the state was to overthrow the theory of gravitation, and its founders asserted that "the planetary systems were to be rearranged" by it.[30] In 1907 the trustees of Brigham Young University threatened to dismiss some members of its staff because their teaching was not in harmony with church doctrines, and four years later the trustees of that institution declared that nothing was to be taught that was "not in harmony with the revealed word of God."[31] There are not readily available authoritative sources that indicate the extent of Mormon control over intellectual pursuits and education. Has the authority of this sect in such areas declined like that of other religious groups in recent years?

Religious fervor was a primary factor in making the Mormon

[27] E. E. Ericksen, *The Psychological and Ethical Aspects of Mormon Group Life* (1922), p. 53; Werner, *Brigham Young,* p. 437.

[28] Bancroft, *History of Utah,* p. 651.

[29] The same, pp. 753-54; Ericksen, *The Psychological and Ethical Aspects of Mormon Group Life,* p. 71; Gardner, *Quarterly Journal of Economics,* Vol. 37, p. 461.

[30] Bancroft, *History of Utah,* p. 324.

[31] Ericksen, *The Psychological and Ethical Aspects of Mormon Group Life,* p. 65.

experiment possible. "Obedience to the leaders of the church was considered a supreme duty."[32] The whole attitude of the Mormons was conditioned by their belief that they were the chosen people. As a result of this conviction they were set off completely from all non-Mormons. To the members of the faith "the great sin was disloyalty. This was a sufficient cause for ex-communication."[33] Such an attitude tended to stultify the critical faculties. As a further consequence, the resulting attitude of superiority over other people provoked persecution, and such harassment further stimulated the sense of group solidarity.

SHAKERS

The Shakers constitute an old communist community that has declined rapidly in recent years. They are a celibate branch of the Quakers established late in the eighteenth century. At one time the group had as many as 5,000 members,[34] but by 1936 it numbered only about 60 residing in settlements in Massachusetts and New Hampshire. Since it was a celibate order, it was confronted with the difficult task of perennial recruitment, for their number was not replenished as a consequence of natural increases.

This is a real theocracy that has practiced communism for religious purposes. New members surrender all their possessions to the specific community that they join. Title to property is vested in each community and not in the order as a whole.[35] Each group constitutes a separate entity for the purpose of property ownership as well as for the control of production. A board of four, composed of two men and two women, runs each community. The members of these boards are appointed by the central authority of the church, and the supreme head of the church designates his own successor. Each board has full

[32] The same, p. 405.
[33] The same, p. 83.
[34] Morris Hillquit, *History of Socialism in the United States* (1910), p. 29.
[35] Alexander Kent, "Cooperative Communities in the United States," U. S. Department of Labor, *Bulletin 35* (1901), p. 566.

control over the affairs of the community and the activities of its members.[36] Throughout its government religious and civil functions are completely fused.

The life of the members is thoroughly organized; the times of rising, work, and meals are all prescribed.[37] The work to be performed by each member is specifically determined. Musical instruments and pictures are forbidden. All books to be read and all letters written by members are subject to censorship.[38] Being a celibate order any growth must come through outside recruitment. The failure of such an organization to attract new members obviously has resulted in its general decline.

ONEIDA

The Oneida Community of New York, despite its small size (never more than 300 members), was probably better known than many of the other experiments because of its attitude on marriage. This religious organization was founded in Vermont by John Humphrey Noyes in the second quarter of the nineteenth century. Early in its existence the sect moved to Oneida, New York in 1848. Then it consisted of 51 members, and its total assets were only $9,400.[39] Theologically, it was greatly influenced by the Shakers. Very shortly after the formation of the sect the members began to practice a form of polygamy that they called "complex marriage." The widely publicized opposition to ordinary marriage was based on theological grounds, and this was also true of its belief in communism. Complete communal ownership of property prevailed after the removal to Oneida. All members lived as a family group in one large dwelling house; meals were taken in common; and even clothing was owned communally.

Little formalized government existed in this community, and as long as Noyes remained a member he practically ran it. The main means for exerting control over the members was through

[36] The same, p. 570.
[37] The same, p. 574.
[38] William A. Hinds, *American Communities and Cooperative Colonies* (1908), p. 46.
[39] The same, p. 183.

a device called mutual criticism. "Every member of the group was encouraged at regular periods to submit silently while associates analyzed his habits, his virtues and his vices, and pointed the way to character development."[40] Even Mr. Noyes is said to have submitted to the ordeal of mutual criticism.[41] For a time the task of criticism was performed by a special committee rather than the whole membership. One observer commenting on this means of control said: "Here was scandal reduced to a system and made infinitely more effective and delightful than it is elsewhere."[42] Of course sanctions of such a form could only have been effective with a group of like-minded people who were held together by a strong bond of religious sentiment.

The management of the community was practically entirely in Mr. Noyes' hands. He determined what was to be produced and how, as well as who was to perform specific tasks. He not infrequently shifted individuals from task to task as the situation required. One member who previously had been a lawyer worked for the group at no less than twelve different occupations, varying from laundryman to cook, and from pipe fitter to editor.[43] So far as possible work was done through the use of organized bees.

The community engaged in both agricultural and industrial activities; but since its agricultural ventures did not prove to be highly successful, industrial pursuits were stressed. The manufacture of steel traps produced real profits. The group also got into the business of canning some of the farm produce it grew, and the manufacture of silverware was commenced just before the association dissolved.

Community control extended to even the petty things in life. Tobacco was forbidden by unanimous consent. The use of any form of stimulant or even highly seasoned food was avoided as being abnormal and unnecessary.[44] Although Pierpont Noyes,

[40] Robert A. Parker, *A Yankee Saint* (1935), p. 215.
[41] The same, p. 218.
[42] The same, p. 220.
[43] Allan Westlake, *The Oneida Community* (1900), p. 68.
[44] The same, pp. 61-62.

the son of the founder, claimed there was little regimentation in this community,[45] he admitted the existence of some very petty forms of regulation. For example, he pointed out that "Community boys were forbidden even to speak to 'outside' boys,"[46] and that "conformity [in dress], as with many details of conduct, was enforced by public opinion or desire for the approval of Father Noyes."[47]

The dissolution of the community was a consequence of both internal and external forces. Some of the younger men of the group had been educated at Yale and other colleges, and after such an exposure to the outside world occasionally they were critical of the leadership as well as the general philosophy of the movement.[48] At the same time widespread criticism of the sect developed in central New York, largely aroused because of the opposition of the group to marriage. Finally, in the summer of 1879 as a consequence of these two sources of difficulty, Noyes fled to Canada. He feared that his position in the community would be jeopardized by the criticism developing in the group as well as by the outside opposition that was re-enforcing the internal dissension.[49] After his departure disintegration was rapid, and on January 1, 1881 the few who remained in the community reorganized it as a joint stock company.[50] It appears that this small religious sect was held together only by the personality of its leader. When his influence waned its demise was but a matter of a brief time.

THE ORDER OF ZOAR

This German sect, which settled in Ohio in 1819, carried on its experiment in communal living for almost 80 years. Its membership, never exceeding 225, was composed entirely of German immigrants or their descendants. "No American is known to have entered the society."[51] The organization bought

[45] Pierpont B. Noyes, *My Father's House* (1937), p. 12.
[46] The same, p. 115.
[47] The same, p. 79.
[48] The same, p. 159.
[49] The same, p. 158.
[50] The same, p. 187.
[51] E. O. Randall, *History of the Zoar Society* (1900), p. 11.

5,500 acres of agricultural land in central Ohio, and its cultivation was the primary but not exclusive pursuit of the members.

Only after migrating to this country did the group accept complete communism. Before their settlement here, communism was not a part of their religious teaching Upon arrival in the New World they realized that many of their members, inexperienced in agriculture, would have to seek work in the cities. The leaders feared that the scattering of the little band in the strange land would tend to destroy group solidarity. Consequently, communism of property was developed to cement the group.[52] All members surrendered their worldly goods to the society, and the group assumed responsibility for clothing, feeding, and sheltering them. No accounts were kept of the amount of money or goods received by anyone. Equality of treatment for all was the rule. The community benefited greatly from the construction of the Ohio Canal through its land, and largely as a result of this fortunate circumstance, its assets totaled $1,000,000 by 1845.[53]

Although several different constitutions were adopted at various times, during most of its life the group was run by a board of three trustees elected by the full membership. A treasurer and agent general were similarly chosen. The board of three trustees together with the agent general practically ran the community, and most of the time the agent general was the actual controlling force. This single official "controlled and managed everything."[54] He assigned the tasks to be performed by each individual member; he determined what was to be produced and what was to be sold to the outside world. As long as the founder of the colony lived he held this significant office. The social and intellectual life of the community was rigidly controlled. Practically all amusements were denied to the members—dancing was forbidden, and there was no social or literary activity. German was the language in general use.

[52] The same, p. 7.

[53] George B. Landis, "The Society of the Separatists of Zoar, Ohio," *Annual Report of the American Historical Association for 1898* (1899), pp. 196, 199.

[54] The same, p. 80.

Education was not highly prized. Artists, musicians, preachers were not encouraged by the Separatists. "No genius could here find the means for carrying on his work unless he took some underhanded expedient."[55]

When younger members came in contact with the uncontrolled world, disintegration commenced. They were unwilling to remain in the group once they realized how pleasant life was outside of it. Apparently these younger people had little use for communism, and many of them drifted away. With the loss of the more vigorous youngsters, the older members, although they liked their self-contained communal society, were ultimately unable to carry on the agricultural work by themselves. As a consequence, the income of the group declined while its debts increased. Finally, in 1898, the colony voluntarily dissolved. At its end there were but 136 members each of whom received about $2,500 in final settlement. The death of their original leader and the attraction of freedom in the outside world for the younger members brought about the decay and disintegration of this religious sect.

SUMMARY

In all of these religious societies there was thoroughgoing control over the individual. With the exception of the Mormons, complete communism was the rule. The members of the different groups, again with the exception of the Mormons, were expected to turn over all of their property. The members were guaranteed a living in all of the communistic organizations. No system of wage payments existed, and the various skills all received the same compensation.

Generally speaking, the primary objective on the economic level was to make the community self-contained and independent of the outside world, and the ultimate objectives were usually religious. Trade with the outside world was minimized. This was especially noticeable among the Hutarians. Commerce with the surrounding area was more fully developed at Amana and Oneida than was true with other sects.

[55] The same, p. 200.

The extent of control over the details of personal life was not uniform. In the Shaker groups all of the members live in one household. The same was true of the Oneida community. Obviously, living as one household increased the extent of group control. In the Amana community, families lived separately. Generally speaking, simplicity in dress, food, and housing was stressed. In some groups uniform clothing was prescribed. This was especially true with the Shakers and the Hutarians. With the exception of the Mormons there was complete central control of the goods to be produced by the organization and the tasks to be performed by each member. In many of the groups, for example at Oneida, occupations were changed frequently and the development of high skills did not seem to be appreciated.

The government of these settlements was generally autocratic, and obedience was secured through religious sanctions. In most of the communities the government was highly paternalistic, and often it was actually paternalistic in structure. Even where democratic forms were observed the government was really autocratic in substance. Frequently, the original leader of the group was actually the controlling influence as long as he lived, especially at Oneida, Zoar, Amana, and among the Mormons. Religious obedience constituted the essential element of social compulsion, and a careful student has concluded:

> . . . A compact community life, common religious ideals, agreement on economic principles, uniformity in economic and social practises, expulsion into the outside world as a potential punishment for nonconformists—these were the bases of social order. To conform meant complete acceptance and approval. To deviate meant swift social isolation. . . .[56]

Many restraints and limitations were freely accepted by the members because "they wanted to preserve their eternal souls. . . . They wanted little of life because they believed that it had little to offer." Salvation was their main interest, and the freedom they lost was insignificant as compared to this

[56] Dorothy W. Douglas and Katherine Du Pre Lumpkin, "Communistic Settlements," *Encylopaedia of the Social Sciences,* Vol. 4 (1931), p. 98.

objective. Their right to practice their own religion in their own way was the one liberty that they demanded of the ordinary civil authority. "They were willing to sacrifice everything for the common good, except their personal right to interpret God's word as they individually wished."[57]

II. THE NONRELIGIOUS EXPERIMENTS

The nonreligious utopias generally have been less successful than the religious experiments. Probably more than 60 nonreligious communistic or socialistic experiments have been organized in this country. Most of them were developed in the second quarter of the nineteenth century, but at least 20 more attempts were made at the close of that century. Obviously most of the communities cannot be considered here; some of them were very short lived, and others were purely faddist.[58] In this section only a few idealistic nonreligious settlements will be surveyed—the experiments of Robert Owen, the Fourier colonies, and the Icaria group.

THE OWENITE EXPERIMENTS

Robert Owen, a Scotsman who did much to stimulate the co-operative movement in Great Britain, was the inspiration for the establishment of at least 19 communistic groups in this country in the period following 1825.[59] He was a successful industrialist who was disturbed by the effects of the industrial revolution on many of the workers and who had great faith in co-operation. Starting from the belief that the human character was formed by environment, he concluded that the individual would show immediate improvement with a change in his physical, economic, and social surroundings. To him the en-

[57] Victor F. Calverton, *Where Angels Dared to Tread* (1941), pp. 169-71.

[58] For example, Fruitlands. See Sears, *Bronson Alcott's Fruitlands.* This was a strange communistic community that survived but for one year. It rested on the hypothesis that human nature would be improved by changes in dress and diet. No animal labor or animal products would be used. The leaders of the experiment never thought about what they would do for shoes when their footgear wore out in the inclement climate of Massachusetts.

[59] Lockwood, *The New Harmony Communities,* p. 216.

vironment of the communistic group was ideal for individual development.

His major American experiment at New Harmony in Indiana was an admitted failure within less than two years. The colony, founded on the banks of the Wabash River in 1825, was entirely financed by Mr. Owen, and at its height had about a thousand residents.[60] It was a completely communistic group—all tasks were allocated by the central authority, and housing was distributed similarly. Members lived in individual houses but took meals together. Remuneration was absolutely uniform without regard for skill or effort. As payment of wages each member was given a credit in the community store, and on this he could draw for his food and clothing.[61] The type of government utilized by the group changed frequently. At first it was a complete dictatorship under Owen's personal control; then various forms of direct democracy were tried; and near the end of the experiment it once again became a dictatorship under Owen.[62]

The most important reason for the short life of this group was the failure to select the members carefully. Apparently, almost any person who sought admission was accepted. Many of the recruits were ill-suited for an experiment in group living. Property and religion also constituted major causes of dissension. Only Owen's personal enthusiasm and his private funds kept the group going for two years, and in 1827 even Owen, despite his normal optimism, had to admit that the experiment was a failure. Other communities similarly inspired were established subsequently in Indiana, New York, Ohio, and Pennsylvania; but like the first one, they were all short lived.[63]

THE FOURIER GROUPS

The more than forty Fourier colonies organized in this country during the 1840's all failed.[64] These groups were a prod-

[60] The same, p. 118.
[61] The same, p. 108.
[62] The same, pp. 122-67.
[63] The same, pp. 199, 206-07, 216.
[64] Hillquit, *History of Socialism in the United States,* p. 117.

uct of the thinking of Louis Fourier. This Frenchman was a person of some means whose basic objective was the creating of a system of social harmony. His ideas were popularized in this country largely through Arthur Brisbane's writings in Horace Greeley's *New York Tribune*.

Fourier started not from the belief that there was a maldistribution of wealth but from the conviction that modern production suffered from anarchy and wastefulness, and he was motivated by "the repellant condition of labor."[65] He believed that God originally created a harmonious universe in which the basic drives of man served legitimate and useful purposes. When these fundamental personal drives were permitted to have free play, a harmonious society would result. The problem then was to give man a real opportunity to develop. This dreamer envisaged that such an opportunity could be given by a program of planned communities. As Fourier outlined his ideas the colonies were to be financed through the sale of shares to prospective members. The members of each community should be able to buy as many shares of stock in the undertakings as they desired. Thus there was not to be common ownership of capital. The earnings from the enterprise were to be distributed on the following basis: five twelfths for labor, one third for capital, and one fourth for talent.[66] Capital was not to be owned in common, and remuneration was not to be based on need; and as thus developed Fourierism was far from true communism.

Probably the most successful and long-lived Fourier group, or phalanx as they were called, was the North American Community founded at Red Bank, New Jersey, in 1843. Even this undertaking lasted for only 11 years, and at no time did it have more than 90 members. Starting with an investment of only $8,000, in less than ten years its assets increased tenfold, and the colony generally paid dividends of 5 per cent on the stock. Agriculture constituted the principal occupation of the group. The majority of its members were substantial persons of "cul-

[65] The same, p. 78.
[66] The same, p. 84.

ture" and "refinement."[67] When the undertaking began, the members displayed much enthusiasm; but as time passed this spirit waned and dissension developed over problems of administration and the distribution of earnings. When its mill was destroyed by fire in 1854, the group disbanded. The $12,000 loss involved was not the cause for such a decision, however, because Horace Greeley was willing to advance the funds for rebuilding the structure.[68]

The Ceresco, Wisconsin, phalanx was the only other Fourier experiment that met with even moderate success. This was founded in 1844 and ultimately numbered about 180 members.[69] What success it enjoyed was due in part to the facts that it paid cash for its land and that it was free from debt. Another contributing factor was the great care that was exercised in selecting members. The group refused to take in anyone who did not have adequate means and proper physical capacity. Although successful from a financial standpoint, the community always suffered from a lack of internal harmony and enthusiasm. Some of the members desired to establish a unitary farm that would have involved cultivating as a unit all of the land owned by the group, while others desired to divide the land into family-size farms.[70]

Probably the most widely known Fourier phalanx was the Brook Farm Colony. Although this group was founded in 1841, it really did not become a true phalanx until 1844. Included among its members were such important transcendental literary lights as Hawthorne, Charles Dana, Ripley, Channing, and Margaret Fuller. It was primarily a dairy farm located in West Roxbury, Massachusetts. It was run by four committees of three persons, all chosen by the full membership. These committees dealt with general direction, agriculture, education, and finance. Despite an increase in membership from a mere 20 to some 70 persons "the financial success of the Farm was but very mod-

[67] The same, p. 102.
[68] The same, p. 103.
[69] Hinds, *American Communities and Cooperative Colonies,* p. 283.
[70] Hillquit, *History of Socialism,* pp. 110-12.

erate, and the life full of toil and devoid of earthly comforts."[71] The romantic members had a great knack for covering their poverty with an attractive veil of poetry.[72] With the destruction by fire of their main building in 1846, the experiment came to an end.

ICARIA

Although suffering many vicissitudes and frequent reorganization this group persisted for about 40 years. It consisted of a group of French artisans who came to this country without either capital or experience. Under the leadership of Étienne Cabet, they first attempted to settle in Texas, and in 1849 moved to Illinois, taking over the old Mormon settlement at Nauvoo. Agriculture was their primary occupation, though they had no experience in the field. They also operated flour and saw mills, and a distillery was a major source of income.[73]

Cabet, their leader, was effectively clothed with all real power over the colony irrespective of the nominal form of government. He was generally re-elected president each year. For a period after 1850 there were also six directors named annually; each of these was charged with the management of a specific department of community activity. This central board had the authority to assign tasks to each member and to enforce its decisions by denying food to any who did not perform his designated stint.[74]

Dissensions plagued the Icarians throughout their existence. In 1855 trouble resulted from Cabet's desire to end the board of six directors and to regain all power for himself.[75] As a consequence of this difference of opinion, Cabet and a number of followers seceded and moved to St. Louis where only for a short time did they persist as a group. The 239 persons remaining in the old community at Nauvoo subsequently moved to southwestern Iowa and there acquired agricultural lands that proved

[71] The same, p. 107.
[72] For a romantic picture see Katherine Burton, *Paradise Planters* (1939).
[73] Shaw, *Icaria, A Study in Communistic History,* pp. 47-50.
[74] The same, p. 58.
[75] The same, p. 55.

to be valuable.[76] During the initial period in Iowa members rapidly drifted away from the community so that in 1863 only 35 remained. Ultimately, this new settlement managed to make considerable money by selling land to the Chicago, Burlington, and Quincy Railroad, and as a result of the Civil War, they were able to profit from raising wool.[77]

Even with prosperity in Iowa, dissensions continued. The conservatism of the majority of its members was a source of difficulty since the younger members were very anxious to introduce new agricultural and business methods. They also desired to give the vote to women, and they sought to make the community a haven for European communists.[78] Since the younger members were a minority in a group that temporarily was organized democratically, the innovators were unable to get their ideas adopted. After their failure to win control and change the policies, the younger members withdrew and set up a new settlement on another part of the same tract of land.[79] This new section assumed the original name of Icaria, while the conservatives took the name of the New Icarian Community. The latter group composed of the older members declined rapidly and finally moved to California in 1884.[80] During all of its life the Icarian Community was marked by a lack of able direction and leadership. This contributed to the dissension and personal squabbles that always characterized it.

SUMMARY

The form of government of most of the nonreligious communities was clearly autocratic. Frequently, the original leaders assumed a position of complete dominance and exercised absolute control. When the organizer gifted with the capacity to inspire left or died, disintegration was rapid. Where democracy was practiced, as in Icaria, policies were continually in a state of flux, and no leadership was long accepted. Generally speak-

[76] The same, pp. 77-78.
[77] Hillquit, *History of Socialism,* p. 134.
[78] Shaw, *Icaria, A Study in Communistic History,* p. 95.
[79] The same, p. 102.
[80] The same, p. 139.

ing, the nonreligious associations have been shorter lived than the religious communities. Other than the Icarian group and the North American Colony among the Fourier phalanxes, none of them lasted for more than a few years. Uniformly the nonreligious groups have been failures.

One of the most important causes of failure has been a lack of money. This was noticeably true of most of the Fourier phalanxes, and it was also a contributing factor in most of the Owenite communities. The poverty accompanying the initial period of economic trial and error was met by them with dogged perseverance and closer communal unity.[81] Another reason for failure was that most of the communities suffered from an oversupply of land. Again, difficulties of recruitment were prevalent. Persons with business acumen and skilled artisans usually were not attracted to these visionary experiments. Not infrequently, the agricultural groups had a dearth of skilled farm workers. Finally, they lacked the great all-prevailing drive that carried many of the religious groups through periods of difficulty. When dissatisfaction developed from the restraints imposed by an autocratic leader or an equally autocratic majority, the members were quick to flee from the narrow confines of group life.

III. CONCLUSION

What impact did these small controlled societies have upon their individual members? A number of writers have sought to answer this question. In 1875 Charles Nordoff attempted to investigate the problem through an analysis of the American communist experiments. Being highly sympathetic with the endeavors, he believed that they stimulated honesty, cleanliness, and efficiency among their members. He also was pleased to discover that "the communists do not toil severely,"[82] because their "life is full of devices for personal ease and comfort."

But he did go on to point out several of their unfavorable repercussions on the members. "Some things the communist must

[81] Douglas and Lumpkin, *Encyclopaedia of the Social Sciences,* Vol. 4, p. 101.

[82] Charles Nordoff, *The Communistic Societies of the United States* (1875), p. 400.

surrender; and the most precious of these is solitude." Again, the environment was not stimulating to the more able members, and because of this he believed that intellectual persons of good circumstances could not succeed in such communities. To Nordoff it appeared that the great stress on conformity encouraged mediocrity. "The communal life appears to be at first view, inexorably dull and dreary."[83] He feared that the inhabitants of the colonies did not make nearly as much of their lives as was possible. "Most of them are ascetics, who avoid the beautiful as tending to sin; and most of them, moreover, out of force of old habits, and a conservative spirit, which dreads change, rigidly maintain the old ways."[84] Success was possible for such an experiment, he concluded, only when the participants felt that anything would be better than the life in the outside world. "Success depends . . . upon a feeling [among the participants] of the unbearableness of the circumstances in which they find themselves."[85] Thus the communities attracted primarily individuals who were badly adjusted to their environment, and many groups suffered from such membership.

Early in the twentieth century another detailed study of the American communistic communities was made by Frederick A. Bushee.[86] His analysis of the causes of the failure of these experiments brings out some of their effects upon their members. This authority concluded that most of the communities failed because of disharmony and that the rigid controls imposed were the main cause of inharmonious relations. "The underlying cause of dissension as illustrated by recent experiments is the rigid character of the communist organization." Rigidity is a consequence of the fact that the "opinion of the majority . . . must prevail even in details."[87] He also found that the great emphasis on equality had undesirable consequences. "The ambitious members are harmed more than the others are helped," Bushee believed. To this author it appeared that "intellect in

[83] The same, pp. 405, and 409-10.
[84] The same, p. 416.
[85] The same, p. 408.
[86] Bushee, *Political Science Quarterly*, Vol. 20, p. 625.
[87] The same, p. 652.

communist colonies is not highly valued." "There is a lack of individual freedom and individual responsibility," he concluded. Competition is suppressed and "the desire for distinction is generally weakened."[88]

William A. Hinds in his exhaustive study of such communities[89] found that the religious groups were more successful than the others, and as a result he concluded that for such experiments to succeed "agreement is indispensable, and thus far it has most surely come through the religious life."[90] He did not believe that any one specific religion was superior for this purpose; but a strong spiritual drive was indispensable. A desire for co-operation was, in his opinion, second best to religion as a cohesive force.

Thus it is agreed that it is difficult to secure a high degree of individual conformity in voluntarily organized, controlled societies. Students are generally agreed on the need for a major drive or directing force to bring about such conformity from the members. The forces promoting compliance were most effective in religious groups or in communities where the members felt that the controls imposed by the group were preferable to their maladjusted life in the everyday world. Where such a drive to conform was absent, the freedom of the great outside world apparently was too attractive and the group disintegrated.

Despite the voluntary nature of these communities, most of them failed. It should be remembered that all of the persons in the various communities (whether agricultural or not) voluntarily joined or remained in the group. Frequently, those who were born in the association left of their own free will after reaching maturity. Membership was the result of a conscious choice. Adherence was not forced upon anyone by a central state. Therefore, it must be assumed that the groups were basically composed of likeminded people. They believed generally that there was a real community of interest among themselves.

In most instances the members did not for long have to ex-

[88] The same, pp. 658, 660; and Calverton, *Where Angels Dared to Tread,* p. 172.

[89] *American Communities and Cooperative Colonies.*

[90] The same, p. 592.

perience the restraints resulting from control before freedom became more attractive. The members always could leave if they found the controlled society was not to their liking, and in practically every instance, other than the Mormons, Amana, and the Hutarians, most of the people left. They escaped into the vast sea of freedom that surrounded the experimental groups. Whatever may have been the advantages that resulted from extensive control, they apparently did not outweigh the disadvantages arising from restraint. To most members the security that resulted from conformity was not a sufficient good of itself. In preference to this security and the concomitant controls in the group, most of the members preferred the relative freedom that surrounded them in the outside world. For such groups to flourish either there must be a great driving force to bind the members together or the freedom to withdraw must be denied by force. When such experiments have succeeded "such success was acquired at a spiritually exorbitant price. All individuals had to sacrifice themselves to the cause, dedicate themselves to the apostolic ideal. Their individualities were immolated upon the altar of group success. They ceased to be individuals, became parts of a social organization."[91]

[91] Calverton, *Where Angels Dared to Tread,* p. 349.

CHAPTER VIII

COMPARISONS AND CONCLUSIONS

The preceding chapters indicate that various forms of authoritarian regimes have sought by a multitude of devices to regiment their individual members in an almost unlimited number of ways. No activity of an individual appears to be beyond the purview of such societies. Personal beliefs, intellectual activities, matters of dress and style, the right to work, the freedom to form associations for almost any purpose, as well as economic activities—including production, distribution, and consumption—all have been subjected to a never-ending series of controls.

This chapter, to round out the analysis, does three things: (1) it summarizes the philosophy, tacit or explicit, on which each totalitarian society relates the individual to society and to the state; (2) it demonstrates how controls over the individual in each society flow inevitably from these philosophic principles; and (3) it marks off the main differences between the early and modern totalitarian systems, showing how modern conditions permit far fuller application of all-inclusive controls than early rulers could achieve.

The first section shows why individual dignity and liberty are incompatible with the basic principles of totalitarianism, since each of these systems treats the individual as only a means to the ends of society or of the state. The second section shows that these principles cannot be dismissed as the megalomaniac fantasies of a gang that has seized power; the principles are rigorously and logically applied in practice. The third section shows how technical developments and the rise of the masses as a major aspect of modern politics allow these principles and practices to be driven to their ultimate conclusions.

I. PRECONCEPTIONS

Both the relationship of the individual to society and the

real freedom of the individual depended on certain dominant interests and beliefs current in each totalitarian system. Under *feudalism* individual protection and salvation were of paramount significance. The absence of any central authority strong enough to maintain public order made it imperative for some group or person in each area to have sufficient power to protect individuals from violence. The overwhelming need for a form of social organization that could give to each person at least the rudiments of physical protection made people willing to put up with many arbitrary restraints to attain it. The value of security made people willing to give up their freedom of person and property to a powerful man in return for his promise of protection. As a part of this process the authority to govern became confused with rights over property, and ultimately it was considered to be a property right itself. Under such conditions government was completely irresponsible to its subjects; and being irresponsible, the government could in effect (if not in theory) be absolute. The power of the lord to govern was as extensive as his rights over the property included within his domain. The picture of feudalism here presented differs from that of idealists who depict it as resting on alleged mutual reciprocal feudal contracts. Since no legal means existed to restrict the governing authority to the terms of such agreements, it is believed that this analysis is a closer approximation to the actual practice than is such an idealistic reconstruction.

The other basic element in feudal society was the universal desire for salvation in the next world. This objective, primarily sought through the Church, was so compelling that the Church could go far in forcing the state to harmonize its policies with those the Church prescribed for saving souls.

While it would be stretching matters to argue that the desires for protection and salvation shaped each and every act of those who wielded public power, these two primary objectives basically conditioned the attitude of feudal society toward the individual. Salvation was not within the hands of each communicant; it was exclusively in the control of the Church. Similarly, protection was received by the subject not as a right but as a gratuity from an absolutist, irresponsible, governing authority. Thus in both the spiritual and temporal fields, the complete dependence of the individual on outside authority was a primary assumption.

The *absolute monarchies* considered that the power of the state was an end in itself. State power was largely measured in physical terms, and the state primarily utilized its might to promote external aggression and to protect itself from the attacks of others. International rivalry was accentuated because of the prevailing view that the quantity of goods available in the world was static and that no human action could increase their sum total. Hence if the power of one state was increased through the augmentation of its physical wealth, this could only be secured at the expense of other states with a consequent reduction of their power. Since the relative might of each state was of pre-eminent importance to its rulers, the practice of viewing power in material terms tended to foster international rivalries and ultimately wars. It was generally assumed that extensive public regulation of the individual was imperative to increase the power of the state to make war. To promote this all-pervading objective, nothing was considered to be beyond the wisdom and competence of the state. All aspects of the life and resources of the people were subject to such degree of control as the holders of government authority considered to be necessary to augment the power of the state. The interests of the state as interpreted by the government always were superior to those of the subject. The unchallenged acceptance of this philosophy facilitated the imposition of restraints that aided special interests more than they enhanced the might of the nation.

The *idealistic communities* of the nineteenth century were of two types, religious and social; but religious objectives were commonly the primary concern. Their members believed that earthly existence was directed only toward a single objective—salvation in the hereafter; the attainment of this objective conditioned all the activities of the group and justified any controls that might have to be imposed on the individual. In the nonreligious groups rigid application of a social or economic theory was the major motivating force. Here, again, the whole life of the group was shaped by the demands of that philosophy. Since all of these communities were voluntary in nature and were composed of like-minded people, the problems of control differed from those in the ordinary state because no real question of compliance existed.

The position of the individual under *communism* is governed by three aspects of communist philosophy: materialist determinism, the notion of social class and the class struggle, and the concept of a political party.

According to materialist determinism, every important aspect of the life of the individual is determined by his material surroundings—in particular by the economic processes of society. The individual has no significant range of choice in any field. Acting alone, he has no control over his economic, cultural, social, or political position. Only as his material environment changes will his condition and way of life be modified. Material environment will change according to "scientific" historical laws completely without regard to his wishes and efforts. As this material substructure changes, the whole superstructure of ideas, of culture, and of law will change. According to materialist determinism, even the thought of the individual changes without regard to the individual himself. Such a degree of determinism is obviously incompatible with any sort of individualism.

Classes and the class struggle are rooted in this determinism, and conspire further to subordinate the individual. Each member of society is significant only as a member of a class. A class is not merely a collection of individuals promoting what the majority of constitutents believe to be their common interests. It is an entity created by economic conditions which inexorably determine its interests. There interests are fixed entirely apart from the wishes of its members. According to materialist theory they are determined by history; in practice, they are announced by the ruling hierarchy.

Economic conditions inevitably create two great antagonistic classes: the capitalist and the proletariat. Between them a class struggle is inevitable. Only through this class struggle can the individual hope to change his fundamental position. The victory of the proletariat is taken as inevitable; it ushers in the "dictatorship of the proletariat," the forerunner of the classless society. But at no stage in this historically determined process is the individual as such of any importance. He is only a pawn in the hands of a ruling group which steers society along its predetermined way.

The communist idea of a party completes the apparatus for subjugating the individual to the group. The party monopolizes the power to express individual and class interests, and centralizes that power at the top within the party. Then the party uses determinism to prevent any other individual or group from attempting to say what its interests at any time may be. Given determinist principles, there can be only one correct formulation of interest at any time. If the individual agrees with the party, that merely means the individual correctly reflects his material environment. If he disagrees, he is simply wrong. He recants, or the party crushes him. Consequently, there is no basis for the formation of more than one political party, since it could only be founded on error, and hence either counter-revolutionary or contrary to the true interest of the class. Within the Communist party, there is room only for one view.

Materialist determinism robs the individual of all freedom. By denying the validity of his opinion and his judgment, it chains him to a class and a party which he is powerless to control. It is therefore completely incongruous for the Communist to permit the individual any freedom to develop himself in his own way.

In *national socialism* the basic underlying conceptions resulted in a society wherein the individual was purposely submerged in the mass. The Germany of Hitler was patently and blatantly totalitarian in the most extreme sense of the word. Everything was considered to be within the orbit of the state, and nothing was regarded as being beyond its competence. Its basic ideas of significance to the position of the individual were those of race (or *Volk*), leadership, and movement.

The *Volk* was considered to be a living organic force that fundamentally determined the role of the individual in society. Solely as a part of his race did an individual have reality; he attained his fulfillment only as a part of the *Volk*. The individual was born into the *Volk;* no acquired legal citizenship could bring a person into the tribal community, and no oath could alienate the ties of blood. The race as a whole was considered as being something different from and superior to the totality of its parts—and only as a part of the *Volk* could the individual fully realize himself. Although the living entity of the race had its being in its individual members, nevertheless "The individual was bound to his people not only physically but mentally and spiritually and he was influenced by these ties in all his manifestations."[1] The German *Volk* was claimed to be the superior *Volk,* and to have been the only creative cultural force in the West. The *Volk* was the paramount form of social organization; its needs and requirements determined the nature of all other organizations including the state. In fact, the state was envisaged as being only an instrument of the *Volk*.

The nazi concept of the leader also involved the suppression of individualism. In the minds of the nazi theorists the mass of people itself could never be politically active. Only through its leader could it have political reality. He alone embodied the will of the people and was independent of all groups. "In his will the will of the people is realized. He transforms the mere feelings of the people into a conscious will. . . . His will is not the subjective, individual will of a single man, but the collective national will is embodied within him in all its objective, historical greatness."[2]

The idea of party or organization was the third major ele-

[1] Gottfried Neesse, as quoted in Raymond E. Murphy, Francis B. Stevens, Howard Trivers, and Joseph M. Roland, U. S. Department of State, *National Socialism* (1943), p. 26.

[2] Ernst Huber, as quoted in U. S. Department of State, *National Socialism,* p. 35.

ment in national socialist thought, and here again the submergence of the individual in the social mass was a logical consequence of the basic philosophy. The party was viewed as constituting the elite of the racially pure; only 10 per cent of the population of any area could be members and only racially pure Germans could be admitted. Its major tasks were the education of the people, propaganda, and the control of the state. The party was the prime device of the *Volk* for ensuring that the state furthered the objectives of the race.

The net consequence of these ideas of *Volk,* leader, and party was the development of a totalitarian state avowedly vested with unlimited authority to control all phases of the individual's life. No aspect of the existence of the citizen was beyond its competence; no phase of his personal liberty was protected from inroads by its agents. ". . . The concept of personal liberties of the individual as opposed to the authority of the state had to disappear; it is not to be reconciled with the principle of the nationalistic Reich. There are no personal liberties of the individual which fall outside the realm of the state and which must be respected by the state."[3]

Fascism, unlike communism and national socialism, made little use of secondary concepts to justify the domination of the individual by society; the avowed and bold search for power was the supreme objective of Mussolini's Italy. To the fascist leaders, the nation as exclusively manifested in the state had ends, life, and being superior to those of its individual members. In the mind of Il Duce the state was the supreme embodiment of history and culture. Of the individual, "it demands a discipline and authority which descends within the spirit and then dominates unchallenged." Mussolini asserted that the individual was to be regimented as in an army. "The individual in the Fascist State is not annulled but rather multiplied, just in the same way that a soldier in a regiment is not diminished but rather increased by the number of his comrades."[4]

[3] The same, p. 50.

[4] Carnegie Endowment for International Peace, *International Conciliation* (1935), p. 15.

The rights remaining to each member of society were only such as might serve the purposes of the state. Thus in the words of Rocco: "Individual rights are only recognized in so far as they are implied in the rights of the state. In this preeminence of duty we find the highest ethical value of Fascism."[5]

Where the Fascists left wide economic rights to the individual, they did this only because they believed that the purposes of the state would be served best thereby.[6] According to Mussolini "Fascism makes of the individual an economic instrument for the advancement of society."

Generally, controlled societies have assumed that the individual should be submerged completely in the social organism and that he existed only as a means of furthering the superior objectives of society. In fact a belief in the individual as the supreme end of society is the thing that is surprising and unusual rather than the attitude that he is but a means to a higher objective. The idea of individualism came into prominence with the rise of utilitarian thought and the revolutions in America and France. The very word individualism did not enter the English language until the English translation of De Tocqueville's *Democracy in America* appeared in 1840,[7] and De Tocqueville disapproved of the whole idea of individualism.[8]

II. APPLICATIONS

These broad philosophical foundations on which authoritarian societies rested had reality only insofar as they shaped or influenced specific types of individual restraints imposed by the all-embracing regimes. In this section illustrations are presented of how these foundations actually were related to specific phases of individual control. The examples selected include such problems as governmental responsibility, the rule of law, equality, economic controls (mainly in the field of labor), and restraints on freedom of thought and expression.

[5] The same (1926), p. 403.

[6] The same, p. 404.

[7] See A. D. Lindsay, "Individualism," in *Encyclopedia of the Social Sciences*, Vol. 7 (1932), p. 674.

[8] Vol. 2, Book 2, Chaps. 2-4.

GOVERNMENTAL RESPONSIBILITY

The various authoritarian views of the relationship of society to the individual have had repercussions on the form of government of the various states, and thereby they have greatly affected the political rights of the individual. All of these regimes denied any responsibility to their citizens or subjects either for specific acts or for general policies. Under the feudal system since the right to govern was regarded primarily as the property of those holding authority, there was no idea of government responsibility to the subject. Was it not proper that the owner should use his property as he pleased; and besides to whom should the property owner be respsonsible for the disposition and management of what belongs to him?

Another factor influencing the problem of responsibility was the limited role of government in a society that generally conceived of law as a product of immemorial custom rather than as a result of overt legislative action. In the Middle Ages law was considered to be found and not made; and, as a result, government could not be responsible for the law that it merely discovered to be already in existence—and in fact that actually existed independent of the government. The government only revealed what the pre-existing custom was, and its sole responsibility was correctly to discover custom. When the basic function of making law was generally considered to be beyond the authority of those who held public authority, and when the possession of public power was a property right, there was no problem of governmental responsibility for the consequences of its actions. This absence of responsibility had direct repercussions not only on political rights (a right to vote would be meaningless) but it had a bearing on the significance of the freedom of the individual to criticize the government.

Under the absolute monarchies the state was not considered to be any more responsible to its subjects than was the feudal state. The authority of the king to govern was largely justified as a divine right conferred upon him by the deity acting through the religious authority that was regarded as being supreme in that area. The king was answerable to God alone since it was from Him that he derived his earthly power. Under such a theory popular participation in government was incongruous. Even when late in the seventeenth century the British Parliament wrested much of the king's power from him, the elective house of that body had no idea of responsibility to its constituents.

In Communist Russia, governmental responsibility as we normally understand it is completely inverted. Although communist leaders constantly idealize the "people"—a propaganda abstraction referring to what is left in society after the revolution has absorbed, exiled, or killed everyone hostile to the party—these leaders destroyed any machinery by which the lower elements in society could hold party or government officials responsible to constitutional principles or public opinion. Since interests are determined in communist society not by independent individual judgment, constitutional prescription, or public opinion, but are announced from the top, there is no reason why individuals as such should expect the regime to listen to their views.

Responsibility in Russia is of two types: all organizations, government or not are responsible to the Communist party; within all organizations, including the party, responsibility runs from below to above. Thus, the government official at any level is responsible both to his hierarchical superior and to his communist opposite number. In the last analysis, all officials are responsible to the communist hierarchy, ultimately, that is, to Stalin. To whom is Stalin responsible? Nobody.

In Nazi Germany there existed no problem of government responsibility to the public. The government was responsible only to the party, and the head of the state and the head of the party were the same person, Hitler. Law was the product of the will of the leader, and he was solely responsible to history for what he did. The only political role for the great mass of the people was to support the government and to obey its orders. Public opinion was something to be watched and manipulated by the party and the government as convenience required.

Elections degenerated into scattered occasions for registering overwhelming public approval of handpicked figureheads, or of decisions already taken.

THE RULE OF LAW

In a free society, law has two main facets important to the individual. First, it is a body of rules accepted in the society as a whole, which governs the conduct of the individual and of the groups which he forms. Second, it is a body of rules which controls the scope, actions, and methods of government. The principle which brings these forms of control into harmony with freedom, is the rule of law. This principle means first that the individual is answerable only to a law which has already been enacted, and second that government can properly act only in conformity with existing statutes.

In the light of communist philosophy, the absence of the rule of law is not surprising. Law, to the Communists, is an instrument of the class struggle. In bourgeois society, it is an instrument for the suppression of the proletariat in the interest of the capitalist. In socialist society, it is an instrument for achieving the ends of the dictatorship of the proletariat: the consolidation of the proletarian victory over the capitalist class and its allies; the suppression of counter-revolution, and the control and governance of society pending the achievement of ultimate communism. This instrument is not limited by any bourgeois standards of justice; it is unlimited, arbitrary if necessary, and not to be trammeled simply because it has not been written out before it is used for the purposes of the ruling regime. In communist theory, the individual proletarian need not worry about the justness of law under socialism. With the abolition of classes, and thus of the class origin of injustice in law, law becomes simply the expression of the interest of the dominant proletarian class. Hence no individual proletarian can urge an individual right against it, for it represents the superior interest of his class. The Soviets have not used law as a major means to control the scope or functions of government organs; they have used the party. Hence the individual could rarely look to the courts to protect him from arbitrary or unauthorized acts of the government. The courts were openly and avowedly instruments of *class* justice, of political education, and of government control.

The idea of the rule of law was also inconsistent with the basic ideas underlying the absolute monarchies. In these states it was assumed that law was that which pleased the king, and where such a philosophy prevailed, any action taken in the name of the king was lawful. Obviously, the individual had no means of protecting his interests against public officials since any act done under cloak of royal authority was by definition legal. It would be out of place to limit the authority of the state to control the individual.

Under feudalism there was wide divergence between theory and practice concerning the rule of law as a means of protecting the individual. In theory the feudal contract between lord and vassal embodied a system of reciprocal rights and obligations that supposedly could be enforced legally. Yet in reality there was a complete absence of effective legal machinery for their enforcement. The villeins who constituted the great mass of the population were subject to the seignorial jurisdiction of their lord, and not infrequently he was also vested with the authority to administer the king's justice in cases involving them. For the villeins there existed no remedies by which they could appeal to the royal jurisdiction from the judgments of their feudal lord when he was administering seignorial justice; even when he dispensed royal justice, their means of appeal were hardly more effective. The whole idea that government was a property right made inapplicable the idea of the rule of law for the overwhelming mass of subjects.

In Nazi Germany the political and civil liberties that were permitted to the individual had little reality. They could not be enforced effectively, and they could be abolished at will by administrative action. This was largely a product of the nazi idea of law. For them law was the will of the *Volk* as expressed by the leader; and it was defined as consisting of "what is useful for the German nation." The only test of what constituted law was that the leader believed it to be useful for the German people. As a result the law was no protection to the individual in restricting arbitrary and discriminatory acts of the government. Thus whatever rights remained for the individual were determined by administrative action and were subject to political and administrative blackmail. This absence of the rule of law was a logical outcome of the idea of the *Volk* and of the leadership principle.

In view of the fascist attitude toward the individual, logically there was no place in Mussolini's Italy for the idea of the rule of law. As against the state the individual had no rights that needed to be protected. Law was only regarded as a means of ensuring the proper execution of the will of the state. In any appeal to the courts by an individual as against the government, the problem was not the protection of his rights; the only issue was whether the interests of the state had been properly determined by the administrator.

EQUALITY

Personal equality before the law has been generally absent in controlled societies. In feudalism different classes with dissimilar rights were the rule. Villeins were supposed to be free in their relations to everyone except their liege lord, but in fact they never enjoyed absolute equality with free men. Their peculiar position was largely an outgrowth of the concept of government as a property right, which in turn evolved out of the need of weak people for personal protection at all costs. The nobility had many personal and political privileges, again largely related to their property rights and status resulting therefrom. The Catholic clergy generally had a preferred position, especially in matters of crime and taxation. The discriminations visited upon the Jews were a consequence of the Church. Since the Jews were outside the religious pale, they could not take an oath, and as a result they were largely excluded from the feudal and guild system.

Under the absolute monarchies class differentiations and formal inequalities were somewhat less than in the feudal period; but nevertheless special privileges were enjoyed by many people. With government regulation widespread and in the absence both of adequate administrative machinery and of the rule of law, discriminatory treatment was widely accepted as almost normal. It was legal in sixteenth and seventeenth century England for the king to sell or give royal dispensations that freed designated individuals from the operation of specific laws. Such a practice gave rise to a general climate of opinion among those charged with law enforcement. As long as government was considered to be primarily a personal matter, why should public officers treat all people as equal?

Personal inequalities and racial discrimination were an inherent part of the system of national socialism as it was practiced in the Third Reich. Since the German *Volk* was regarded as the almost exclusive source of culture, it was logical for the government both to give special favors to members of that race and to impose limitations and restrictions on persons of other races that were considered to be inferior. It was entirely in accord with basic nazi principles for the state to take steps to prevent the inferior attributes of lesser races from being spread to members of the superior Germanic race.

ECONOMIC CONTROLS

The economic activities of individuals were limited in a multitude of ways by these authoritarian groups. All forms of industrial and agricultural production and distribution were brought under government direction and control exercised in various ways. Space precludes a complete summary of the types of economic control that were employed. The restraints imposed in the field of labor will be considered in more detail because they clearly reveal that no aspect of the individual's economic activity was too insignificant to be controlled, and the limitations in this field clearly had their origin in the basic premises or assumptions on which the society rested. Another reason for discussing them is because they obviously and directly affected many more people than did controls on management.

Germany brought all aspects of labor under state authority for it was but "the living arrangement under which the workman becomes a part in the machine of collective national production."[9] With such a philosophy, complete control over wages and all other aspects of employment was a necessary and a logical part of the picture. Under the leadership philosophy the determination of the conditions of employment and the place of work for each employee, became state functions, for no phase of human activity could be beyond the authority of the state. The independence of labor organizations was intolerable in a frankly totalitarian regime. Where service to the higher purposes of the state and the *Volk* constituted the supreme objective rather than the development and satisfaction of the individual, state control of the whole labor market and all forms of labor organizations was entirely consistent with the basic policy.

Thorough government control over all phases of labor also has been the rule in Communist Russia. Here again the all-prevailing public direction of labor was no accident; it was a logical outcome of the basic first principles on which this totalitarian regime rests. Free trade unions have ceased to exist largely because under communism they were left no real role to perform. As genuinely independent organizations differing from the party in interest and policy they could only nurture heresy. In theory, labor organizations could no longer be significant instruments, for with the proletarian revolution achieved, they were not required to curb exploitation because by definition exploitation did not exist. Instead they have now become instruments of the state for attaining its totalitarian goals; today they are used by the proletarian dictatorship to secure greater labor efficiency. In the existing planned economy there is no room for unions to engage in collective bargaining

[9] Ernst Huber, as quoted in U. S. Department of State, *National Socialism,* p. 167.

to fix wages. With all resources being distributed by state action, a central planning authority allocates to each plant a definite fund for the payment of wages, and therefore in any establishment there is only a narrowly restricted area in which wages can be determined by bargaining or negotiation. The major terms of employment are set by bureaucratic action—wages, hours, as well as all other working conditions. Collective agreements could only constitute a record of the conditions of work as fixed by the government. Strikes and boycotts are not only unnecessary, they are treason, for by definition the terms of employment are fixed by a worker's own government. Forced labor and the control over the place and the type of work are a logical part of a philosophy which proclaims that the proletarian revolution must be spread to the capitalistic world by war if necessary. As long as any capitalistic states exist, the Kremlin will insist that a war economy is needed in Russia, and with it will go complete and unremitting labor control.

The labor policy of the absolute monarchies was largely shaped by the desire of the various nations to have large exports so as to secure the maximum amount of goods and bullion useful in war. Labor costs had to be kept low to make possible a large surplus of exports over imports, and to do this a large and impoverished population was considered to be in the public interest. The fixing of maximum wages and the imposition of minimum hours of work was to the national advantage under such conditions. Labor organizations and concerted action by workers might have tended to raise costs, and consequently they had to be forbidden. Since urban labor was more attractive than farm work many steps were taken to hamper the movement of workers from the land to the towns where greater freedom and higher wages were prevalent. Thus the control of labor was a consistent part of the general pattern of mercantilism.

The feudal attitude toward labor was characterized largely by the belief that there was an obligation to work, rather than a right to work. This resulted from the fact that in exchange for protection large masses of people had given up their liberty by placing themselves under the authority of a lord. In return for his protection against attack by other lords or foreigners, the villeins committed themselves to perform certain services for him—thus they were duty bound to work for him. As a part of the agreement the worker generally received the right to till certain land for himself.

Another basic factor affecting labor in the Middle Ages was the general commingling of government or jurisdiction with general property rights. Since the right to govern was considered to constitute property, and the area over which it extended was measured largely by the extent of the realty possessed by the person exercising the power, the control over the right to work on a manor or in a town was a property right to be disposed of by the holder of the authority to govern the area concerned. Thus in either case the authority to confer the right to work was in the hands of those vested with government power.

Under feudalism all forms of labor activities were regulated as the situation required. On manors the fixing of wages or the hours of work was not a significant problem, for very few persons worked for wages; most people were required to labor in exchange for the use of land. But when the scarcity of workers made wage fixing important, maximum wages were determined by public officials. The mobility of labor generally was highly restricted. For example, the villeins were tied to their manors and to their land. Labor organizations did not generally exist, and where they showed signs of developing, they were quickly suppressed. It was unthinkable that a lord would permit any organization of the villeins on his manor for the purpose of changing the conditions under which they utilized his land, for such activities really would have amounted to treason against the manorial lord, and he had sufficient authority in his own hands to put down such traitorous activity.

CONTROL OF THOUGHT AND EXPRESSION

The regulation of the speech and opinion of the individual whether the views expressed were of a scientific, political, or a religious nature, has been an integral part of controlled societies. In imposing such restrictions some of these groups showed greater moderation than others; but always the authoritarian regimes have considered the imposition of such limitations to be within their appropriate sphere of action.

Since feudal Europe did not recognize the modern differentiation between the state and the church and since many functions now performed by civil governments were then performed by the Church, it should not be surprising that at that time much of the process of thought control was carried on by the Church directly with the support and assistance of the regular government authorities. The Church was intent upon maintaining its supremacy as against rival beliefs and upon protecting those who held authority under its regime. The religious ideas of its professed adherents were subject to minute control to ensure unflagging orthodoxy. Not only were non-Christian religious groups (chiefly Jews and Mohammedans) permitted to function solely under most burdensome limitations, but onerous political, economic, and social restrictions were imposed upon all who were not in the good graces of the Roman Church. All forms of intellectual activity, research, and publication were also regulated to ensure conformity to orthodox religious teaching. Individuals carrying on research and writing in fields, such as physics, chemistry, astronomy, biology, and medicine were carefully controlled in order to preclude anyone from questioning religious tenets. We hear little of direct political censorship as such, except in some of the Italian cities; but this does not prove that it was nonexistent. There are obvious reasons why formal political censorship was not mentioned in this period; the power of a feudal lord over his vassals and villeins was so great and so summary that it could readily be used to check any form of criticism. A lack of effective remedies against arbitrary imprisonment meant that formal charges and a trial were not always needed to cope with such unpleasantness as the suppression of political criticism.

The control of thought, expression, and religious beliefs was fully developed under the absolute monarchies. With the state constituting an end in itself, its authority was considered to be inherently good, and any criticism of the rulers and their policies was therefore intolerable and basically inconsistent with the major assumptions of the age. Political censorship was the rule. The control over religious beliefs became even more imperative with the diversity of beliefs resulting from the Reformation. Since the rulers of the state used religion (the divine right of kings) as one of their primary symbols of authority, any divergence from the established religion amounted to a reflection on the authority of the ruler. As a result, religious tolerance was incompatible with the very nature of the absolutistic state. Most of the controls over scientific and intellectual activities were motivated by religious considerations, for the religious foundations of political authority could not be questioned.

The idealistic religious and social experiments in this country imposed strict doctrinal conformity on all of their members. Of course these were voluntary groups recruited from among like-minded persons who were so attracted by the basic ideas of the specific movement concerned that they were willing to withdraw from the free society and to submerge themselves in the narrow confines of the specific association involved. From the regular civil government these communities demanded freedom of speech and of religion, and they were able to exist only because such liberty was an actuality. Although they demanded and required for their successful operation that the religious, economic, political, and social views of their members should be completely removed from the control of the ordinary government, these groups were almost uniformly insistent on absolute and unswerving intellectual and religious conformity on the part of their adherents. The slightest divergence from the teachings of the leader was generally punished by the prompt expulsion of the doubting Thomas. When thus expelled the member generally had to sacrifice such property as he had contributed to the group.

In Communist Russia the control over all phases of intellectual activity primarily results from the idea of economic determinism and secondarily from the belief in the inevitability of war against the capitalistic world. Religion is regarded as a capitalistic opiate of the people. Consequently, it was entirely logical for the communist state to wage a sustained militant anti-religious campaign to purge its people of such sedative residues from an earlier order. Very limited religious tolerance has been permitted only when the state believed that this might be advantageous in the current struggle with the capitalistic nations. Such tolerance can be permitted temporarily by the Communist since he believes that religion will wither away once the economic basis for it is altered under socialism.

Thought control in Russia has permeated many other fields. The entire educational program has been turned into an instrument of propaganda designed to consolidate and further the socialist organization of society and the plans of its leaders. The whole school system has been used to inculcate belief in current socialist dogma, and to distort or cast scorn on anything outside the approved items of knowledge or belief. Scholarly research, even in the field of pure science, has been made into a vehicle of party propaganda. Where the scholar fails to serve the prescribed ends of the state, his work is suppressed. Not objective observation and clear reasoning but the ideological dictates of the Communist party determine the permissible fields and results of scientific inquiry. Where all research is financed by the state as in Russia, it is inevitably subjected to government control, and in Russia this has meant direct supervision by party authorities.

All literature and music are controlled in Russia to make certain that they are used only as positive instruments of propaganda. Freedom of speech and of the press are absolutely unknown. The primary purpose of the complete censorship of books, periodicals, and newspapers is to secure absolute conformity with the basic communist philosophy, and a secondary objective is to prevent the Russian people from being exposed to any contrary points of view—let alone to subversive capitalistic propaganda and information.

In Germany under national socialism the control of thought and expression was brought about by the belief in the supremacy of the *Volk* over the individual and by the assumption that the German *Volk* was pre-eminent as compared to all other races. With the great stress placed upon the *Volk* and the belief in the pre-eminence of the Nordic race, it was almost inevitable that the government ultimately would permit only the publication of Nordic thought and ideas. The thoughts of non-Nordics could not be allowed to pollute the *Volk*. Everything was done to make certain that the mind of the German people developed in strict conformity with the leader's concept of what constituted the appropriate thought pattern for the superior Nordic *Volk*. Academic freedom was destroyed; fields of research and investigation were restricted to those that supported the accepted idea of the *Volk* or that were required for war.

Although in theory, the Nazis accepted the idea of religious liberty, in practice they permitted it only insofar as the religious bodies concerned "are not a danger to" the state and "do not militate against the moral feelings of the German race." Religion had to be subordinated to the state and the *Volk*. In fact the idea of the *Volk* amounted to a religious faith in itself—and an exclusive faith. Religious groups, such as the Jews, that did not support the idea of the Nordic *Volk* were completely destroyed. In addition the Nazi idea of the party further helped to mold the religious attitude of the government, for as Dr. Ley said, "the party claims the totality of the German people." Also the leadership principle required that if religious bodies were permitted to function they must be brought under the leader's control to make certain that they supported the *Volk*. The only Christian churches that were tolerated were those that yielded to far-reaching state control. Thus the ideas of *Volk*, party, and leadership consistently led to the utter destruction of religious liberty for the individual under national socialism.

III. FREEDOM AND THE MASS STATE

The foregoing two sections have demonstrated the extent

and inclusiveness with which historical and modern totalitarian systems have constricted the freedom of the individual. They have shown many of the philosophical and practical reasons why controls of such compass are inevitable in, and integral with, the political systems they sustain. At the same time, however, they have shown that the degree of practical freedom was larger in the earlier systems; the broad sweep of history undeniably indicates that genuine individualism and wide freedoms evolved out of the decay of the earlier systems.

We must now inquire why this is so. The reasons fall into two broad categories: those related to technological development, the elaboration of skills and tools in many fields, and increased diffusion of literacy and information; and those related to the rise of the masses as a major political force.

Feudalism and the absolute monarchies set no theoretical bounds to the controls they exercised. In practice, however, these controls were limited by the special interests of particular rulers and by slow, cumbersome machinery of control. The rivalry of church and state, fought within an inclusive, harmonious ideology, accustomed subjects to the idea that there were fields where the king's whim was not the final standard. These gaps in control made it possible for society to elaborate its structure far beyond the sphere of the state. Voluntary groups flourished. Through the Reformation, the Renaissance, and the great political revolutions, the individual came to be the center of ethics, of economics, and of politics. His dignity and position were epitomized in Kant's declaration that man must always be treated as an end, never merely as a means.

While the nineteenth century thus marked a new height for the individual, it also witnessed fundamental regressions culminating in the modern totalitarian movements.

The elaboration of society and its concomitant advances in knowledge, skills, and tools had a double significance. While they offered new scope for the individual to live a free and full life, they were at the same time an invitation to unlimited control and indispensable prerequisites to it.

First, the prerequisites: economic, intellectual, and administrative changes made it possible for modern totalitarians to match their ambition by their success in total regulation. The earlier totalitarians dealt with a relatively simple, largely domestic economic structure. The modern ones are founded on a highly centralized economic system dependent on minute division of labor. Thus they can use the economic system as a means to assure domination over the individual in every field. The earlier totalitarians knew no education for the masses; literacy was the exception, and means of communication rudimentary. The modern totalitarians founded their controls on mass education and literacy, and the most modern systems of communication. If, as in Tsarist Russia, the masses were not yet literate, the Soviet rulers hurried to make them so. Only thus could they fully utilize propaganda to get their subjects to support their own subjugation. The earlier totalitarians held sway before administrative machinery was sufficiently developed to assure that the King's writ was immediately known to all in his realm, and that it was efficiently executed. The modern ones rely on advances in administrative machinery, supplemented by those in education and communication, to support intricate and involved programs of control over great areas and tremendous numbers of people.

Second, the invitation: the very complexity of society seemed to call for a system of government adequate to cope with it. The industrial revolution brought in its wake economic consequences which ate at the foundations of individualist society. Division of labor robbed the craftsman of his sense of integration through his craft. Economic fluctuations beyond the comprehension or control of the average individual undermined his faith in the institutions he had taken for granted. On the other hand, the great productivtiy of the new system made possible the tremendous rise in the total population, with a proportionate increase in those who lived in cities as specialized servants of the new economic system. The rational and critical spirit loosed in the great revolutions undermined the faith of many in their political and spiritual order. As a result, masses arose. These masses were not distinguished by their unprecedented number, but by their beliefs, demands, and attitudes. These in turn were related to the fundamental conditions of the mass mind. Uprooted from their traditional foundations, the masses during the nineteenth century discovered their need for new loyalty, for new idols, for new beliefs. They discovered the strains of freedom. Many appeared who could not stand the stress of independent thinking, independent judgment, independent action. In consequence, they sought for a new orthodoxy, a new hierarchy of leaders which would fit them back into society in some definite way, think for them, judge for them, tell them what to do. The mass man thus appeared as the antithesis of the free man.

The rise of the masses called into being the characteristic modern totalitarian leader, who gratifies the mass, fills its emotional needs, and uses it as a means to seize and maintain power.

The ruling gangs of the modern totalitarian systems are interested first and foremost in the perpetuation of their control. By their rise through elaborated societies they schooled themselves to high skill in the arts of conspiratorial seizure of state power. During their rise they discovered how to spread disaffection among the masses of modern societies and to use them as a major instrument for revolution. Thus they became specialists in the maintenance of power in the mass state. Skill, ruthlessness, and modern technique combine with the conditions of power-management in the mass state to snuff out freedoms remaining after revolution, and to close any gaps through which freedom might infiltrate anew.

The most important condition for keeping control over a mass state is to atomize social structure outside the state and to dominate every form of social grouping within the state. This process of atomization is the primary device of the totalitarian state for subjecting the individual to its will. Thus to the Russians man under freedom is "an undisciplined, unoriented entity"; while under communism "each person becomes 'a particle of the Soviet system.' "[10] And Goebbels in the same vein said, "to be a socialist is to submit the I to the thou; socialism is sacrificing the individual to the whole."[11]

No modern totalitarian system permits any organization whatsoever outside those it authorizes and controls. Thus totalitarian gangs protect themselves in power by ensuring that no opposing group can ever take form, in no matter how innocuous guise, and raise the remotest threat of new revolution. Those with supreme power recognize that the easiest way to prevent revolution is to rub out any possible source of its organization at the earliest possible moment. Hence the first victim of modern totalitarian gangs is the freedom of association.

Although these gangs are experts in violence, and know well how to provide outlets for mass sadism, they are as interested as any type of ruler in rooting their dominance in mass loyalty and devotion. Hence religious freedom is attacked for two reasons: first to control or smash an association which might germinate and nurture rebellion, second to divert to the totalitarian leader those streams of loyalty and devotion given by most humans to divine objects. The modern totalitarians do not share an ideology with the church; they set up their single ideology in opposition to the church. They attack the church as severely as they can, and still retain their power. They seek to reduce the church to an institution which serves the state, so long as the church must persist. In propaganda and in daily life, the modern totalitarian seeks to possess those areas of the human personality which are normally the province of the church. No commissar ever went to Canossa, even for reasons of state. By controlling the material base of the church, and much of its social base as well, he seeks to shackle and then to smash the church.

The struggle of the totalitarian gang to monopolize loyalty

[10] Quoted from Marshal Zhukov and Konstantin Simonov, by Arthur M. Schlesinger, Jr., *The Vital Center* (1949), p. 54.
[11] As quoted in the same.

and devotion also results in its characteristic propaganda and censorship. Thus it destroys all freedoms of speech, of publication, of intellectual inquiry, and of culture. Since the mass rulers use the unarticulated masses as means to smash any incipient movement toward overthrow, they must regiment their thought to ensure loyalty, and must gratify their emotions as means to ensuring enthusiastic execution of the tasks of the state. The mass rulers cannot suppress thought, but by suppressing the means whereby thought can be circulated and tested, they can do much to wither and restrict it. They put about or circulate only those versions of news or history calculated to keep the masses ripe to execute the decrees of the state. The masses function themselves as a control instrument over those specially gifted individuals who might attempt to produce something original, something outside of the command of the state. The mass rulers apply rigorously the conservative standards of the mass to everything in the field of music, of art, of literature. Art is not solely bent to the purpose of inciting masses to worship the central symbols of power; music is not solely used to speed the rhythm of production. They are kept to the limited standards of what the masses are accustomed to and will accept. Art may not disturb the new orthodoxy by innovations which may be interpreted as deviation from the norm, or wandering beyond the range of state authority. The older totalitarians permitted much unorthodoxy, if there was no clear or immediate transgression of the will or interest of the ruler. The modern totalitarians permit no unorthodoxy whatsoever.

There can be no political freedom in the mass state, because its characteristic form is that of a one-party state in which the rule of law is abolished. The single permitted political party in a modern mass state is the instrument whereby the control of the ruling gang is extended to every crack and corner of the life of the people. The rule of law has no place; in the early period of revolution, it is necessary to get rid of the legal basis whereby the old class ruled, and whereby it might organize a threat against the new regime. Gradually, regularity may reappear in the totalitarian state, for reasons of expediency and convenience. But so long as the new state is ruled by men who are interested first and foremost in power, the elements of stability and regularity are never preferable to action taken to maintain that power.

The single party, as the instrument of power, brooks no competitor. It penetrates all permitted organizations, government or otherwise, as leader and regulator. Since the political power it wields is unlimited, there is no case for a system in which branches of government are balanced off against one another. All such branches are conceived as elements of an all powerful whole, to be used or not according to the judgment of the leader as to which branch is the most convenient and appropriate for various portions of the task of governance.

Finally, since the political atom, the individual, is regarded as of no value in himself, there is no basis for allowing to him any significant area of political choice. He cannot choose between parties as instruments of his will; he cannot organize voluntary groups to impress political parties with aspects of his interest; he cannot choose between candidates for legislative, executive, or judicial office.

Modern totalitarian states have stooped to abysmally low levels in their use of unbridled and irresponsible force. Every state, in the last analysis, rests on a combination of force and consent. Free states are limited in their use of force, both as to the occasions on which and the manner in which force is used as an instrument of government. Force so regulated by the consent of the community is accepted as a legitimate means to guarantee the peace and interests of the society as a whole. Force not so regulated is unjust; it is pure violence. Modern authoritarian regimes combine both force and violence to such an all-encompassing degree that few or no actions of the individual can be taken without thought as to the probability of sanctions. These regimes, instead of protecting the individual from violence, play upon his fear that he will be attacked or harassed, either by agents of the state or the party, even though he has never violated any promulgated law of the land. In their conscious use of incontinent violence, the recent totalitarian regimes differ from other authoritarian and from democratic states.

Under the modern totalitarian systems, fear of arbitrary action becomes a major instrument of government. Their practice far transcended the fascist cry to "live dangerously." Internally, the state assures conformity to its demands by the threat of public or secret police, by savage judicial and administrative penalties for the slightest *lèse majesté* or such specialized faults as "crimes against socialist property," and by a web of official and unofficial espionage which encompasses the whole of society. What real freedom is there in a state which by its apparatus of oppression makes it possible for the citizen to be denounced, broken, or eliminated on the basis of unchecked rumor, nonproletarian or foreign origin, or mere relationship or association with a suspect person? Given the characteristic ruthlessness of the ruling gang to stamp out any conceivable source of counterrevolution, it becomes possible for party fanatics to threaten any man or his family, on real or imagined grounds. Competitors for place and power can use secret denunciation to eliminate those who block their rise in the hierarchy. The citizen lives under the constant threat that any of his neighbors may denounce him to the secret police, merely to avenge a real or fancied injury.

Externally, the modern totalitarian state deliberately risks new wars. Masses require scapegoats. Sometimes scapegoats are conveniently available from within, and those which do exist can serve beyond their numbers because of their symbolic role. But so far, no modern totalitarian state has been able to get along without exploiting real or fancied external threat as a means to increase internal cohesion. Mass rulers divert the frustrations and consequent aggressions of their masses onto foreign enemies. Thus they protect themselves, justify monolithic controls, and energize their societies. They assuage guilt among their masses which might otherwise arise because of their own aggressions and war preparations, by propaganda asserting the preparations and aggressions of potential enemies. In so doing, they perpetuate the conditions out of which new wars arise, and postpone the epoch in which the individual can live in peace and safety.

Mass societies by their very nature deny economic freedom. They can no more allow economic groups than any other form of group to go their way untrammeled. As societies devoted to the perpetuation of control, they manipulate economic goods and operations to see to it that all forms of societal activity are kept within prescribed channels. Ownership is not critical; both communist and fascist systems see to it that economic operations are conducted according to the interest of the state. Modern totalitarians allow and welcome technological initiative from subordinates, but in every case arrogate fundamental economic decisions to themselves. The prizes of domestic power and the rewards of external aggrandizement are not left to the improvisation of anyone from below.

We have now catalogued various ways in which mass societies deny individual freedoms, because of the very nature of those societies and of the leadership which rules them. More than anything in the catalogue is the final way in which these societies trammel the individual: they deny him his individuality, his potentiality of self-directed development. On this basic denial the detailed controls are built up. The mass society cannot prevent the individual from experiencing independence in the world of his own mind, but it can and does take every step to see to it that even this most private and subtle form of individuality is hemmed in. The state puts so much demand on the individual's time and imagination; it moves so inexorably to monopolize his waking attention, and it strikes so severely to prevent any outward manifestation of inward individuality that it sears back the private freedom of any but the most fanciful or most obdurate. By regimenting his education, it thins out and dulls the tools of thought. By regimenting public expression, it restricts the challenges to the individual's thinking. It puts a premium on monotonous uniformity and conformity, while weighting versatility and the expression of differences with the risk of savage sanctions. By catching up his entire outward life in its own mad career of revolution and world domination, it enforces its philosophy that the state is everything, and the individual as such no more than one of the atoms which make the state possible. Thus the totalitarian state denies in practice not only the perfectibility, but also the ultimate value of the individual. On this double denial rests the permanent slavery of the individual.

INDEX

INDEX